bal, and in places so remote and
ers' would be likely to pass some
st curious explorers would penetrat
that passing travellers woul d spend
clambering up the rugge d preci
han 6000 feet high, carrying with th
he useless object of carving inscript
the eye of man—and that too, in
avine discovered by Mr. B tler ev
with them ?
that most of those which saw
an climbing on another shoul
ow any man balan ing hin
maintaining his posi
ock, could at the
which would
ccels su
re as

la l
ate of
by At
brother
Inaccessible
see those
skill, dispo
an lines o
in letters
high—forming
it s—ot the one

full description, the
Sinaitic Inscriptions, p.

TRADITIONS OF EDEN.

TRADITIONS OF EDEN;

OR,

Proofs of the Historical Truth

OF THE

Pentateuch,

FROM EXISTING FACTS, AND FROM THE CUSTOMS
AND MONUMENTS OF ALL NATIONS.

BY

H. SHEPHEARD, M.A.,

LATE FELLOW OF ORIEL COLLEGE, OXFORD.
AUTHOR OF "THE TREE OF LIFE," "ITHURIEL'S SPEAR," AND
"SILVERDALE TRACTS."

LONDON:
JAMES NISBET & CO., 21 BERNERS STREET.
1871.

PREFACE.

IT is one of the most saddening as well as most striking signs of the times that there is at the present moment a more widely spread, active, and determined opposition to the Word of God than at any former period since the Reformation.

I say, the Word of God—for such is THE BIBLE, and such it will be found at last to be, whatever may be thought and said against it now.

The question is of such overwhelming importance—the blessedness of a right faith so transcendent—the consequences of error so appalling—that it is impossible to overrate the value of any testimony by which the truth can be vindicated and established.

In the *methods* of attack employed against the Holy Scriptures there is an almost endless variety. Criticism—pretended Science—antiquarian research—every resource of genius and learning—and an assumed supremacy of human reason, as if it were able to sit in unerring judgment upon the veracity of the sacred writers—all are brought to bear in these our days against the truth and Divine authority of the Bible.

The design of the present work is to call attention to numerous facts—some not generally known, others familiar enough but seldom duly weighed—which offer irresistible evidence of the historical and prophetic truth of the Scriptures;

and especially that part which has been most industriously
disputed—the Book of Genesis.

We are told by modern sceptics that "Science has proved
the Bible not to be true"—that "Genesis is poetry, not
history"—and that "the whole of the first eight chapters of
Genesis are now generally admitted by scholars to be made
up of earlier books or earlier traditions, belonging, properly
speaking, to Mesopotamian rather than to Jewish history"[1]—
and the like. The meaning and intent of all these assertions
is one and the same— *to deny the truth of the Bible.*

In behalf of the two last assertions not a syllable of proof is
even attempted. It is not the manner of unbelievers to
adduce proofs. A fair and candid enquiry into the evidences
of the Bible must inevitably result in conviction of its truth—
for those evidences, when impartially and intelligently weighed,
are irresistible. But it is a charge justly urged against unbelievers of every grade, that their mode of enquiry is not fair or
candid. Attempts to invalidate the Scriptures are invariably
one-sided. There is an evident *animus* in all such attempts,
influencing, perhaps unconsciously, the minds of the enquirers.
They assume the Bible to be untrue, but they evidently *wish*
it were untrue : and the wish is father to the thought. This
is manifest from a very significant fact—that they never take
into account those arguments which make *for* the truth of the
Scriptures, but those only which seem to make *against* it.
For such unfairness there can be but one motive—the *wish*
to find the Bible untrue. Many an enquirer who has sat down
to read that blessed Book with such a wish, and for the sole
purpose of detecting its supposed falsehood, has indeed been
convinced by his studies, in spite of himself, that the Bible is
true : but such a result is more than could be reasonably expected. The very first, the most indispensable requisite for
the discovery of moral truth is the *love* of truth.

---

[1] Fergusson's *Tree and Serpent Worship*, p. 6.

Here, indeed, lies the very heart and core of the whole matter. There is this essential difference between moral or religious truth, and every other kind of truth—that while the study of other truth requires only a good *head*, the study of moral and religious truth requires also a good *heart*. "An honest and good heart"—Luke viii. 15—as the Lord Jesus Himself declared, is that soil which alone receives rightly or successfully the precious seed of truth—the Truth of God. The pilot may steer his vessel strictly according to the compass before him—but if a mass of iron in the ship has diverted the needle from its pole, he will steer only to destruction. "The light of the body is the eye: if therefore thine eye be single (clear), thy whole body shall be full of light. But if thine eye be evil, thy whole body shall be full of darkness. If therefore the light that is in thee be darkness, how great is that darkness!"—Matt. vi. 22, 23.

Now it is just the want of the "single eye"—the "honest and good heart," or sincere desire to know what is right—that produces the one-sidedness and unfairness so characteristic of the arguments of unbelievers. The objections quoted above furnish fair specimens of these.

"Modern Science," say they, "has proved the Bible not to be true."

Now what is Science? Science is *scientia*—KNOWLEDGE.

But scientific knowledge can be obtained only by one method—the method pointed out by the prince of philosophers and father of modern Science, the great Bacon. FACTS must be carefully observed—and general PRINCIPLES laid down by induction from the facts. But facts must be distinguished from merely *apparent* facts—and the facts must be ascertained to be also *universal* facts—universal as far as human observation can reach—before any general principle can be assumed as established by them. The fall of an apple would not alone have warranted Newton in assuming gravitation to be a universal law of matter: but the observation, to which it led him, that all material objects do in fact gravitate towards some centre, established that universal principle which has formed the basis of all astronomical science.

It is obvious that in no other way can Science—that is, the *knowledge* of the laws of Nature—be attained. Any theory which does not proceed upon actually ascertained facts, and universal principles correctly deduced from them, can lead to nothing but error, confusion, and ignorance.

But this is not the method followed by those who impugn the truth of Genesis on pretence that it is opposed to the discoveries of Science.

They frame the wildest theories upon the most irrelevant facts, or upon the merest fancies. Mr. Darwin thinks that whales may be bears which have enormously increased their bulk, washed their paws into fins by constant swimming, and stretched their mouths by keeping them open to catch insects in the water. So also he thinks that men and women may have been developed out of monkeys, monkeys out of mushroms, and mushroms out of "monads," or little clots of jelly. Where is the proof? where is a single instance of a bear-whale, or a man-monkey, to be seen? Of course there is not one. But Mr. Darwin hopes that fossil specimens may yet be dug up in some geological stratum not yet explored! And this is called Science! Geology is a noble and profoundly interesting science; but geologists have small reason to congratulate themselves upon their efforts to prove the Scripture chronology to be untrue, and the antiquity of man to extend to hundreds of thousands of years. In several instances their conclusions have been shown by subsequent discoveries to have been enormous mistakes—geologists perpetually contradict each other, and sometimes themselves—one theory after another is overthrown, and some new one set up in its place—and the latest and greatest of all geologists, Sir Roderick Murchison, declares his belief that all the geological theories of the immense antiquity of man upon the earth are founded upon assumptions utterly false, and that it is impossible, from geological data, to form any opinion at all upon the subject.

He has shown also that Geology itself furnishes a demonstration that "the first living animal of each class was as perfect and composite in structure as any of its congeners in after-times"[1]—and consequently that Darwin's theory is absolutely false.

Thus, with one stroke of a master-hand, the great geologist has swept away the whole accumulated heap of crudities, absurdities, and contradictory theories of geological objectors against the Bible—theories which are a reproach to the very name, the honoured name, of *Science*.

Then, again, Criticism is enlisted as an ally in the attack.

The blunders and puerilities of such writers as Colenso have been amply and sufficiently exposed.

But it is now insinuated, in more courtly guise, that "Genesis is poetry, not history."

The phrase is not distinguished for good logic. The same narrative may surely be both poetry and history at once. Because a history is written in poetical language, it does not follow that it must needs be untrue. The very expression "poetry, not history," indicates in the authors of it a confusion of thought by no means qualifying them to be sound critics, or safe guides in any matter whatever.

But, moreover, we utterly deny that Genesis, (with few exceptions) is poetry at all. No narrative of facts could possibly be written in plainer or more unpretending prose. The assertion that Genesis is "poetry, not history," is merely a mild phrase intended to insinuate that it is *not true*. The sacred history is not objected against as *poetical*, but as *fabulous*.

The same meaning is conveyed in another form, in the assertion that the eight first chapters of Genesis are made up of

[1] *Siluria*, p. 506.

Mesopotamian books or traditions. Why is such an assertion made but for the purpose of representing the *events* of the sacred history as fictions, not facts—and the book itself as altogether human, not divinely inspired? Though even here, the assertion carries absurdity and self-contradiction upon the very face of it—for how could Mesopotamian or any other traditions inform Moses how the first man came into existence? How could the first man himself know how he was created, except by information from his Creator?

And upon what authority is the assertion presented to us? We are told that "the whole of the first eight chapters of Genesis are now *generally admitted by scholars* to be made up of earlier books or earlier traditions," &c. If this be so indeed, then so much the worse—for the scholars. But we utterly deny that it is so: and moreover, whether it be so, or not, does not affect the question in the slightest degree. It is not a question of scholarship at all, but of *fact*, and of the evidence of facts. Nor is it a question in which the majority of scholars must needs be right, and the minority wrong. Truth was never yet decided by the numbers arrayed against or in favour of it, nor ever will be. One good physician is a better guide than a hundred bad ones—and the judgment of one such man as Newton, or Butler, or Brewster, or Tischendorf—all devout believers in the truth of the Bible—is far more than sufficient to outweigh the opposition of a host of smaller "scholars."

Moreover, what *proof* is offered in behalf of the strange assumption that the early chapters of Genesis are Mesopotamian traditions? As usual, not a particle.—The unanimous and unvarying testimony of a whole nation for the space of three thousand three hundred years, from the time of Moses to the present hour, is utterly disregarded and ignored—and the mere fancy of some modern "scholars" is presumed to be a better authority. The whole Jewish people throughout the world, and from Moses downwards, are witnesses to the authenticity and almost verbal accuracy of their Hebrew

Scriptures—a matter in which they could not possibly be mistaken—and also to their historical fidelity, from the time of Abraham downwards: but some modern scholars have, it seems, made the astounding discovery that they were all wrong, and knew nothing about their own countryman Moses, or the stupendous events of which they were eyewitnesses in Egypt and Sinai, and by which Moses was attested to be God's messenger and minister among them!

Anything more preposterous than such pretensions of "scholars", or more utterly subversive of all sound criticism, scientific research, and Scriptural truth, cannot be conceived.

The case, then, stands thus—that all the efforts of unbelievers have signally failed to produce a single fact which really contravenes the truth of Scripture in the slightest degree: while their conclusions have been, over and over again, shown by subsequent discoveries to be gross blunders. Their theories are wild fancies—their "estimates" mere guesses—and their opinions are proved to be worthless by their continual opposition to each other, and even to themselves.

On the other hand, all history, all fact, all true science, are found to confirm the Scriptures, sometimes with even curious minuteness. Not an event recorded in the Bible history has ever been disproved—not a miracle ever detected as fictitious or deceptive—not a prophecy shown to be false. In such a vast number and variety of statements as the Bible contains, this of itself affords the strongest presumption of its truth, seeing that no ingenuity or activity have been spared by its enemies to overthrow it.

But this is only negative evidence. The world is full of facts, and history is full of records, which, taken in connexion with the Bible itself, amount to such a demonstration of its truth as we cannot reject without at the same time rejecting all the records of history, all human testimony, and even the evidence of our own senses. And this, indeed, is what unbelievers really are guilty of. It cannot reasonably be doubted

that those who disbelieve the overwhelming proofs of Revelation, would disbelieve their own senses if a miracle were
wrought before their eyes in demonstration of its truth. It
was so in the days of Christ and His Apostles—and so it
would be again.

The following pages contain a selection, rather than a collection, of some of these significant facts.   The subject is
vast and inexhaustible: and even the facts now extant and
within reach, numberless though they be, are yet but the
sparse relics of the past—the gleanings, as it were, of a harvest
which once covered the whole field of human society.

In order to afford to the reader the means of testing the
accuracy of the statements here adduced, references are constantly given to the authorities on which they are made.

The work is offered to an intelligent public in the hope that
it may serve to confirm the wavering faith of some—to dispel
the prejudices of others—and to excite interest and enquiry
upon subjects the most momentous which can engage the
attention of an immortal being.

To Dr. Forbes Watson, of the Indian Museum, the best
thanks of the author are due for his courteous and kind permission to make use of several Illustrations from Mr. Fergusson's *Tree and Serpent worship*: to A. H. Layard, Esq., M.P.,
and John Murray, Esq., for a similar permission respecting Mr.
Layard's *Nineveh and its Remains:* and to the Rev. Charles
Forster and Messrs. Bentley for copies of Illustrations from
Mr. Forster's works *The One Primeval Language* and *Sinai
Photographed.*

SILVERDALE, CARNFORTH,
   May 1871.

CONTENTS.

CHAPTER I.

CHAPTER XV.

CHAPTER XVI.

CHAPTER XVII.

CHAPTER XVIII.

CHAPTER XIX.

CHAPTER XX.

CHAPTER XXI.

TRADITIONS OF EDEN.

CHAPTER I.

The great subject of Holy Scripture is the Incarnation and Redeeming Work of the Son of God—Inspiration totally different from Intuition and Science—Various Methods of impugning the Truth of Scripture.

THE loveliest character ever seen upon earth was the character of JESUS CHRIST.

This is acknowledged even by those who do not believe Him to have been more than human.

But the fact derives all its importance, and all its interest for us, from another fact—that Jesus Christ is the SON OF GOD—Himself very and eternal God.

If JESUS is JEHOVAH—the God who is our Creator and will hereafter be our Judge—then reason itself tells us that to disown or dishonour Him must be to risk all the fearful consequences of setting at defiance the God who made us, as well as of losing all the blessing and happiness which He is able to bestow upon His creatures.

Now the Bible declares that JESUS IS THE SON OF GOD—and that, not merely by an expression here and there which might mean that He is the Son of God in some lower sense than as being Himself God, but in such a manner that His Divine nature and mission is THE subject of the whole Scrip-

ture from Genesis to Revelation—THE fact which is the foundation of the whole structure of the sacred volume.

This is the express statement of the Book itself: "The testimony of Jesus is the Spirit of prophecy "—Rev. xix. 10; that
is, the Spirit of prophecy, or Spirit of inspiration, which was
given to the servants of God, was given them specially for this
purpose—to enable them to testify concerning Jesus. So also
Christ Himself, in His discourse to the two disciples, "beginning at Moses and all the prophets, expounded unto them *in
all the Scriptures* the things concerning himself."—Luke xxiv.
27. And this testimony of the Scriptures was not the mere
announcement beforehand that a man called Jesus Christ would
be born at a certain time and do certain things. It was the
announcement of *a Divine interposition in human affairs*. It
was the announcement that a work had been planned in the
eternal counsels of God which was to be carried out, in the fulness of time, by One who was expressly designated beforehand
as "Wonderful, Counsellor, THE MIGHTY GOD, the everlasting
Father, the Prince of Peace."—Isa. ix. 6.

If, then, the Bible is true, it establishes the most stupendous
fact that ever happened, or ever can happen, in all eternity—
nothing less than THE INCARNATION OF THE SON OF GOD—
a fact which no created mind could have imagined, and of
which the results may well be believed to be eternal and inexhaustible.

But if, on the other hand, Jesus is not God, then the Bible is
the most extraordinary and the most wicked imposture the
world has ever witnessed.

"IS THE BIBLE TRUE ?" is, therefore, a question the answer
to which involves either all the glorious hopes arising from the
fact that, in the person of Jesus Christ man's nature has been
eternally united to God Himself; or, the heart-sickening discovery that we know absolutely nothing of God beyond the
meagre teachings of the works of creation.

For it is needless to remark that if the Bible is not a revelation from God, then no revelation has been granted by God to mankind—for there is no 'other book pretending to be such a revelation that deserves a moment's consideration.

And when I speak of a revelation from God, I mean something made known to us by God in a supernatural way—not something which we could have discovered for ourselves by the use of our natural faculties or reason. To speak of *Science* as a revelation, or of natural *Genius*, or *Intuition*, as inspiration, is merely to make confusion. Science is one thing, revelation is another; intuition is one thing, inspiration is another thing. To work out a problem in mathematics is a very different thing from receiving a telegram across the Atlantic Ocean; and there is no less difference between a scientific discovery and a revelation from God. Science is knowledge obtained *from within* a man's own mind by the use of his reason and faculties; revelation is information imparted by God *from without*. The two things are not merely different in degree; they are totally distinct and opposite in their nature. No flight of natural genius can ever become Divine inspiration; no amount of scientific discovery can ever be a revelation from God. Science can no more pass into revelation by becoming more advanced than a stone by being thrown into the air can become a star; genius can no more by its loftiest soarings grow into inspiration than the Babel-builders of old could raise a tower whose top should reach to heaven.

To keep these two things perfectly distinct is of the first importance to truth; to confuse them together is one of the strongholds of rationalistic error. Rationalists, by exalting human genius to the level of Divine inspiration, do in reality *deny* inspiration by bringing it down to the level of human genius. By calling science "a revelation," they in fact deny that Divine revelation is anything more than human science.

Now, the Bible everywhere declares itself to be given by inspiration of God. Its utterances are introduced by the express words, "The Lord said unto Moses"—"Hear the word of the

Lord "—"Thus saith the Lord"—and the like. St. Paul says that "*God spake* unto the fathers by the prophets," and that He "hath in these last days *spoken* unto us by His Son."

If, therefore, the Bible is true at all, it is *an actual message to us from God.* For the man who writes, "Thus saith the Lord," when he is uttering merely the ideas suggested by his own mind, is simply "speaking lies in hypocrisy." The writers of the Scriptures were either wilful deceivers, or else what they delivered to us was communicated to them from God in a manner altogether supernatural.

But the Incarnation of the Son of God does not stand in the Bible as an isolated fact. It is inseparably connected with the Temptation and Fall of our first parents as its occasion, and with the Redemption of mankind as its object and result. Man's redemption implies man's previous ruin, and man's ruin alone explains the occasion and need of the Incarnation. Together with the great doctrine of the Incarnation of the Son of God must stand or fall all the great doctrines relating to the salvation of man—such as those of the Atonement, justification by faith alone, the new birth by the Holy Spirit of God, and the necessity of holiness in heart and life which the Holy Spirit alone can operate. These doctrines are all either denied or explained away by those who deny the Incarnation. On the other hand, if we admit that Jesus is indeed " God manifest in the flesh," we cannot consistently refuse to admit that lamentable fact of man's Fall, which alone can account for the stupendous fact of the Incarnation, or the glorious fact of provision having been made for man's recovery by the Father's redeeming love, the Son's atoning sacrifice, and the Holy Spirit's renewing, life-giving, and purifying power.

And our belief of all these doctrines wholly depends on our belief of the Scriptures. If the Bible is true, then all these doctrines are true : if the Bible be not true, there is no proof of the doctrines. This is not a question of opinion. It is a question of *fact*—proved, like other facts, by historical evidence. If the *events* narrated in the Scriptures really took place, it is impossible to deny the *doctrines* of the Scriptures— for these doctrines are just the necessary consequences of the events, or else indeed the very teachings of the persons concerned in the events. If, for example, the history of the Temptation and Fall of Eve and Adam is true, the doctrine of man's sinfulness and ruin follows from it as a necessary consequence. If the narrative of Christ's miracles and sayings is true, it follows as an inevitable inference that He is the Son of God, in the highest sense of being Himself very and eternal God. There is no escaping from the admission of the truth of the *doctrines* of the Bible but by denying the truth of the *facts* it narrates.

Therefore it is, that the adversaries of the Gospel have always directed their busiest endeavours to overthrow the testimony of the Scriptures. Every conceivable device has been employed for this end, from the coarsest derision to the keenest subtlety. The sense of Scripture has been assailed by perversion the most ignorant and the most malevolent: its authenticity has been questioned by speculations equally remarkable for folly and pretension to superior discernment: the miraculous facts of the narrative have been ascribed to natural causes in a way far more incredible than miracles themselves. Every objection has been tried which could be suggested either by ignorance or science, by dulness or by wit, by unwillingness to receive the truth and eagerness to destroy it.

In the present day, the favourite modes of attack appear to be no longer the coarse virulence of former times, but the more artful, and far more dangerous methods of evasion, misrepresentation, and insinuation of doubts. Of these arts there is an endless variety, but a few remarks may be necessary in this place respecting two of them, namely, the *allegorical interpretation* of Scripture, and the device of the "*verifying faculty.*" These will form the subject of the next chapter.

CHAPTER II.

The Allegorical Interpretation of Scripture, and the " Verifying Faculty,"
or Rationalistic Infallibility.

AMONG those who wish to escape from the stringency of
Scripture truth, no subterfuge seems to have found more favour
than the notion that certain parts of the sacred narrative must
be understood in an *allegorical sense.* The early chapters of the
book of Genesis are especially thus treated. It has been
repeatedly and openly proclaimed, of late years, both from the
pulpit and the press—and that by preachers and dignitaries
in the high places of the Church—that the early part of Genesis
is "*poetry, not history.*" The description of Adam and Eve in
Paradise—of the creation of Eve out of one of Adam's ribs—of
the Trees of Life and of the Knowledge of good and evil—of
the Serpent-tempter—of the Fall—is regarded by the allegorizers as a pretty Oriental fable: not as a record of real
events, but a mythical and mystical poem, intended to convey,
under a veil of symbols, certain high lessons of moral truth.

Here, then, is a question raised, upon which depends the very
being of Christianity, the very existence of true religion. If
the history of man's Creation and Fall is a myth or an allegory,
then the very foundation of revealed religion is undermined,
and the whole fabric of Scripture truth falls to the ground.

For the whole system of revealed religion, or Christianity, is
based upon the lamentable fact of the Fall. It is a religion
suited to *fallen* beings. It is a system of *remedies,* a method
of *recovery.* But to say that the history of the Fall is an

allegory, is simply to deny that there was any Fall at all. And if there was no Fall, but mankind have remained in their original and unfallen state, then no remedy is needed, no recovery is either necessary or possible. In this case the whole system of Christianity would be an impertinence, a sporting with falsehood, and a mockery of mankind.

It is part of the design of this work to prove that the narrative of the early part of Genesis is no allegory, but a simple record of actual events, from the universal testimony of the whole world; that is to say, from facts before our eyes, and from customs, traditions, modes of worship, and the like, which are traceable in almost every country and nation under heaven of which any records exist : as well as in the startling discoveries made within the last few years of sculptures at Nineveh, and elsewhere, which throw a new and unexpected light, amounting almost to a demonstration of the literal truth of the Scripture narrative.

Before proceeding to these proofs, it may be briefly remarked in this place, that quite apart from the positive proofs to be hereafter adduced, the very idea of the history of Adam and Eve in Paradise being an allegory, or as it has been expressed, "poetry, not history," is in itself absurd, and contradictory to acknowledged facts. For it is acknowledged that the *later* part of Genesis, and the subsequent books of the Scripture history, are a narrative of real events, and of the lives and actions of real men and women. But where, then, does the allegorical part end, and the historical part begin? "If," says Bishop Horsley,[1] "the formation of the woman out of man be allegory, the woman must be an allegorical woman. The man therefore must be an allegorical man, for of such a man only the allegorical woman will be a meet companion. If the man is allegorical, his Paradise will be an allegorical garden; the trees that grew in it, allegorical trees; the rivers that watered

[1] *Works*, vol. ii. 10.

it, allegorical rivers; and thus we may ascend to the very
beginning of the creation, and conclude at last that the heavens
are allegorical heavens, and the earth an allegorical earth."
And if Adam and Eve were allegorical personages, who were
the parents of the real men and women whose history follows
afterwards?—or indeed of the present inhabitants of the earth?
If Eve was an allegorical woman, who was the mother of Cain
and Abel? or were these also allegorical men, and if so, when
and how did the real men and women of history come into
being? This is a question upon which the allegorizers are
wholly silent: but which certainly reason requires that they
should answer.

To pursue the argument farther is needless; but it is among
the most important uses of history, and the most interesting
subjects of study, to trace out the overwhelming evidences of
the literal truth of the Mosaic narrative. The marks and
effects of those primeval events of man's history are stamped
upon every nation under heaven; the scars of those wounds are
branded upon our very souls and bodies; they can be traced
in the very brutes; they can be seen and heard in earth, air,
sea, and sky. The "philosophy," falsely so called, which
denies the reality of facts under the weight of which all creation
groans up to the present hour, is the worst kind of foolishness
—for it is foolishness which pretends to be the highest kind of
wisdom.

The "verifying faculty" is a name which has been invented
to designate a power supposed to belong in some way to the
human mind, by which we are able to discern what parts of
Scripture are true, and what parts are false—what parts are
genuine, what parts are incorrectly ascribed to the writer whose
name they bear. The advocates of this faculty allege that
though the Word of God is contained in the Bible, yet the
Bible is not wholly the Word of God: and the "verifying
faculty" must be employed to distinguish the parts which
are the Word of God from those which are not so.

That any such "faculty" exists at all is, indeed, not attempted to be proved : much less are any rules laid down by which we may safely guide its exercise. The very absence of any attempt to prove that we possess such a faculty, leaves it to be inferred from the nature of the case what kind of faculty is intended. It must, of course, belong to that class of powers which we call *intuitive*—those powers, of the existence of which no other proof can be given than our own consciousness that we possess them.

We must needs then understand that by the "verifying faculty" is meant a power of discerning intuitively the truth or falsehood, the literal or allegorical meaning, the genuineness or spurious character of each portion of the Scriptures. Less than this cannot be meant by it, since it is made to set aside all the ordinary rules and evidences by which a sound and healthy criticism must always be regulated.

Let reason and common sense decide whether such a faculty does, or does not, exist in our minds. Now, first, it is obvious that such a faculty, to answer its professed object, must be in itself not only intuitive, but also not liable to make mistakes. If it can make mistakes, it is no verifying faculty—for it does not verify. But if it makes no mistakes, it is nothing less than *infallible*. So that under this designation of a "*verifying faculty*," we have in very truth nothing less than a claim to *infallibility*—put forth, not by the Pope, or the self-called infallible Church of Rome, but by those who occupy a position at the very antipodes of church doctors and authority—the Rationalists themselves! Extremes often meet. Errors which start from opposite sides of a question are often found to gravitate to a common centre. Such a common centre belongs to Romanism and Rationalism—and that centre is *Infidelity*. The Romanist finds his principle of infallibility in a Pope, a general Council, or a Church (for it has never yet been agreed on all hands where it resides) ; the Rationalist finds it in the "verifying faculty," which saves all farther discussion, and

solves every doubt, by making every reader of the Scripture a
Pope to himself.

Let, then, the matter be put to the test in a practical way.

If the Bible contains some portions which are the Word of
God, and other portions which are not so, the number of each
kind of portions must be definite and exact—whether counted
by chapters, verses, or words. No verse, no sentence, no word,
can be both the Word of God, and also *not* the Word of God.

The two kinds of verses, or sentences, must be perfectly distinct, and capable of being separated. And to make the
separation is the business of the "verifying faculty"—which of
course must always be able to perceive to which kind any particular sentence or verse belongs, and assign it to its proper
place accordingly, as being either the Word of God or not the
Word of God.

Now let the trial be made upon the first five books of the
Bible. Let any hundred persons believing in the "verifying
faculty," be set to make a division of all the verses of these
five books into two parts, the one part consisting of those
which they think to be the Word of God, the other of those
which are not so. Would all these hundred persons be found
to have made exactly the same division? Is it likely that even
any two of them would agree in all points? But if not, what becomes of the "verifying faculty?" The chances would be
thousands of millions against an agreement among even one
hundred persons respecting the Pentateuch alone: what then
would be the probability of agreement among all the readers
of the whole Bible throughout the world, if each should have no
other guide than the "verifying faculty"?

If we suppose for a moment that such a result had been
obtained as that the "verifying faculty" had led all the readers
of the whole Bible throughout the world to a perfect agreement as to which parts of it are inspired and which uninspired, we should have before us, in so extraordinary a fact, a
most convincing proof that the inspiration we claim for the

writers of the Scriptures certainly existed in the *readers:* for nothing less than a supernatural guidance could possibly lead to so singular a harmony of judgment.

Those objectors, therefore, against the inspiration of the Bible who advocate the criticism of it by the "verifying faculty," make use of an engine which recoils upon themselves. In their attempt to throw doubt upon the inspiration of the Scriptures, they actually make it appear that there is infallibility in the readers of them.

But this is not all. To throw doubt upon the inspiration of the Holy Scriptures, either in whole or in part, is to throw doubt upon the *truth* of the Scriptures, and also upon the *character* of the sacred writers themselves.

For the Scriptures everywhere speak *of God*—and that, as *from* God. They record the acts and words of the Almighty. They declare too that these acts and words were made known by God Himself—that what they speak, they speak by His authority and commission.

Now these constant assertions of Divine communications and Divine commission are either true or false. If they are true, it follows of necessity that the whole Bible is inspired. If they are false, it follows that the writers of them are guilty of wilful and deliberate lying and imposture; and, moreover, of the most awful blasphemy and presumption.

From these considerations the conclusion is inevitable. Either the whole Bible is the inspired Word of God, or it is the work of the most worthless and wicked impostors. It is either the inspired Word of God, or it is a base and impudent forgery.

Hence, again, it follows that a *partially* inspired Bible is simply impossible. In one or two places, indeed, St. Paul expressly says that the judgment he gives is his own, and not commanded by God—that is, not inspired. But the very exception is the strongest confirmation of the rule. When he says, as in 1 Cor. vii. 6—"But I speak this by permission, and

not of commandment," it follows inevitably that the rest of
his injunctions in the matter *are* "of commandment." This is
also expressly stated—"And unto the married I command,
yet not I, but the Lord," &c. So again, v. 25 : "Now concerning
virgins I have no commandment of the Lord : yet I give my
judgment, as one that hath obtained mercy of the Lord to be
faithful." If any thing were wanting to clench the nail of conviction that the *whole* of any book is inspired by God, it is
supplied by the special notice so carefully given when any
exception is made to the otherwise universal rule.

It is thus perfectly clear that the notion of a *partially* inspired book, *containing* the Word of God, but not *being wholly*
the Word of God—the two different portions requiring to be
distinguished by the "verifying faculty"—is self-destructive
and absurd.

It need hardly be remarked that it is in direct contradiction
of the Scripture itself, which declares that, "*All* Scripture is
given by inspiration of God"—*God-breathed.*—2 Tim. iii. 16.

CHAPTER III.

IF our appeal is to be made to reason and common sense, the
proofs adduced in the last chapter are sufficient to show that
the allegorical interpretation of plain historical parts of the
Bible, such as Genesis and the Pentateuch in general, is inadmissible ; and also that the notion of a book partly inspired
and partly human, with a "verifying faculty" to distinguish
the inspired part from the human, is self-contradictory and
irrational.

But here another question arises—How are we to know what
is Scripture and what is not so ? Though we should admit
that "all Scripture " is inspired, yet how can we be sure that
all is Scripture which goes under the name of Scripture ?

Again the appeal must be to reason and common sense.

How do we know that the whole contents of any other book
are the work of the author whose name it bears ? How do we
know that the book called *Cæsar's Commentaries* was all
written by Cæsar ; or, that *Gibbon's History of the Decline and
Fall of the Roman Empire* was all written by Gibbon ?

Recourse, no doubt, will be had by the sceptical objectors
to the "verifying faculty." Bishop Colenso has laboured to
show that the Pentateuch was not all written by Moses, but
parts of it by one writer whom he calls "the Elohist," other
parts by another whom he calls "the Jehovist." So, another
writer tells us that the sacred songs introduced into the Scripture history are nothing different from old ballads and battle-

songs. He includes in his list of passages thus treated part of Psalm lxviii., and the Lamentations of Jeremiah, and regards them all as "examples of a lay, a ballad, a dirge, a battle-song," such as we meet with in our own early literature. "The *compiler*," he adds, "whoever he was," who rescued these fragments from oblivion, "was the precursor, by direct anticipation, of Bishop Percy, when he collected the Reliques of Ancient English Poetry,—of Walter Scott, when he treasured up the remains of his own Border Minstrelsy."[1] We are here distinctly told that the Lamentations of Jeremiah and part of Psalm lxviii.— to say nothing of such passages as the Song of Moses, Deut. xxxii. 1-43; the Song of Moses and Miriam, Exod. xv. 1-19; the Blessing of Jacob, Gen. xlix. 1-28, and many others—are no more inspired than a collection of old English ballads, and that, "though belonging to secular occasions, they have been incorporated for our instruction into the Sacred Books," by a "compiler," who was no more inspired than Bishop Percy or Sir Walter Scott!

To say nothing of the futility of such idle speculations, is this way of treating any book, sacred or profane, a way which reason and common sense can tolerate? We are told that a great German composer of music, in his declining health, used sometimes to fall asleep while composing, and then wake up again and continue his work; and that there are critics who pretend that their musical instinct enables them to detect the exact places where the great composer began to nod. The musical critics are far more modest in their pretensions than the sceptical critics of the Holy Scriptures—their musical genius is tame compared with the professed powers of the "verifying faculty."

Now in the name of reason and common sense, we ask what would become of all history, and all scientific and literary records, if this be a sound method of criticism? If it be a thing

[1] Dean Stanley, in an article in *Good Words* for February, 1863.

doubtful and uncertain whether each of the Sacred Books was written wholly, or only partially, by the writer whose name it bears, then there is not a book in the world which can be relied upon. If a "verifying faculty" is required to detect interpolations in the Scriptures, much more is it necessary in the case of other books—for no other book was ever guarded with one thousandth part of the jealous vigilance which from the very first has watched over the Scriptures. But who ever dreamed of a necessity for scrutinizing *Cæsar's Commentaries*, or *Gibbon's Decline and Fall*, in hopes of detecting, by a difference of style or phraseology, a plurality of authors in each work?

The whole matter is a question of *fact* and of *evidence*. It is simply absurd to pretend to a "verifying faculty" which is able to discern intuitively the genuineness and authenticity of any and every passage in any and every book. But if there is no faculty which can enable us to do this in other books, much less is there any which can do so in the case of the Bible. This argument applies with peculiar force to the Old Testament, in proportion as writings so ancient are more difficult of criticism than others.

There are two kinds of evidence by which alone every ancient book must be tested :—1. The testimony of all time since the book was written, that it was written by the author whose name it bears.—2. The collation of manuscripts, to ascertain the integrity of the text.

Why do we receive without doubting the Grecian history of Herodotus, or the Odes of Horace? Simply because the authors of these works were known at the time when the works first appeared, and have been attested by an unbroken stream of testimony ever since.

And if Horace, for example, had allowed any other hand to insert in his collection of Odes a poem not composed by himself, and had given it forth to the world as his own, he would have been guilty of a falsehood and a fraud. To attribute such conduct to Moses, for instance, is to represent Moses as a person devoid of truth and unworthy of credit. And if Moses allowed the Pentateuch to be attributed wholly to himself as the writer of it, he made himself responsible both for the authorship and the truth of the whole narrative it contains, without any exception whatever.

Now, both in respect of the testimony of all time to the fact that the several books of the Scriptures were delivered by the writers whose names they bear, and also in respect of the care with which the text has been guarded from alteration or addition, there is no ancient book in the world which can bear a comparison with the Bible.

To enter upon the proof of this in detail would be beyond the design of this volume, and the work has been abundantly performed elsewhere. But the matter must not be dismissed without a few remarks.

And it may safely be asserted that the proofs of the genuineness and authenticity of every book in the Bible are such as to amount to nothing less than moral certainty. We must believe them to be true, because in the nature of things it is morally impossible they can be false. And this can be proved even without taking into account the overwhelming evidence of *Prophecy*—that grand demonstration of the Divine inspiration of the sacred writers, which is gradually and majestically unfolding itself before our eyes in the continual fulfilment of the predictions written.

The proof, in the case of the Pentateuch for example, may be stated as follows :—

The work *exists*, at the present moment—and is by common consent attributed to Moses—it might be said by universal consent, but that a few objectors, with an evidently hostile feeling against the doctrines it involves, have laboured to create doubts respecting parts of it.

But there is *one* people—and that one the people of Moses himself—who with one voice, and one heart and soul, claim the work as their own—written by the hand of their country-

man and one of their ancestors, Moses—written, as it is, in their
own ancient and cherished language, and regarded by them
with an almost idolatrous veneration. This national testimony
of the Jews is absolutely universal. Wherever Jews are found
under the whole heaven there is found the Pentateuch—held
sacred and inviolable as "*the Law of Moses.*" And this,
though some of the known portions of the Jewish people
have been separated from the rest for many hundreds of years,
having little, if any, communication with their brethren—some
probably even as far back as the captivity of the Ten tribes,
more than twenty-five centuries ago.

Moreover, this universal and unvarying testimony of a whole
nation is not a mere oral testimony—a mere tradition. The
"Law of Moses" has been THE *Law* of the whole Jewish
people from remote antiquity to the present hour. It is the
bond which has held them together as a people distinct and
exclusive, however scattered among the nations. It is the law
which moulds their whole mind, and regulates their daily life—
not only written upon their memory, but interwoven with their
whole history and stamped upon their very flesh. Its authority
is acknowledged, and its ordinances, as far as possible, are
observed by them, even to the present moment. It is their
pride, their treasure, and their trust.

Now, the question to which reason and common sense must
supply the answer is this :—If the Pentateuch, whole and unbroken, was not delivered to the Jewish people by Moses, how
are we to account for the fact that every Jew throughout the
world believes and obeys it? We may go farther, and ask—
How is it that the Jew is a Jew at all? for it is the "Law of
Moses" that has made him a Jew. The Jew, as a Jew, and
the whole nation, as a distinct nation, owe their very existence
to "the Law of Moses."

When, then, did this unvarying national testimony first
begin? It must be traced to its very fountain. If any time
later than the time of Moses can be pointed out when the

B

Pentateuch first began to be called the "Law of Moses," and to be obeyed as the national Jewish law, then we may admit the possibility that it was the work of some later author, and not of Moses.

But this, from the very nature of the case, is simply impossible. If any person since the death of Milton should have given himself out to be the author of the *Paradise Lost*, what sort of treatment would his pretensions have met with, and what chance would there have been that any one but Milton himself could come to be the reputed author?

But the argument for the authorship of the Pentateuch is a thousand-fold stronger than this illustration. We may ask— What chance would any one but the Duke of Wellington have had of being believed, if he had chosen to pretend that he was the conqueror at Waterloo? Even this absurdity would bear no comparison with the impossibility that any one but Moses could ever have obtained credit for being the writer of the Pentateuch.

In order to appreciate the nature of the case, we must consider all its circumstances. Moses was not merely the writer of a book—not merely even the chief actor in the events related in by far the greatest part of the book. He was all this and far more—he was the Lawgiver who obtained *obedience* from the whole people to the code of laws which the book contains.

Now this obedience absolutely depended upon the reality of all those most extraordinary events which the narrative records —all the stupendous miracles by means of which the people of Israel were rescued from Egypt, delivered from Pharaoh's host, and maintained and conducted during the forty years' wandering in the desert, till they entered the Land of promise. To those miracles, and above all, to the supernatural and stupendous terrors amidst which the Ten Commandments were delivered to Moses from the hand of God Himself on Mount Sinai, Moses invariably appealed as the credentials of His Divine mission, and the proof that the Law he delivered was given by God. If those miracles were real, then Moses was a divinely commissioned Lawgiver and ruler, and the law which he delivered was the Law of God. If those miracles were not real events, then Moses was an impostor, and the law which he delivered was a mere invention of his own. "For ask now of the days that are past, which were before thee, since the day that God created man upon the earth, and ask from the one side of heaven unto the other, whether there hath been any such thing as this great thing is, or hath been heard like it? Did ever people hear the voice of God speaking out of the midst of the fire, as thou hast heard, and live? Or hath God assayed to go and take him a nation from the midst of another nation, by temptations, by signs, and by wonders, and by war, and by a mighty hand, and by a stretched out arm, and by great terrors, according to all that the LORD your God did for you in Egypt before your eyes? Unto thee it was showed, that thou mightest know that the LORD he is God; there is none else beside him. Out of heaven he made thee to hear his voice, that he might instruct thee: and upon earth he showed thee his great fire; and thou heardest his words out of the midst of the fire. . . . . Thou shalt keep therefore his statutes and his commandments, which I command thee this day, that it may go well with thee, and with thy children after thee," &c. —Deut. iv. 32-40. Then, after reciting the Ten Commandments, he adds, " *These words the* LORD *spake unto all your assembly in the mount out of the midst of the fire, of the cloud, and of the thick darkness, with a great voice: and he added no more. And he wrote them in two tables of stone, and delivered them unto me.*"—Deut. v. 22. Moses appealed to their own eyes and ears for the truth of what he said, and for the Divine obligation of the Law which he had delivered to them. Could a whole people be persuaded to believe they had seen and heard these most stupendous wonders, when nothing of the kind had ever taken place? Yet upon this ground, and nothing less, was the Law of Moses established as the law of the people of Israel, and upon this ground has it been received and acknowledged

by that people for more than thirty-three centuries. The
creed and customs of every Jew at the present moment con-
nect themselves with the scenes of Egypt and Sinai. The
very existence of the Jews as a nation is a proof of the reality
of these scenes—for it is a consequence and result of them.
Without his peculiar creed and exclusive customs, the Jew must
inevitably have been lost by intermixture with all the nations
of the earth, and disappeared from sight thousands of years
ago. But that creed and those customs could not by any
possibility have been established but by the actual occurrence
of those miraculous events upon which they are expressly
grounded in the very book itself which contains the account of
them. Had the national creed of the Jews originated in any
other manner than in the miraculous events detailed in the
Pentateuch, the " Law of Moses," instead of being enshrined in
every Jewish heart with the deepest religious reverence, would
carry in itself its own condemnation as a gross and ridiculous
forgery. Every Jew throughout the world is thus a living
monument of the truth of Exodus and Deuteronomy, the
Divine origin of the " Law of Moses," and the Divine mission
and inspiration of Moses himself: for if these things were not
true, the faith of the Jew would be an impossibility, the
Pentateuch would contain its own condemnation, and the
legislator, Moses, would have proclaimed himself, with his
own mouth, to be a base deceiver and an impudent impostor.

It is, therefore, not possible in the nature of things that
Moses could be other than a divinely commissioned messenger
and inspired teacher to the people of Israel.

But, admitting this, what ground have we for believing that
the Pentateuch, as we now have it, is word for word the same
" Law of Moses," which this man of God left with the Jews?

The answer is, that we have proof not less conclusive of the
integrity of the Pentateuch than we have of its authenticity
and inspiration.

First—it is expressly declared that Moses wrote it with his own hand. "It came to pass, when Moses had made an end of writing the words of this law in a book, until they were finished, that Moses commanded the Levites, saying, Take this book of the law, and put it in the side of the ark of the covenant of the LORD your God, that it may be there for a witness against you."—Deut. xxxi. 24-26.

From which passage we learn, secondly—that the manuscript of this book was laid up, doubtless by the command of God Himself, by the side of the Ark, beneath the very Mercy-seat of God, with the express injunction that there it should always remain.[1] It is reasonable to believe that this injunction was religiously observed from generation to generation, and that accordingly the "book of the law of the LORD by Moses," which was found in the Temple by Hilkiah the priest, in the reign of the good king Josiah, was this very manuscript —the Sacred Original written by the hand of Moses himself. —2 Chron. xxxiv. 14. "It was," says Dr. Wordsworth, "the sight of that venerable volume, written by the great Lawgiver, and the sound of the Divine words recited from that holy oracle, which affected the tender heart of that youthful pious prince with awe and penitential sorrow for the sins of the people committed to his charge, and with godly fear of the Divine judgments hanging over their heads."

Thirdly—it was ordered by the express command of God that every king that should reign over Israel should write for himself a copy of this Law from the sacred original preserved in the Holy of Holies. "It shall be, when he sitteth upon the throne of his kingdom, that he shall write him a copy of this law in a book out of that which is before the priests the Levites: and it shall be with him, and he shall read therein all

---

[1] "That this command concerned the whole Pentateuch is shown by Hävernick, *Einleitung*, 1, p. 19."—Dr. Wordsworth, *On the Inspiration of the Bible*, p. 45.

the days of his life: that he may learn to fear the LORD his God, to keep all the words of this law and these statutes to do them."—Deut. xvii. 18, 19.

Fourthly—this "book of the Law," the Pentateuch, was ordered to be read in public every seven years before the whole assembled people at the Feast of Tabernacles.—Deut. xxxi. 10-13. It was read also at other times. Very soon after the entry of the people into the Land of promise, Joshua "read all the words of the law, the blessings and cursings, according to all that is written in the book of the law. There was not a word of all that Moses commanded, which Joshua read not before all the congregation of Israel, with the women, and the little ones, and the strangers that were conversant among them."—Josh. viii. 34, 35. Moreover, it was afterwards constantly read every Sabbath-day in the synagogues, both in Palestine, and in other countries where the Jews had settlements. It is obvious that for this purpose a large number of copies must have been made—all transcribed from the one original manuscript of Moses. The practice of publicly reading the "Law of Moses," has thus been continued by the Hebrew nation from the very time the book was written down to the present hour.

Now, with all these facts before our eyes—and the additional fact that all the best manuscripts of the Hebrew Scriptures agree in all essential points—will any reasonable man hesitate to believe that we possess the very words written by Moses himself at the command of God, without any material addition or alteration?

It is of course obvious, that the manuscript of Moses, and the parting words addressed by him to the people, which may have been taken down from his lips by dictation, did not extend beyond the thirty-third chapter of Deuteronomy: the thirty-fourth and concluding chapter containing merely the account of his death and burial, and of course having been added by a later hand—no doubt by Joshua. With this obvious exception, it is beyond reasonable doubt that the whole Pentateuch is indeed the very writing of Moses himself.

Let any person weigh well the whole nature of the case, and all the circumstances under which this sacred book has been transmitted to us, and the proof of its being *all* written by Moses and no one else, will appear not merely conclusive but absolutely overwhelming. When, or how, could any alteration or addition possibly have been made? The book, from the moment of its completion, was committed, as a sacred trust, to the keeping of the Levites, who had charge of the Tabernacle, and afterwards of the Temple. It was deposited in the Holy of Holies, into which no person but the High Priest could enter, on pain of death: who then could have access to it without the knowledge of its appointed guardians? From the time of Ezra, the Holy Scriptures were watched and guarded with such jealous care, that not only every section, but every verse, every word, and every letter of each book were diligently counted, and the number of them registered; the middle letter of the Pentateuch, the middle verse of each book, and how many times each letter of the alphabet occurred in the whole Hebrew Scriptures, were accurately noted at the end of each portion respectively. A book so guarded could no more be corrupted than Magna Charta or a modern Act of Parliament.

Farther—Moses being thus proved to be the writer of the Pentateuch, and the inspired Lawgiver of the Hebrews, and the sacred Text being thus shown to have come down to us without material alteration, it follows of necessity that the Pentateuch is *true*—historically and literally true.

For if not, Moses must either have been deceived himself, or he must knowingly have written what was false.

But he could not himself have been deceived, because when God commissioned him to govern and instruct His people, He would certainly preserve him from error. To suppose that Moses wrote what was false, is to suppose that he was not inspired— and therefore contradictory to what has been already proved.

Neither could he have deceived others wilfully; for this is no less contrary to the truth that he was inspired by God.

We conclude, therefore, from irresistible evidence, that the Pentateuch is an inspired and true narrative of facts, extending from the creation of the world to the death of Moses.

The same mode of reasoning which has here been applied to the Pentateuch is applicable, though under varied circumstances, to all the other books both of the Old and New Testaments. The testimony of the whole Jewish nation respecting every one of the former is, and always has been, unanimous and unvarying. And this testimony must of necessity have originated at the very time when each book was written; for in no other way than by each book having been recognized as true when it first appeared was it possible that it could ever be acknowledged as true at all. A book professing to be a history of real events, but speaking of events which no one had ever heard of before, would be such a manifest forgery, that it is impossible it should ever be believed at all. The fact therefore that all the books of the Old Testament *are* believed, by the whole Jewish people at the present moment, to be true and authentic, is a real proof that they are so: for had they been *untrue*, the falsehood must have been detected as soon as each book appeared, and the detected falsehood would inevitably have doomed the book to immediate infamy and speedy oblivion.

There is one proof of the truth of the whole of the Old Testament so overwhelming and unquestionable, that the whole weight of the argument might safely be laid upon it alone without any addition—namely, the express sanction of the Lord Jesus Christ Himself. But as the force of this proof depends upon the recognition of the Godhead of Christ—and as this must not be taken for granted, but proved—it would be premature to enter upon it in this place.

CHAPTER IV.

*Is it a thing incredible that God should grant a Revelation of Himself
to man?*

IT may be objected that *any* revelation of Himself by God to
man is a thing in itself so wholly improbable—so utterly incredible—that *no* amount of testimony can overcome the difficulty we find in believing that such a thing has ever taken
place.

This objection has, in fact, been urged by Hume and other
infidels against *Miracles*, which are inseparably connected with
Revelation, and must stand or fall together with it. If miracles
have not been really wrought, then no revelation can have
been given; for revelation is in itself of the nature of a
miracle, and miracles are the necessary and indispensable
proof, to the world, of a revelation made to any one individual.

It will therefore be proper to treat of the probability and
credibility of Revelation and Miracles together: since the probability of the one involves and implies the probability of the
other. The inquiry of course comprises the whole question of
the "*supernatural*" in religion.

It is contrary to experience, say the Sceptics, that miracles
should be true, but it is not contrary to experience that testimony should be false. And the conclusion they draw from this
statement is, that therefore it is not to be believed that
miracles have ever been wrought, however great the weight of
testimony by which they are attested.

It is truly surprising that men of acute and powerful

minds should have been misled by so transparent a fallacy. The argument, stated in plain English, is this :—Miracles are contrary to experience, therefore they have never taken place. And this must mean either that miracles are contrary to *our* experience, or that they are contrary to the experience of *all mankind*, in all ages of the world.

If it is meant to say that miracles are incredible because they are contrary to *our* experience, this is the same thing as to say that nothing can ever have taken place except what we have ourselves seen or heard—an absurdity so monstrous as not even Rationalists will venture to maintain.

But if the other alternative be meant—that miracles are incredible because they are contrary to the experience of all mankind—this is merely to assert in other words that miracles have never taken place *because* they have never taken place. To maintain that miracles are incredible because they are contrary to all experience, is to take for granted the very point under debate—which is, *whether* miracles are contrary to experience or not. If they have ever really been wrought, then they are not contrary to experience.

It is evident also that, supposing miracles to have been wrought, the only means by which they could possibly be made known to us is the testimony of those who were eye-witnesses of them. To say, then, that no testimony is sufficient to make miracles credible is the same thing as to say that, even though miracles have really been performed, it is impossible we could ever know the fact.

But it may be answered—If miracles are necessary at all, why are they not wrought in the sight of every individual—so that no one should be left in any doubt as to the fact of God having indeed interposed in human affairs ? This argument, presumptuous and foolish as it is, has actually been put forward by infidels. It has been demanded that if we are to believe in a Divine revelation, the truth of it should be proved to each one of us by ocular demonstration—by miracles wrought before our eyes. But those who argue thus, seem to forget that they are demanding an impossibility. A miracle is something extraordinary—something out of the usual course of nature. Now if miracles should become matters of daily occurrence, they would cease to be miracles. They would come to be regarded as common events, and would be so in reality. The very frequency of their recurrence would deprive them of their miraculous character, and reduce them to the level of things happening in ordinary course.

It is plain, therefore, that human testimony, so far from being inadmissible in proof of miracles, is the only proof by which mankind in general could possibly be assured of them. It is in the very nature of miracles that the eye-witnesses of them could be but few out of the many, and that the rest of mankind must depend for their knowledge of them upon the testimony of those few.

We recur then to the question—Is a Divine revelation a thing in itself so improbable that no amount of testimony can make it credible?

In order to answer this question, we must consider what is meant by *improbable*.

The nature of *probability* is well conveyed by the word *likely*—that is, *like* what has happened before in similar circumstances. The only reason of our judging that such and such an event will *probably* happen—or is *likely* to happen—is that it has been observed always, or often, to happen in like circumstances before. We know no reason in the nature of things why the sun should rise to-morrow; but we expect it will rise, because it has risen regularly heretofore. We consider it certain that every man will die; but (independently of revelation) this could only be inferred from the fact that men have died hitherto. There is no reason in the nature of things why men should die. Physicians tell us that the structure of the human frame is so perfect that their science can discover no reason why it should not last for ever. For anything we can see, men need never

die. The Scripture history tells us that some have never died ;
yet we expect that every man will die, because (with two exceptions only) all men in times past, so far as we know, have
died.

It is clear, then, that the highest probability, even to moral
certainty, rests on nothing more than the constant, or frequent,
recurrence of like events.

It follows, therefore, that anything which happens *for the
first time*, cannot be said to have been probable beforehand.
A thing of such a nature as has never yet happened cannot be
said to be *likely* to happen ; for it is like nothing that has ever
happened before.

If, then, miracles are incredible because they are improbable,
we must admit the strange conclusion that *nothing can ever
happen for the first time!* Nothing is probable except what
has happened before ; consequently, whatever has happened at
all must have been improbable before it happened for the first
time.   And if we are to disbelieve every thing that is improbable, we must disbelieve many things besides miracles—we
must disbelieve the very existence of the heavens and the earth,
sun, moon, stars, and all creation.   There was a time when the
only Being in existence was God Himself—a time when no
created thing had been called into existence by His Almighty
word.   At that time, the very existence of our world, and of
man upon it, was not probable ; for no world had yet been
created.   Must we therefore refuse to believe our own existence? We must do so, if every thing that is improbable is
therefore incredible.

It cannot, therefore, reasonably be argued that miracles are
really more improbable than any thing else.   It was once improbable that God would create the world ; yet the world was
created.   Therefore, even if it should be granted that miracles
were improbable, this would not have the weight of a single
atom as a proof that miracles would not be wrought.

But this is not all.

There is another view of the matter—and it is the true view
—which will show that it is really more probable that miracles
would, than that they would not, be wrought.

For it is probable—nay, certain—that God would always act
according to those principles of goodness and benevolence
which we see displayed in His works. From the *works* of God
we gather the *attributes* of God. From the wisdom and goodness shown in the works of nature, we naturally and unavoidably
infer that God is wise and good.

Now is it probable that God would create man upon the
earth and leave him completely to himself—without the means
of knowing for certain either who was his Maker, or what was
his own duty and destiny? Is it consistent with God's wisdom
and goodness that He should have sent mankind into the
world like outcasts, and left them to shift for themselves,
without affording them either help for this world, or hope for
another? Yet this is what we must believe that God did, if we
disbelieve a revelation attested by miracles.

If it is probable, and even morally certain, that God would
deal with mankind according to those attributes of wisdom and
goodness which we see that He manifests towards the rest of
His creatures, it is probable, and even morally certain, that
He would impart to mankind a knowledge of Himself—since
He has made man *capable* of knowing Him—and this knowledge is a want of man's nature, and necessary to his happiness.

But this argument derives still greater force from the fact
that man is—and feels himself to be—a responsible moral
agent. We have a *conscience*, and this conscience not only
speaks within us as *a law*, but also forewarns us that its own
dictates are *the* law by which we are bound under obedience to
our Maker. It both tells us that right is right, and wrong is
wrong, and also warns us that there is a Judge over all the
earth who will one day reckon with us, and call us to account
for our doings. The Scripture account that " as Paul reasoned
of righteousness, temperance, and judgment to come, Felix

trembled "—Acts xxiv. 25—is in exact accordance with the
sentence of conscience which every man may find within himself if he will only attend to it.

Now, this being so, reason would of itself lead us to think
that God would not leave mankind without an express revelation of that duty which their own conscience tells them they
owe to Him.   And as the natural conscience, while warning us
of our duty, is plainly no sufficient guide to direct us into all
the particulars of it, a strong probability arises—amounting
perhaps to moral certainty—that God would enlighten His
responsible creatures by some better means than the natural
conscience supplies.   Hence, then, we might reasonably conclude that a Divine revelation, enlightening mankind as to
their duty to their Maker, was a matter not only of high probability, but even of moral certainty.   The works of God
everywhere show *adaptation* to their intended use and object.
The eye is evidently made for the purpose of seeing, and the
ear for hearing; and the very fact that they are so implies
that there must be things to be seen and sounds to be heard.
The foot implies ground to walk upon, the hand implies something to be handled.   And in like manner a moral *conscience*
implies a moral *command*, and implies, farther, that this moral
command would certainly be supplied by the same Creator
who implanted in the mind a moral conscience.

The expectation, therefore, that God would grant to His
intelligent and responsible creature, Man, a supernatural revelation of Himself, and a divinely imparted knowledge of what
He requires of us, and of our own future destiny, is no more
than the whole analogy of His works warrants and even en-
forces.

It thus appears that a revelation from God to man, attested
by miracles, is so far from being improbable, that it is highly
probable, and even morally certain, that in some way or other
such a revelation would be made.

CHAPTER V.

*A Revelation from God must be probable in proportion to its Necessity
for Man—Reason and Natural Conscience insufficient—Instinct of
Immortality — Ennui — Lord Chesterfield's Testimony — Colonel
Gardiner's—Hume's—Lord Byron's.*

IT cannot reasonably be denied that if mankind stand in need
of some farther information than nature supplies, then there is
a probability that such a revelation would be granted as should
supply that need. So much, at least, as this we are bound to
believe by the manifestation of God's goodness and wisdom
displayed in all created things.

Now, does the state of the world at large go to prove that
man does need a revelation or not ?

If mankind need no revelation, this can only be because man
is self-sufficient to inform himself of all that he needs to know,
and all that he ought to do ; and, moreover, so entirely well
disposed as always and invariably to do what is right according
to that knowledge. But this is what no one certainly would
venture to assert.

It is true that to some extent nature itself, and our own
reason and conscience, do inform us both concerning God and
ourselves. That there is a God—that He is the Maker of all
things—that He ought to be honoured and worshipped as the
Giver of all good, and the Governor over all the world, are
truths which may certainly be perceived by the light of nature
—so as to leave men without excuse if they overlook and
neglect them. There are also plain moral duties which even

heathen writers have set forth with much labour and acuteness
—such as justice, temperance, humanity, and the like.

But what is the actual state of the world at the present
moment with regard either to the acknowledgment of these
truths, or the practice of these duties?   There is not a religious
or moral truth, from the very existence of a God to the
commonest moral precept, which is either universally acknowledged or universally obeyed ; and the result is that the whole
world is a very Babel of confused creeds and opinions, and a
very Sodom of all iniquities—a bane and a blot on the face of
God's creation.   To say that man's own reason and virtue
have proved sufficient guides to his conduct and happiness,
even in this world, would be to assert what is manifestly contrary to facts.

But there are questions which must needs force themselves
sometimes upon the mind of every one who ever thinks at all,
to which human reason supplies no answer ; such as these—
What am I?   For what was I born into this world?   Is this
life to be the whole of my being, or will death but introduce
me into another state of existence which may last for ever?
And if so, what will be my condition there—and is it depend-
ing on my conduct here?   May there not be awaiting me
hereafter a weight of happiness or a depth of misery incon-
ceivably greater than any degree either of pleasure or pain I
can experience in this life?

To a mind of any reflection these questions unanswered—
these doubts unsolved—these apprehensions unappeased—are
nothing short of torture inexpressible and intolerable.

Is it reasonable—is it possible—to believe that the God who
made us, and who has filled our world with manifest tokens of
His care for all His creatures, has left the noblest of them all
—the lord of creation here below—in such a condition of hopeless ignorance and helpless alarm as might make him envy the
very beasts that perish?

Against such a conclusion reason revolts.   It cannot be.

Whatever may be the cause of the ignorance, error, misery, and wickedness of the world, it cannot be owing to any neglect on the part of God towards the creatures of His hand. To impute such neglect to the Creator would be to charge Him with cruelty to His creatures, and to make Him, at least indirectly, the author of evil.

Moreover, the supposition that God has made no revelation to man of his duty and his destiny involves in itself an inconsistency which we cannot attribute to the good and wise Creator.

There is a spirit in man superior to the mere interests of this lower world. There is within us the instinct of *immortality*— the consciousness that we are not made to die eternally, and be no more for ever. We shrink from the thought of utter extinction ; and one of the strongest impulses of human ambition is the desire to be held in remembrance after death—to achieve a name and reputation which shall not die with us. There is also a sense of want—a craving for some undefined good—a feeling of destitution, of emptiness of soul—of which the most thoughtful and reflecting minds are usually the most conscious. There is a weariness of heart, which even the most thoughtless persons are compelled to confess under the name of *ennui*—and which is in truth the very same described in the Scripture itself as "vanity and vexation of spirit." It is the heart-sickening experience that this world contains nothing which can satisfy the aspirations of a human soul.

The fact is unquestionable that this incongruity between our desires and our position *exists*. It is for those who reject Revelation, and trust to human philosophy and science, to explain the *reason* of this fact, if they are able.

There is nothing like it to be found in the case of any other creature besides man. Other animals find themselves placed in circumstances suitable to their nature, and are satisfied. Man alone is an unsatisfied and unhappy being. With a mind capable of knowing God, he is left—if there be no revela-

C

tion—without the means of even understanding himself. With a soul thirsting for immortality, he must go down into the grave unable to penetrate the darkness which lies beyond it. With a heart ready to burst with the greatness and intensity of its own emotions, he is doomed to pine and sink under perpetual disappointment—and, like the fabled Tantalus, must bear the lifelong torture of seeing the cup of happiness apparently presented to his acceptance, but always dashed from his lips.

Such feelings as these are not mere vapourings of a disordered imagination. They are the recorded experiences of those whose testimony can neither be rejected as spurious nor charged with partiality or prejudice. The men who have drunk most deeply of the cup of this world's pleasures are precisely those who have the most bitterly complained that they had not found it to be the cup of happiness.

Shall we hear, and believe, the confessions of one who had certainly denied himself nothing which the world could offer? In old age, and failing health, he wrote thus :—" I have enjoyed all the pleasures of this world, and consequently know their futility, and do not regret their loss. I appraise them at their real value, which in truth is very low, whereas those who have not experienced always over-rate them. They only see their gay outside, and are dazzled with their glare ; but I have been behind the scenes. . . I look upon all that has passed as one of those romantic dreams that opium commonly occasions, and I do by no means desire to repeat the nauseous dose for the sake of the fugitive dream. When I say that I have no regret, I do not mean that I have no *remorse*. I have been as wicked and as vain, though not so wise, as Solomon ; but am now at last wise enough to feel and attest the truth of his reflection, that '*all is vanity and vexation of spirit*.' This truth is never sufficiently discovered or felt by mere speculation ; experience in this case is necessary for conviction. When I reflect upon what I have seen, what I have heard, and what I have done myself, I can hardly persuade myself that all that frivolous hurry and bustle, and pleasures of the world, had any reality, but they seem to have been the dreams of restless nights. I see the folly and absurdity of mankind without indignation or peevishness. I wish them wiser, and consequently better, than they are."

Such were the acknowledgments of the most well-bred, and the most admired man of his time—the clever, witty, accomplished, but profligate, Lord Chesterfield.

Again, we are told concerning another of the world's favourites, that "his fine constitution, than which perhaps there hardly ever was a better, gave him great opportunities of indulging himself in excesses; and his good spirits enabled him to pursue his pleasures of every kind in so alert and sprightly a manner that multitudes envied him, and called him by a dreadful kind of compliment, *the happy rake*. Yet still the checks of conscience, and some remaining principles of so good an education as he had received, would break in upon his most licentious hours; and I particularly remember he told me, that when some of his dissolute companions were once congratulating him on his distinguished felicity, a dog happening to come into the room, he could not forbear groaning inwardly, and saying to himself, *Oh that I were that dog!* Such was then his happiness, and such perhaps is that of hundreds more, who bear themselves highest in the contempt of religion, and glory in that infamous servitude which they call *Liberty*."[1]

David Hume, one of the greatest luminaries of infidel "science," was forced at last to confess that his light was darkness. In his book on Human Nature, vol. i. p. 458, he says—"I seem affrighted and confounded with the solitude in which I am placed by my philosophy. When I look abroad, on every side I see dispute, contradiction, and distraction. When I turn my eye inward, I find nothing but doubt and

---

[1] Dr. Doddridge's *Life of Colonel Gardiner*.

ignorance. Where am I? or what am I? From what cause do I derive my existence? To what condition shall I return? I am confounded with these questions. I begin to fancy myself in a most deplorable condition, *environed with the deepest darkness on every side."*

"Habemus confitentem reum."—The most acute and clever among infidels is thus obliged to confess that mere human reason, even with all the culture, all the resources, of "philosophy," leaves him in the deepest darkness and ignorance concerning those vital questions which he cannot avoid asking himself, yet cannot answer, and trembles to leave unanswered.

Once more—who can mistake either the character of *Byron,* or the mournful complaint which his genius could clothe in words as beautiful as they are melancholy—

> " Alas! it is delusion all—
>   The future mocks us from afar;
> Nor can we be what we recall,
>   Nor dare to think on what we are.
>
> " No—for myself, so dark my fate
>   Through every turn of life hath been,
> Man and the world so much I hate,
>   I care not when I quit the scene.
>
> " Count up the joys thine hours have known,
>   Count up thy days from anguish free—
> And know, whatever thou hast been,
>   'Tis something better not to be."

Such was the portion of this man of the world—his hope a delusion, his desire annihilation!

Here, then, we find that there is in the experience of mankind an incongruity between our natural wants and our actual circumstances, such as we cannot in reason suppose to have been according to the design of God in our creation. It is *contrary* to our reason. It is contrary to our natural sense of the fitness of things—contrary to the ideas we naturally entertain of the goodness and wisdom of the Creator—contrary to the whole analogy of His dealings with the lower animals, to the beautiful order and harmony displayed in all His works, and the exquisite adaptation of every part to every other part, and of each part to the whole.

And this undeniable fact is altogether inexplicable—a dark and dreary maze of perplexity and despair—unless we admit the countervailing fact that God has made to man in the Bible a revelation, which reveals God to man, and man to himself. Admit this, and all is clear—the ways of God with man are justified, and shown to be worthy of God—and a prospect is held out to man of happiness and blessing, not merely equal, but far superior, to his fondest hopes and loftiest aspirations.

Just in proportion, therefore, as we highly estimate the wisdom and goodness of God, we must admit the high probability that He would pity and relieve the mental misery of which the most powerful and reflecting minds are the most painfully conscious, arising from the felt inaptitude of their circumstances in this world to satisfy the wants and longings of an immortal soul.

CHAPTER VI.

Nature of Proof from Facts, that the Bible is true.—The present observance of the Sabbath, both by Jews and Christians, a Proof of the Literal Truth of Genesis.

FACTS are, proverbially, stubborn things; and no inquiry after truth can possibly be successful which either ignores facts, or fails to recognize their bearing on the points under debate.

The Bible professes to give an account of the origin and early history of mankind. It must needs be thought that the facts of such a history, if truly narrated, would be found to be in accordance with all other authentic histories.

If this is found to be actually the case, then there is positive evidence, of a circumstantial kind, in proof of the correctness of the Scripture narrative.

But this is a very small part of the nature of the proof derivable from facts in favour of the narrative of man's Creation, Temptation, and Fall—and of the promise of a Redeemer, and the attendant circumstances—contained in the early chapters of Genesis. These facts are of a nature so extraordinary that they could not possibly have taken place without producing the most prodigious *consequences* upon the whole state and history of mankind from that time to the present, and for all time yet to come—and that too, throughout the whole world. The effects of those events must have been felt in every part of man's nature, body, soul, and spirit—

in every department of earth, his habitation—in soil, climate, produce—in healthiness, fertility, and adaptation to the natural state and wants of mankind. They must of necessity tell upon the whole condition of human society—physical, moral, intellectual, social, and political. It must needs be that we should find in every country and every clime the traces of a change so appalling—of circumstances so strange and singular —as those recorded in the book of Genesis.

But, on the other hand, we may and must reason backwards from the present to the past. We must not only expect to find causes so portentous producing corresponding effects, but we must also argue from the effects to the causes. If we find in history—in the traditions and customs of the nations of the world—in actual facts daily before our eyes, consequences such as *could* be produced only by some such events as those narrated by Moses, then we are bound by logical necessity to infer that those events must really have taken place. When we find facts existing which *could* only have arisen from such and such causes, the inference is inevitable that such causes must have existed to produce them. A coin dug out of the earth, bearing the name and effigy of the Roman emperor Trajan, or the English king Edward III., is an indisputable proof that those sovereigns really lived and reigned—but why? Simply because the existence of the coin can be *accounted for* by nothing else than the *fact* of their having lived and reigned.

And facts are like coins, in the cogent and inevitable force of their testimony. Every effect must have had a cause. When, therefore, an effect is found existing which can only be accounted for by such and such a cause having previously existed, it is as certain that such a cause *did* once exist as that the effect is visible at the present time.

Of this nature, for example, are national customs and traditions. A tradition of a Deluge, found existing among all nations, is irresistible evidence that a Deluge once happened— because on no other supposition can the universal tradition

be accounted for. The Jewish Passover, always kept as a
memorial of the Exodus, is an absolute demonstration that
the Exodus took place—for otherwise the institution of such a
memorial would have been simply impossible. In like manner,
if facts exist at the present moment, or well authenticated
accounts of them, which are altogether inexplicable on the
supposition that Genesis is "poetry, not history," but which
are natural and necessary results of the events therein recorded, if Genesis is history and not "poetry"—then we must
in all reason conclude that those events really happened as the
history relates.

It will be convenient, in reviewing the facts in connexion
with the record, to take them in order pretty much as we find
them suggested by the narrative.

The *Sabbath* is an institution existing at the present day.
It is recognized both by Jews and Christians—and observed,
in name at least, wherever there is a professing Christian
church. By the Jews it is kept with punctilious and religious
reverence—and that, notwithstanding that, in Christian countries, their voluntary observance of their own Sabbath on the
seventh day of the week, besides the enforced keeping of the
first day, subjects them to the loss of two days for business
instead of one.
This difference between the Jewish and Christian Sabbath
is in itself the strongest confirmation of the truth both of the
Old and New Testaments. The change of day is clearly
traceable to the Resurrection of the Lord Jesus Christ on the
first day of the week—in consequence of which circumstance
the first day of the week was from that time forward kept as
the Christian Sabbath instead of the seventh day. The
change was evidently made from the very time of the Saviour's
Resurrection, and must have been made with the sanction, if
not by the express direction, of Christ Himself. It is called

in the New Testament "*the Lord's Day,*" evidently with reference to the Lord's Resurrection.

But as the Jews never, as a nation, acknowledged the truth of the Saviour's Resurrection, their adherence to the ancient observance of the *seventh* day is in exact accordance both with the Gospel histories, and also with their own national and immemorial custom.

That custom can be traced, for its origin, to no later a date than the Creation itself.

In the Jewish polity it was ordered by the Fourth of the Ten Commandments delivered by the hand of Moses.

But this was not its beginning. The Fourth Commandment is introduced, unlike any of the others, by the significant word *Remember*—"Remember the seventh day, to keep it holy." Why "*remember*"? Just because the commandment was not new, and the observance of it was already an established institution. The word "*Remember*" is positive proof that the Sabbath was observed before the giving of the Law from Mount Sinai.

When did it begin? It began when "God blessed the seventh day, and sanctified it: because that in it he had rested from all his work which God created and made."—Gen. ii. 3.

Will any sceptic have the face to assert that the seventh-day Sabbath of Genesis was "poetry, not history"—in other words, that the institution of the Sabbath was merely an allegory, not a fact? If so, when did it become a fact, and not an allegory? To-day, it is a fact. It has been a fact for 3300 years—it was a fact already when, 3300 years ago, Moses delivered the commandment, "*Remember* the seventh day to keep it holy." When did it *begin* to be a fact, if at its first announcement in Genesis it was an allegorical fable?

The universal and invariable observance of the seventh-day Sabbath by the Jews, and of the Lord's Day by the Christian professing churches, throughout the whole world—linked to-

gether as they are by the Gospel history, the Fourth Commandment, and the appointment of the Sabbath in memory of
God's resting from the work of creation—forms a chain of
evidence, extending back from the present hour to the creation
of the world, which amounts to nothing less than a demonstration of the historical and literal truth of Genesis in this particular.

And every such proof in a particular instance has a value
beyond the particular instance itself. For it is an instance,
and a specimen, of the *general character* of the Book. It is one
of a *series* of things narrated, which, taken together, make up
the whole narrative. Any one of these things, therefore, being
proved to be an actual fact, and not an allegory or poetical
figure, affords a presumption that the other things also, narrated
in the same connexion, are of the same kind—actual facts, not
poetical or imaginary. For a narrative of successive incidents,
some actual and historical, others allegorical and poetical,
would be so far from being according to reason and common
sense, that it would be incoherent and absurd.

The week of creation, and the hallowing of the seventh day
as a Sabbath, were well known and remembered among the
ancients.

"With regard to the particular number of days which were
employed in the creation of the world," says Mr. Faber, "it
has been already shown that the ancient Persians and Etrurians
were not unacquainted with it. The use of the Sabbath, and
the division of time into weeks, which can only be accounted
for on the supposition of a remote tradition of the grand week
of creation, seems to have pervaded nearly every part of the
globe. Eusebius in his *Præparatio Evangelica* cites several of
the ancient poets who speak of the seventh day as being holy.[1]
Hesiod and Homer both unite in ascribing to it a degree of
superior sanctity; and Callimachus asserts that upon it all

---

[1] Euseb. *Præp. Ev.* lib. 13, cap. 13.

things were finished. The Sabbath is said to have been observed among the ancient inhabitants of Arabia, previous to
the era of Mahomet;[1] consequently, though that impostor
confirmed the observation of such an ordinance, he could not
be said to have first enjoined it to his followers, from the knowledge which he possessed of the Books of Moses. Thus also
the natives of Pegu assemble together for the purposes of
devotion on one fixed day in every week;[2] and the people of
Guinea[3] rest from their accustomed occupations of fishing and
agriculture every seventh day throughout the year.

"As for the division of time into weeks, it extends from the
Christian states of Europe to the remote shores of Hindoostan,
and has equally prevailed among the Jews and the Greeks, the
Romans and the Goths; nor will it be easy to account for this
unanimity upon any other supposition than that which is here
adopted.

"Even the Mosaical method of reckoning by nights instead
of by days has prevailed in more than one nation. The
polished Athenians computed the space of a day from sunset
to sunset;[4] and from a similar custom of our Gothic ancestors
during their abode in the forests of Germany,[5] words expressive of such a mode of calculation have been derived into our
own language—such as *fortnight, sen'night.* The same custom, as we are informed by Cæsar, prevailed among the Celtic
nations. 'All the Gauls,' says he, 'conceive themselves to be
sprung from father Dis, and they affirm it to have been handed
down to them by the Druids. For this reason they measure
time not by the number of days, but of nights. Accordingly, they
observe their birthdays, and the beginnings of months and years,
in such a manner as to cause the day to follow the night.'[6]"[7]

---

[1] Purch. *Pilg.* b. 3, c. 2.   [2] Ibid. b. 5, c. 5.
[3] Ibid. b. 6, c. 15.   [4] Aul. Gall. *Noct. Attic.* lib. 3, cap. 2.
[5] Tac. *de Mor. Germ.* c. 11.   [6] Cæs. *de Bell. Gall.* lib. 6, cap. 18.
[7] Faber, *Hor. Mos.* b. 1, ch, 2.

So again, "Throughout the whole of this kingdom (Pegu) Monday is set apart for religious worship, and on that day their priests, whom they call *Talapoins*, preach sermons to the people."[1]

At Delphi, it was the custom to *sing a hymn to Python on every seventh day.*[2]

A custom, so singular in itself, of observing every seventh day as holy—and this observed from immemorial antiquity among the remotest nations, can be accounted for on one supposition only—viz., that the Scriptural account of its institution is historically and literally true.

There are two circumstances which furnish collateral proof of the strongest kind in confirmation of the Divine institution of the Sabbath in Eden—first, its wise and beneficent adaptation to man's nature—and secondly, the constant opposition which it has nevertheless encountered from mankind. That "the Sabbath was *made for man*"—and that, too, by One who knew man's constitution and wants—is a truth attested by facts as well as pronounced by the Saviour. The highest medical authorities declare that the machinery of the human frame is not made to work more than six days in seven—that the seventh-day rest is an indispensable necessity both for mind and body.

At a meeting of the Medical Society of the county of New York, held not long since, a resolution was passed that "one day's rest from labour in seven is necessary for the health both of the body and mind."

The late Sir Robert Peel also is remembered to have said, "I never knew a man to escape failures, in either body or mind, who worked seven days in the week."

All experience proves that, *with* this rest, both mind and body are kept healthy and vigorous, and capable of an inde-

[1] Hurd's *Rites and Ceremonies*, p. 73.

[2] Deane on the *Worship of the Serpent*, p. 90—and authorities there quoted.

finite amount of labour—and that too for the term of a long life ; but that *without* it, health is impaired, the mind enfeebled, strength broken down, the constitution early worn out, and life cut short by premature decay. It thus becomes evident that there is a perfect *adaptation* of the seventh-day rest to the requirements of man's constitution. But it is equally clear that this adaptation has become known to *us* only by experience ; so that the Sabbath could not have been devised by *man* for the sake of its beneficial effect on man's health—for this effect was not discovered till after the Sabbath had been long observed.

Moreover, the Sabbath is so necessary for the moral and religious welfare of mankind, that wherever it is neglected or abused, there religion almost entirely disappears, and morality suffers in proportion.

We have then, on one hand, the fact that the Sabbath is an actual institution observed at the present day, and traced through the Scripture history to the very time of the Creation —and, on the other hand, the fact that it is indispensable to the bodily, mental, and moral well-being of mankind, though this beneficial effect of it could be known to us only by the actual observance of it. Was it then devised by man, or ordained by God ? Is it more likely that an institution of so singular a nature should have been thought of by some one man, and adopted by others, without any reason at all—or that it should have been appointed in mercy and benevolence towards man by the God who made man, and knew exactly what was good for His own creature ? Genesis affirms that it was ordained by God. Those who think otherwise are bound in reason to show cause why it is more probable that it was devised by man.

But the improbability of this latter idea grows into moral impossibility when it is considered, farther, that always and everywhere men have rebelled against it, instead of adopting it willingly. It has never anywhere been observed otherwise

than as a religious obligation : and never anywhere has it
been obeyed without an evident reluctance, and often active
opposition, on the part of men in general. Not that men in
general would have any objection to a seventh-day *holiday*—if
nothing were lost by it from their gains or convenience. But
this is not the nature of the Sabbath. It was expressly
enjoined to be "*kept holy*"—that is, set apart from all worldly
business for the special service of God. In this its proper
sense and aim, when and where has it ever been generally and
willingly observed ? By the Jews it was grossly and continually
profaned. They said, "When will the Sabbath be gone, that
we may set forth wheat ?"—Amos viii. 5. And the case at
the present day among professing Christian nations is yet
worse. "A continental Sunday," is become a bye-word as
meaning just a general holiday : and it need hardly be remarked
that in our own country there is a continual struggle to bring
about the same state of things among ourselves—and that the
number of persons, of all clases in society taken together, who
really "keep the Sabbath *holy*," is a small minority. Mankind
in general are so far from desiring to observe it, notwithstanding the experience of its benefits, that they are impatient of
its restraints, and averse to its holy employments.

Yet—notwithstanding impatience, opposition, and dislike—
the Sabbath *exists*—as an institution recognized, however it may
be abused, wherever Jews or professing Christians are to be
found, throughout the world. The fact must in all reason be admitted as a proof that it is not of man, but of God. *When*, and
how, was it first appointed otherwise than as Genesis declares ?

But the Sabbath of our days is a real fact, not a myth or an
allegory. So, therefore, must have been the Sabbath of
Genesis—a real and literal seventh-day rest, and a memorial
for evermore of the real and literal event of God's having
"rested on the seventh day from all his works which God
created and made."

CHAPTER VII.

Traditions of Eden—"Paradises" of Assyrian Kings—The Garden of the Hesperides—Easter Eggs and Oranges—Eve deified and worshipped.

THAT the garden of Eden was a real place, and not an allegorical figure, is evident from the fact that the memory of it was handed down in Eastern countries from generation to generation. It appears even to have been actually imitated by Eastern monarchs. They used to have enclosed gardens, or parks, attached to their palaces—with trees, and a river flowing through them, in accordance with the description of Eden. And these parks, or gardens, were called *Paradises.*[1] Now the term *paradise* is an Oriental word, found both in Sanskrit, Hebrew, and Arabic: and it is the very word employed, in its Greek form, by the translators of the Septuagint for the garden of Eden in Gen. ii. 8. It is abundantly clear that the coincidence was not accidental. There can be no reasonable doubt that these parks, or *paradises*, were imitations of the lovely place · prepared by God Himself for man's abode in the happy days of his innocence. The fact that the word *paradise*, already familiar as the appellation of the royal gardens or parks, was used by the Septuagint translators, nearly three centuries before Christ, to designate the garden of Eden, is positive proof that the parks were understood to be *similar* to Eden : and this fact, conjoined with other circumstances hereafter to be noticed, forms with them a train of circumstantial evidence,

[1] As in Xen. *Hellen.* 4, 1, 15.—*Cyr.* 1, 3, 14.

too strong to be reasonably questioned, that they were in reality intended as *imitations* of Eden.

It would be absurd to suppose that the royal parks of Eastern monarchs were laid out to embody an idea suggested by a mere allegory in a Hebrew "*poem*"! especially when in all probability that "poem," so called, was not yet in existence when those ancient Eastern kings first planted parks or gardens. For when it is considered how enduring and unvarying are Eastern customs from age to age, even for thousands of years, the park of the Assyrian monarch, which existed in the days of Xenophon, will be seen to have been most probably as old as the Assyrian monarchy itself. And no time could be pointed out, as the date of its construction, more probable than those early times after the Flood, when the memories of Eden were most fresh in the minds of men.

Those memories were never wholly lost among the nations. The traditions of Eden, the garden of "Delight," though distorted by various wild imaginations, are among the most interesting records of earth's scattered tribes. "Arab legends," for example, "tell of a garden in the East, on the summit of a mountain of jacinth, inaccessible to man; a garden of rich soil and equable temperature, well watered, and abounding with trees and flowers of rare colours and fragrance."[1] So also the Hindû tradition says that, "in the centre of Iambo-dwipa, the middle of the seven continents of the Puranas, is the golden mountain Méru, which stands like the seed-cup of the lotus of the earth. On its summit is the vast city of Brahmá, renowned in heaven, and encircled by the Ganges, which, issuing from the foot of Vishnu, washes the lunar orb, and falling thither from the skies, *is divided into four streams*, that flow to the four corners of the earth. . . . In this abode of Divinity is the Nandana, or grove of Indra; there too is the Iambu tree, from whose fruit are fed the waters of the Iambu river, which *give*

---

[1] Smith's *Dict. of the Bible*, art. "Eden."

life and immortality to all who drink thereof." [1] Again—"The enchanted gardens of the Chinese are placed in the midst of the summits of Houanlun, a high chain of mountains farther north than the Himálaya, and farther east than Hindukush. The *fountain of immortality* which waters these gardens is *divided into four streams*, the fountains of the supreme spirit Tychin." One ancient tradition has preserved even the very name of *Eden*—"The Zend books mention a region called *Heden*, and the place of Zoroaster's birth is called *Hedenesh*." [2]

Traditions coinciding so strangely with the narrative of Genesis cannot be accounted for but by the truth of that narrative. To say that such coincidences are accidental is idle and evasive. The garden of delicious fruits and flowers—the *four* streams watering it—the tree whose fruit conferred *immortality*—the very name of *Eden*—the circumstance that this garden was become *inaccessible* to man—are features of the traditions which are almost repetitions of the sacred history in other words.

The classic fable of the garden of the Hesperides is another legend of Eden. In that garden the *golden apples* of the goddess Hera were said to be kept by the Hesperides nymphs with the aid of the dragon (or *serpent*) Ladon : the serpent was overcome—some accounts say killed—and the apples recovered, by Hercules—but not without the aid of the giant Atlas, who was fabled to bear the heavens upon his shoulders. Hercules employed Atlas to fetch the apples, and in the meanwhile bore the weight of the heavens for him. Now Hercules is a character of Pagan mythology under which is concealed a tradition of the world's Redeemer promised to Adam. It may, or may not be, that in the fable of his being able to recover the golden apples *only by bearing the weight of the heavens upon his shoulders* in the absence of Atlas, there is a covert allusion to the under-

[1] *Vishnu Purana*, trans. Wilson, pp. 166-171, cited by Smith, *ibid.*
[2] See Smith, *ibid.*

D

lying truth that the Redeemer could only recover man's lost Paradise by taking the world's sin upon Himself. However this may be, the other points of similarity between the garden of Eden with its Tree of Knowledge, the Serpent, and the promised Redeemer, on the one hand—and the garden of the Hesperides, the golden apples, the guardian serpent, and the deliverer Hercules on the other,—are striking and conclusive. In Smith's *Classical Dictionary* there is a group of " Hercules and the Hesperides, from a bas-relief at Rome," which, but for the additional figures, might stand for an illustration of the Tree of Knowledge with Eve and the Serpent-tempter. It represents a tree with fruit hanging on it, and a serpent intertwined among the branches: while Hercules is seated under it between two nymphs.

But there is much more wrapped up in this fable of the Hesperides and the golden apples. Straws, as it were, cast upon the stream of tradition at its very fountain-head are picked up floating on its waters at the distance of six thousand years, and bear witness to the unbroken continuity of the stream which has brought them down from the remotest antiquity to our time.

Bishop Gillis, of Edinburgh, some years ago went through the vainglorious ceremony of washing the feet of twelve ragged Irishmen at Easter. He concluded by presenting each of them with *two eggs and an orange*.[1] Who would have guessed that under so simple and apparently trifling an act there lurks a mystic meaning of mingled truth and superstition running back to the very scene of Eve's temptation and man's ruin? Yet so it is.

The *Easter egg* is a commemoration of the *Ark*, in which during the time of the Flood the human race were shut up, as the chick is enclosed in the egg before it is hatched. This

---

[1] This statement and the explanations following are taken from Mr. Hislop's work, *The Two Babylons*, p. 161, &c.

mystic egg was afterwards adopted and consecrated by the
Romish Church as a symbol of Christ's Resurrection.

But the *orange* used at this Popish Easter ceremony has
another meaning. " This use of the orange as the representative
of the fruit of Eden's 'dread probationary tree,' be it observed,
is no modern invention; it goes back to the distant times of
classic antiquity. The Gardens of the Hesperides in the
West are admitted by all who have studied the subject just
to have been the counterpart of the paradise of Eden in the
East. The description of the sacred gardens, so situated in the
isles of the Atlantic, over against the coast of Africa, shows
that their legendary site exactly agrees with the Cape Verd or
Canary Isles, or some of that group; and of course that the
'golden fruit' on the sacred tree, so jealously guarded, was
none other than the *orange.* Now let the reader mark well:—
According to the Pagan classic story there was no serpent in
that garden of delight in the ' Islands of the blest' to *tempt* mankind to violate their duty to their great benefactor by eating of
the sacred tree which He had reserved as the test of their
allegiance. No—on the contrary, it was the Serpent, the symbol
of the Devil, the Principle of Evil, the Enemy of man, that *prohibited* them from eating the precious fruit—that strictly
watched it—that would not allow it to be touched. Hercules,
one form of the Pagan Messiah—not the primitive, but the
Grecian Hercules—pitying man's unhappy state, slew or subdued the serpent, the envious being that grudged mankind the
use of that which was so necessary to make them at once perfectly happy and wise—and bestowed upon them what otherwise would have been hopelessly beyond their reach. Here,
then, God and the devil are exactly made to change places.
Jehovah, who *prohibited* man from eating of the Tree of Knowledge, is symbolized by the serpent, and held up as an un-
generous and malignant being : while he who emancipated
man from Jehovah's yoke, and gave him of the fruit of the
forbidden tree—in other words, Satan under the form of

Hercules—is celebrated as the good and gracious Deliverer of the human race. What a mystery of iniquity is here! Now all this is wrapped up in the sacred *orange* of Easter!"[1]

But this ceremony of the orange can be traced up to Eve in Paradise by another channel.

The orange is a substitute for the *Pomegranate*[2]—the *Rimmon* of Babylonian mythology, and the symbol assigned to the principal goddess of Babylon. The word *Rimmon*, in Hebrew signifies *a pomegranate;* and the "house of Rimmon," in which Naaman the Syrian attended his master the king of Syria when he went to worship there, was in all likelihood a temple of this Babylonian goddess, who was the same as *Ashtoreth*, or Astarté. Bryant gives a figure from the antique representing the goddess Hera, (or Juno or Rhea) with a dove sitting on a staff or sceptre which she holds in one hand, and a *pomegranate* held in the other. Now Juno, or Hera—otherwise called Rhea or Cybele—was worshipped with these emblems as the *Mother of mankind.* She was also called *Idaia Mater*, the "Idæan Mother"—and the sacred mount in Phrygia most famed for her worship was called Mount *Ida.* Now, in the Chaldee—the sacred language in which her mysteries were conveyed—"Mount Ida" signifies the *Mount of Knowledge*, and *Idaia Mater* signifies the *Mother of Knowledge.* In other words,

---

[1] Hislop, *Two Babylons*, as above.

[2] The Pomegranate is the Sacred Tree of the Eastern legends of Paradise: and Mr. Forster has shown that there is express evidence, both pictorial and written, that the Tree of Knowledge was believed to have been a pomegranate. The Tree in the picture of the Fall in Plate I. (see Chapter 8) answers accurately to the appearance of the pomegranate—the *flowers* sculptured in the legend of the large tablet in Mr. Forster's work *The Monuments of Egypt*, p. 184, are those of the pomegranate—the *fruit* on the head of the basilisk, or serpent, in the picture, is a pomegranate—and Mr. Forster reads, in the scroll surmounting the picture, both the word *raman*, a pomegranate, *with the pomegranate flowers beside it*—and also, in the hieroglyphics, the word *marmar*, a "*juicy pomegranate.*"

Ashtoreth, or Astarté, or Rhea, Cybele, Juno, or the Idæan Mother, are but different names under which was deified and worshipped *our mother Eve*—who first coveted the *"knowledge"* of good and evil, and actually obtained it by eating of the forbidden *fruit*. When therefore the Ashtoreth of the Babylonian worship—the Cybele or Idaia Mater of the Greeks and Romans —is represented holding forth in her right hand the *pomegranate*, with the symbol of the dove, which identifies her as the *Mother of mankind*—what else is presented to us but a legendary picture of Eve inviting mankind to taste of the fruit of the *Tree of Knowledge ?*—" that very

> ————'Tree, whose mortal taste
> Brought death into the world, and all our woe.'

"The knowledge to which the votaries of the Idæan goddess were admitted was precisely of the same kind as that which Eve derived from the eating of the forbidden fruit—the practical knowledge of all that was morally evil and base."[1]

So curiously was the tradition of Eve in Paradise, and the Tree of Knowledge, interwoven with the Pagan idolatry—and so strangely are its traces found lingering among us to this very day. Such facts afford nothing less than historical demonstration that Eden was a reality, and not a myth. Nothing less than the actual occurrence of the events recorded in the sacred narrative—thrilling through the very hearts of men from generation to generation—could account for traditions and idolatries so evidently of identical origin, so generally diffused, and so tenaciously remembered, among the principal nations of antiquity.

[1] *Two Babylons*, ibid.

CHAPTER VIII.

*Traditions of the creation of Adam and Eve—their first state of inno-
cence—the descent of all mankind from them alone—the Flood and
kindred subjects.*

A WRONG turn taken at the *beginning* of a journey is that
which leads the traveller farthest astray.

The early chapters of Genesis are the very starting-point of
the whole course of revealed religion—the very fountain-head
of all our knowledge of our own state and destinies.

Hence arises their peculiar importance. A mistake here is
a mistake at the very outset of the whole inquiry, and involves
of course the continual propagation of error at every subsequent stage. Such a mistake is of the nature, not of an isolated wrong conclusion upon which nothing depends beyond
itself—but of a false assumption at the beginning of an argument, which vitiates everything beyond it. It is like a wrong
figure, not in the last line of an arithmetical calculation, but in
the first—or a crumbling stone laid, not on the coping of a
building, but as a corner-stone at the foundation. The effect
of any material error in interpreting the history of the origin
of our race will be to shake, and eventually overthrow, the
whole fabric of belief in Revelation.

And such an error is that which assumes that mankind are
not the offspring of a single pair, but of many, or several,
brought into being (we are not told *how*) at different times and
places.

Now this is a question which touches the very vitals of Christianity—the very life of our souls. If it be once granted that the Mosaic account of man's creation is not an account of the origin of *the whole race of mankind*, then farewell at once to all Revelation. There is an end of all belief in the Fall of man by sin, and the Redemption of man by Jesus Christ, if the narrative of Adam's disobedience concerns only a *part* of mankind—just that part which was descended from Adam— while another and perhaps a larger part has no connexion with him whatever.—Any doubt, therefore, cast upon the literal truth of the creation of Adam and Eve, and of the descent of all mankind from them alone, is an axe laid to the root of all belief in Revelation and the doctrines of Christianity.

If only a part of mankind are the offspring of Adam and Eve, then the whole Bible must be false—which everywhere speaks of *all* mankind as their posterity, and bound up with them both in their Fall and in their Redemption.

Or if, again, the account of Adam's formation by the finger of God, and of Eve's being made of a rib taken from his side, is " poetry, not history "—that is, in plain English, a fable and a falsehood—then we know nothing whatever of the origin of mankind, of our own standing before God, or of our eternal destiny. Then we are left in as complete ignorance of all that it most concerns us to know, as the very heathens them- selves—in as total darkness as if the Bible had never been written.

These points, then, must be studied, and the question settled, once for all, as for our very life.

Those who deny that mankind are all the family of Adam, must of course deny the truth of the express statement of Genesis concerning the sons of Noah—" These are the three sons of Noah, and *of them was the whole earth overspread."*— Gen. ix. 19. This statement, at least, is history—and as it is not, and cannot be, denied that the whole family saved in the Ark were sprung from Adam and Eve, the statement establishes the descent of the whole existing human family from the one first pair.

The same remark applies also to the earlier statement respecting the origin of Eve's name—"Adam called his wife's name Eve; *because* she was the mother of all living,"—Gen. iii. 20,—the word *Eve* signifying, in the Hebrew, *living*. This text, like the former, is too plain to be evaded. It makes a statement which, if it be not historically true, is simply and absolutely false—for the words are incapable of any figurative meaning.

St. Paul, too, expressly affirmed the unity of origin of all mankind when, on the memorable occasion of his being brought before the Areopagus at Athens, he declared that "*God hath made of one blood all nations of men* for to dwell on all the face of the earth."—Acts xvii. 26. This text, whether it be received as true, or rejected as false, can have but one meaning. It can mean nothing but that all mankind are the offspring of a single pair of parents. And this is the uniform and unvarying tenor of the whole Bible. The proof of the unity of origin of the whole human race rests upon precisely the same basis as the truth of the Scriptures. Those who deny the former must equally reject the latter.

Now it is a fact that the traditions of various and widely scattered nations confirm the literal truth of the Mosaic history of man's creation and first state of innocence.

"The idea of a terrestrial Paradise, the abode of purity and happiness, has formed an element in the religious beliefs of all nations." . . . .

"All these and similar traditions[1] are but mere mocking echoes of the old Hebrew story, jarred and broken notes of the same strain: but, with all their exaggerations, they intimate how in the background of man's visions lay a Paradise of holy joy—a Paradise secured from every kind of profanation, and made

---

[1] See the quotations at p. 48.

inaccessible to the guilty :—a Paradise full of objects that were calculated to delight the senses and elevate the mind—a Paradise that granted to its tenant rich and rare immunities, and that fed with its perennial streams the Tree of Life and Immortality." [1]

It is fully allowed—and that by authorities certainly not prejudiced in favour of Revelation—that traditions of Paradise, and even the very name of *Eden*, were handed down among various nations from remote antiquity.

But these traditions were not derived from the writings of Moses. They were unquestionably far more ancient: and moreover, while they are too much like the description of Eden in Genesis to relate to any thing else—and while also the very name identifies the Paradise of tradition with the Paradise of Scripture—yet they are too unlike it to have been derived from it. The similarity of the description, and the identity of name, prove the identity of the Paradise of Hindû, Persian, and Chinese tradition with the Paradise of Genesis : but the variations of the traditional accounts prove that the traditions themselves are independent descriptions of the same original.

We may cite also an authority much prized by some who yet make light of Scripture—namely *Plato :* who in discoursing of the primitive condition of mankind gives a description which, with all its Grecian cast of thought and historical inaccuracies, could have had no other original than the Paradise of Eden.

"Divine beings," he says, "had distributed the animals also according to their kinds and tribes, so that there was nothing of a savage nature, nor any preying of one upon another ; and there was no war among them, nor quarrelling, at all: but it would be endless to describe all the accompanying circumstances of such an order of things. We have already spoken of mankind, and their life thus naturally sustained. God

---

[1] Smith's *Dict. of the Bible.*—art. " Eden."

Himself tended and presided over them ; just as now man, himself a more godlike animal, governs other kinds of animals inferior to himself. Under His guidance, there were no civil polities : and they had abundance of fruits from the trees and bushes, not produced by agriculture, but springing spontane- ously from the earth. They lived naked, and without covering at night, for the most part in the open air ; for the seasons were so tempered as to cause them no inconvenience, and they had soft couches of grass growing abundantly from the ground.

"If then the foster-children of Saturn, having thus abundant leisure and ability for conversing not only with men but also with the beasts, employed all these opportunities in the culture of philosophy, discoursing both with the beasts and with each other, and enquiring of every kind if any one endued with a peculiar faculty perceived any thing different from the rest, with a view to collecting wisdom, it is manifest that the men of that time had an infinite advantage over those of our day for happiness. These subjects, however, we must dismiss, until there may appear some competent informant to tell us whether the men of that time had their desires directed to science and the practice of reasoning."[1]

In this very curious passage there is an evident tradition of the serpent's having conversed with Eve—for to no other fact can we refer the origin of the belief that mankind could hold discourse with the beasts. The whole account here given by Plato of the first state of mankind, their abode, the absence of all violence and ferocity even among the brute creation, and the power of mutual converse between mankind and the lower animals, cannot in reason be regarded in any other light than as a direct tradition of Eden and its blissful Paradise :—and therefore as a direct proof of the literal and historical truth of Genesis.

[1] Plato, *Polit.* fol. 272, Ed. Steph., Stallbaum's Pl. Op. Om., vol. ix. p. 194.

PLATE I.

THE FALL.

It is evidently the same tradition that is so frequently alluded to by the classic poets of antiquity, when they describe in such glowing terms the "Golden Age," as the reign of innocence, peace, and plenty upon earth. The accounts they give of the creation of the world, and the primitive condition of the earth and of mankind, are too strikingly like the Mosaic narrative for us to suppose that they were the produce of mere imagination. It is not reason or common sense that will ever lead any one to deny that they are just echoes of the traditions handed down from the very days of Adam himself.

There exists, however—and that among *heathen* works of art—a monumental record of the events of Paradise which, if monuments have any historical value, is absolutely conclusive as to the literal truth of the narrative of Gen. iii. 1–5.

This is nothing less than an actual delineation of the scene there described.

Plate I. represents the central tablet of a large sculpture in the temple of Osiris at Phylæ, "which at once tells its own story as, beyond a rational doubt, an Egyptian delineation of the Temptation and Fall of our first parents. Every particular of the Mosaic account is here depicted to the life : the man, the woman, the serpent, the tree, the forbidden fruit : only the fruit was not on the tree, but in the hands of the man and the woman, and upon the serpent's head—a basilisk, standing erect, as though the sentence 'upon thy belly shalt thou go, and dust shalt thou eat, all the days of thy life,' had not yet been passed." [1]

But this central tablet, demonstrative as it is of the facts, is yet but a part of the demonstration.

It stands between two other tablets, with accompanying hieroglyphics ; the whole forming one composite picture in three compartments.

[1] *The Monuments of Egypt*, by the Rev. C. Forster, p. 185.

The first compartment represents, apparently, a *basilisk*—or serpent of that peculiar species so famed in the legends of antiquity.

The second compartment, or central tablet, is the Tree, with the man, woman, and basilisk, or serpent, already mentioned.

The third compartment represents a *jackal*, holding between its paws a *bone*, which it seems to be in the act of gnawing or sucking.

Over each of these three tablets are hieroglyphic inscriptions, which are thus deciphered and described by Mr. Forster.

Over the first compartment, containing the basilisk, "I first noticed," he says, "three hieroglyphics of men's heads, two of them set upon poles, with the figure of a serpent across each pole. The word besides these emblems of death was *wahar*, and its primary definition, 'Casting a man into something from which he cannot get out.'

"The second word was *wated*, 'a pile or stake driven into the ground'—a term standing beside the two upright poles, supporters of the human heads.

"The third was *fani*, 'perishing.'

"The fourth, *hak*, 'smiting with the sword.'

"Then follows, 5, *rajas*, (Satanas?) or *rahh*, 'a curling serpent'—

"6. *Rai*, dissembling, acting hypocritically,' and

"7. *Namas*, 'one guilty of imposture, a deceiver, an accuser.'"

Over the second, or central tablet, follows, next in order—
"8. *Raman*, 'the Pomegranate tree'—
"9. *Hatt*, 'lost and ruined men'—
"10. *Badu*, 'transgressing the bounds of moderation'—
"11. *Haja*, 'eating, giving to another to eat.'

"These words, be it observed, from 8 to 11 inclusive, stand over the picture of the Fall. Then follow,

" 12. *rahak*, 'wandering from the right way, perishing :' and,

" 13. the figure of a crouching lion, with a word under it of a double sense, and awfully self-interpretative, viz., *naham*— 1. 'Satan,' and 2. 'a lion.' This all-important word is determined by the hieroglyphic lion : if connected words have connected senses, in this place it is Satan as 'a roaring lion.'

" The next words, 14. *ârm*, 'stripping the bone bare of flesh,' and 15. *natan*, 'fetid, ill-odoured,' with the significant figure of a *vulture*, seem to tell but too significantly, so far as words can tell—

> ' Of man's first disobedience, and the fruit
> Of that forbidden tree, whose mortal taste,
> Brought death into the world, and all our woe.'

" The concluding words,

" 16. *auah*, 'manifesting great sadness ; peculiarly, through grief on account of sins, and imploring the mercy of God,' and,

" 17. *dari*, 'conscious,' illustrated by a human figure crouching on the heels, a well-known Egyptian attitude of devotion and homage—at least are well in unison with the repentance of our first Parents.

" I give the words as they presented themselves on first consulting the lexicon, and leave the application with my readers.

" Below the last four words, beginning with *ârm*, 'denuding a bone of the flesh,' is the figure of a jackal crouching on a tomb, with an unknown hieroglyphic between the fore-paws, which I mistook for *a torch*. A glance into the lexicon undeceived and enlightened me. The words over the jackal's head, in the plainest characters, were *namar har*, 'howls the angry dog,' and *machar*, 'sucking the marrow out of a bone.'

" The rest of this short inscription, being only the repetition of the vulture, with the words, ' *ill-odoured, gnawed by famine*,' the burden of this part would most plainly seem to be, the fatal consequences of the Fall, (the scene of which stands depicted at hand) indicated by the tomb, the human bone, and *the bird and beast of death."*

There is another sculpture in the same temple, similar to the central tablet above described, in which there are two short inscriptions, containing together a description of the subject matter.

Both tablets alike represent the figures in the act of *watering* the tree; while in the hand of one is held one piece of the fruit, another being apparently *offered* to them by the serpent, by being held up on its head.

The two hieroglyphical inscriptions, as deciphered and translated by Mr. Forster, give the following sense—"Diligently watering" (the tree).—"Promising a future good, he plunges (them) into evil."

Could words convey a more striking parallel to the sacred narrative?

"The LORD God took the man, and put him into the garden of Eden, *to dress it and to keep it."*—Gen. ii. 15.

"And the serpent said unto the woman, Ye shall not surely die: for God doth know that in the day ye eat thereof, then your eyes shall be opened, and ye shall be as gods, knowing good and evil."—Gen. iii. 5.

The reader who desires thoroughly to study this most startling monumental record, should not fail to inspect the Plates in Mr. Forster's work, and carefully read the marvellous comments on them contained in the subsequent pages.

It may be worth while to consider here, before proceeding farther, what must have been the channels by which such traditions flowed from the fountain-head throughout the world.

It is obvious that they came through Noah and the Ark family. How may they have been communicated to them?

The long lives of Adam, and his posterity before the Flood, gave a singular facility for the transmission of all the particulars of his own earliest recollections to later times. Between the death of Adam and the birth of Noah there was but an interval of one hundred and fifty-six years. Methuselah was contemporary with Adam about 245 years, and with Noah 600 years. It is simply impossible that the numberless persons who must have heard from Adam all that he could tell them —and must have heard the thrilling tale a hundred times over —could have been ignorant of the real facts, or that Noah could have been misinformed respecting them. As well might we suppose that at the present day we are all in ignorance of the reality of the great French Revolution or the battle of Waterloo.

Well then, Noah had the facts from those who had them from Adam himself. How would they be communicated to posterity ?

Noah lived 350 years after the Flood—and 250 years after the dispersion at Babel, which is supposed to have taken place about 100 years after the Flood. The fathers of the human race therefore went forth from Babel, to people the earth, with their minds and memories stored with the same startling history which Noah himself had received from Adam's contemporaries.

Shem lived 500 years after the Flood—and 150 years after the death of his father. We can form but very inadequate ideas of the correctness and stability with which traditions would be handed down in the times when men lived for centuries in intercourse with each other—and when one generation overlapped for centuries the generations following. Thus, Shem was contemporary 150 years with Abraham, and 50 years with Isaac. Isaac lived to see his grandson Levi 33 years old: Levi lived 103 years after Isaac's death, and Jochebed, his own daughter, was the mother of Moses. And we may be sure that she would carefully instil into the young mind of Israel's future Lawgiver what she had herself heard from the lips of her father Levi—he from Isaac—and Isaac from Shem—of the eventful history of man's creation, first abode, and fall. The wondrous tale would thus reach Moses' own mother from the lips of Adam himself through no more than *five* intermediate narrators—and that, too, confirmed and corrected by multitudes of others, contemporaneous with each generation through long periods of years, so that the accuracy of the narrative could hardly fail to be maintained.

And all this strong ground for believing the truth of the Scripture narrative is independent of its *inspiration*—save indeed so far as it relates to the *creation* of the world and of mankind, which, of course, could be known to Adam himself only by express revelation from God.

Events so marvellous could hardly fail to be stamped upon the minds of successive generations, and the story of them carried by the dispersion from Babel throughout the habitable world. Yet it is only in accordance with the nature of tradition that, through time and distance, it should become corrupted and distorted, specially through the perverse and degrading tastes and passions of mankind, the extravagances of fancy, and the influence of local circumstances. And this is precisely what has happened. The traditions of almost all nations preserve traces of the original truth which cannot be mistaken— yet mixed up with various distortions and additions, which it is necessary to distinguish from what bears the stamp of authenticity.

From the Scandinavian poem called the *Voluspa*, and the *Edda*, which is a kind of paraphrase of it, the following curious legends are gathered. "In the day-spring of the ages," says the poet, "there was neither sea, nor shore, nor refreshing breezes. There was neither earth below, nor heaven above, to be distinguished. The whole was only one vast abyss, without herb, and without seeds. The sun had then no palace, the stars knew not their dwelling-places, the moon was ignorant of her power." This abyss, toward the north, became full of scum and icy vapours. "Then a warm breath coming from the south melted those vapours, and formed of them living drops, whence was born the giant Ymer. It is reported that, while he slept, an extraordinary sweat under his arm-pits produced a male and female, whence is sprung the race of the giants; a race evil and corrupt, as well as Ymer their author. Another race was brought forth, which formed alliances with that of the giant Ymer: this was called the family of Bor, so named from the first of that family, who was the father of Odin. The sons of Bor slew the giant Ymer, and the blood ran from his wounds in such abundance that it caused a general inundation, wherein perished all the giants except one, who, saving himself in a bark, escaped with all his family. Then a new world was formed. The sons of Bor, or the gods, dragged the body of the giant in the abyss, and of it made the earth. . . . . The days were distinguished, and the years were numbered. They made the earth round, and surrounded it with the deep ocean. One day, as the sons of Bor, or the gods, were taking a walk, they found two pieces of wood floating upon the water: these they took, and out of them made a man and a woman. The eldest of the gods gave them life and souls: the second, motion and knowledge: the third, the gift of speech, hearing, and sight, to which he added beauty and raiment. From this man and this woman, named Askus and Emela, is descended the race of men who are permitted to inhabit the earth."

The observant reader will not fail to trace, amidst this confused heap of mingled truth and fable, the "earth without form and void"—"the Spirit of God moving upon the face of the waters" (the abyss)—the sleep of Adam, during which Eve was produced from his side—the race of "the sons of God" intermarrying with "the daughters of men"— the Flood—the saving of Noah and his family in the Ark— and the descent of all mankind from Adam and Eve.

E

There is also a noticeable coincidence of the legend with the doctrine of the Holy Trinity.

Not less remarkable, and more unexpected, is the tradition of the future destinies of the wicked, the just, and the world itself.—"There will come a time," says the Edda—"a barbarous age, an age of the sword, when iniquity shall infest the earth, when brothers shall stain themselves with brothers' blood, when sons shall be the murderers of their fathers, and fathers of their sons, when incest and adultery shall be common, when no man shall spare his friend. Immediately shall succeed a desolating winter." Then follows a description of a convulsion of all nature, amidst which the great *Dragon* shall roll himself in the ocean, so that the earth shall be overflowed and shaken with his motions, and he shall vomit forth upon the waters and into the air great torrents of venom. Then "fire consumes every thing, and the flame reaches up to heaven. But presently after, a new earth springs forth from the bosom of the waves, adorned with green meadows; the fields there bring forth without culture, calamities are there unknown, a palace is there raised more shining than the sun, all covered with gold. This is the place that the just will inhabit, and enjoy delights for evermore. There the POWERFUL, the VALIANT, HE WHO GOVERNS ALL THINGS, comes forth from his lofty abodes, to render divine justice. He pronounces decrees. He establishes the sacred destinies which shall endure for ever. There is an abode remote from the sun, the gates of which face the north; poison rains there through a thousand openings: this place is all composed of the carcases of *Serpents*—there run certain torrents, in which are plunged the perjurers, assassins, and those who seduce married women. A black-winged *Dragon* flies incessantly around, and devours the bodies of the wretched who are there imprisoned."[1]

[1] Mallet's *Northern Antiquities*, vol. i. p. 105, &c.

Let the former of these legends be compared with Genesis, and the latter with St. Paul's predictions of the *"perilous times"* of *"the last days,"* and of Christ's being "revealed in flaming fire taking vengeance on them that know not God"— 2 Tim. iii. 1, &c., and 2 Thess. i. 8—with St. Peter's description of the future burning of earth and heavens, and "the new heaven and new earth, wherein dwelleth righteousness" —2 Pet. iii.—with that of the coming forth of Christ to execute judgment—Rev. xix. 11., &c.—and of the final abodes of holiness and happiness—Rev. xxi.-xxii.—and it must be evident that among the traditions derived from Adam to his posterity there was far more than the mere knowledge of man's creation and the propagation of all mankind from a single pair. There was also a knowledge of the promised *Seed of the woman who should bruise the Serpent's head*—and of that conflict between Christ and "that old serpent, the devil, and Satan," which is to issue in the complete and final victory of the Redeemer over the adversary, and the setting up of His blessed and eternal kingdom.

CHAPTER IX.

Same Subjects continued.—Traditions of the Karens—Fijians—and New Zealanders.

THOSE who call in question the historical truth of Genesis are certainly bound in reason to show how it is that the facts recorded in Genesis have been believed and remembered in all parts of the known world, and from the time of Adam to the present hour. From the farthest East to the farthest West— from the snows of Scandinavia to the sunny shores of the South Sea Islands—the thrilling story of man's Creation, Fall, and promised Redemption have been familiar as household words for six thousand years. The fact is utterly unaccountable upon any other supposition than that those events actually took place. If those events had not taken place, the existence of these traditions would have been simply impossible.

What else could have given rise to such traditions, for instance, as the following, found among the semi-barbarous *Karens* in *Burmah,* and translated from their legendary verse :—

> " In ancient times God created the world ;
> All things were minutely ordered by Him.
> In ancient times God created the world ;
> He has power to enlarge, and power to diminish.
> God created the world formerly ;
> He can enlarge and diminish it at pleasure.
> God formed the world formerly ;
> He appointed food and drink.

He appointed *the fruit of trial*—
He gave minute orders.
Satan deceived two persons;
He caused them to eat the fruit of the tree of trial.
They obeyed not, they believed not God;
They ate the fruit of the tree of trial :
When they ate the fruit of trial,
They became subject to sickness, old age, and death.
Had they obeyed and believed God,
We should not have been subjected to sickness.
Had they obeyed, and believed God,
We should have prospered in our doings.
Had they obeyed and believed Him,
We should not have been poor."

The dispersion at Babel is thus remembered :—

"O children and grandchildren ! men had at first *one father and mother;* but because they did not love each other, they separated. After their separation they did not know each other, and their language became different ; and they became enemies to each other and fought."

"The Karens were the elder brother,
They obtained all the words of God.
They did not believe all the words of God,
And became enemies to each other :
Because they disbelieved God,
Their language divided.
God gave them commands,
But they did not believe Him, and divisions ensued."

In the following words there is an unquestionable tradition of the *resurrection* to come :—

"O children and grandchildren ! you think the earth large. The earth is not so large as the entada bean. *When the time arrives, people will be more numerous than the leaves of the trees, and those who are now unseen will then be brought to view.* O my children, there will not be a hiding-place for a single thing on earth."

Idolatry and sin are thus denounced, and love to enemies enjoined :—

"O children and grandchildren ! do not worship idols or priests. If you worship them, you obtain no advantage thereby, while you increase your sins exceedingly."

"O children and grandchildren ! if a person injure you, let him do what he wishes, and bear all the sufferings he brings upon you with humility. If an enemy persecute you, love him with the heart. *On account of our having sinned against God from the beginning*, we ought to suffer."

The *curse of God upon sin*, and the promise of its *removal by a Redeemer*, are thus commemorated :—

"O children and grandchildren ! formerly God loved the Karen nation above all others, but they transgressed his commands, and in consequence of their transgressions we suffer as at present. Because God cursed us, we are in our present afflicted state, and have no books. But God will have mercy on us, and again he will love us above others. God will yet save us again ; it is on account of our listening to the language of Satan, that we thus suffer."

> "At the appointed season God will come ;
> The dead trees will blossom and flower :
> When the appointed season comes, God will arrive :
> The mouldering trees will blossom and bloom again :
> God will come and bring the great Thau-thee ; [1]
> We must worship, both great and small.
> The great Thau-thee, God created ;
> Let us ascend and worship.
> There is a great mountain in the ford,
> Can you ascend and worship God ?
> There is a great mountain in the way,
> Are you able to ascend and worship God?

---

[1] A mountain so called, which is to be the seat of future happiness, according to some statements.

You call yourselves the sons of God—
How many evenings have you ascended to worship God?
You call yourselves the children of God—
How often have you ascended to worship God?"[1]

In these remarkable traditions, preserved among the jungles and mountains of the poor unlettered Karens, we have a summary of the principal subjects of the early chapters of Genesis —the creation of the world by God—the *one father and mother* of mankind—the Tree of Knowledge—the deceiver Satan— the temptation and fall of Eve and Adam—the infliction of sickness and *death* in consequence—the curse of God upon the earth—the promise of a Redeemer—the confusion of tongues and dispersion at Babel—and the hope of the restitution of all things as the Redeemer's blessed work hereafter. It is idle to say that such a coincidence is accidental—or that traditions so marvellously distinct are mere poetical fictions, and not traditions of actual facts.

The savage inhabitants of the *Fiji Islands* were found to have preserved, amidst the lowest barbarism, traditions in which several of the same events are very distinctly traceable.

Of the creation of man they give the following account. "A small kind of hawk built its nest near the dwelling of Ndengei (their principal deity); and when it had laid two eggs, the god was so pleased with their appearance that he resolved to hatch them himself; and in due time, as the result of this incubation there were produced *two* human infants, a boy and a girl. He removed them carefully to the foot of a large *vesi* tree, and placed one on either side of it, where they remained till they had attained to the size of children six years old. The boy then looked round the tree and discovered his companion, to whom he said, 'Ndengei has made us two that we may people the earth.' Becoming

---

[1] *The Gospel in Burmah*, by Mrs. Macleod Wylie—p. 8, &c.

man and wife they had a numerous offspring, which, in process of time, peopled the world."

They speak also of a *deluge*, which, according to some of their accounts, was partial, but in others is stated to have been universal. At the command of Ndengei the dark clouds gathered and burst, pouring streams on the devoted earth. Towns, hills, and mountains were successively submerged. All agree that the highest places were covered, and the remnant of the human race saved in some kind of vessel, which was at last left by the subsiding waters on Mbengga ; hence the Mbenggans draw their claim to stand first in Fijian rank. The number saved —*eight*—exactly accords with the Scripture record !

" The highest point of the island of Koro is associated with the history of the Flood. Its name is *Ngginggi-tangithi-Koro;* which conveys the idea of a little bird sitting there and lamenting the drowned island. In this bird the Christians (converted natives) recognize Noah's dove on its second flight from the ark.

"Near Na Savu, Vanua ,Levu, the natives point out the site where, in former ages, men built *a vast tower*, being eager for astronomic information, and especially anxious to decide the difficult question as to whether the moon was inhabited. The tower had already risen far skyward, when the lower fastenings suddenly broke asunder, and *scattered the workmen* over every part of Fiji." [1]

The identifying of the scenes of the events thus remarkably recorded by the Fijians, with localities in their own neighbourhood, is quite in accordance with the usual practice of all nations in similar cases. Adam and Eve peopling the earth—the Deluge—the saving of eight persons in a vessel—

[1] *Fiji and the Fijians*, by Thomas Williams, late Missionary in Fiji, vol. i. p. 252.

the Dove—the Tower of Babel and the dispersion—are not to be mistaken as the originals of the wild Fijian traditions. Even the association of the *tree* with the two children seems clearly connected with the memorable Tree of Knowledge, which has never been forgotten in the legendary creed of the remotest tribes of earth.

Few of these tribes have been found sunk in deeper darkness than the *New Zealanders*. It is therefore the more remarkable that even among these savages there existed traces of the truth respecting the Creation, and even the Trinity. "The New Zealanders attribute the creation of man to their *three principal deities*, acting together; thus exhibiting, in their barbarous theology, something like a shadow of the Trinity. What is still more extraordinary, is their tradition respecting the formation of *the first woman*—who, they say, *was made of one of the man's ribs;* and their general term for *bone* is *hevee*, or, as Professor Lee gives it, *iwi*—a sound bearing a singular resemblance to the Hebrew name of our first mother." [1]

"*The conversation of Eve with the serpent* seems to have made more impression upon the memory of man than almost any other event in primeval history: as from the singularity of the circumstance we might expect. It is remembered in the mythologies of Egypt, Greece, Syria, Hindûstan, Northern Europe, and North and South America. And it is one of the very few rays of truth discoverable in the darkness of the New Zealander's mind."

The first European that broke in upon that darkness by imparting to these poor savages the light of the Gospel was the Rev. Mr. Marsden, a missionary of the Church Missionary Society. The report he sent home respecting the native tradi-

---

[1] *Library of Ent. Knowledge*, quoting Nicholas's *Voyage*, vol. i. p. 59, and *New Zealand Grammar*, p. 140.

tions is thus given in the *Christian Observer* of November 1810.—" The following is the substance of the information obtained by the Rev. Mr. Marsden from Duaterra the New Zealander, and communicated to this (the Church Missionary) Society.—The New Zealanders believe that *three gods* made the first man, and that the first woman was made of *one of the man's ribs.* The general name for *bone* is *Eve ;* and Duaterra asserts that all his countrymen believe that the first woman was made of an *eve*, or bone, taken from the side of the first man : . . . and they believe that at some former period, *the serpent actually spoke with man's voice."* [1]

Again—"The natives (of the Tokelau or Union Group Islands, in Polynesia) say that men had their origin in a small stone on Fakaafo (one of the islands). The stone became changed into a man. After a time he thought of making a woman. This he did by collecting a quantity of earth and forming an earth model on the ground. He made the head, body, arms, and legs, all of earth, then *took a rib from his right side*, and thrust it inside of the earth model ; when suddenly the earth became alive, and up started a woman on her feet. He called her *Ivi* (Eevee), or *rib ;* he took her to be his wife, and from them sprang the race of men. This reminds us of Prometheus and his clay models ; but it is more interesting still as a manifest fragment of the Divine doings as recorded in the Mosaic cosmogony." [2] Who can doubt that it is so ?

[1] Deane on *The Worship of the Serpent*, p. 355.
[2] *Nineteen Years in Polynesia*, by the Rev. G. Turner—p. 526.

CHAPTER X.

The Woman and the Serpent—the Tree of Knowledge—the Temptation—the worship of the Serpent in various parts of the world.—The Hierogram of the Circle, Serpent and Wings.

IF the world-wide traditions of the Creation, and of the first state of man, are remarkable, much more so are those of the Temptation and Fall of man through the supernatural subtlety of the Serpent. In these traditions *a tree* is almost constantly mixed up with the story.

It is a most significant fact, that there is hardly a people upon earth among whom the Serpent has not been made an object either of direct worship, or at least of superstitious veneration. The fact is extraordinary in any case: but upon the supposition that the Mosaic narrative is not literally true, it is absolutely unaccountable. The existence of such a fact is in itself sufficient to stamp the character of truth upon the Scripture history of the Fall—and to brand also with the character either of culpable ignorance, or wilful blindness, those who, in the face of such a fact, neither admit the literal truth of Genesis, nor account for the fact upon any other rational theory.

It is abundantly proved, that every idolatrous system of worship throughout the world has had its origin in a *perverted tradition of the events recorded in the early chapters of Genesis.* And among these events the conversation between Eve and the Serpent, resulting in her being beguiled to her ruin, has evidently made the deepest impression upon mankind, and has been remembered with the most tenacious superstition. It would be begging the question, and arguing in a circle, to assume at starting that the serpent's form was the mask under which Satan concealed his approaches to our first mother. But such is the intimation of Scripture—and it is a startling confirmation of this, that the very same arts by which Satan is declared to have beguiled Eve have apparently been employed to deceive her posterity :—by whom so probably as by the same enemy of God and man ?—According to Genesis, Satan beguiled Eve by an assumption of *supernatural wisdom*, as well as of goodwill towards herself. And it is just in accordance with this lying profession that the Serpent has been, throughout the world, regarded as a supernatural being. The lie has been believed by Eve's descendants as it was by Eve herself—and the Serpent accordingly has been *worshipped*—by some nations as the symbol of the *evil spirit*, but by others as that of the *good deity:* and every where with the effect of plunging mankind into deeper sin, degradation, and misery.

The proofs of this statement are so voluminous that to detail them would require, not a separate chapter merely, but a separate and large treatise. A brief summary is all that can be here attempted. In a case of which the evidence lies broadcast over the whole face of the world, the difficulty consists, not in finding proofs, but in selecting from the overwhelming number a few of the most striking.

The mere fact that a loathsome and venomous reptile has been made an object of worship any where, is one of which a reasoning mind would justly require an explanation. But the fact that it has been made an object of *universal worship throughout the world*, challenges the "philosophers." They must either explain it, or confess that their philosophy is utterly at fault. *Some* cause there must have been to produce so marvellous an effect. And the cause must have been *coextensive with the effect*—that is, coextensive with the whole race of mankind. How could this have taken place? At what period of man's history would it have been possible for *one* such cause to reach the whole race? Evidently, only at a time when the whole race were gathered together in one society. And this has happened at no time since that immediately following the Deluge. But as there was nothing at that time to give rise to Serpent-worship, it must be traced to an earlier date. And what event is known to us, that could originate such a worship, between the Deluge and the Fall? If any such event had happened at any time after mankind had dispersed themselves from Eden's gate, the chances are incalculably against the probability that Noah and his family would have known of the existence of Serpent-worship at all. It is a moral certainty that it never would have become *general*, even before the Flood—much less afterwards. The conclusion is irresistible that it arose from the scene of Eve's temptation, and consequently that Genesis is historically true.

That the Serpent was an object of worship in every part of the world is expressly stated by the poet Lucan, in the following lines :—

> " Vos quoque, qui *cunctis* innoxia *numina* terris
> Serpitis, aurato nitidi fulgore Dracones"——.[1]

> " Ye Serpents[2] too, who, gay with golden bands,
> Crawl, harmless *gods*, in *all* earth's many lands "——.

Tracing this universal Serpent-worship from the cradle of the human family in Asia, we find that, at *Babylon*, the national god *Bel*, *Belus*, or *Baal*, was symbolized by, if indeed not iden-

---

[1] Lucan's *Phars.* ix. 727.—Much of the information here given is selected from Mr. Deane's curious volume on the *Worship of the Serpent*, and Mr Hislop's still more elaborate work *The Two Babylons*.
[2] The word *draco*, "*dragon*," signifies a large serpent.

tical with, the Serpent. If we may suppose the apocryphal book *Bel and the Dragon* to have any historical value, there must have been at least a tradition that live serpents were kept at Babylon as objects of worship—as was the case at Thebes in Egypt, and at Athens.

The Chaldæan word *Abadon*, a title of the Prince of darkness, is thought to signify the *Serpent-lord*—and would thus be identical in meaning with Bel, Baal, and Belial. It is identical also with the Hebrew *Ob*, and the Greek names *Python*, the Pythian *Apollo*, and *Apollyon*—the "angel of the bottomless pit, whose name in the Hebrew tongue is *Abadon ;* but in the Greek tongue hath his name *Apollyon*"—Rev. ix. 11 ;—elsewhere called also " the dragon, that old serpent, which is the devil and Satan."—Rev. xx. 1, 2.

The "familiar spirit" of the woman of Endor—1 Sam. xxviii. 7—is called, in the Hebrew, *Oub*, or *Ob*.—"Seek me," said Saul to his servants, "a woman full of *Ob*"—that is, possessed by the spirit Ob, or Satan.

The "spirit of divination," mentioned Acts xvi. 16, is in the Greek a "spirit of *Python*," or the "spirit Python."

And the most celebrated of the heathen *oracles* was that of the Pythian Apollo—where the priestess was believed to be possessed by the god as the inspiring deity. But this god, Apollo, was said to have been called "Pythian" from *Python*, the name of a huge serpent which had formerly guarded the sacred cavern where the oracle was erected. Apollo killed the serpent Python, and took possession of the oracle.[1]

Among the negroes, the *Obi-man* or *Obi-woman* is habitually applied to as Saul applied to the *Oub*-woman or Ob-woman of Endor, for an oracle.

And in the Egyptian language the Serpent is called *Oub* or *Ob :* a word which is certainly the same as *ophis*, the Greek term for serpents in general.

[1] Potter, *Arch. Græca*, ii. 272.

From all these coincidences it is clear that the Serpent has been from the remotest antiquity regarded as a supernatural being, especially as possessed of supernatural *knowledge*—and has been worshipped accordingly. The coincidence with the history of the serpent in Paradise is conclusive as to the fact that *Serpent-worship* arose from the scene of Eve's fall through being deceived by the Serpent-tempter. Only, through human perverseness, the Tempter has been handed down, not as the *deceiver* of the woman and her posterity, but as the *divine giver of knowledge* not attainable by human power.

Respecting Serpent-worship in *Persia*, Eusebius says that the Persians "all worshipped the *first principles* under the form of serpents, having dedicated to them temples in which they performed sacrifices and held festivals and orgies, esteeming them *the greatest of gods*, and *governors of the universe.*" These "first principles" were *Ormuzd* and *Ahriman*, the good and evil deities, whose contention for the universe was represented by *two serpents contending for the mundane egg*, which denoted the *universe* in the Indian, Egyptian, and Persian mythologies. The two serpents are depicted standing on their tails, and each has fastened with his teeth upon the object in dispute.

Among the most curious and prevalent symbols of Serpent-worship is the hierogram of the Circle, Wings, and Serpent—a circle, with wings proceeding from its upper part, and a serpent projecting from the lower, the head on one side, the tail on the other. "It forms a prominent feature in the Persian, Egyptian, and Mexican hieroglyphics. China, Hindûstan, Greece, Italy, and Asia Minor, as distinctly though more rarely exhibit it; and it has been found even in Britain. It appears over the portals of the Egyptian temples, and may be recognized even in those of Java." [1]

The Druids, with the rude grandeur which characterized

---

[1] See Chapter XIV.

their rites, instead of placing the Circle and Serpent over the entrance to their temples, erected the whole building itself in the form of the Serpent hierogram, shorn of the wings. The Serpent-temples at Abury in Wiltshire, and Stanton Drew in Somersetshire, are interesting examples of this construction: the former represents the hierogram with one serpent, the latter with two.

In the *Mexican* form of this hierogram, the two serpents, intertwining, form the Circle with their own bodies; and *in the mouth* of each is the singular and significant addition of a *human head!*

The Caduceus, or wand, of the classic heathen god Mercury is but another form of the same hierogram of Serpent-worship —consisting of two serpents intertwining round the staff, and thus forming the Circle.

It is certain that the triple emblem, of the Serpent, Wings, and Circle, was a hieroglyphic of the DEITY—a fact which establishes the reality of the Serpent having been made an object of *worship.* " *The Serpent of Paradise was the Serpent-god of the Gentiles.*"[1]

In *Hindústan* various traces remain of the ancient prevalence of Serpent-worship. " The natives looked upon serpents as endued with divine spirits."[2] In Forbes's *Oriental Memoirs* it is stated that certain gardeners in Guzerat would never suffer snakes to be molested, calling them " father," " brother," &c.; and the head-gardener " paid them religious honours." Many similar instances are mentioned by travellers. The king of the evil demons also is called in Hindû mythology " the king of the *serpents.*" His name is *Naga*, and he is the prince of the Nagas. "In which appellation," observes Maurice, " we plainly trace the Hebrew *nachash*—the very word for the particular

---

[1] Deane's *The Worship of the Serpent*, p. 60.
[2] Purch. *Pilgr.* part I. p. 565, *ibid.*

serpentine Tempter, and in general for all serpents, throughout the Old Testament." [1]

In *Cashmere* there were no less than seven hundred places in which carved images of serpents were worshipped.[2]

The natives of *Ceylon* conceive that the hooded snake belongs to another world—that it possesses great power—and is somewhat akin to the gods and superior to man.[3] These serpents are supposed by them to have been once human beings, who forfeited their estate by indulging the sin of malice.

In *China*, the great Dragon, or Serpent of ancient mythology, is the common and conspicuous national emblem—the stamp and symbol of royalty, sculptured on the temples, blazoned on the furniture of the houses, and interwoven in the garments of the chief nobility.[4] They call him "the Father of happiness," and erect to him temples shaded with groves.[5]—" Here we perceive the union of two primeval superstitions, *Serpent-worship* and *Grove-worship*—each of them commemorative of the Fall in Paradise." [6]

" The superstition of *Japan* was in all respects similar to that of China. The Dragon was held in equal veneration in both countries."

In *Burmah* also and in *Java*, where, as in China, the Buddhist superstition prevailed, there are distinct traces of the ancient prevalence of Serpent-worship.

In *Arabia*, the same word denotes both " *adoration*" and " *serpent*"; from which Dickinson infers that the Arabians formerly worshipped serpents." [7] And Philostratus attributes

---

[1] Maurice, *Hist. of Hindústan*, 1. 343, *ibid.*
[2] Maurice, 1. 291.
[3] Dr. Davy's *Account of Ceylon*, p. 83, *ibid.*
[4] Maurice, 1. 210.
[5] Cambry, *Monumens Celtiques*, 163, quoting Father Martin, one of the Jesuits who obtained a settlement in China. *Ibid.*
[6] Deane, p. 71.
[7] *Delphi Phœnicizantes*, c. 2. p. 10. *Ibid.*

both to the natives of Arabia and Hindûstan the same superstitious practice of eating the heart and liver of serpents, for
the purpose of acquiring a *knowledge of the thoughts and languages of animals.*[1]

In *Pegu*, when a child is born, they tie a little bell round its
neck, and within the bell they put the tongue of a snake."[2]
What a confirmation of the fact that the Serpent was believed
to be the giver of wisdom and eloquence!

In *Canaan*, the *Hivites* were not only the primitive Serpent-
worshippers, but even derived their name from this practice.
This name, according to Bochart, is derived from *Hhivia*, a
serpent, the root of which is *Eph* or *Ev*—one of the variations
of the original *Aub*.   For this word was variously pronounced
in different dialects, Aub, Ab—Oub, Ob—Oph, Op—Eph or
Ev—the Greek *ophis*, a serpent, being formed from the same
root. *Ephites* or *Evites*, being aspirated, would become
Hevites or *Hivites*—which is equivalent to the term *Ophites*,
by which the Greek historians called the worshippers of the
Serpent. The fact of these Hivites being Serpent-worshippers,
and of the Israelites having intermarried with them and
"*served their gods*," throws a curious light upon Hezekiah's
having "removed the high places, and cut down the groves,
and broken in pieces the brazen serpent that Moses had made;
—for unto those days *the children of Israel did burn incense to
it:* and he called it Nehushtan"—that is, a piece of brass, in
contempt.—2 Kings xviii. 4.

These Serpent-worshippers, however, seem to have maintained their practices in secret even to the times of the Gospel
—for they are mentioned by Clement of Alexandria, and by
Tertullian, as heretics professing Christianity even in their
own time, and as giving to the Serpent an equal or even
greater reverence than to Christ Himself. The Nicolaitans

---

[1] Philostratus *de vitâ Apollonii*, lib. 2. c. 9.
[2] Hurd's *Rites and Ceremonies*, vol. 2. p. 74.

and Gnostics seem to have been infected with the same superstition. These Gnostic Ophites are stated by Epiphanius to
have profaned the Lord's Supper by ceremonies evidently
borrowed from the orgies of the Bacchanalian mysteries, in
which the worship of the serpent had a prominent place.[1]

In *Asia Minor* Serpent-worship was universal. "A female
figure, holding in her right hand a serpent, and in her left the
beak of a ship, was the symbol of Asia."[2] At Hierapolis in
Phrygia a large live serpent was kept and worshipped. In
short, the Serpent was the *genius loci* of this whole region and
the surrounding islands, as is testified by the coins and medals
of many of the towns.

It appears, then, that the worship of the Serpent pervaded
Babylonia, Assyria, Mesopotamia, Persia, India, Cashmere,
China, Japan, Java, Ceylon, Arabia, Syria, Colchis, and Asia
Minor—a tract of country over which (the worship of the Sun
alone excepted) no other superstition was so uniformly spread.
It entered also into the religion of the Vandals, who had a
flying Dragon for their deity, and bore it on the royal banners.[3]
·It was carried with them probably to the river *Obi*—a river in
whose name is preserved to the present day a memorial of the
sacred Serpent *Ob*. It is a recorded fact that the *Ostiackes*,
who inhabited the banks of the Obi, among their other idols,
worshipped the image of a *Serpent*.[4]

---

[1] Epiphan. lib. 1. tom. 3. p. 268, &c.
[2] Beger, *de Num. Creten. Serpentif.* 8.
[3] Koch, *de cultu Serpentum*, p. 30, also Suidas.
[4] Deane.

CHAPTER XI.

THE Serpent was venerated, in *Egypt*, as an emblem of Divinity—as a charm—as an oracle—and as a god.

It was especially symbolical of the gods *Cneph* and *Thoth*, and the goddess *Isis.*

Cneph was regarded as the "architect of the universe," and was worshipped as "the good demon." He was sometimes represented as *a serpent with an egg in his mouth.* The egg denoted the mundane elements as proceeding from him.— Thoth, the supposed founder of the first colonies in Phœnicia and Egypt after the Flood, taught the Egyptians a mixed system of worship, of which one tenet was that Cneph was "*the original, eternal Spirit, pervading all creation*"[1]—and the symbol of Cneph was *a serpent.*

Thoth, after his death, was deified by the Egyptians, on acconnt of his many services, as *the god of healing, or health*— and became the prototype of the classic deity Æsculapius.[2] But of Æsculapius the well-known and constant symbol was

---

[1] Jablonski, *Panth. Ægypt.* lib. i. c. 4. p. 81, Frankfort, 1750.
[2] Ibid. lib. v. c. 6.

the Serpent. Thoth was himself symbolized by this reptile, which he had taught the Egyptians to consider as a general emblem of Divinity.

The Serpent was also symbolical of Isis, and formed a considerable feature in her mysteries.

This reptile appears indeed to have been adopted as the very symbol of Deity itself. The *Serpent, Globe,* and *Wings* were sculptured on the porticoes of the temples, and on the summits of obelisks. The temples of Luxor, Esnay, Konombu, Dendara, and Apollinopolis, are thus ornamented.[1] On the Pamphylian obelisk the Serpent appears, with or without the Globe and Wings, fifty-two times.

One city and prefecture of Egypt was called *Onuphis,* concerning which Kircher remarks—" In the Coptic language this city was called Pihof or Nouphion, which signifies *a serpent.* This prefecture is called Onuphis, because here they *worshipped the asp :* as Pausanias, when speaking of the worship of animals in Bœotia, says, ' As in the city of Onuphis, in Egypt, they worship the asp.' "

This Serpent-worship was adopted by the Gnostic heretics, as before mentioned—and has lingered even till modern times —for Bishop Pococke, when he visited Egypt, was shown on the banks of the Nile a cleft in the rock where the famous serpent *Heredy* is said to have lived ever since the time of Mahomet. Before the door of the mosque, which is built against the rock, there was much blood, and the remains of beasts lately killed, which had evidently been offered in sacrifice to the serpent.[2]

The *Shangalla,* a race of negroes on the northern frontier of *Abyssinia,* retain to this day their primitive superstitions : they worship *serpents, trees,* and the heavenly host.[3]

---

[1] Plates to Maurice's *Ind. Antiq.*, vols. 2, 3, 4,—London, 1800.
[2] Pococke, *Descr. of East,* vol. 1.
[3] Bruce, vol. 2. 554.

In Western as well as Eastern Africa, Serpent-worship has existed from time immemorial; and was found in actual practice, and in its grossest forms, by the first European discoverers of *Whidah* and *Congo*. From the complete dissimilarity of the negroes of these regions to the Egyptians, and the simplicity of the worship itself, it appears to have been aboriginal—and introduced at the first colonization of the country, probably by the earliest descendants of Ham who reached these shores by sea from Phœnicia. It thus supplies another independent presumptive proof of Serpent-worship having had its origin in a perverted tradition of the Serpent-tempter in Paradise.

The gods of Whidah are *the Serpent, tall trees,* and *the sea:* and of these the Serpent is the most celebrated and honoured. The snake, which the Whidanese thus honour and worship, is perfectly harmless, and may be seen in all their houses, leaving its young in their very beds, from which it is thought the height of impiety to dislodge them.

This Serpent they invoke under all the difficulties and emergencies of life. The king especially, at the instigation of the priests, under every national visitation, makes great offerings and entertainments at the Serpent's shrine. The most celebrated temple in the kingdom they call "*the Serpent's House;*" to which processions and pilgrimages are often made, and victims daily brought, and *at which oracles are sought.* Here there is a vast establishment of priests and priestesses, with a pontiff at their head. The priestesses call themselves "the children of God," and have their bodies marked with the figure of the Serpent.[1]

In Purchas's *Pilgrims* the following statement occurs:—
" The negroes of Congo worshipped serpents, which they fed with their daintiest provisions. Snakes and adders envenomed

---

[1] Deane, p. 164—quoting *Modern Universal History,* and Astley's *Voyages,* ch. 5, sect. 3, 4.

their souls with a more deadly poison than they did their bodies."[1]

In Lander's *Records* of Capt. Clapperton's expedition[2] it is stated that "the worship of the snake still prevails in Central Africa. Among the idols in a temple of the Yaribeans is one with the image of a snake upon his head; which reminds us of the Egyptian priest with the *asp* of Isis."

One tribe of the Whidanese are called *Eboes*—a word of the same import as *Oboes*, which might mean the people or worshippers of *Ob*, the Serpent-god. These people still practise a kind of Serpent-worship—they worship the *guana*, a species of lizard.

A neighbouring tribe, the Koromantynes, adore and propitiate as the evil spirit a god whom they call *Oboni.*

The Eboes affirmed that the most acceptable offering at the shrine of the guana was a *human victim:* and the Koromantynes maintained that when Oboni was angry, nothing could appease him but a human sacrifice!

From whence could such extraordinary superstitions originate—such startling coincidences with the great truth that victory over the Serpent-tempter could be obtained only by the suffering of *the Seed of the woman*—but from the very facts recorded in Genesis?

Either from Phœnicia or Egypt the worship of the Serpent appears to have been carried into *Greece* by Cadmus—who was one of the earliest colonists of that country mentioned in history, and is said to have introduced letters and other improvements there. Cadmus and his wife Harmonia are said to have been in the end changed into serpents—a fable which with other legends makes it not doubtful that Cadmus taught his countrymen, as Thoth did the Egyptians, to worship the Serpent—and was himself honoured after death as the Serpent-

---

[1] Purch. *Pilg.* pt. 1, p. 768.   [2] Vol. 2. p. 198.

god. There is a well known classical story of his killing the
dragon which guarded the well on the spot where he afterwards
built Thebes—and of his sowing the dragon's teeth by the
advice of Minerva—out of which sprang up armed men, called
Sparti or *the Sown*. These all killed one another except five,
who became the ancestors of the Thebans. The story is evidently of the same import as the former—both have arisen
from the fact that Cadmus was at first the promoter, and afterwards, at his death, the deified object, of Serpent-worship
among his countrymen.

The very name of *Eubœa*, according to Bryant, is just
Aubaia, the land of Aub, or the serpent—as we might say,
Serpent-land—a name given to the island by Cadmus and his
followers, by whom it is said to have been colonized.

Cecrops, who founded Athens, appears to have been another
Ophite leader. His name seems to involve the word Ob, or
Ops,[1] the name of the Serpent-god of antiquity : and Cecrops
himself was said to have been of twofold form, human and
serpentine. The first king of Athens also was said to have
been called *Draco*, a dragon, or serpent. The first altar erected
by Cecrops at Athens was to *Ops*, the Serpent-god. Cecrops
and Draco would seem indeed to have been but two names for
the same person, and that person the author of Serpent-worship in Attica.

The worship of the Serpent was, in short, so mixed up with
the whole of the Grecian mythology that Justin Martyr ac-
cuses the Greeks of making it the symbol of all their gods.[2]

It may be traced in connexion with Bacchus, Ceres, Minerva,
Jupiter, Diana, Cybele, Hercules, and very specially with
Apollo.

---

[1] Allwood, *Lit. Ant. of Greece*, p. 259, derives the name *Cecrops*
from *Ca-cur-ops*, "The Temple of the Supreme Ops"—which in the
Attic dialect became Ce-c'r-ops.

[2] *Apolog.* lib. 1. p. 60.

In the mysteries of *Bacchus* a procession of noble virgins carried in their hands golden baskets which contained sesamum, small *pyramids*, wool, *honey-cakes* marked with the sacred *omphalos*, grains of salt, and a *serpent*.[1]

These symbols show the connexion of the Bacchic orgies with the worship of the Serpent, combined, as was very generally the case, with that of the Sun. This appears likewise from other facts to have been the form in which Serpent-worship prevailed in Greece—especially in the worship of Apollo.

The *pyramids* were intended to represent the *rays of the sun*. They are seen, in a representation among the Egyptian Antiquities in the British Museum, held in the hands of priests kneeling before the sacred Serpent.

The *honey-cakes* were the offerings made to the Serpent-god. The guardian serpent kept in the Acropolis at Athens was fed, as Herodotus states, on cakes of honey once a month.[2] These honied cakes are mentioned as the food and offerings presented to the dragon of the Hesperides[3]—and to the guardian serpents in the cave of Trophonius. They were evidently the universal offerings made to the Serpent by his worshippers.

These cakes were stamped with a singular device, which appears to have been wholly misunderstood by the ancient Greeks and Romans themselves. This was the sacred *Omphalos*, or navel, as it was universally understood in classic antiquity. The device itself was a boss marked with a *spiral line;* which, together with the obvious absurdity of the meaning assigned to it, speaks for itself as to the true meaning of the emblem. It cannot reasonably be doubted that it was intended to represent a *coiled serpent*—for it was the constant accompaniment of Serpent-worship. The story of the *om-*

---

[1] Clem. Alex., cited apud Gronov., 643.
[2] Herod. 8. 41.   [3] Virg. *Æn.* 4. 483.

phalos being kept at Delphi because that place was supposed to be the centre of the earth is too absurd to be seriously entertained : besides which, if this was the meaning of the symbol, the earth must have had two centres—for there was another *omphalos* at Phlius in the Peloponnesus.

An "ingenious writer" quoted by Deane, describes similar devices discovered upon some rude stones at New Grange in Ireland, and remarks that "they appear to be the representations of serpents coiled up, and probably were symbols of the Divine Being." The remark is confirmed by Quintus Curtius, who says that the temple of Jupiter Ammon in Africa had a rude stone, whereon was drawn a spiral line, the symbol of the deity.[1]

The word *omphalos* is derived by Bryant from *Omphiel*, which signifies the *oracle of the Sun*. The term thus interpreted exactly describes the characters attributed to Delphi, the supposed "centre of the earth": for that place was the seat of the renowned oracle of Apollo, the Grecian Sun-god ; who was likewise the reputed slayer of the great serpent Python at the same spot, and was in consequence surnamed the Pythian god, or Serpent-slayer. The sacred *omphalos* thus combined in itself an apt symbolism of Apollo as the *oracular Serpent-Sun-god*. Here, as elsewhere, the Serpent was employed as *a symbol of Deity*.

The carrying of serpents in the Bacchanalian worship speaks for itself. Archbishop Potter[2] says that "in these consisted the most mysterious part of the solemnity." The serpent was, in fact, the characteristic mystery of the Bacchic orgies. Catullus,[3] in describing the Bacchanals, says that they "wreathed themselves with twined serpents."

---

[1] Deane, p. 191, quoting Beauford in Vallancey's *Collectan. de reb. Hibern.* vol. ii. p. 174.

[2] *Archæol. Græc.* ii. 383—9th Ed.

[3] *Nupt. Pel. and Thetidis*, 256.

Similar baskets were carried also in the mysteries of Ceres, Isis, and Osiris—a fact which, together with abundance of other proofs, indicates the identity of these deities, though bearing different names.

The goddess *Minerva* also was often represented with a *dragon*, or serpent—in statues, medals, and the like. The city of Athens was specially consecrated to her—and in the Acropolis there was kept a *live serpent*, which was regarded as the guardian of the place. In her temple at Tegea there was a sculpture of Medusa's head which was said to have been given by the goddess herself as a talisman to preserve the city. The hair of the head was *intertwined with serpents*.

It is remarkable that the Serpent should be thus found as a characteristic symbol of the goddess of *wisdom*—and in like manner also of Bacchus the god of *drunkenness*. May not the one fact be traced to the tradition of the Serpent in Paradise having conferred on the first human pair the gift, as it was supposed, of *wisdom*—and the other to a recollection of the *prostration of mind* caused by their having listened to the Serpent-tempter?

Something, perhaps, of the same kind may be involved in the fact that the Serpent was sacred also to *Æsculapius*, the god of *health*—as it was likewise to *Hygeia*, the goddess of health, who was said to be his sister. When a pestilence had broken out at Rome, the oracle at Delphi being consulted advised the Romans to send an embassy to Epidaurus, where was a celebrated temple of Æsculapius, to fetch *the god* from thence. While the ambassadors were gazing on the superb statue of the god, a *serpent* glided from his lurking-place, and sought the Roman vessel, where he coiled himself up, and so was conveyed to the Tiber. Here he leaped upon an island and disappeared. The Romans erected a temple on the spot, and the plague was stayed " with wonderful celerity."

Jupiter was said to have changed himself into a *dragon*, to deceive Prosperine—a striking travestie of the story of Paradise, where *Eve was deceived by a spiritual being, who assumed the form of a serpent.*

But the god most intimately associated with the worship of the Serpent was *Apollo*, the Sun-god—and the most noted seat of that worship was Delphi, where was also the most celebrated temple and oracle of Apollo. Strabo says that Delphi was originally called *Pytho,* from Python, the serpent said to have been slain there by Apollo. This serpent Python, according to Hyginus and Ælian, used to give oracles in Mount Parnassus *before* the oracle of Apollo was established at Delphi.

. From all this it is clear that ancient tradition attributed the power of giving supernatural oracles to the *serpent Python*— and in accordance with this belief Hyginus calls Python *the divine dragon,* or *serpent.*

The priestess of Apollo delivered the oracles sitting upon a tripod, which was formed of a serpent of bronze coiled spirally upwards in the form of a *cone,* and terminating in three heads. The *cone,* or pyramid, being a symbol of the *sun's rays,* there was here signified the union of the worship of the *Sun-god,* Apollo, with that of the *Serpent,* under the name of Python. These two forms of idolatry were usually combined in all parts of the world—though more rarely, as in Western Africa, the Serpent-worship was sometimes found alone. This tripod of bronze, or brass, according to Gibbon, was carried by Constantine from Delphi to Constantinople, where it may still be seen. Lucian says, that "*the dragon* (or serpent) under the tripod *spoke*"—another striking reminiscence of the Serpent in Paradise speaking with a human voice. Live snakes were kept in the temple at Delphi—an additional proof that the Serpent was an object of religious veneration there.

At *Delos* was also a celebrated oracle of Apollo—and here too the Serpent was associated with him, for there was an image erected to him in the shape of a dragon.[1] Here was

---

[1] Potter, *Archæol. Græc.* 2. 283.

likewise an oracular fountain, called *Inopus*—i.e. *Ain-opus*, the fountain of *Oph*, the Serpent-god.[1]

There were besides several other "*Serpent's-fountains.*" One in Palestine is mentioned by Maundrel; another was a celebrated stream at Colophon, in Ionia, which communicated prophetic inspiration to the priest of its guardian deity Apollo —the name Colophon being *Col-oph-on*, i.e., "*collis serpentis solis*"—the "Hill of the Serpent of the Sun."[2] There was a fountain also at Ismenus, the guardian of which was a dragon —near the spot where Cadmus was said to have sown the dragon's teeth.[3]

In the cave of *Trophonius*, in Phocis, was another noted oracle. The name itself is derived by Bryant from *Tor-oph-on*, the "Temple of the *Serpent of the Sun.*" In this cave were two figures, of a man and a woman, holding in their hands sceptres encircled by *serpents*. Live serpents were kept there—which were propitiated by offerings of cakes : and there was attributed to them the power of striking into those who entered the cave a *stupor*, or *seizure of mind*—in like manner as the votaries of Bacchus were believed to be possessed by their presiding deity.

The coincidence of all these superstitions concerning the Serpent, with the narrative of Eve and the Serpent in Paradise, cannot be mistaken. The fatal promise of the gift of *knowledge*—the ambiguous *prophetic* utterances of the Serpent to Eve—the *perverting*, and, as it were, *paralysing* influence on the minds of our first parents—the Serpent *speaking* with a human voice—are all facts to which the human voice and oracular and supernatural powers attributed by the popular belief to *the serpent*, are just the natural counterparts.—The belief was perfectly natural, conceivable, and probable, if the Scripture narrative is literally true ; but perfectly inconceivable, unaccountable, and impossible, if it be false.

[1] Bryant, 1. 257.   [2] Bryant, 1. 256.
[3] Pausanias, Book 9. p. 556, 557.

The *Peloponnesus* and the islands of the Ægean Sea were overrun by Serpent-worshippers. The very name Peloponnesus, or "the Island of Pelops," denotes its Ophite origin. Pelops is *P'-el-ops*, the *Serpent-god*[1]—so that Peloponnesus is just the "*Island of the Serpent-god.*"

The traces of Serpent-worship in this part of Greece are so numerous, and so similar to those already mentioned, that it would be perhaps wearisome as well as needless to recount them. Some sculptures, however, may be mentioned which have been figured by Fabretti,[2] and which are remarkable.

One of these represents a *tree* encircled by a *serpent*—an altar appears in front, and a boy on horseback approaches it. This is a monumental tablet.

Another shows a tree with a serpent entwined about its branches. A priestess stands by the altar.

A third has in the centre a tree with a serpent enfolding it. To the right of the tree is a naked female, holding in her hand a chalice under the serpent's mouth, and near her a man in the attitude of supplication to the serpent.

This last appears to illustrate a statement of Ælian, (Hist. Anim. lib. ii. 2,) that the husbandmen of the country used to proceed annually to the temple where live serpents were kept, and approached by naked priestesses. The object of this annual solemnity was to supplicate the Serpent-gods for a good harvest. If the serpents received the food offered to them, the omen was a good one, and *vice versâ*.

In *Epirus* there was a grove of Apollo, where sacred serpents were kept, within a walled enclosure. An annual festival, exactly like that just mentioned, was celebrated here also, and for the same purpose.

Who can doubt that in these remarkable sculptures, and the

[1] Allwood, *Lit. Antiq. of Greece*, p. 182, and Faber, *Cabiri*, 2. p. 212.

[2] *Inscript. Antiq.* p. 61, &c.

festivals which so strikingly explain their import, there was a real commemoration of the Paradisal scene of the Tree of Knowledge—the Serpent—and Eve in her innocence?

Turning now to *Italy*, we find that *Campania* was colonized by Ophites, who were called *Ophici* or Opici, from the Serpent —*ophis*—which they worshipped. They were also called *Pitanatæ*—a term of the same import as *Ophici*, being derived from *Pitan*, another form of *Python*—both being derivatives from the same Hebrew root signifying a serpent.

The Romans, in the time of Marcus Aurelius, had a *dragon*-standard at the head of each cohort, ten in every legion—a fact which, interpreted by the usual custom of the ancients of having for their military ensigns images of the gods they worshipped, indicates that the Serpent was regarded by the Romans, even then, with religious veneration. The *Parthians* had the same dragon-standards—from whom it has been said by some that the Romans borrowed them. The bearers of these standards were called *draconarii*—from which in all probability is derived our term *dragoons*—the word having been in time diverted from its original meaning to designate a particular kind of cavalry.

Various other traces remain which show that in Italy generally the Serpent was an established object of religious veneration, and regarded as oracular or ominous of coming events.

In *India*, even to the present time, the Hindûs observe one day in the year as sacred to the worship of serpents. It is thus noted in their calendar :—" On the fifth of the light half of (the month) *Srawan*, is the birth-day of the Snake-king. On that day they worship snakes. In Benares is a well called the Snake-well ; there on this day the people bathe. By worshipping snakes, there is no fear of snakes." At Muttra men look out for snake-holes long beforehand, and women pour milk into them. They also make a charcoal drawing of a snake on the walls of their houses, and worship it.

Sir William Jones says, this day is "sacred to the Demigods in the form of serpents, who are enumerated in the Padma and Garuda Puranas. Doors of houses are smeared with cow-dung and Nim leaves, as a preservative from poisonous reptiles."

Both in the Padma and Garuda we find the serpent Kaliya, whom Krishna slew in his childhood, among the deities worshipped on this day; as the Pythian snake was adored with Apollo at Delphi.

" Perhaps," says another writer, "there is no superstition more ancient and more universal than Ophiolatry. The great dragon, which, as we learn from one of the apocryphal books, was worshipped in Babylon : the figure of this reptile, as it is found sculptured in the temples of Egypt, Persia, India, Greece, and Rome : its occupying a place in the mythology of the Scandinavians, the Mexicans, and even of the rudest nations inhabiting Africa and America, are indisputable proofs both of that antiquity and universality. These proofs are evidently derived from the patriarchal tradition of the fall of our first parents—a tradition which the descendants of Noah would carry into the uttermost parts of the earth. Hence it is that this animal has ever been regarded as the symbol both of subtlety and evil, and in many countries as a personification of the great enemy of man.

"The snake is also introduced into the mythology as *Sesh Nág*, the thousand-headed serpent, supporting the universe according to some, and to others as the couch and canopy of Vishnu, as may be seen in paintings on the walls in all Upper India ".[1]

---

[1] *The Missionary's Vade Mecum*, p. 217, by the Rev. T. Phillips. See authorities there quoted.

CHAPTER XII.

Same subject continued.—Serpent-worship among the Sarmatians—
Livonians—in the North of Europe—among the Vandals and Lom-
bards—the Druids—in Ireland—in Britany.—Serpent-temples at
Carnac—in Britain, at Abury, Stanton Drew, Dartmoor, and
Shap—Stone-circles at Stonehenge and others in Britain—in Arabia
—in America—Mexican and Peruvian Serpent-worship.

RETURNING again to the cradle of the human family in Central
Asia, and tracing their steps as they wandered northwards, we
may distinguish two great divisions of the inhabitants of
Northern Europe—the *Sarmatians*, occupying the country
now comprised under the Eastern part of Poland and the
Southern part of Russia—and the *Scandinavians*, inhabiting
the countries now called Lapland, Finland, Norway, Sweden
and Denmark. To these may be added the Vandals and
Lombards, who were of the same stock and religious creed.

All these tribes were Serpent-worshippers from unknown
antiquity.

"From Ouzel [1] we learn that the Serpent was one of the
earliest objects of worship in Sarmatia. He cites Erasmus
Stella *de Antiq. Borussiæ.* 'For some time,' says this author,
'they had no sacred rites;[2] at length they arrived at such a

---

[1] *Not. in Minuc. Fel.*, p. 267.

[2] Erasmi Stellæ *de Borussiæ Antiq.* lib. ii. p. 175—in Grynæi *Nov.*
Orb. reg., &c.—This author, however, must certainly have been

G

pitch of wickedness that they worshipped *serpents and trees.'*
The connexion between serpents and trees we have already
had occasion to notice more than once.   They are united on
the sepulchral monuments of the Greeks and Romans, on the
coins of Tyre, and among the Fetiches of Whidah.   We shall
find them in the same union pervading the religion of the
Hyperboreans of every description, the superstition of the
Scandinavians, and the worship of the Druids.   They are
closely connected in the mythology of the heathens of almost
every nation : and the question is not unnatural, Whence arose
this union ?   The coincidences are too remarkable to be un-
meaning ; and I have no hesitation in affirming my belief that
the Paradisiacal Serpent and the Tree of Knowledge are the
prototypes of the idolatry." [1]

The *Livonians* are said to have been wont to sacrifice the
most beautiful of their captives to their dragon-gods [2]—as was
done also at Whidah.

Olaus Magnus [3] states that in the extreme parts of Northern
Europe serpents were considered as *household gods*—they were
fed on milk with the children, and it was a heinous offence to
hurt them.

The *Vandals* worshipped their principal deity under the
form of a *flying dragon.*

The *Lombards* worshipped a *golden viper and a tree,* on
which the skin of a wild beast was hung.   Barbatus, bishop of
Benevento, found this custom prevailing among them, notwithstanding their profession of Christianity, as late as A.D. 663.
He prevailed to cut down the tree, and having melted the
golden viper made a sacramental chalice of it. [4]

misinformed as to the origin of Sarmatian Serpent and Tree-worship. The
religious rites of a country are never mere inventions, but have always
some traditional origin.

[1] Deane, p. 244.   [2] Koch, p. 39, cited ibid.
[3] *Hist. Gent. Septentor.* 21. c. 48.
[4] Milner, *Church Hist.,* Cent. 7. Chap. 2.

In *Britain*, the Druids were notorious worshippers of the Sun-god, here as elsewhere symbolized by the Serpent; and also of the Serpent itself, independently of this connexion.

In an ancient Bardic poem there is a remarkable description of Serpent-worship—which not only identifies the Druidical rites with those of Isis in Egypt, but also proves that the Serpent-god worshipped by the Druids was identical with the Bel, Belus, or Baal, of Assyria and Canaan. The poem itself is called "*The Elegy of Uther Pendragon*"—that is, of *Uther the Dragon's Head*. The ancient British word *Draig* signifies both a fiery *serpent* or *dragon*, and also the Supreme Being.[1]

The passage in this poem is as follows :—

> With solemn festivity round the two lakes,
> With the lake next to my side :
> With my side moving round the sanctuary,
> While the sanctuary is earnestly *invoking*
> *The gliding king*, before whom the *fair one*
> Retreats, upon the veil that covers the huge stones :
> While the Dragon moves round over
> The places which contain vessels
> Of drink-offering :
> While the drink-offering is in the golden horns :
> While the golden horns are in the hand ;
> While the knife is upon the chief victim :
> Sincerely I implore thee, O victorious *Beli*, &c.

This most curious and instructive passage furnishes coincidences which form a chain of evidence linking the far West with the far East—and the Druidical sacrifices of Britain with Eve and the Serpent in Paradise. Here is—depicted "upon the veil which covers the huge stones"—a *fair one* pursued by the *gliding king* or Serpent—in other words, a poetical and pictorial commemoration of Eve and the Serpent. Beneath this veil,

---

[1] Owen's *Dict.*, Art. *Draig.*

within the well known Druidical sacred circle of huge stones, is "the *dragon that moves round over the places which contain vessels of drink-offering*"—that is, a *live serpent*, moving round the *altar-stone*—which is thus shown to have been a part of the Druidical sacrificial rites, as it was of the worship of the Egyptian goddess Isis.

Ovid describes this ceremony in the following imprecatory lines addressed to Isis :—

> Per tua Sistra precor, per Anubidis ora verendi,
> (Sic tua sacra pius semper Osiris amet,
> Pigraque *labatur circa donaria serpens* [1]—.)

"By thy Sistra I implore thee, by the presence of the revered Anubis—(so may Osiris ever love thy sacred rites, and so may the *serpent* always *glide around the offerings*—.)"

From which it must be inferred that in the temples of Isis also live serpents were kept, which were made to *glide about the offerings*, to consecrate them.

The Gnostic Ophites of Canaan, who polluted the profession of Christianity by mingling with it their wretched idolatry of the Serpent, practised a similar rite in connexion with their pretended observance of the sacrament of the Lord's Supper. "The Ophites," says Epiphanius, "attribute all wisdom to the Serpent of Paradise, and say that he was the author of knowledge to men."—"They keep a *live serpent* in a chest ; and at the time of the mysteries they entice him out by placing bread before him upon a table. Opening his door he comes out, and having ascended the table, *folds himself about the bread.* This they call a *perfect sacrifice.* They not only break and distribute this among the votaries, but whosoever will, may *kiss* the serpent. This the wretched people call *the Eucharist.*

[1] Ovid, *Amor.* lib. 2. Eleg. 13.

They conclude the mysteries by singing a hymn *through him* to the Supreme Father."[1]

" In the Bacchanalian mysteries also there was a consecrated cup of wine handed round after supper, called the cup of the Agatho-dæmon (the good deity,) which was received with much shouting."—" The hymn addressed *through the serpent* to the supreme Father is a memorial of *the hymn sung to Python on every seventh day at Delphi.*"[2]

Thus, Druids in Britain—Gnostic Ophites in Syria—and the ancient votaries of Isis in Egypt, are all found to have had the identical custom of consecrating their idolatrous offerings by the *gliding of the serpent* round them—an irresistible evidence that their worship of the Serpent proceeded from one common origin. What could that origin be but the perverted history of the Serpent in Paradise?

But there is another coincidence with the Druidical rites described above, too remarkable to be passed by unnoticed.—A Danish peasant woman, in the year 1639, found a *golden horn* near Tundera in Denmark, which is without doubt one of the very same kind as those described in the lines above quoted— and supplies the key to the meaning and origin of the Druidical as well as the Danish Serpent-worship.

This horn is embossed in parallel circles, of rude workmanship, seven in number. In the first compartment of the *first* circle is represented a naked female figure kneeling, with the arms held up to heaven. On each side of this figure is a large serpent in the attitude of attack. In the second, the same figure is *fleeing from a serpent which pursues.* The third represents the serpent with its head turned away from the figure, who holds up both hands as if in thanksgiving for deliverance.

---

[1] Epiphan. lib. i. tom. 3, p. 268. The *kissing* of idols is well known to have been a custom of the heathens. The Papists, to this day, in like manner kiss the toe of St. Peter's image, and of the Pope.

[2] Deane, p. 90, citing Nicolaus in Gronov., and Bryant.

In the second circle, the figure is seen seated upon the ground, with the hands brought together, as if in the act of prayer to the serpent. Another serpent is coiled behind the figure, with head and neck erect. The next compartment of this circle represents the same figure *in conversation with the serpent.*

In three others of the seven circles the serpent appears again in different ways.

Can there be a reasonable doubt, when all these remarkable facts are compared and combined, that the events of Paradise were the real origin of these idolatrous rites—so widely diffused, and so strangely alike—so natural if Genesis be true, so utterly unaccountable upon any other supposition? The *"gliding king before whom the fair one* retreats," described in the Bardic poem, is exactly depicted to the eye on the golden horn of Tundera—and this golden horn itself is beyond reasonable doubt just a specimen of the *"golden horns"* mentioned in the poem, and used for the very same sacrificial drink-offerings in Denmark which are celebrated by the Bard in Britain.

In *Ireland*, a large cavern has been discovered at New Grange, in the county Meath, "whose consecration to Mithras is indisputable." *This deity was the Apollo or Sun-god of the Persians, and was symbolized by a serpent.* Here were dug up three remarkable stones, on which were rudely carved spiral lines like coiled serpents, as mentioned above.

Mr. Deane thinks that the legend of St. Patrick having destroyed all the serpents in Ireland is a traditional record of his having, by preaching the Gospel, abolished the *worship* of the Serpent throughout the country: just as Mr. Bryant has concluded that the stories of the destruction of serpents in the Grecian Archipelago and Peloponnesus relate in reality not to the serpents themselves, but to their worshippers.

One of the most curious and striking testimonies to the historical truth of the Scripture narrative of man's Fall in Paradise, is the connexion found to have existed between *Serpent-worship* and *agriculture.*   One immediate consequence of the Serpent's successful temptation of our first parents was that a *curse* was pronounced upon *the ground and its produce.*

With that perversion of the truth which everywhere led mankind to *worship* the Serpent who had been the author of all our miseries, it was supposed that *the Serpent had power over the fruits of the earth.*

This idea is plainly traceable in heathen mythology.

In the Grecian and Roman idolatry, *Ceres*, the goddess of *agriculture*, was represented *sitting in a chariot drawn by serpents.*   And Triptolemus, when instructed by her in the arts of agriculture, was immediately presented with the *serpent-chariot* to convey him through the world that he might diffuse the benefit among mankind.

Traces of this idea, and of the worship of Ceres the Serpent-goddess of agriculture, linger among us to this day.   The following account, taken from a London journal, is an illustration of the fact :—

" A Relic of Paganism.—An interesting observance of an ancient custom took place on the 29th instant (Sept. 1867) in the harvest-home celebration at Hughenden Manor, the seat of the Chancellor of the Exchequer. At the close of the speech of the Right Hon. gentleman in responding for his health being drunk, a village maiden stepped up and presented him with what the report oddly terms ' a cereal, doll-shaped figure ': its head was of oats, its arms were of barley, its feet were wheat, and it had a dress or frock of blue paper.   The presentation of this figure, Mr. Disraeli explained, was one of the most ancient customs in England ; it being a representation of the goddess Ceres, such as for centuries had been brought forward on these occasions to personate the golden harvest for which the parishioners of Hughenden are deeply grateful.   Their *Bona Dea* may have been a rude personation, but not a whit less earnest on this account.   Hentzner records an image, richly dressed, to represent the Roman Ceres, in 1598, in a harvest-home at Windsor, not many miles from Hughenden; and the custom is doubtless one of the many observances traceable to the Roman occupation of Britain. Hutchinson records a similar custom at Easington, Durham, among others evidently derived from the Romans. Rollin thinks Ceres 'the same Queen of Heaven to whom the Jewish women burnt incense, poured out drink-offerings, and made cakes for with their own hands.'—Jerem. xvii. 16." [1]

In the Pythian Serpent-temple of Epirus, and at Lanuvium in Italy, sacred serpents were kept to whom the *farmers* of the vicinity resorted for an omen *of a good or bad harvest*—as already mentioned.

Now, in *Ireland*, the name *Tat, Taith,* or *Tait,* was well known to the ancient Irish. By this word they designated the first day of the month of August, that being the month of harvest, and *Tait being the god who presided over agriculture.* The month which among the Egyptians corresponded with August was called by the name of the god *Thoth.*" [2]

Among the *Celts* the same god was called *Theutates;* among the *Goths Teut* or *Tuisto.*

But the Egyptian *Thoth* or *Teuth*—the Celtic *Theutates*—the Irish *Tat, Tath,* or *Tait*—the Gothic *Teut*—was identical with the Grecian *Hermes* or *Mercury;* [3] whose Caduceus or *serpent-wand* has been already mentioned as connecting him with the worship of the Serpent.

---

[1] *Illustrated London News.*—The supposition that this curious custom is derived from the Romans, however, is a gratuitous conjecture. It is probably far more ancient than the Roman occupation of Britain, and traceable to the Druidical system—which, as is abundantly proved, was identical with the Babylonian worship of the " Queen of Heaven," and the false Messiah as the Sun-begotten Seed of the Woman. Rollin's belief is the correct one.

[2] Faber, *Pagan Idolatry,* vol. 2. 362, 365.—London, 1816.

[3] Ibid.

Thus is found a most curious connexion between *agriculture*, and the worship of the *Serpent* as being believed to preside over the produce of the earth—and this extending from the East to the remote regions of Western Europe. Whence could such a notion originate, as that *serpents have any connexion with good or bad harvests*, but from the events of Paradise?

A curious relic of Serpent-worship in *Gaul* has been preserved in a sculpture on the front of a temple at Montmouillon in Poitou, of which an engraving may be seen in Montfaucon.[1] It represents, among other sacerdotal figures, a naked female with two serpents twining round her legs. This figure evidently represents the priestess of the Serpent-god—according to the customs already mentioned as prevailing in the Serpent-temples of Epirus and Lanuvium.

In *Britany*, where the ancient Celtic idolatry found refuge when banished from other parts of Gaul by the Romans, there is still to be seen *an oracle of Bel*, the Serpent-god of Assyria and the East. It is situated in the island of St. Cado, and consists of a small rectangular enclosure three feet long by two feet wide, contained by four stone slabs. The parish in which it stands is still called *Belz* or *Bels*—that is, *Belus*. The peasants devoutly believe in the miraculous powers of this hole —a relic probably of its ancient reputation for oracular responses.

But Britany contains a memorial of the Serpent-worship which once prevailed there, as stupendous in its magnitude as it is significant in its indications. This is the great Serpent-temple at *Carnac*, in the department of the Morbihan.

This remarkable relic, like Stonehenge and other Druidical remains, consists of huge stones, set up in rows, the course of which is sinuous, describing the figure of an enormous serpent moving over the ground. There were originally eleven rows

[1] Suppl. to vol. 2. 249.

of stones, about ten thousand in number—more than three
hundred of them being from fifteen to seventeen feet in height,
and from sixteen to thirty feet in girth—one measuring even
forty-two feet in circumference. The whole length of this
huge temple, following its windings, is *eight miles*.

At Erdeven, where the temple commences, an annual dance,
describing the Ophite symbol of the *Circle and Serpent*, is still
kept up by the peasants at the Carnival : and, as is also the
case in England, various superstitious legends are believed by
the people respecting these stones.

Near that part of the temple which approaches Carnac there
is a lofty mound, the upper part of it being evidently artificial.
This mound was probably used for the same purpose as those
which are common in Persia, and the "high places" mentioned
in Scripture. The worship of the Serpent was commonly,
though not invariably, combined with that of the *Sun*, as already noted : and these mounds, or "high places," were the
spots on which was kept burning on the altars the perpetual
fire kindled by the sun, according to the rites of the ancient
Fire-worshippers, or Sun-worshippers, in Persia and elsewhere.
The very name *Carnac* is just *Cairn-hac*, the *Serpent's Hill*—
cairn being a word still in use in the north of England to signify a *mound or heap of stones*, and *hac* being an old Celtic
word signifying a *serpent*. In the north of England snakes are
to this day called by the common people *hag*-worms. The
term *hag*, meaning an old woman believed to be a *witch*, is
doubtless from the same origin—and is a singular memorial of
the world-wide and ancient belief in the *oracular powers* conferred by the Serpent on his votaries. In this usage the word
hag, properly meaning a *serpent*, was applied to the woman
who was believed to be possessed or inspired by the supernatural being, whether good or evil, supposed to reside in the
Serpent. And this is in exact accordance with the general
practice among the heathens of calling the priestesses of their
idolatry by the name of the god they served. The priestess

of *Aub*, the Serpent-god of Canaan, was called *Oub*—that of *Python*, the oracular Apollo, was called *Pythia*, the Pythoness —and the same analogy would lead to a witch being. called a *hag*, or serpent-prophetess, as being supposed to be inspired by the evil spirit in the serpent.

In the *Ile aux Moines*, in the Morbihan, are the scanty remains of what appears to have been another Serpent-temple, of smaller size. The avenues terminated in an oblong mound which is still called *Penab*—that is *Pen-ab*, the "head of *Ab*," the sacred Serpent of the East!

There was at the head of this mound an *obelisk*—the familiar symbol of Sun-worship—the *obelisk, pyramid*, or *cone*, being adopted as an emblem of the Sun, from its resemblance to the sun's rays, as before noted. The word *pyramid* itself means a *ray of the sun*—being from the Coptic *Pi-ra-mu-e*.[1]

In like manner the word *obelisk*, according to Bryant, is derived from Obel—which is *Ob-el*, the "Serpent-god," the Apollo of Syria—to whom they were dedicated.

Britain, however, was the head-quarters of the Druidical worship—and here accordingly were several vast Serpent-temples, of which the remains are still to be seen.

The most remarkable of these is at *Abury*, or Avebury, in Wiltshire, about five miles west of Marlborough, on the Bath road. The very name of this village seems to be derived from that of the *Sun-serpent-god*. The present form of the name is Avebury; but in the books of Malmesbury Abbey it was found by Mr. Aubrey written *Aubury*. This word is almost without alteration *Aub-ur*: that is, the "Serpent-sun"—*aub* being the Eastern name of the *serpent*, and *aur*, or *ur*, signifying *light*, and being a title of the *Sun-god* of the East.

This most interesting monument of Druidical idolatry was visited and described by Dr. Stukeley in 1723; whose work,

[1] Deane, p. 363, quoting Jablonski, *Panth. Ægypt. Proleg.*, 82.

and Sir Richard Colt Hoare's *History of Ancient Wiltshire,*
contain all that is known on the subject. The temple consisted of a circle of upright stones, set up at equal distances,
from which proceeded two avenues in a wavy course in opposite directions. The circle was the symbol of the Sun-god—
the two avenues were the fore and hinder part of the serpent's
body : the whole forming the usual *Ophite hierogram,* or sacred
symbol of the *Solar-serpent* deity. Within the large circle
were two smaller ones.

The *head* of the serpent was formed of two concentric ovals,
and rested on an eminence called Overton Hill, which is the
southern promontory of the Hakpen hills. But *Hak-pen* is
just " *Serpent-head*" *!* so that in all probability the whole range
of hills was so called from this very *head of the serpent* of Druid-
stones.

From this *Serpent-head* or *Snake's-head* promontory to the
end of the serpent's tail, in a valley towards Beckhampton, is
about two miles. The whole figure was so contrived as to
have the appearance of a vast snake creeping over hill and
dale.

Midway between the extremities of the serpentine avenues
is a remarkable artificial mound, of very great elevation, called
Silbury Hill—the *"Hill of the Sun"*—corresponding with the
Mont St. Michel mound at Carnac.—The whole structure is
thus identified as sacred to the *Sun-god* and the *Serpent.*

Another ancient Serpent-temple was situated at Stanton
Drew, in Somersetshire—near the village of Pensford, about
five miles west of Bristol, of which however the remains, when
seen by Mr. Deane in 1831, were but scanty—the stones, as
elsewhere, having been ruthlessly and ignorantly broken up
and removed for building and mending roads.

A third locality of similar structures is at Merivale Bridge,
on Dartmoor, four miles from Tavistock. Here are the remains of four temples—two serpentine, two circular.

A fourth is Shap in Westmorland, where was a Serpent-temple formed of smaller stones than those at Abury, the largest now remaining being but eight feet in height—but in extent it was the largest in Britain, having once, as tradition says, reached from about one mile south of the village of Shap to Moor Dovey, a distance of *eight miles.*

The description of the Snake's-head promontory, and Silbury Hill, and of the temple at Avebury, may be compared with a statement of Pausanias that "in the road between Thebes and Glisas you may see a place *encircled by select stones,* which the Thebans call *the Serpent's head."* To complete the resemblance, there is, near this Theban temple, a lofty hill corresponding to Silbury, upon which was erected a temple to Jupiter, the same god as the Syrian Belus or Baal.

The affinity between these Serpent-temples, and *Sun-circles* such as those at Stonehenge, and near Keswick, and others, is so close that they must be regarded as little more than varieties of the same kind of structure, and dedicated to essentially the same kind of worship. Though there has been much discussion and difference of opinion as to the nature and purpose of these stone circles, there is no room for doubt that they were temples of Sun-worship.

This is not a matter of mere conjecture, or probability from the analogy of their circular form or other circumstances with the known symbols of Sun-worship. There is express testimony, as conclusive as any that can come down to us from pre-historic times, that these stone circles were temples of the Sun.

They are found in many places in *Peru,* as well as elsewhere; and the following account of them is given by a writer in the *American Naturalist.*—"But it is not in the early sepulchral monuments of Peru that we have absolute coincidences with the remains which are now accepted as among the primitive monuments of mankind. As we find in both Europe and Asia the rude monuments of religion existing side by side with

those of sepulture, so we find in Peru the Sun-circle, or primitive, open, symbolical temple, side by side with the Peruvian
chulpa. In many places we discover circles defined by rude upright stones, and surrounding one or more larger upright stones
placed sometimes in the centre of the circle, but oftener at one-
third of the diameter of the circle apart, and on a line at right
angles to another line that might be drawn through the centre
of the gateway or entrance on the East. In connexion with
the group of *chulpas* at Sillustani, or rather on the same promontory on which these occur, are found a number of such
Sun-circles, which seem strangely to have escaped the notice
of travellers. The tradition of their original purpose is preserved in the Quichua name they still bear, of *Intihuatana,*
'where *the sun is tied up*'."[1]

In *Arabia* also, there may be seen to this day similar monuments of Sun-worship. "Hardly," says a modern traveller,
"had we descended the narrow path where it winds from ledge
to ledge down to the bottom, when we saw before us several
huge stones, like enormous boulders, placed endways perpen-
dicularly on the soil, while some of them yet upheld similar
masses laid transversely over their summits. They were arranged in a curve, once forming part, it would appear, of a
large circle ; and many other fragments lay rolled on the
ground at a moderate distance : the number of those still
upright was, to speak by memory, eight or nine."—The transverse stones are described as being about 15 feet from the
ground.

"Pointing towards Rass, our companions affirmed that a
second and similar stone circle, also of gigantic dimensions,
existed there ; and lastly, they mentioned a third towards the
South-west.

---

[1] *The Primeval Monuments of Peru compared with those in other
parts of the World*"—by E. G. Squier, M.A., *American Naturalist* for
March 1870.

"That the object of these strange constructions was in some measure religious, seems to me hardly doubtful; and if the learned conjectures that would discover a planetary symbolism in Stonehenge and Carnac have any real foundation, this Arabian monument, erected in a land where the heavenly bodies are known to have been once venerated by the inhabitants, may make a like claim : in fact, there is little difference between the stone-wonder of Kaseen and that of Somersetshire except that the one is in Arabia, the other, though more perfect, in England."[1]—Kaseen is in the province of Lower Mejed.

These stone circles are monuments of the old Sabæan worship, which is identified with the Sun-worship of the ancient Chaldæans.—"These Sabæans," adds this author, "worshipped the seven planets, and pre-eminently the Sun".—"They had a special veneration for the two great Pyramids of Egypt:"—another link of connexion between the Pyramids and Sun-worship.

Sun-worship among the Arabs is not, however, a thing only of the past. "The sun rose," says the same writer, "and then for the first time I witnessed what became afterwards a daily spectacle, the main act of Bedouin worship in their own land. Hardly had the first clear rays struck level across the horizon, than our nomade companions, facing the rising disk, began to recite alternately, but without any previous ablution or even dismounting from their beasts, certain formulas of adoration and invocation, nor desisted till the entire orb rose clear above the desert edge. Sun-worshippers as they were before the days of Mahomet, they still remain such; and all that the Hejaz prophet could say, or the doctors of his law repeat, has been entirely thrown away on those obstinate adherents to ancient customs."[2]

---

[1] Palgrave's *Journey through Arabia*, vol. 1., 251, and vol. 2., 258.
[2] Ibid., vol. 1. p. 8.

The worship of the Serpent as well as the Sun was not confined to what we call the Old World. There have been discovered clear traces of it even in the remote regions of South America.

In *Mexico*, as we are informed by an intelligent traveller,[1] the *rattle-snake* was an object of veneration and worship: and representations of this reptile and others of its species are very commonly met with among the remains of their ancient idolatry. "The finest known to exist is to be seen in a deserted part of the cloister of the Dominican convent, opposite to the palace of the Inquisition. It is coiled up in an irritated erect position, with the jaws extended, and in the act of gorging an elegantly dressed female, who appears in the mouth of this enormous reptile crushed and lacerated." A cast of this terrific idol was brought over to England by Mr. Bullock.

The Spaniards who first visited Mexico asserted that the people of that country worshipped an idol in the form of a serpent. Bernal Dias del Castillo, who accompanied Cortez, was introduced by Montezuma into the principal temple, and saw "the large stones whereon were placed the victims who were to be sacrificed. Here was a great figure representing a dragon, and much blood spilt."

Acosta[2] says that "the temple of Vitziliputzli was built of great stones in fashion of *snakes* tied one to another, and the circuit was called *the circuit of snakes*", because the walls of the enclosure were covered with figures of snakes. This god, Vitziliputzli, held in his right hand a staff cut in the form of a serpent; and the four corners of the ark, in which he was seated, terminated each with a carved representation of the head of a serpent.[3]

There was also in Mexico a temple dedicated to "*the god of*

----

[1] Mr. Bullock.
[2] Ch. 13. London, 1604.
[3] Faber, *P. I.*, vol. i. 455, citing Purchas's *Pilgrims*, b. 8. ch. 11, p. 796.

the air"—and the door of it was so formed as to resemble a *serpent's mouth*[1]—a curious coincidence with the fact that St. Paul calls *the devil* "the *prince of the power of the air.*"—Eph. ii. 2.

It is stated also that the Mexicans, like other Serpent-worshipping nations, used to keep live serpents in their dwellings as *household gods*.

M. Aglio's work on *Mexican Antiquities* contains fac-similes of nearly all the Aztec paintings known to be in Europe, with lithographs of sculptures, and other monuments of these aboriginal inhabitants of Mexico. "These paintings and sculptures abound with evidences of Mexican Serpent-worship, and prove that there was *scarcely a Mexican deity who was not symbolized by a serpent or a dragon*. And—to confirm the original connexion of all the Serpent-worshippers throughout the world—the Mexican paintings, as well as the Egyptian and Persian hieroglyphics, describe the *Ophite hierogram* (or sacred symbol) of the intertwined serpents, in almost all its variations."

There is scarcely indeed a feature in the mystery of Serpent-worship which may not be recognized in the Mexican superstitions.

"We perceive therefore that in the kingdom of Mexico the Serpent was sacred, and emblematical of *more gods than one*"—a fact which "proves the Serpent to have been a symbol of *intrinsic divinity*, and not a mere representative of peculiar properties which belong to some gods and not to others."

"The Serpent also entered into the religion of the Mexicans as a *charm*. Whenever a person was ill, a priest was immediately sent for, who having perfumed the patient, and shaved off his hair, hung *snake's bones* about his neck."

"In Couliacan, Nunnez de Gusman found, in the year 1531, the houses filled with thousands of serpents mingled together.

---

[1] Faber, *P. I*, 2. 285, citing Purchas.

H

The inhabitants showed great reverence to these serpents, because, as they said, *the devil often appeared to them in that form.*[1]

The *Peruvians* also were Serpent-worshippers.

It is stated in Purchas's *Pilgrims*,[2] that they "worshipped snakes, and kept them pictured in their temples and houses."

Acosta[3] says that "in the temple of Pachamana, near Lima, tradition states that *the devil did speak visibly*, and gave answers by his oracles; and that sometimes they did see a *spotted snake*."

In the province of Topira in Peru, the Spaniards saw a temple, in front of which was a moat containing a vast image of "a serpent of divers metals, with his tayle in his mouth. A man was sacrificed before it every year."[4]

Mr. Deane gives a plate representing an Indian priest of the Solar-serpent worship in the country north-west of *Louisiana.* The Sun and the Serpent are tattooed upon his breast; and in his hand he holds a kind of instrument shaped like a tadpole, on the rounded head of which is a figure of the Sun, penetrated by the head of a Serpent—the tail of which forms the waving handle of the instrument. These "stigmata," or devices, borne on the body of the priest, denote the gods to whose worship he was consecrated—in exact accordance with the universal practice among all the ancient sects of idolaters, and with that of the Brahmins and the votaries of the various Hindû idols at the present day. To this custom St. Paul alludes in Gal. vi. 17.

The reader who desires to follow out this very curious subject will find ample details and authorities in Mr. Deane's valuable work, from which the foregoing statements are for the most part extracted.

---

[1] Deane, p. 301, citing Ogilby, and Voss, *de Idol.*
[2] Part 4. p. 1560.
[3] Acosta, c. 5.
[4] Purchas, part 4. 1478.

The result of such enquiry is an overwhelming mass of evidence that there is hardly a people or country in the world in which the Serpent has not been from the remotest antiquity an object of worship, and an emblem of Deity. The very fact of the reptile having held with Eve an actual and literal conversation in human language, has been so remembered as to prove beyond reasonable doubt the literal truth of the narrative of Genesis.

We are thus reduced to this alternative—that we must either admit that Genesis is history and not "poetry", or we must blot out the universal history of the world. If *any* history is true, Genesis is true—for it lies at the very fountain-head of *all* history. If the account of Eve and the Serpent in Paradise is not a record of actual facts—and if the whole race of mankind did not spring from Eve and Adam, how is it that all history is full of these very facts—that all the nations of earth have preserved the memory of them, and recorded them in medals, and sculptures, and traditions, and poems, and written documents of various kinds? How is it that these facts have sunk so deep into the universal mind of man that they have moulded the religious creed and worship of the nations of the whole world—that they have left their impress not only on the literature and religious history of almost every country under heaven, but even upon the natural features of the lands themselves—upon plain and promontory, hill and dale, rock and mountain—in the huge structures of Carnac, and Avebury, and other monuments—and in the very names of the places where Serpent-worship once prevailed—names which will perpetuate its memory as long as language shall remain?

But the evidences of primeval truth expand and multiply the more in proportion as they are more fully investigated—as will appear in some degree in following chapters.

CHAPTER XIII.

*Sun-worship combined with Serpent-worship—its origin in the Baby-
lonian apostasy and priestcraft—the worship of Nimrod as a false
Messiah—and of Semiramis and her son as the Mother and the
Child—the Seed of the Woman worshipped as the Seed of the Sun.*

THE worship of the Serpent was almost invariably conjoined
with that of the Sun. Both were symbolized together in one
and the same composite hierogram, or sacred device—both
were celebrated together in one and the same temple.

It may well seem unaccountable how two objects so totally
unlike each other as the grovelling reptile and the glorious sun
should not only both be worshipped, but also *both worshipped
together*, as if inseparable—as if one without the other would
have been incomplete.

This indeed was not invariably the case. Sometimes, as in
Whidah and Congo, the Serpent was worshipped without the
Sun—sometimes the Sun without the Serpent. And sometimes the two sects of votaries became bitter rivals and deadly
enemies of each other, and bloody wars arose between them.
This, however, is no more than might be expected to happen,
human nature being what it is. We are unhappily too well
acquainted with the *odium theologicum*, in our own day, to be
surprised that what has happened even under the light of
Christianity should have been found to exist amidst the darkness of Pagan superstition.

Still, however, the fact remains, that in the earliest ages of

Serpent-worship and Sun-worship *the two were combined*—and that they continued for many ages to be celebrated jointly in those parts of the world where the simple rites of antiquity remained least corrupted by subsequent alterations and additions —as, for example, in Britain and the North of Europe.

This combination, so unaccountable in itself, is however not difficult to be explained in connexion with the events recorded in Genesis.

It is an indisputable fact, that the mythology of all nations can be traced to *one* source—*Babylon and its apostasy.* The apostate and idolatrous Church of Rome itself is no exception —as Mr. Hislop has proved by overwhelming evidence in his admirable work *The Two Babylons.* " Profane antiquity— Jewish tradition—Christian commentators—historic research —alike attest the truth of the Mosaic record, and prove that, when the Lord confounded the language of the idolatrous builders of Babel, and dispersed them, those Chaldæan mysteries which had been instituted in the plains of Shinar were carried thence into the uttermost parts of the earth. Each separated tribe, bearing, under its ostensible leader, Osiris, Brahmah, &c., the sacred ark of their favourite deity, and travelling under their supposed miraculous guidance, compulsorily fulfilled the Lord's command in distributing themselves over the face of the whole earth, and reaching the most distant countries. Consequently, these mysteries, which sprang originally from the same poisoned fountain, became universal, and were everywhere the same; the same divinities being worshipped as at Babylon, though under different appellations.[1]

---

[1] The fact that all the numerous deities of the ancient heathen world were originally one and the same is expressly attested. Bryant quotes among other authorities the following—

     Εἷς Ζεὺς, εἷς Ἀίδης, εἷς Ἥλιος, εἷς Διόνυσος,

     Εἷς Θεὸς ἐν πάντεσσι.—*Orphic. Fragment.*, 4. p. 364, ed. Gesner.—" One and the same is Jove, Pluto, the Sun, Dionysus (or Bacchus)—one god is in them all."—And again—

And so true to the primitive Chaldæan model was the apostasy of Rome as to be designated by our Lord Himself in the Revelation, " Babylon the great, the mother of harlots and abominations of the earth." [1]

To *Chaldæa*, then, we must look for the explanation of the strange association of the worship of the Serpent with that of the Sun.

The explanation is found in the fact of *Man's fall by sin together with corrupted traditions of God's promise of a Redeemer.*

We have seen how the circumstances of Eve's temptation and ruin by the Satanic Serpent—distorted by the perverse ingenuity of human pride, and by an imagination doubtless aided by the same Satanic subtlety—gave rise to the worship of the *Serpent*, as symbolizing Deity.

It was a similar perversion of the Lord's promise of a Redeemer to ruined man that led to the worship of the *Sun*.

"The woman said, The serpent beguiled me, and I did eat. And the LORD God said unto the serpent, Because thou hast done this, thou art cursed above all cattle, and above every beast of the field: upon thy belly shalt thou go, and dust shalt thou eat all the days of thy life: and I will put enmity between thee and the woman, and between thy seed and her

> Πλούτων, Περσεφόνη, Δημητὴρ, Κύπρις, Ἔρωτες,
> Τείτωνες, Νηρεὺς, Τηθὺς καὶ Κυανοχαίτης,
> Ἑρμῆισθ', Ἥφαιστός τε κλυτὸς, Πὰν, Ζεύς τε καὶ Ἥρη,
> Ἄρτεμις, ἠδ' Ἑκάεργος Ἀπόλλων, εἷς Θεὸς ἐστίν.

—Hermesianax, quoted ibid., *Ancient Mythol.* vol. 1. p. 310.

" Porphyry acknowledged that Vesta, Rhea, Ceres, Themis, Priapus, Proserpina, Bacchus, Attis, Adonis, Silenus, and the Satyrs, were all one and the same. Nobody had examined the theology of the ancients more deeply than Porphyry. He was a determined Pagan, and his evidence on this point is unexceptionable."—Ibid. 1. 335, and 395.—And this one deity, according to Bryant, was the *Sun*. He quotes to the same purport Selden *de Diis Syris*, p. 77.

[1] *Armageddon*, vol. ii., 203.

seed; IT *shall bruise thy head, and thou shalt bruise* HIS *heel.*"
—Gen iii. 14, 15.

Satan, in the form of a serpent, prevailed by his malicious
cunning first to bring "death into the world and all our woe"
—and then, so to misrepresent the matter as to procure himself to be worshipped as if he had been the *benefactor*, instead
of the *destroyer*, of mankind.

God's promise of mercy and redemption to His guilty children
was next, by the same arts, *evaded*, and eventually lost to all
mankind, (save only the chosen people the Jews,) by a kind of
jugglery which has, from the first, always characterized the introduction of error in religion.

There was a jugglery of *words*, and a jugglery of *creeds*—
the one aided by the other.   There was also some confusion of
ideas—such as might be expected, and such as is almost inseparable from error.

Thus much however is certain—that *there was a false Messiah set up in ancient Babylon, and worshipped as the promised*
SEED OF THE WOMAN—and that this delusion grew into the
world-wide system of *Sun-worship*, or *Fire-worship*, which was
almost everywhere found associated with the worship of the
Serpent.

And from this fountain of bitter waters was derived the
mythology of the whole heathen world.   The Serpent was
sometimes worshipped as a beneficent deity, sometimes regarded as the enemy of mankind, to be destroyed by the
promised Deliverer.   Either way he was worshipped—as a
benefactor he must be honoured with offerings, as an evil deity
he must be propitiated with sacrifices.   *Devil-worship* was as
common a feature of heathen superstition as *god-worship*.

But the expected Deliverer himself was worshipped as the
Sun-begotten SEED OF THE WOMAN—for a reason which will
appear presently.

It is abundantly evident that the promise of the Seed of the
Woman who should bruise the Serpent's head was well under-

stood as to be fulfilled by the INCARNATION *of the Son of God.*
To this fact must be traced that remarkable feature of heathen
mythology, the idea of *the gods becoming incarnate* in various
human personages. The classic mythology of Greece and
Rome is full of this idea. The incarnations of Vishnu form a
large part of the Hindû superstitions. The animal-worship of
Egypt was little else but a symbolical and mystical representation of the same notion.

But it was in *Babylon* that the whole system took its rise.

The great hero of the heathen world, and the great object of
heathen worship, was *Nimrod,* the first king of Babylon:—and
the great leader of the Babylonian apostasy after his death was
his beautiful but ambitious and abandoned queen *Semiramis.*

When the Jesuit missionaries first penetrated into the East,
they were astounded to find every where, in the Hindû and
Buddhist temples of India and China, the images of the
Mother and the Child—exactly similar to their own Madonnas.

And this worship of the Mother and the Child was everywhere conjoined with the worship of the *Sun* and of the
Serpent.

How are all these extraordinary facts, and this strange
association of ideas, to be accounted for?

Nimrod, according to ancient tradition, died a violent death.
His widow Semiramis, far from being daunted by her loss,
took advantage of it to raise herself to higher dignity. "In
life her husband had been honoured as a hero—in death she
will have him worshipped as a god, yea, as the woman's promised Seed—'*Zero-ashta*'—who was to bruise the Serpent's
head, and who in doing so was to have his own heel bruised.
The patriarchs, and the ancient world in general, were perfectly acquainted with the grand primeval promise of Eden,
and they knew right well that the bruising of the heel of the
promised Seed implied his death, and that the curse could be
removed from the world only by the death of the grand
Deliverer. If the promise about the bruising of the Serpent's

head, recorded in Genesis as made to our first parents, was actually made—and if all mankind were descended from them, then it might be expected that some trace of this promise would be found in all nations. And such is the fact. There is hardly a people or kindred on earth in whose mythology it is not shadowed forth. The Greeks represented their great god Apollo as slaying the serpent Pytho, and Hercules as strangling serpents while yet in his cradle. In Egypt, in India, in Scandinavia, in Mexico, we find clear allusions to the same great truth. 'The evil genius,' says Wilkinson, 'of the adversaries of the Egytian god Horus,[1] is frequently figured under the form of a snake, whose head he is seen piercing with a spear. The same fable occurs in the religion of India, where the malignant serpent Calyia is slain by Vishnu, in his *avatar* (incarnation) of Crishna; and the Scandinavian deity Thor, was said to have bruised the head of the great serpent with his mace.' 'The origin of this,' he adds, 'may be readily traced to the Bible'.[2] In reference to a similar belief among the Mexicans we find Humboldt saying that 'The serpent crushed by the great spirit Teotl, when he takes the form of one of the subaltern deities, is the genius of evil—a real Kakodæmon'.[3]

"Now, in almost all cases, when the subject is examined to the bottom, it turns out that the serpent-destroying god is represented as enduring hardships and sufferings that end in his death.

"This is particularly the case with the Indian god Crishna, to whom Wilkinson alludes in the extract already given. In the legend that concerns him the whole of the primeval promise

---

[1] Horus was the Egyptian Apollo, the same deity as the Assyrian Tammuz, &c., the Hindû Vishnu, the Scandinavian Thor, &c. His mother Isis answered to the Queen of heaven of Assyria and Greece. He was, in short, the Egyptian form of the false Messiah.

[2] Wilkinson, vol. 4, p. 395.

[3] Humboldt's *Mexican Researches*, vol. i. p. 228.

in Eden is very strikingly embodied. First, he is represented in pictures and images *with his foot on the great serpent's head*, and then, he is fabled to have died in consequence of being shot by an arrow *in the foot;* and, as in the case of Tammuz, great lamentations are annually made for his death.[1] Even in Greece also, in the classic story of Paris and Achilles, we have a very plain allusion to that part of the primeval promise which referred to the bruising of the conqueror's *heel.* Achilles, the only son of a goddess, was invulnerable in all points *except the heel*, but there a wound was deadly. At that his adversary took aim, and death was the result.

"Now if there be such evidence still, that even Pagans knew that it was *by dying* that the promised Messiah was to destroy death and him that has the power of death, that is the Devil, how much more vivid must have been the impression of mankind in general in regard to this vital truth in the early days of Semiramis, when they were so much nearer the fountain-head of all divine tradition."[2]

In order, then, to set up Nimrod as a *false Messiah*, it was necessary to represent his violent death as having been *voluntarily submitted to for the benefit of mankind.*

Accordingly, this was actually done. "The Chaldæan version of the story of the great Zoroaster (*Zero-ashta*) is, that he prayed to the God of heaven to take away his life; that his prayer was heard; and that he expired assuring his followers that if they cherished due regard for his memory the empire would never depart from the Babylonians."[3]

Thus, then, was *a false Messiah set up in Babylon.*

It appears, however, that afterwards this false Messiah came to be regarded as the *son* as well as the husband, of Semiramis. Nimrod is proved by the representations of him in ancient

[1] Coleman's *Indian Mythology*, plate 12, p. 34.
[2] Hislop's *Two Babylons*, p. 84 &c., from which work most of the information here given is derived.   [3] Ibid.

monuments, and the testimony of Plutarch, to have been *black*, with thoroughly *negro* features.[1] But, (as there is reason to believe), this deformity being found to make his worship unpopular in some quarters—or for some other unexplained reason—Semiramis seems to have pretended that one of her many posthumous children, of a fair complexion, was an incarnation of the departed spirit of her husband. This device enabled her to represent herself to be *the Woman*, whose Seed, or Son, was to bruise the Serpent's head, and her posthumous child to be the promised Deliverer, and at the same time a *Nimrod redivivus*—Nimrod in a new body—according to the Eastern notion of the transmigration of souls.

The plan was ingeniously devised. If successful, it would renew and perpetuate the influence of Semiramis, which her husband's death had cut short: and its success would be promoted by the double advantage it presented, of the re-appearance of Nimrod in the person of her son, and also of its being believed to realize the fulfilment of the primeval promise of the Deliverer. "The scheme, thus skilfully formed, took effect. Semiramis gained glory from her dead and deified husband: and in course of time, both of them, under the names of Rhea and Nin, or 'Goddess-Mother and Son,' were worshipped with an enthusiasm that was incredible, and their images were every where set up and adored."[2]

But how was this connected with the worship of the *Sun?*

The Chaldee word *Ashta* signifies both *woman*, and *light* or *fire: Zero* signifies *seed:* hence *Zero-ashta*, the *Seed of the woman*, would signify, to the uninitiated, *the Seed of fire*—or of *the sun*, as the great central fire of the universe.

Hence Nimrod, under the title of *Zero-ashta*—or in its Greek form *Zoroaster*—came to be regarded as the *Sun-born* deity, himself the progeny of the Sun, and the object as well as author of the whole system of *Fire-worship*, or *Sun-worship*.

---

[1] Ibid, p. 62, 99.   [2] Ibid.

The deception was aptly aided by the natural properties of
the sun, as the great centre of light and heat, and the instrument of life and activity, to the whole natural world—wherein
it was a striking *emblem* of the Deity, as indeed it is employed
even in the figurative language of Scripture.

This fact of Fire, or the Sun, having been regarded as the
fountain of life—and so, the symbol of Deity, if not itself
actually a god—is fully attested. In the Zoroastrian verse,
quoted in Cory's *Fragments*, p. 212, it is said, "*All things are
the progeny of one Fire.* The FATHER perfected all things,
and delivered them to the *second mind*, whom all nations of
men call the first." Here *Fire* is declared to be the *Father* of
all ; for all things are said to be its *progeny*—and it is also
called the "*perfecter* of all things." The *second mind* is
evidently the Child who displaced Nimrod's image as an object
of worship ; but yet the agency of Nimrod as the first of the
gods, and the Fire-god, was held indispensable for '*perfecting*'
men. And hence, too, no doubt, the necessity of the fire of
Purgatory to '*perfect*' men's souls at last, and to purge away
all the sins that they have carried with them into the unseen
world."[1] The name of *Tammuz* (who was identical with
Nimrod) signifies, "*Fire the perfecter*," or "the *perfecting fire*"
—being derived from *tam*, "to make perfect," and *muz*
"fire."

This idea of *perfecting by fire* gave rise, beyond a doubt, to
the savage practice of sacrificing children to Moloch, by making them "pass through the fire." It was also the cause of
Hindû widows burning themselves in the funeral pile of their
husbands, by which they thought they would become "*Suttee*"
—that is, "*purified by fire*," or "*pure by burning*."

Thus was Nimrod, the Babylonian false Messiah, worshipped
both as the promised "*Seed of the Woman*"—and also as the
Seed of the Sun—the Sun being regarded as the Creator and

---

[1] *Two Babylons*, p. 259.

Father of all things, and the Divine parent of this pretended Messiah.

Now there is express historical testimony that this was the vulgar belief of the ancient heathen nations.

"Almost all the *Tartar* princes, says Salverte, trace their genealogy to *a celestial virgin*, impregnated by a sunbeam, or some equally miraculous means.—In *India*, the mother of Surya, the Sun-god, who was born to destroy the enemies of the gods, is said to have become pregnant in this way."

Again, *Orion* was identical with Nimrod, who was fabled to have been changed into the constellation of that name. But the wife of Orion was called *Aurora*. Now the word Aurora signifies, in one sense, the "*awakener* of light"—but in another and no doubt the *mystical* sense, known only to those who were initiated into the mysteries, it signified "*pregnant* with light."[1]

We have now a complete unravelling of the curious enigma that the worship of the Mother and the Child—the Sun—and the Serpent, has pervaded the world: and that these three objects of idolatry have been almost everywhere associated together.

The idolatry of the Israelites, so frequently denounced in Scripture, was entirely of the same kind.

The Golden Calf made in the Wilderness, when in revels like those of the heathen "the people sat down to eat and drink, and rose up to play", or dance, has been already mentioned: as also the fact that the *Bull*, or Calf, was sacred to the Sun, and that accordingly the young *Apis* in Egypt used to be fed by the priests in a house facing the rising sun. The worship of the sacred bull Apis was celebrated with great festivities, and dances, and revels: of which the scenes presented at the worship of the Golden Calf were undoubtedly imitations.

To the same intent also were the two Calves of Gold set up

[1] *Two Babylons*, p. 144.

by Jeroboam in Bethel and Dan: and it cannot be doubted that the worship thus established as a national practice of the kingdom of Israel was of the same licentious and debasing character as the Egyptian festivities.

That the worship of the Sun was a part of the national Jewish apostasy, is not only indicated by their sacrifices and festivals in honour of the Golden Calves in Sinai and Bethel, but expressly stated in Scripture. We read of " the idolatrous priests whom the kings of Judah had ordained to burn incense in the high places in the cities of Judah, and in the places round about Jerusalem; them also that burned incense unto Baal, to *the sun*, and to the moon, and to the planets, and to all the host of heaven"—2 Kings xxiii. 5;—likewise of " the horses which the kings of Judah had given to the sun", and "the chariots of the sun",—v. 11:—and "sun-images"—2 Chron. xiv. 5, (marginal reading). And among the abominations shown "in the visions of God" to Ezekiel, as practised in the very temple at Jerusalem, were "about five and twenty men with their backs toward the temple of the LORD, and *their faces toward the east; and they worshipped the sun toward the east.*"—Ezek. viii. 16.

There is hardly room to doubt that this idolatrous custom was the real origin of the practice of *turning to the East* in Christian churches at the recital of the Creed; and of the practice therefore also of building churches with the great window towards the East, under which was placed the so-called "Altar", and the consecrated "Host," or wafer, believed by Romanists to be the very material Body and Blood of Christ. For it was thus contrived that the heathens might still be indulged in the adoration they had been wont to pay to the Sun, and yet should seem to be venerating the Presence of Christ on the "Altar"—another instance of the famous policy of Pope Gregory I. in "meeting the heathens half-way."

The identity of the Jewish idolatry with the Babylonian system is farther apparent from their worship of the "Queen of Heaven." Thus the LORD denounced their practices to the prophet—"The children gather wood, and the fathers kindle the fire, and the women knead their dough, to make cakes to the queen of heaven, and to pour out drink-offerings unto other gods, that they may provoke me to anger."—Jer. vii. 18.

The prohibition to the priests of the LORD to "make any baldness upon their head"—Levit. xxi. 5—was no doubt in reference to another practice of the Sun-worshippers, with whom it was an indispensable ceremony that their priests should receive the *circular tonsure* on their heads.

Maurice, referring to this usage in India, says that "it was an old practice of the priests of Mithra (the Persian name of the Sun-god), who *in their tonsure imitated the solar disk.*"[1] And Herodotus expressly states that the Arabians acknowledge no other gods than Bacchus (identical with Nimrod the Sun-god, Tammuz, Adonis, &c.), and Urania, (the Queen of Heaven); and they say that their hair is cut in the same manner as Bacchus's is cut: now they cut it in a *circular form*, shaving it round the temples."[2]

Of the constant combination of the worship of the false Messiah, the Sun, and the Serpent, the classical deity Apollo may serve as an example. Apollo was, first, the same as Crishna, and Nimrod, in the character of the promised *Deliverer*, who was to bruise the Serpent's head: and in this character he is said to have killed the great Serpent Python.— Next, he was the god of the *sun*—as is familiarly known to every schoolboy.—Thirdly, he was the god of *oracles*—which were universally believed to derive their supernatural knowledge from the *Serpent-god*—the spirit, good or evil, supposed to inhabit the Serpent.

The circumstance that the Serpent was regarded as the Evil one destroyed by the great Deliverer, and yet was worshipped as a god, need cause us no surprise. The one view

[1] *Antiquities*, vol. 7. p. 851.   [2] Herod. lib. 3. c. 8.

of the matter was handed down by direct tradition of the
primeval promise—the other arose from that ingenious perversion of the facts, by which the forbidden knowledge was
represented as the good gift of a benefactor, instead of the
bait of a malignant and designing enemy.   Such contradictions
are usual concomitants of every erroneous creed, and every
system of idolatry.

CHAPTER XIV.

Same subject continued.—Sun-worship in Egypt—symbolized by Obelisks and Pyramids—in Persia—in America.—Nimrod the Leopard-tamer and " Spotted One."—Modern Sun or Fire-Worship in Chaldæa—in the Midsummer Baal-fires of France, Switzerland, Ireland, Scotland, and Cornwall—in the Ramazan in Turkey—in the Romish Mass, Altars, Wafers, and priestly Tonsure—the Sun-goddess of Japan.—Union of Sun and Serpent-worship in the hiero-gram of the Circle, Serpent, and Wings.

To trace the practice of Sun-worship, or Fire-worship, through-out the world, would be tedious after what has been advanced on the kindred subject of Serpent-worship. The two were almost invariably found prevailing in the same regions.

But some notices of the more striking features of Sun-wor-ship in different parts of the world may be interesting.

In *Egypt*, it was a great national institution. The vast *Pyramids*, which have been the wonder of ages—and the *Obelisks*, which were of kindred origin, may be regarded as gigantic indications of this idolatry.

For they were both imitations of *rays of the sun*, as already stated. " The word *Pyramid* itself means ' *a ray of the sun* ', from the Coptic *Pi-ra-mu-e*."[1] Pyramids were frequently used as sepulchres. In Mexico they united the purposes both of sepulchres and temples.[2]

---

[1] Deane's *Worship of the Serpent*, p. 363.   [2] *Ibid*, p. 362.

I

"The word *obelisk*, according to Bryant, is derived from
Obel, the name of the god to whom they were dedicated." [1]
But Obel is just *Ob-el*—the *Serpent-god.* An obelisk, therefore, symbolizing a *ray of the sun*, especially by the small
pyramid in which it always terminated at the top—and dedicated to the *Serpent-god*, is another proof of the *same* god
being regarded both as the Sun-god and the Serpent-god.

This fact, indeed, is evident in the very name of the classic
god *Apollo*—or, in its Greek form, *Apollon.* For this word is a
compound of *Ap*, or *Ab*, a serpent—*El*, a god—and *On*, the
sun ; the whole name Apollo thus signifying the *Serpent-Sun-
god.*

Now it was just a series of *obelisk-like* stones that formed
the rude temples dedicated by the ancients to these favourite
deities.

The worshippers of the Sun arranged theirs in a *circle*, to
represent the *sun's disk*. Stonehenge was a temple of this
kind, and it is observable that the rude upright stones are
somewhat *pyramidal:* though the transverse stones which
rest upon the upright columns are thought to indicate that
this structure is of a later date than other Druidical remains.

The Serpent-worshippers, again, had the upright stones
placed in *serpentine avenues*, to represent the sinuosities of an
enormous snake moving over hill and dale—as in the remarkable Serpent-temple at Carnac in Britany, and in that described
by Ovid as passed by Medea in her flight from Attica to
Colchis—

> Factaque de saxo longi simulachra draconis :—
>
> "A long-drawn serpent's image made in stone."

The votaries of the Sun and Serpent *conjointly*, made their
temples in the form of *a circle with serpentine avenues running
through it.* Of this kind the temple at Abury was a notable
specimen. [2]

---

[1] Ibid. p. 361.   [2] Deane, p. 363, &c.

But the greatest monument, and head-quarters, of Sun-worship in Egypt was the city of *On*—in Greek *Heliopolis*—both names signifying the *City of the Sun*. Here was a temple of the Sun, and a large and flourishing establishment of priests, with colleges for their education. This city was, indeed, the University of Egypt, and appears to have been the centre of Egyptian science and learning.

The Sun-deity was called by the Egyptians *Ré*, or *Phra*. The name of Potipherah, priest of On, whose daughter Asenath was given in marriage to Joseph,[1] is "evidently compounded of Phré or Phra, the Sun; and answers to the Egyptian Petphré, or Heliodotus," ("*given to the Sun*"): and the title *Pharaoh* borne by the kings of Egypt, was derived from the same root.[2]

"The god Ré was usually represented as a man, with a hawk's head, surmounted by a globe or disk of the Sun, from which the Uræus *asp* issued."[3]

The hawk, according to Porphyry, and also the Scarabæus or Beetle, were sacred emblems of the Sun-deity. The Beetle, with its wings expanded, was thought to present an image of the sacred *Circle and Wings*.[4]

This Sun-god Ré was the same as the Syrian Baal, and the Babylonian Belus or Bel—this name itself being probably an abbreviation of *Ob-el*, the Serpent-god.

"There is reason to believe," says Wilkinson, "that the god Ré corresponded to the Syrian Baal, a name implying *Lord*, which was given *par excellence* to the Sun: and the same idea of peculiar sovereignty vested in that deity may have led the Egyptians to take from Ré (Phra) the regal title of their kings.

---

[1] Gen. xli. 45.

[2] In like manner *Mithridates*, a name common to several Persian kings, signifies *given by the Sun*, or given to the Sun.

[3] Wilkinson's *Ancient Egyptians*, vol. i., p. 295—from which these particulars are taken.

[4] Deane, p. 43.

Heliopolis in Syria still retains the name of *Baalbek*, "the city of (the *lord* or) the Sun": and the same word occurs in the names of distinguished individuals among the Phœnicians and their descendants of Carthage, as Annibal, Asdrubal, and others."

In the above account of the Egyptian Sun-worship, the reader will not fail to observe the usual association of the *Sun* and the *Serpent*—both being identified with the Babylonian Belus or Bel.

In Wilkinson's *Ancient Egyptians* there is a plate (No. 30) of "the king and queen praying to the Sun." The Sun is represented by several concentric circles, or rather oval figures, with divergent rays proceeding from the outermost ring.

The *Persians* were Sun-worshippers. "They are wont," says Herodotus, "to offer sacrifices to Jupiter, ascending to the highest parts of the mountains, calling the whole circle of the heaven Jupiter: and they sacrifice to the *sun*, and the moon, and the earth, and *fire*, and water, and the winds."—"And when they have divided the victim into parts, and boiled the flesh, they spread out grass as smooth as possible, especially *trefoil*, and place all the flesh upon it".[1]—This passage seems to point out the origin of sacrificing upon "high places", so often mentioned in Scripture. The custom would appear to have arisen from the "*circle of the heaven*" being taken as an *emblem of deity*—the "high places", of course, being those from which the largest expanse of heaven could be seen.—There is also in this curious passage an evident indication that the doctrine of the *Trinity* was known to the ancient heathens. The selection of *trefoil* grass, which has the form of *three leaves in one*, cannot be otherwise explained.

We may pass from one side of the earth to the other, and find that there also the same worship was prevalent.

In *America* there are still remaining, in various places,

---

[1] Herodot, i. 131, 132.

ancient structures of a *pyramidal* form. One of these is thus
described by a modern traveller. It "is called *El Sacrificatorio*,
or 'the place of sacrifice'. It is a quadrangular stone structure,
sixty-six feet on each side at the base, and rising in a pyramidal
form to the height, in its present condition, of thirty-three feet.
On three sides there is a range of steps in the middle—on the
side facing the west there are no steps, but the surface is
smooth, and covered with stucco, grey from long exposure.
By breaking a little at the corners we saw that there were
different layers of stucco, doubtless put on at different times,
and all had been ornamented with painted figures. In one
place we made out part of the body of a *leopard*, well drawn
and coloured."[1] On the top of this pyramid a human sacrifice
was offered from time to time. "The barbarous ministers
carried up the victim, and extended him upon the altar. Four
priests held the legs and arms, and another kept his head firm
with a wooden instrument made in the form of *a coiled serpent*."
The head priest then approached, and with a knife made of
flint cut an aperture in the breast, and tore out the heart, which,
yet palpitating, *he offered to the Sun*, and then threw it at the
feet of the idol."

Not only is the strange combination of Sun and Serpent-
worship here illustrated, but there is another coincidence too
curious and significant to be passed over—namely, the discovery, on the painted stucco, of the figure of a *leopard*.

It has been already remarked, that the real original object
of Sun-worship was *Nimrod*, who was regarded in after times
as *Zero-ashta*, the Seed of the Woman—and then, by a double
meaning of the word, favoured doubtless by priestcraft, as the
Seed of *Fire*, or of the *Sun*. He thus united both ideas, and
was venerated as the *Sun-begotten Seed of the Woman*.

But it has not yet been mentioned that Nimrod was every
where throughout the ancient heathen world known as *the*

[1] Stephens's *Incidents of Travel in Central America*, &c., vol. 2. 184.

Leopard-tamer—and was always represented as *clothed in a leopard's skin.* That he was "a mighty hunter" we know from Scripture: but it is expressly stated by Sir William Jones, "from the Persian legends, that Hoshang, the father of Tahmurs, who built Babylon, was the first who bred dogs and *leopards* for hunting.[1] As Tahmurs, who built Babylon, could be none other than Nimrod, the legend only attributes to his father what, as his name imports, he got the fame of doing himself."[2] "When Nimrod, as the Leopard-tamer, began to be clothed in the leopard-skin, his spotted dress and appearance must have impressed the imaginations of those who saw him; and he came to be called not only the ' *Subduer of the Spotted one* ' (for such is the precise meaning of *Nimrod*[3]), but to be called 'the Spotted One' himself."

Nimrod was identified with the Egyptian *Osiris*, the Grecian and Roman *Bacchus*, the Syrian *Tammuz*, the classic *Adonis:* and the worship of all these gods or demi-gods was accompanied, in one way or another, by the symbol of *the Spotted One*—either the *leopard*, or, as in Greece, the *spotted fawn*.[4] And "the existence of this worship," says Mr. Hislop, "can be traced not merely in the annals of classical antiquity, but in the literature of the world from Ultima Thule to Japan."

Let all these facts be taken together — and then, how startling to find the records of them all grouped together in one single structure in the far West—at the very antipodes of the places where the facts themselves occurred! Deeply must those facts have been graven on the memory of mankind, thus to have been remembered and recorded in the religious rites, the temples, the monuments, or the traditions, of every nation under heaven.

---

[1] *Works*, vol. 12. p. 400.   [2] *Two Babylons*, p. 64.

[3] The name *Nimrod* is from the Hebrew *Nimr*, a leopard, and *radah*, or *rad*, to subdue.—Ibid. p. 66.

[4] For full proof of this curious fact see the details and authorities produced by Mr. Hislop, *Two Babylons*, p. 62, &c.

But the reader will perhaps hardly be prepared to hear that not merely the traces, but the actual *practice*, of Fire-worship or Sun-worship, exists to this very day:—and that, too, not only in foreign lands, but even in our own country !

As a specimen of the practice in *foreign* lands, we may take the description given by Mr. Layard of what he himself witnessed in Chaldæa in 1842. "Below the cluster of buildings assigned to the people of Semil is a small white spire, springing from a low edifice, neatly constructed, and like all the sacred places of the Yezidis, kept as pure as repeated coats of white-wash can make it. It is called the sanctuary of *Sheikh Shems*, or *the Sun ;* and is so placed that the first rays of that luminary should as frequently as possible fall upon it. Near the door an invocation to *Sheikh Shems* is carved on a slab. The interior, which is a very holy place, is lighted by a few small lamps. At sunset, as I sat in the alcove in front of the entrance, a herdsman led into a pen, attached to the building, a drove of *white oxen*. I asked a Cawal, who was near me, to whom the beasts belonged. 'They are dedicated,' he said, 'to *Sheikh Shems*, and are never slain except on great festivals, when their flesh is distributed among the poor.'[1]

"As the twilight faded, the Fakirs, or lower order of priests, issued from the tomb, each bearing a light in one hand, and a pot of oil with a bundle of cotton wicks, in the other. They filled and trimmed lamps placed in niches of the walls of the court-yard, and scattered over the buildings on the sides of the valley, and even on isolated rocks and in the hollow trunks of trees. Innumerable stars appeared to glitter on the black sides of the mountains, and in the dark recesses of the forest. As the priests made their way through the crowd to perform their task, men and women *passed their right hands through the*

---

[1] "The dedication of the *bull* to the *Sun*, so generally recognized in the religious systems of the ancients, probably originated in Assyria, and the Yezidis may have unconsciously preserved a myth of their ancestors."

flame, and then devoutly carried them to their lips, after rub-
bing the right eyebrow with the part which had been *purified
by the sacred element.* Some who bore *children* in their arms
anointed them in like manner, whilst others held out their hands
to be touched by those who, less fortunate than themselves,
could not reach the flame.

" As night advanced, those who had assembled—they must
now have amounted to nearly five thousand persons—lighted
torches, which they carried with them as they wandered
through the forest. The effect was magical; the varied groups
could be faintly distinguished through the darkness; men
hurrying to and fro; women with their children seated on the
house-tops; and crowds gathering round the pedlars who exposed their wares for sale in the court-yard. Thousands of
lights were reflected in the fountains and streams, glimmered
amongst the foliage of the trees, and danced in the distance.
As I was gazing on this extraordinary scene, the hum of
human voices was suddenly hushed, and a strain, solemn and
melancholy, arose from the valley. It resembled some majestic
chant, which years before I had listened to in the cathedral of
a distant land. Music so pathetic and so sweet I had never
before heard in the East. The voices of men and women were
blended in harmony with the soft notes of many flutes. At
measured intervals the song was broken by the loud clash of
cymbals and tambourines; and those who were without the
precincts of the tomb then joined in the melody."—" The
chant gradually gave way to a lively melody which, increasing in measure, was finally lost in a confusion of sounds. The
tambourines were beaten with extraordinary energy; the flutes
poured forth a rapid flood of notes; the voices were raised to
their highest pitch; the men outside joined in the cry; whilst
the women made the rocks resound with the shrill *tahleel.*
The musicians, giving way to the excitement, threw their in-
struments into the air, and strained their limbs into every
contortion, till they fell exhausted to the ground. I never

heard a more frightful yell than that which rose in the valley."

The Yezidis, says the same author, " are accustomed to kiss the object on which the sun's first beams fall ; and I have frequently, when travelling in their company at sunrise, observed them perform this ceremony. For *fire*, as symbolical, they have nearly the same reverence; they never spit into it, but frequently pass their hands through the flame, kiss them, and rub them over their right eyebrow, or sometimes over the whole face."—" Their Kubleh, or the place to which they look while performing their holy ceremonies, is that part of the heavens in which the sun rises, and towards it they turn the faces of their dead."[1]

These people are reputed to be Devil-worshippers. They combine with their worship of the Sun an extraordinary and reverential dread of *Satan*—though nothing is said of their using the symbol of the Serpent. " When they speak of the Devil, they do so with reverence, as *Melek el Kout*, the mighty angel. So far is their dread of offending the Evil principle carried, that they carefully avoid every expression which may resemble in sound the name of Satan, or the Arabic word for ' accursed '." They also " hold the Old Testament in great reverence, (though not Christians), and believe in the cosmogony of Genesis, the Deluge, and other events recorded in the Bible ".[2]

Thus it appears that, however the facts of Genesis may be discredited by European sceptics, they are believed to this day

[1] Layard's *Nineveh*, chap. 9.

[2] Ibid.—It is a significant remark made by Mr. Layard that "the mysteries of the sect have been traced to the worship introduced by *Semiramis* into the very mountains they now inhabit—a worship which, impure in its forms, led to every excess of debauchery and lust."—*Nineveh and its Remains*, vol. i. p. 271.—The fact is a striking confirmation of the accounts of the Babylonian system given in the present work.

among the inhabitants of the countries nearest to the very localities where Eden was planted, where the Ark rested after the Deluge, and where the building of Babel's Tower was interrupted by the confusion of tongues. The national creed and customs of the Chaldæan Yezidis attest at once both the truth of Genesis, and the corruption of that truth after the Flood, which, by means of the dispersion from Babylon, became the fountain-head of all the idolatrous systems of the whole earth.

The classical reader will not fail to be struck with the similarity of the nocturnal torch-bearing ceremonies of the Yezidis with the rites of Bacchus and Cybele among the Greeks. They had, in fact, a common origin; for Bacchus was identical with Nimrod the Babylonian false Messiah, and the real Serpent-Sun-god of all the nations: and Cybele was identical with Semiramis, the real wife of Nimrod, but the reputed mystical Mother of the Child—whose worship was usually associated with that of the Serpent and the Sun, from the very fact that the Babylonian false Messiah was worshipped both as her Child, the Seed of the woman, and also (as has been already shown) as the *Seed of Fire*—the Sun-begotten Seed of the woman.

But there are unconscious successors to the ancient worshippers of the Sun, or Fire, nearer home.

The *Midsummer Fires*, annually lighted by the Roman Catholics on the Eve of St. John the Baptist, are nothing else but *a continuation of the Baal-fires of old*—the fires of the Babylonian Nimrod or Zoroaster, and of the Canaanitish Moloch.

One of the grand original festivals of Tammuz (or Nimrod) was celebrated on the 24th June—which in Chaldæa, Syria, and Phœnicia was called the "month of Tammuz".

"When the Papacy sent its emissaries over Europe, towards the end of the sixth century, to gather in the Pagans into its fold, this festival was found in high favour in many countries.

What was to be done with it? Were they to wage war with it? No. This would have been contrary to the famous advice of Pope Gregory I., that by all means *they should meet the Pagans half-way*, and so bring them into the Roman Church.[1] The Gregorian policy was carefully observed, and so Midsummer-day, that had been hallowed by Paganism to the worship of Tammuz, was incorporated as a sacred Christian festival in the Roman Calendar."

For this purpose the *Nativity of St. John the Baptist* was aptly selected. Another Pagan festival, that of the Birth of the Babylonian false Messiah, had always been kept on the 25th of December—and was observed as *Yule-day*, or the "Child's Day," in ancient Britain, for ages before any Christian missionary set foot in our island. That the "Yule-day" festival was of Babylonian origin is proved by the fact that *yule* is the Chaldee term for an *infant* or little child.

"Now for the purposes of the Papacy nothing could be more opportune than this. John the Baptist was born six months before our Lord. When, therefore, the Pagan festival of the winter solstice had once been consecrated as the birth-day of the Saviour, it followed as a matter of course that if his forerunner was to have a festival at all, his festival must be at this very season: for between the 24th June and 25th of December there are just six months." Moreover, "one of the many names by which Tammuz or Nimrod was called, when he reappeared in his mysteries after being slain, was *Oannes*. The name of John the Baptist, on the other hand, in the sacred language adopted by the Roman Church, was *Joannes*. To make the festival of the 24th of June, then, suit Christians and Pagans alike, all that was needful was just to call it the festival of Joannes (pronounced *Yoannes*); and thus the Christians would suppose that they were honouring John the Baptist,

---

[1] Bower's *Lives of the Popes*, vol. 2. p. 523, quoted in *Two Babylons*, p. 163, which see for these statements.

while the Pagans were still worshipping their old god Oannes,
or Tammuz. Thus the very period at which the great summer
festival of Tammuz was celebrated in ancient Babylon, is at
this very hour observed in the Papal Church as the feast of the
Nativity of St. John. And the fête of St. John begins exactly
as the festal day began in Chaldæa. It is well known that in
the East the day began in the *evening*. So though the 24th
be set down as the Nativity, yet it is on St. John's *Eve*, that is,
on the evening of the 23rd, that the festivities and solemnities
of that period (St. John's Nativity) begin.

"Now if we examine the festivities themselves, we shall see
how purely Pagan they are, and how decisively they prove
their real descent. The grand distinguishing solemnities of
St. John's Eve are the Midsummer *fires*. These are lighted
in France, in Switzerland, in Roman Catholic Ireland, and in
some of the Scottish Isles of the West, where Popery still
lingers. They are kindled throughout all the grounds of the
adherents of Rome, and flaming brands are carried about their
corn-fields. Thus does Bell, in his 'Way-side Pictures', describe the St. John's fires of Britany, in France. 'Throughout
the day the poor children go about begging contributions for
lighting the fires of Monsieur St. Jean, and towards evening,
one fire is gradually followed by two, three, four; then a
thousand gleam out from the hill-tops, till the whole country
glows under the conflagration.—The young people dance with
a bewildering activity about the fires; for there is a superstition among them that if they dance round nine fires before
midnight, they will be married in the ensuing year.—Fragments of the torches on these occasions are preserved as spells
against thunder and nervous diseases; and the crown of
flowers which surmounted the principal fire is in such request
as to produce tumultuous jealousy for its possession.'[1] Thus
it is in France.

[1] *Wayside Pictures*, p. 225.

"Turn we now to Ireland. 'On that great festival of the Irish peasantry, St. John's Eve,' says Charlotte Elizabeth, describing a particular festival which she had witnessed, 'it is the custom, at sunset on that evening, to kindle immense fires throughout the country, built, like our bonfires, to a great height, the pile being composed of turf, bog-wood, and such other combustible substances as they can gather. The turf yields a steady, substantial body of fire, the bog-wood a most brilliant flame, and the effect of these great beacons blazing on every hill, sending up volumes of smoke from every point of the horizon, is very remarkable. Early in the evening the peasants began to assemble, all habited in their best array, every countenance full of that sparkling animation and excess of enjoyment that characterize the enthusiastic people of the land. The fire being kindled, a splendid blaze shot up.—After a short pause, the ground was cleared in front of an old blind piper, who, seated on a low chair, with a well-plenished jug within his reach, screwed his pipes to the liveliest tunes, and the endless jig began. But something was to follow that puzzled me not a little. When the fire burned for some hours, and got low, an *indispensable part of the ceremony* commenced. *Every one present of the peasantry passed through* it, and *several children* were thrown across the sparkling embers.' 'Here', adds the authoress, 'was *the old Pagan worship of Baal, if not of Moloch too*, carried on openly and universally in the heart of a nominally Christian country, and by millions professing the Christian name! I was confounded; for I did not then know that Popery is only a crafty adaptation of Pagan idolatries to its own scheme'.[1] Such is the festival of St. John's Eve, as celebrated at this day in France and in Popish Ireland."[2]

Who can fail to be reminded, by the foregoing descriptions, of the *singing* and *dancing* of the Israelites around the molten

---

[1] *Personal Recollections*, Letter 5. [2] *Two Babylons*, p. 163, &c.

Calf in the desert of Sinai, when "the people sat down to eat and drink, and rose up to play"?

There can be no doubt that this worship of the Golden Calf by the Israelites was just the same which they had been wont to see practised in Egypt, and that it was, in fact, the worship of the Sun-god—the Baal of Canaan, the Bel or Belus of Babylon, the Zoroaster of the Fire-worshippers—the Bacchus and also the Adonis of the Greeks—all these being but different names for Nimrod, the Babylonian false Messiah, the Sun-begotten Seed of the woman. In Egypt this same god was worshipped under the name of Osiris : and the *sacred Bull* Apis was consecrated to Osiris, and appears to have been regarded as a kind of incarnation of this deity. But Herodotus, in describing the Apis, says that "he is a young bull, whose mother can have no other offspring, and who is reported by the Egyptians to *conceive from lightning sent from heaven,* and thus to produce the god Apis."[1] Plutarch says that "they call the Apis the living image of Osiris, and suppose him *begotten by a ray of generative light* from the moon.[2]

But there is extant a still more complete and striking identification of the Egyptian Apis with that object of world-wide idolatry, the Serpent-Sun-god. Wilkinson gives an engraving of a bronze figure of the Apis, "in the possession of Miss Rogers," on which is seen the indispensable sacred mark on the back of the bull—which is none other but the *Circle and Wings,* already mentioned as the well-known symbol of deity : and curled between the horns is *a serpent,* rising above their points and *forming a circle.* And at the funeral obsequies observed when the Apis died, the coffin, placed on a sledge, was followed by the priests, "*dressed in the spotted skins of fawns,* bearing the thyrsus in their hands, uttering the same

[1] Herod. 3, 28.
[2] Plut. *de Is.* s. 43, quoted by Wilkinson, *Anc. Egypt,* vol. i., 348, second series.

cries, and making the same gesticulations as the votaries of Bacchus during the ceremonies in honour of that God."[1]

When the young Apis was discovered, it was fed by the priests in a house *facing the rising sun.* "It would be tedious," says the historian, "to relate what pompous processions and sacred ceremonies the Egyptians perform on the celebration of the rising of the Nile, at the fête of the Theophania, in honour of this god: or what *dances, festivities,* and joyful assemblies are appointed on the occasion, in the towns and in the country."[2]

No doubt, therefore, can remain as to the nature of those idolatrous rites celebrated by the Israelites in honour of the Golden Calf, at the very time when Moses was on the Mount, receiving the Divine Law from the hand of God Himself. That Calf was the same idol as the Egyptian Apis, the Serpent-Sun-god of all heathen nations—the same, among many others, as the Bacchus of the Greeks and Romans. These dances and festivities were of the same nature as the licentious revels of the Egyptians, and the Bacchanalian orgies of the Greeks. The Moloch-fires were only another phase of the same idolatry ; the relics of which are still to be seen in the Baal-fires of the Yezidis in Chaldæa, and the Roman Catholics in Britany, Ireland, and the north of Scotland.

These latter are, in fact, a continuation of the *Druidical* rites of our forefathers.

"Before Christianity entered the British Isles, the Pagan festival of the 24th of June was celebrated among the Druids by blazing fires in honour of their great divinity, Baal. 'Of the fires we kindle in many parts of England at some stated times of the year', (says Borlase, in his *Antiq. of Cornwall,* pp. 135, 136), 'we know not exactly the rise, reason, or occasion ; but they may probably be reckoned among the relics of the

---

[1] Plut. *de Is.* s. 35, quoted by Wilkinson, ibid, p. 353.
[2] Ælian, xviii., 10, quoted ibid.

fore-mentioned Druidical superstition. In Cornwall, and all over Cumberland, the Festival Fires, called Bonfires, are kindled on the Eve of St. John the Baptist; and Midsummer is thence, in the Cornish tongue, called Goluan, which signifies both *light* and *rejoicing*. At these fires the Cornish attend with lighted torches, tarred and pitched at the end, and make their perambulations round their fires, going from village to village, and carrying their torches before them. *This is certainly the remains of Druid superstition'.*"[1] And it is thus a confirmation of the fact that the Druids were Sun-worshippers or Fire-worshippers.

So also in Scotland.—"The late Lady Baird of Fern Tower in Perthshire, says a writer in *Notes and Queries*, thoroughly versed in British antiquities (the Right Hon. Lord John Scott) told me, that every year at Beltane (or the first of May) a number of men and women assemble at an ancient Druidical circle of stones, on her property near Crieff. They light a fire in the centre, each person puts a bit of oat-cake in a shepherd's bonnet, they all sit down, and draw blindfold a piece from the bonnet. One piece has been previously blackened, and whoever gets that piece has to jump through the fire in the centre of the circle, and pay a forfeit. This is, in fact, a part of the ancient worship of Baal, and the person on whom the lot fell was (previously) burnt as a sacrifice. Now the passing through the fire represents that, and the payment of the forfeit redeems the victim."[2]

The fact that the first of May is still called *Beltane*,[3] and that it is on that day that this custom is observed in Scotland, is a further proof that the custom is a remnant of Baal-worship.

And the fact that the fire is kindled "in an ancient *Druidical circle* of stones, is a confirmation of the other evidences that

---

[1] *Armageddon*, vol. 2, p. 223.		[2] *Two Babylons*, p. 148.
[3] See Oliver & Boyd's *Edinburgh Almanac*, 1860.

the Druidical worship was of Babylonian origin, and that Fire
or Sun-worship was one of its essential elements.

"'These Midsummer fires and sacrifices,' says Toland in his
account of the Druids, 'were (intended) to obtain a blessing
on the fruits of the earth, now becoming ready for gathering.'
Again, speaking of the Druidical fires at Midsummer, he thus
proceeds: 'To return to our carn-fires, it was customary for
the lord of the place, or his son, or some other person of distinction, to take the entrails of the sacrificed animal in his
hands, and walking barefoot over the coals thrice, after the
flames had ceased, to carry them straight to the Druid, who
waited in a whole skin at the altar. If the nobleman escaped
harmless, it was reckoned a good omen, welcomed with loud
acclamations; but if he received any hurt, it was deemed un-
lucky, both to the community and himself.'—'Thus I have
seen the people running and leaping through the St. John's
fires in Ireland; and not only proud of passing unsinged, but,
as if it were some kind of *lustration*, thinking themselves in an
especial manner blest by the ceremony—of whose original,
nevertheless, they were wholly ignorant, in their imperfect
imitation of it.'"[1]

"Among the Druids, also, fire was celebrated as the *purifier*.
Thus, in a Druidic song (called the *Song to the Sun*) we read,
'they celebrated the praise of the holy ones in the presence of
the *purifying fire*, which was made to ascend on high.'"[2]—"It
is evident that this very same belief about the '*purifying*'
efficacy of fire is held by the Roman Catholics of Ireland, when
they are so zealous to pass both themselves and their children
through the fires of St. John. 'I have seen parents,' said the
late Lord John Scott in a letter to me, '*force* their children to
go through the Baal-fires.' Now, if Tammuz was, as we have
seen, the same as Zoroaster, the god of the ancient Fire-wor-

[1] *Two Babylons*, p. 168, quoting *Toland's Druids*, pp. 107, 112.
[2] Davies's *Druids*, p. 360.

K

shippers, and if his festival in Babylon so exactly synchronized with the feast of the Nativity of St. John, what wonder that that feast is still celebrated by the blazing 'Baal-fires'—and that it presents so faithful a copy of what was condemned by Jehovah of old in his ancient people when they 'made their children pass through the fire to Moloch'"?[1]

This notion of fire being the *purifier* was not only laid down as the essential principle of the Chaldæan system of Zoroaster, but was derived thence throughout the heathen nations of antiquity. Therefore it was that children were 'made to pass through the fire to Moloch'—Jerem. xxxii. 35—to purge them from original sin; and through this purgation many a helpless babe became a victim to the bloody divinity. Among the Pagan *Romans* this purifying by passing through the fire was equally observed; for, says Ovid, 'Fire purifies both the shepherd and the sheep.' Among the Hindoos, from time immemorial, fire has been worshipped for its purifying efficacy".[2]

"In *Turkey*, the feast of Ramazan, which begins on the 12th of June, is attended by an illumination of *burning lamps*. And it is remarkable that a festival, accompanied with all the essential rites of the Fire-worship of Baal, is found among Pagan nations, in regions most remote from one another, about this very period of the month of Tammuz, when the feast in honour of the Babylonian god was anciently celebrated. In *China*, the *Dragon*-boat festival begins at the summer solstice. In *Peru*, during the reign of the Incas, there was the feast of Raymi at the same period—when the *sacred fire* was rekindled *from the sun* by means of a concave mirror of polished metal. All through *Egypt* the festival of burning lamps took place on this night".[3]

But who would have thought that Sun-worship lingers even to this day in the ceremonies observed at the very altars, and

---

[1] Hislop's *Two Babylons*, pp. 174, 175.
[2] Ibid.   [3] *Armageddon*, vol. 2. 223, 224.

in the most sacred rite, of that professing Christian Church which arrogates to itself the title of Mistress and Mother of all churches? Yet so it is— as will plainly appear from the following facts.

"We read that the servants of the good king Josiah in carrying out the work (of reformation) proceeded thus :—'And they brake down the altars of Baalim in his presence : and the images (margin, *sun-images*) that were on high above them, he cut down.'—2 Chron. xxxiv. 4. Benjamin of Tudela, the great Jewish traveller, gives a striking account of Sun-worship even in comparatively modern times, as subsisting among the Cushites of the East; from which we find that the image of the sun was, even in his day, worshipped on the altar. 'There is a temple,' says he, 'of the posterity of Chus, addicted to the contemplation of the stars. They worship the sun as a god, and the whole country, for half-a-mile round their town, is filled with great altars dedicated to him. By the dawn of morn they get up and run out of town to wait the rising sun, to whom, *on every altar*, there is *a consecrated image*, not in the likeness of a man, but of the solar orb, framed by magic art. These orbs, as soon as the sun rises, take fire, and resound with a great noise, while every body there, men and women, hold censers in their hands, and all burn incense to the sun.'[1] From all this it is manifest that the image of the Sun, above or on the altar, was one of the recognized symbols of those who worshipped Baal or the Sun."

But Hurd, describing the embellishments of the Romish Altar, says, "A plate of silver, in the form of a *sun*, is fixed opposite to the *sacrament* on the altar: which with the light of the tapers, makes a most brilliant appearance".[2]

So then, "here, in a so-called Christian church, a brilliant

---

[1] "Quoted by Translator of *Savary's Letters*, vol. 2. pp. 562, 563, Note."—*Two Babylons*, p. 237.

[2] Hurd's *Rites and Ceremonies*, p. 196, col. 1.

plate of silver, 'in the form of a *sun*', is so placed on the altar that every one who adores at that altar must bow down in lowly reverence before that image of the *sun*.   Whence, I ask, could that have come, but from the ancient Sun-worship, or worship of Baal?   And when the wafer is so placed that the silver *sun* is fronting the *round* wafer, whose roundness is so important an element in the Romish mystery, what can be the meaning of it but just to show, to those who have eyes to see, that the wafer itself is just another symbol of Baal or the Sun?

"If the Sun-divinity was worshipped in Egypt as 'the Seed', or in Babylon as the 'Corn', precisely so is the wafer adored in Rome. 'Bread-*corn* of the elect, have mercy upon us,' is one of the appointed prayers in the Roman Litany, addressed to the wafer, in the celebration of the Mass.   And one at least of the imperative requirements as to the way in which that wafer is to be partaken of, is just the very same as was enforced in the old worship of the Babylonian divinity.   Those who partake of it are required to partake absolutely *fasting*."[1]

Again—the priests of Bacchus, Mithra, Osiris, and of the whole Babylonian worship every where,[2] were distinguished by the *circular tonsure ;* and so also are the priests of the modern Babylon at the present day.   "The tonsure is the first part of the ceremony of ordination" of the priests of Rome ; "and it is held to be a most important element in connexion with the orders of the Romish Clergy."

Now this indispensable mark of the Romish priesthood is just nothing more nor less than a continuation of the Babylonian custom.   One of the most important parts of the Chaldæan mysteries was the *mutilation* suffered by Tammuz, or Nimrod—the same with the Grecian Bacchus, and Adonis, the Egyptian Osiris, the Scandinavian Balder, &c., as before observed.   In memory of this, he was lamented every year with bitter weeping as "Rosh-Gheza", *the mutilated Prince.*

---

[1] See *Two Babylons*, p. 235, &c.   [2] Ibid, p. 324.

But "Rosh-Gheza" also signified the *clipped or shaven head.* Hence he was represented with his head clipped or shaven : and his priests, at their consecration, underwent the same process. The tonsure was made circular in honour of this deity as the Sun-god. The mark which distinguished the priests of the Babylonian Sun-god or false Messiah is the mark adopted by the priests of Rome at the present day.

And as in the far West, so it is in the far East. In *Japan,* the principal and most highly honoured deity of the Sintoo mythology, the most ancient creed of the Japanese, is the *Sun-goddess*—the Sun being here, as in Scandinavia and elsewhere, regarded as a female divinity. And among the duties enjoined by this ancient superstition, the first is the "preservation of *pure fire,* as the emblem of purity and means of purification".[1]

The fact, then, is indisputable that throughout the known world the worship of the Sun, in conjunction mostly with that of the Serpent—and associated with that of the Mother and the Child—has prevailed from the remotest antiquity ; and its relics are found to this day even in our own country.

In the hierogram of the Circle, Serpent, and Wings, already noticed, these combined objects of worship are clearly symbolized.

The Circle, as already observed, denotes the Deity—which was symbolized among the ancient Persians by the circle of the heavens, or horizon. It would also aptly represent the *Sun,* as an object of worship ; and is so found, in its separate form, in the Egyptian monuments.

The forming of this circle *with the serpent itself,* would amount to an expression of the deification of the Serpent.

"The Serpent *emerging* from the globe was the *vivifying*

---

[1] Steinmetz's *Japan and her People,* pp. 227, 229.

power of God, which called all things into existence. This he named *the Word.*

"The *Wings* implied the *moving or penetrative power* of God, which pervaded all things. This he called *Love.*

"The *whole* emblem was interpreted to represent the Supreme Being in his character of *Creator and Preserver.*"[1]

In *Persia*, this emblem has been found in the form of a human figure whose waist is encircled with a zone, while the wings appear on each side, and the serpent traverses the circle. This is identified as the god *Azon*, whose name, according to Bryant, signifies "the Sun." The sacred girdle round his waist was esteemed an emblem of the orbit described by *Zon*, the *sun.* Hence girdles were called by the Greeks, *Zones.*[2]

Plate II. represents several different forms of the hierogram; each one being merely a variety of the same general symbolism of *Deity.* The introduction of the Serpent amounts to an expression of the belief that the Serpent was an *incarnation* of deity—in other words, it implies the deification and worship of the Serpent.

Fig. 1 is the ordinary symbol of Deity among the *Assyrians;* as found in the Nineveh sculptures.

"According to M. Lajard, this symbol is formed by a circle or crown, to denote time without bounds, or· eternity—encircling the image of Baal, with the wings and tail of a dove, to show the association of Mylitta, the Assyrian Venus—thus presenting a complete triad."[3]

Fig. 2 is the usual *Egyptian* hierogram, taken from the temple of Isis at Dendera in Upper Egypt. It is found profusely ornamenting this and the other Egyptian temples. The serpents issuing from the Circle are *basilisks*—of the same kind as that in the picture of the Fall given in Pl. I.

---

[1] Deane, p. 56, quoting the theory of Trismegistus, from Kircher, *Pamph. Obel.*, 399. [2] Deane, p. 50, quoting Bryant, 2, 407. [3] Layard's *Nineveh and its Remains*, vol. ii. p. 449.

PLATE II.

SYMBOLS OF DEITY.

Fig. 3 is the *Persian* god Azon, described by Bryant.[1]

Fig. 4 is a *Chinese* symbol.

Fig. 5 is one from the ruins of *Naki Rustan,* supposed to have been the ancient Persepolis.

Fig. 6 to 11 are from the Isiac Table.[2]

Among the Assyrian relics discovered by Mr. Layard is a cylinder of green felspar which he believes to have been Sennacherib's own signet or amulet. This cylinder is engraved with a figure of the king in the act of *sacrifice and worship* before the sacred symbol—which here presents a human figure in the circle, with the wings and tail of a bird, and two human heads placed one upon each of the expanded wings, forming a *triad* of human heads. Mr. Layard conjectures that this emblem was "the symbol of *the triune god,* the supreme deity of the Assyrians, and of the Persians their successors in the empire of the East."[3]

On another Assyrian cylinder the same hierogram appears with a remarkable deviation. There are the usual wings and tail of a bird, but, instead of the human figure and circle, there is the *all-seeing Eye of Deity.*[4]

On each of these cylinders the symbol of Deity is placed above the *sacred Tree,* which forms so remarkable a feature in the representations of worship on the Assyrian monuments.

"The Ophite hierogram has been recognized also in *Gaul.* A sculpture of the *Circle, Wings, and two Serpents,* exhibiting a Medusa's face, was found by Simeoni in the sixteenth century at Clermont in Auvergne."[5]

Of the prevalence of Sun-worship even to the present day in *India,* the following testimony may be cited here. "On the seventh of the month *Mágh Sudi,* is the Sun's birthday. On this day the chariot of the Sun, drawn by eight horses, is taken

---

[1] *Anc. Myth.* vol. ii. p. 122.   [2] Ibid. vol. i. p. 488.
[3] Layard's *Nineveh and Babylon,* p. 160.
[4] Ibid, p. 343.   [5] Deane, p. 276.

from the temple dedicated to that orb (in Rajputhana), and there is a grand procession." [1]

We can hardly fail to be reminded of "the horses that the kings of Judah had given to the sun," and of "the chariots of the sun," mentioned 2 Kings, xxiii. 11 : and likewise of the classical fable of the sun-chariot of Apollo, constantly alluded to by the Greek and Roman poets.

Upon the whole subject of the worship of the *Serpent*, the *Sun*, and the *Mother and Child* so intimately connected with them, the reader who desires farther and full information should consult the very curious and elaborate works so often quoted above—Deane *on the Worship of the Serpent*, and Hislop's *Two Babylons*.—The extracts given above are but meagre selections, such as our space admits, from the rich stores supplied by these works.

And with such abundant evidence, there remains no room for reasonable doubt of the literal and historical truth of the Scripture narrative of *Man's creation, and Fall, in Paradise.*

If that narrative is "poetry, not history", then those events never occurred. But if so, how is it that they have been the foundation of the religious creeds and rites of every nation under heaven? How is it that they are found mentioned as real events in the written and unwritten records of every people, from the classic pages of Greek and Roman historians, poets, and philosophers, to the traditions of the savage tribes of New Zealand and the South Sea Islands? How is it that the memorials of those events form the most remarkable and the most enduring monuments of the heathen superstitions of the world—from Scandinavia to Japan, and from the Chinese wall to Western Africa, and even to Mexico? How is it that all history, all mythology, all antiquity, all tradition, are rife with recollections of the events of Paradise, if those events

[1] Tod's *Rajasthan*, quoted by the Rev. T. Phillips, *Missionary's Vade Mecum*, p. 242.

never happened, and if the story of them was but a poet's dream ?

Those events were literal and stern realities—and they sank so deep by their tremendous weight into the very inmost hearts of the first human pair and their posterity, that from the moment of their occurrence to the present hour the impression has been indelible. The pride which rejects all that is humbling to our nature, and seeks out all that is flattering, has distorted the truth and perverted the real bearing of those events—the arts of Satan which deceived our first parents have prevailed to keep up the deception among their posterity —but the events themselves, faithfully recorded in the Word of God, are traceable, amidst all the corruptions by which they have been defaced, in a chain of evidences which has literally girdled the world.

CHAPTER XV.

Tree and Grove-worship—generally joined with Serpent-worship—one of the sins of Israel—practised by the aboriginal Canaanites.—Tree-worship in Assyria— Greece—Italy—Germany.—Origin of the custom of the Christmas Tree and Misletoe Branch—the Yule Log, Christmas Boar's head and Goose, and Yule cakes.

No form of idolatrous worship has been more remarkable than the veneration paid in all ages and countries, to *Trees* and *Groves*—and the use also of groves in the celebration of heathen rites and orgies.

Frequent mention of this practice has already been made in connexion with Serpent-worship. The two were almost always combined. Tree-worshippers were usually Serpent-worshippers—and Serpent-worshippers were usually Tree-worshippers. The combination was not accidental. The same primeval events which gave rise, by perverse and corrupt tradition, to the one gave rise also to the other—the never forgotten events of Paradise the garden of "Delight"—the Temptation and the Fall.[1] Viewed in this light, the con-

---

[1] A contrary theory is put forward in a recently published volume on *Tree and Serpent-worship* by James Fergusson Esq.; a work so full of valuable information that the errors with which it abounds are the more to be lamented.

He assigns as the cause of the Serpent's being worshipped, the singular celerity and gracefulness of its motion without legs—and its terrible spring and deadly attack. Trees he considers to have been

nexion of the two is natural and almost inevitable ; upon any
other supposition it is absolutely unaccountable.

Suppose, for a moment, that in some one of earth's many
tribes the Serpent had become an object of worship from
some accidental cause, or some peculiar and strange fancy of
the people—yet how came it to be universal throughout the
world ?

The same question may be asked, and with like reason,
concerning Trees.

But how are we to account for the constant *combination* of
the two ? Is it to be imagined that every nation and people
under heaven, separately and independently of each other, and
by mere accident, happened to fix upon the Serpent as their
god ? Such an accidental and universal coincidence would be
more marvellous than any miracle.—Or is there anything in
the Serpent so godlike that it might seem natural to superstitious minds to attribute to it something divine ? The
answer is, there is nothing of the kind. To the eye of reason
and common sense a grovelling and mischievous reptile would
surely appear one of the last objects likely to be thought
worthy of veneration.

But if the separate and accidental choice, by every nation
under heaven, of the Serpent *singly* as an object of worship, is
incredible, what must be the thought of the idea that not only

worshipped on account of their wondrous beauty, their welcome shelter
and shade, their grateful fruits, their multifarious uses for buildings,
furniture, implements, and fuel. Not only, however, is this theory
utterly inadequate to account for *worship* being offered either to Serpents or Trees, but it is entirely opposed to the testimony of history.
We have abundant and express statements of various writers that the
Serpent was worshipped on account of the *supernatural wisdom* and
oracular powers it was believed to possess—and not on account either
of its rapid motion, elegance, or deadly spring. In like manner it was
not the beauty or usefulness of Trees that led men to worship them,
but the belief that *one certain Tree*, of which tradition spoke, had once
possessed the property of *conferring Life, and Immortality.*

might this have happened, but that in like manner, by pure accident, every nation might *also* have chosen to venerate *Trees*, and unite the two in one universal system of Tree and Serpent-worship? If the accidental selection of the *one* is incredible, the accidental selection of *both* is too absurd a theory to be made a subject of argument. There is nothing in Trees to suggest the propriety of venerating them as gods. They are beautiful, delightful, and most useful to mankind—in their forms and foliage, shade and fruits, timber and fuel—but multitudes of other objects are beautiful and useful which have never been worshipped throughout the world.

But great as is this improbability, it is but a fraction of the whole case.

The worship of Serpents and Trees has been almost universally conjoined with the custom of offering animal *sacrifices*.[1]

But in connexion with these three, there are also found other particulars so mixed up with them—not universally, but with an evident significancy as parts of the same rites—that the coincidence cannot be accidental. The nude *priestess* employed in Serpent-worship, and the similar figures found in ancient carvings, as already mentioned—the world-wide worship of the *Sun*, intimately connected with that of the Serpent, and embodying the tradition of the promised *Seed of the woman*, as will be shown hereafter—and the *Cherubic figures* so frequently associated with Tree-worship, as seen in the Assyrian monuments, and also in the interesting plates of Mr. Fergusson's work and elsewhere—all these are indissolubly united in one and the same system. In other words, Tree and Serpent-worship—Sun or Fire-worship—the traditions of Eve in Paradise, and of the promised Seed of the woman—animal sacrifice, including its cruel abuse in *human* sacrifices—were

---

[1] Mr. Fergusson himself states that *human* sacrifices and Serpent-worship were generally found conjoined—so that where the one prevailed there also did the other.—*Tree and Serpent-worship*, p. 27.

all just so many parts of one traditional system of idolatry, derived from the never-dying memories of Paradise and Eden's gate. This system pervaded the world—just because it originated in the cradle of the whole human family. To speak of this singular and world-wide association of things having no natural connexion, as an accidental coincidence, is worse than trifling. It is tampering with the most important truths, and with the gravest interests of mankind.

The oldest history in the world is the Pentateuch—and in that book we find the earliest mention of *Groves* as used for the purposes of worship. Nearly 1500 hundred years before the Christian era, and not more than about 850 years after the Flood, Moses charged the Israelites concerning the idolatrous practices of the Canaanitish tribes whose land they were to inherit—"Ye shall destroy their altars, break their images, and cut down their groves; for thou shalt worship no other god : for the LORD, whose name is Jealous, is a jealous God." —Exod. xxxiv. 13, 14. The Israelites were expressly forbidden to follow the example of heathen nations in planting groves or trees near their places of worship :—"Thou shalt not plant thee a grove of any trees near unto the altar of the LORD thy God which thou shalt make thee."—Deut. xvi. 21.[1]

---

[1] Yet Mr. Fergusson misrepresents Abraham's " planting a grove in Beersheba,"—Gen. xxi. 33,—as the earliest instance of "a *form of worship* to which continual allusions are afterwards made in Jewish history": though " there is apparently no mention of *serpents* in connexion with Abraham ". The worship of Trees, not less than that of Serpents, was *idolatry*—a practice altogether abhorrent to the character of faithful Abraham, and of which he most certainly was never guilty.

Concerning Moses he says—"With the Brazen Serpent in the Wilderness we tread on surer ground : it is *the first record we have of actual worship being performed to the Serpent.*" There is, however, no record whatever of any worship being paid to the Serpent in the Wilderness. There was simply a direction given to *look* at it—being, as is expressly declared in John iii. 14, a type of Christ's crucifixion.

Notwithstanding these strict and often repeated commands, the worship of Groves became one of the most common sins of the Jews in the time of their apostasy from God—as is familiarly known to every reader of the Bible.

Truly, Grove-worship was "a form of worship to which," as Mr. Fergusson remarks, "continual allusions are made in Jewish history"—but the allusions are only and always by way of the severest condemnation, and declaration of the anger of God against it. One of the crying sins for which Israel, and Judah also, were finally cast out from their own land into banishment and bondage is declared to have been their having "*made a grove*," and having "set them up images and *groves* in every high hill, and under every *green tree*."—2 Kings xvii. 10, 16.

The fact that the worship of the *Asherah*, or Groves, was an established custom among the Canaanites before the entrance of Israel into Canaan, has an important bearing upon the *origin* of Tree or Grove-worship—which were evidently one and the same thing.

The Canaanites were already settled in the country called Canaan (from their progenitor, the son of Ham) before the call of Abraham—about 400 years after the Flood. Now one of the most remarkable characteristics of Eastern nations is the

Again, he considers Exodus iii. 5 as intimating that the tree or bush in Horeb, from which the Lord appeared to Moses as a flame, had been *considered sacred before that time*"—and that "it was *apparently* in consequence of its sanctity that it was chosen for the delivery of the oracle ".—*Tree and Serpent-worship*, p. 7.

A more groundless and gratuitous assumption could not be made than is here conveyed. There is not even the shadow of an apparent sanctity of the bush—for not a word is to be found in the Scriptures on the subject. It is lamentable to find a learned and ingenious writer propounding ideas not only utterly fanciful, but which also make the faithful servants of God guilty of the most degrading idolatry—and, worst of all, which actually make God Himself command or sanction it.

singular tenacity with which they cling to the customs of their fathers ; so that to this very day the habits and manners of the East are just what they were in the days of Abraham and Job. But of all customs, the most tenaciously preserved are national rites of worship. It is, therefore, morally certain that the Tree or Grove-worship found existing in Canaan by Joshua and the Israelites was the same that had been practised there from the very first settlement of the aboriginal Canaanites. But the Canaanites migrated direct from the cradle of the human family—their ancestor Canaan being the grandson of Noah. The origin of Tree and Grove-worship in the land of Canaan is thus traced back to the very family who issued from the Ark, and to whom all the traditions of Paradise were familiar as household words. Is it possible to believe that it had any other origin but those very traditions ?

Canaan was one of the earliest centres also of Serpent-worship. Sanchoniathon, "an author supposed to have lived before the Trojan war," is quoted by Eusebius as expressly stating that it was taught to the Phœnicians by Taautus.[1] It may therefore fairly be assumed to have been conjoined in Canaan, as elsewhere, with Tree-worship, from the very earliest times. Taautus, as already stated, is doubtless the same person as Thoth, who was the patron of Serpent-worship in Egypt, and was deified there after his death as *the god of health*, or *healing;* and became the prototype of the Greek and Roman Æsculapius.[2] He was probably the leader of one of the first colonies after the Flood who found their way down the sea-board of Syria into Egypt, where he was venerated in after ages as one of their greatest legislators, and was even identified with the Grecian god Hermes—the Roman Mercury.

We have thus a chain of circumstantial evidence that Tree

---

[1] Fergusson, *Tree and Serpent-worship*, p. 10.
[2] Deane *on Serpent-worship*, p. 121.

and Serpent-worship in Canaan were introduced there by the very first settlers in the country after the Flood. That both were consequently derived from the antediluvian tradi-tions of the Trees and Serpent in Paradise is an inference too obvious to need farther argument.

And such a fact as this casts a flood of light upon the origin of Tree and Grove-worship, as well as its usual accompaniment Serpent-worship, throughout the world.

It is reasonable to believe that such events as the Tempta-tion and Fall of man in Paradise, and the attendant circum-stances, would never be forgotten—but that the memory of them would be carried by the scattered posterity of Noah into every country of the world.

And the fact that Trees and Serpents were objects of popular worship in *one* country among the very first settlers there after the Flood—as was the case in Canaan—would lead us to expect that the same thing would happen in other countries also.

And this is just what did happen—doubtless from the same cause, the perverted traditions of the supernatural properties attributed to the Trees and the Serpent of Paradise.

The universality of Serpent-worship throughout the world has been shown in previous chapters :—that Tree or Grove-worship was almost equally wide-spread we have the testimony of Mr. Fergusson himself, as well as that of universal history.

The constant occurrence of the Sacred Tree, and its wor-shippers, in the sculptures of *Assyria*, has been already noticed above. It is represented in Plate III.

In *Greece*, several of the most popular legends shadowed forth the same ideas.

"The Argonautic Expedition was undertaken to recover a fleece that hung on a *sacred Tree*, guarded by a *dragon*" (or great serpent), "that Jason and his companions would have been unable to cope with, unless they had been aided by the enchantments of Medea. But the great destroyer of serpents

PLATE III.

ASSYRIAN FIRE-WORSHIP.

in those days was Hercules. Most appropriately was he represented as strangling two serpents sent by Juno to destroy
him while he was yet in his cradle. His adventures in the
Garden of the Hesperides is the Pagan form of the myth that
most resembles the precious *serpent-guarded* fruit of the Garden
of Eden, though the moral of the fable is so widely different."[1]

In Athens, the centre of Grecian learning and politeness,
"there can be no doubt," says Mr. Fergusson, "that the
ancient Tree and Serpent-temple stood where the Erectheum
now stands."—"The Tree, I believe, occupied the Caryatid
Portico, the Serpent the lower cell adjoining.

"The traces of Tree-worship in Greece are even fuller and
more defined than those of the Serpent Cultus.

"As each succeeding Buddha in the Indian mythology had
a separate and different Bo Tree assigned to him, so each god
of the classical Pantheon seems to have had some tree appropriated as his emblem or representative. Among the most
familiar are the oak or beech of Jupiter, the laurel of Apollo,
the vine of Bacchus. The olive is the well-known tree of
Minerva. The myrtle was sacred to Aphrodité. The apple
or orange of the Hesperides belonged to Juno. The *populus*
was the tree of Hercules, and the plane tree was the 'numen'
of the Atridæ."—"It would be easy to multiply these instances

---

[1] *Tree and Serpent-Worship*, p. 13.—The fable of the "serpent-
guarded" Tree of the Garden of the Hesperides was a *Pagan* tradition of
Eden. But Mr. Fergusson seems to have adopted it as the *true*
account of the Serpent and the Tree of Knowledge in Paradise—with
that complete rejection of the veracity of the Holy Scriptures with
which he treats the whole of the first eight chapters of Genesis as
"*made up of fragments*" of Mesopotamian "books or traditions".—
He speaks of "the Trees of Life and Knowledge in the garden of
Eden" as having been "*intrusted to the custody of the serpent*"/ No
wonder that he finds "this narrative one of the least intelligible parts
of the Pentateuch."—P. 6.—It is not the sacred narrative, but Mr.
Fergusson's strange and distorted version of it, that is indeed unintelligible, as well as unscriptural.

L

of Tree and Serpent-worship among the Greeks to almost any extent."[1]

In *Italy* "there is every reason to believe that such representations" (of serpents considered as symbols of sacredness) "were much more common than the few remains we possess might at first sight lead us to suppose, and that the serpents were also frequently represented as the *genii loci*, and as mixed up with Mithraic or Tree-Worship."[2]

Among the *Teutonic* races, "the evidences of Tree-worship are numerous and complete".—"Tacitus distinctly states that the Germans have no images, and decline to enclose their gods within walls, but consecrate groves and woods, within which they call on the name of God." The authority of Grimm is cited for the statement that, among the Germans, though "individual gods might have dwelt on hill-tops, or in caves, or rivers, the festal universal religion of the people had its abode in *woods*, and nowhere has another temple been found."[3]

A relic of this ancient superstition, according to Mr. Fergusson, still exists in "the 'Stock am Eisen', in Vienna, the sacred tree into which every apprentice, before setting out on his 'Wanderjahre', drove a nail for luck. It now stands in the centre of that great capital, the last remaining vestige of the sacred grove around which the city has grown up."

The same writer adds that "the festival of the Christmas Tree at the present day, so common throughout the whole of Germany, is almost undoubtedly a remnant of the Tree-worship of their ancestors."

The origin of the Christmas Tree, however, is involved in deeper mystery. It seems certainly to have had a different source, which it is perhaps worth while here to point out.

It is to be noted, that the Christmas Tree is always a *fir*—and this custom is of remote antiquity. "The Christmas

---

[1] *Tree and Serpent-Worship*, p. 15.　　　　[2] Ibid, p. 18.
[3] Ibid. p. 21, quoting Grimm's *Deutsche Mythologie*.

Tree, now so common among us, was equally common in
Pagan Rome and Pagan Egypt. In Egypt that tree was the
palm tree ; in Rome it was the *fir:* the palm tree denoting the
Pagan Messiah as Baal-Tamar, the fir referring to him as Baal-
berith."[1]

Tamar signifies a *palm tree*—and Baal-Tamar " *the lord of
the palm tree.*" And Baal-berith, which was also one of the
titles of the Pagan Messiah, signifying " *Lord of the covenant,*"
was almost identical with Baal-*bereth*, which signifies *Lord of
the fir tree.* It was just another instance of that jugglery of
words by which the cunning priests of Chaldæa mystified the
common people in order to further their own craft, that the
word Baal-berith, "Lord of the covenant," was represented
as Baal-*bereth*, *Lord of the fir tree.* Hence the fir tree became
a symbol of the Babylonian false Messiah.

The palm tree was the well-known symbol of *victory:* and
the title " Lord of the palm tree " was apparently given to the
Pagan Messiah in accordance with the tradition of the primeval
promise that the Messiah, the Seed of the woman, should
"bruise the serpent's head," or be victorious over the Serpent,
that is, the devil.

"The Christmas tree, as has been stated, was generally at
Rome a different tree, even the fir: but the very same idea as
was implied in the palm tree was implied in the Christmas fir:
for that covertly symbolized the new-born god as Baal-berith,
'Lord of the covenant,' and thus shadowed forth the perpetuity
and everlasting nature of his power."[2]

Moreover, the custom of the Christmas *misletoe branch* has a
similar origin. "In the light reflected by the above statement
on customs that still linger among us, the origin of which has
been lost in the mist of hoar antiquity, let the reader look at
the singular custom still kept up on Christmas eve of kissing
under the misletoe bough. That mistletoe bough in the

---

[1] *Two Babylons*, p. 139.   [2] Ibid. p. 140.

Druidic superstition which, as we have seen, was derived from
Babylon, was a representation of Messiah, '*the Man the
Branch.*' The misletoe was regarded as a Divine branch—a
branch that came from heaven and grew upon a tree that
sprung out of the earth. Thus by the engrafting of the
celestial branch into the earthly tree, heaven and earth, that
sin had severed, were joined together; and thus the misletoe
bough became the token of Divine reconciliation to man, the
kiss being the well-known token of pardon and reconciliation.[1] So it is in Ps. lxxxv. 10—"Mercy and truth are met
together; righteousness and peace have *kissed* each other."

But what has all this to do with Christmas?

To understand this, we must trace another winding in that
labyrinth of error, "the Mystery of iniquity."

In Babylon and elsewhere, as already shown, the *Sun* was
an object of worship, as one of the symbols of the Seed of the
woman—by the perversion of the word Zero-ashta, "the seed
of the woman," to signify to the uninitiated the Seed of light,
or fire, or *the Sun.* "It was an essential principle of the
Babylonian system that the Sun, or Baal, was the one only
God. When, therefore, Tammuz was worshipped as God incarnate, that implied also that he was an incarnation of the
Sun. In the Hindû mythology, which is admitted to be
essentially Babylonian, this comes out very distinctly. There,
Surya, or the Sun, is represented as being incarnate, and *born*
for the purpose of subduing the enemies of the gods, who,
without such a birth, could not have been subdued."[2]

Now the winter solstice, when the days begin again to
lengthen, and the Sun appears to enter upon a new course,
was regarded as a fitting symbol of this birth, or incarnation,
of the Sun. The 25th of December, accordingly, "was held

---

[1] *Two Babylons*, p. 141.
[2] Ibid. p. 138, where see authorities quoted for these statements.

as the '*natalis invicti Solis*'—the birth-day of the unconquered
Sun." And in pursuance of this idea, the Christmas festival of
the Sun-god—identical with Nimrod, Tammuz or Adonis, and
also with Bacchus—was celebrated in ancient Babylon for ages
before the Christian era. It was identical with the *Saturnalia*
of Rome, and kept with similar scenes of drunkenness and
revelry. "The wassailing bowl of Christmas, of the dark ages
in Popish countries, had its precise counterpart in the *Drunken
festival* of Babylon."[1]

A farther confirmation and illustration of these facts is
found in the custom of the Christmas *Yule-log.* The word
Yule is the Chaldee term for an *infant* or *little child*—and
hence it was that Christmas-day was called among the
heathens *Yule-day*, or the "Child's day," and the night before
Christmas "*Mother-night*," for ages before the birth of Christ.
"And this entirely accounts for the putting of the Yule-log
into the fire on Christmas eve, and the *appearance of the
Christmas Tree the next morning.* As Zero-ashta, the Seed of
the Woman, which name also signified *Ignigena*, or '*born of
the fire*,' he has to enter the fire on Mother-night, that he may
be born the next day out of it as *the Branch of God*, or the
Tree that brings all divine gifts to men."[2]

"But why, it may be asked, does he enter the fire under the

---

[1] Ibid. p. 139.—It is a curious coincidence, and a striking cor-
roboration of the thoroughly Babylonian character of Popery, that
"the oldest and largest wassail bowl in Christendom is preserved *in
the vestry of the Vatican.* It is never used except when the Pope
has the entire college of Cardinals to supper. On this occasion all
formality is laid aside" (as was the case also in the wassailing festivities of the middle ages, and in the corresponding Saturnalia of
Pagan Rome). "The Pope himself roasts the apples, and the two
youngest cardinals make the toast and grate the nutmeg; while 'hunt
the Pope's slipper' and other sports are freely indulged in till midnight."—*Manchester Courier*, Dec. 22, 1870.

[2] From this idea evidently sprang the custom of hanging *gifts* on
the Christmas tree.

goose and a *thin cake*."[1] At Rome, it was by the cackling of the sacred geese of Juno, kept in the Capitol, that the city was saved from the night attack of the Gauls. But Juno was another form of the Queen of Heaven, and Mother of the Child. In Asia Minor the goose was the symbol of Cupid, the Child of the Mother under the name of Venus—just as it was the symbol of Seb, the father of the gods, and so, identical with Saturn or Nimrod. In India the goose is sacred to Brahma, the Hindû father of the gods.

But *why* was the goose thus sacred to these deities? A symbolical meaning was attached to this bird. "The goose," says Wilkinson, "signified in hieroglyphics a *child* or *son*." "It was chosen to denote a *son*, from its love to its young, being always *ready to give itself up to the chasseur, in order that they might be preserved:* for which reason the Egyptians thought it right to revere this animal." Here, then, the true meaning of the symbol is a *son*, who voluntarily gives himself up as a sacrifice for those he loves—viz., the Pagan Messiah. It is, then, abundantly clear why the goose was sacrificed and eaten at Christmas—the ancient *heathen* Christmas—in honour of the Babylonian false Messiah, whose birth was celebrated at that season.

The modern Christmas *turkey* would seem to be merely a more delicate and luxurious substitute for the Christmas goose.

The " *Yule-cakes*," in like manner, or Christmas cakes, still made in Scotland, and at least remembered in England also, are derived from Babylonian customs and worship. "The cakes then made are called (in Scotland) *Nūr-cakes* or *Birth-cakes*." And in the north of England old people still remember that in their childhood they used to receive presents, on Christmas-day, of cakes, sweetmeats, and an *orange*. The

---

[1] *Satires*, vi., 539.
[2] *Two Babylons*, p. 146, and authorities there quoted.

cakes were made with the figure of a bird upon each, the tail straight and long, touching the cake with its tip. Now this bird, together with the orange, form a double link of connexion between these cakes and Juno, the Babylonian Queen of Heaven—and by consequence, with her son the Babylonian Messiah.

The *orange* has already been noticed as the traditional representative of the forbidden fruit of Eden.[1] But Juno is just the Latin form of *D'Juné*, or "The Dove", one of the titles of the Babylonian goddess. Another form of the name, as found in Latin authors, is Dione, which is applied both to the mother of Venus and sometimes to Venus herself. Now of this goddess, D'Juné, or Juno, or Venus, the characteristic and well-known symbol is the *Dove*. Her earthly representative, Semiramis, was fabled to have been changed at death into a pigeon, or dove ; and the goddess is represented in ancient monuments with the dove as her accompaniment.

Another bird, however, was sacred to Juno—namely, the *Cuckoo*: and it is stated by Pausanias that it is the cuckoo, and not the dove, that was meant to be represented as the symbol of Juno when she was pictured holding the *pomegranate*.[2]

Either way—whether it were the Dove or the Cuckoo—here we have, in the "Nūr-cakes" or "Birth-cakes" of Scotland, and the "Yule-cakes" of England, a note of connexion identifying the Christmas season of modern days with the birth-festival of the Babylonian false Messiah!

There is yet another curious proof of the same thing in the name still given in Scotland to the last day of the year. That name is *Hogmanay*. The term *Hog* is a Chaldee word signifying a *feast*:—*manai* signifies *numberer*, and is akin to *mene*, the first word of the Divine message of judgment written on the wall of the terrified Belshazzar's banqueting hall. *Hog-*

---

[1] See Chapter vii.   [2] *Two Babylons*, p. 160.

manai, therefore, means the *Feast of the Numberer*—that is, the feast of the Babylonian Messiah regarded as the Sun-deity. The reason why this time was selected is obvious. It is the winter Solstice, when the Sun seems to begin a new course of motion, and, so to speak, to enter on a new life: the time from which the days of the New Year begin to be *numbered.* This season was a time of festivity at Babylon as it is at the present day in Scotland.[1] The "*Drunken Festival*" at Babylon—the *Saturnalia* at Rome—and the Christmas Popish revels of the Middle Ages were all identical in origin, meaning, and character: though the custom has been kept up after both its origin and its meaning had for ages fallen into oblivion.

Is, then, the observance of Christmas a thing of Babylonian and heathen origin?

Now whatever may be the propriety of commemorating the Saviour's Nativity, it is certain that the *time* of His birth was not the 25th December, nor any time later in the year than October: for the shepherds in Palestine never "keep watch over their flocks by night" after that time, on account of the coldness of the nights. Nor is it likely that the depth of winter would be appointed for the "taxing," or census, of the people, when women and children would, in many cases, have long journeys to make to and from their respective cities.

Moreover, no such festival as Christmas was ever heard of *in the Christian Church* till the third century: nor was it much observed in the Church till the fourth.

But among the *heathen*, a festival had been celebrated from time immemorial, in honour of the birth of the son of the Babylonian Queen of Heaven, *on the 25th of December*. And it was in order to conciliate the heathen, and to *meet them half way*, according to the celebrated policy of Pope Gregory I.— in order to swell the number of nominal converts to Christianity—that this festival was *adopted* by the missionaries of

---

[1] See more to the same purpose in *Two Babylons*, p. 137, &c.

Rome both in Britain and elsewhere, and *adapted* to the Nativity of Christ—the only change that was made being the change of names.   It was called *Christmas* (that is, the Mass said in honour of Christ) instead of *Yule-day*, the "Child's day"—or, the "Birth-day of the Sun"—or, as among the Arabs, the "Birth-day of the Lord Moon": for "on the 24th day of the tenth month (our December) the Arabians celebrated the *Birth-day of the Lord*—that is, the Moon".[1]   The "Lord Moon" was but another title of the same deity who was otherwise represented as the Sun-god.[2]

---

[1] Stanley's *Sabæan Philosophy*, quoted by Mr. Hislop, *Two Babylons*, p. 135.

[2] For proof of this, see *Two Babylons*, p. 36, in which interesting work the reader will find full information on this intricate subject.

CHAPTER XVI.

Same Subject continued.—Tree and Serpent-worship in Northern and Eastern Europe—the Persian and Indian Homa Tree—Tree-worship in Gaul and Great Britain—in East and West Africa—throughout America—in Asia from the Indus throughout India and China—Hindû traditions of the Tree of Life—the Buddhist Bo Tree—Sculptures in Fergusson's Tree and Serpent-worship.

"If a line," says Mr. Fergusson, "were drawn from the shores of the Caspian Sea north of the Caucasus to the mouth of the Vistula or Dwina in the Baltic, it would be coincident with one of the oldest routes of communication between the East and the West, and one that probably was the road by which Serpent and Tree-worship were introduced into the North of Europe."—"At the far end of this route," Procopius tells us that " in his day the barbarians worshipped forests and groves, and in their barbarous simplicity placed trees among their gods."[1]

Accordingly, Tree and Serpent-worship prevailed from the Caspian Sea to the Baltic. Mr. Fergusson cites the testimony of Olaus Magnus that "the Poles worshipped their gods, Fire, Serpents, and Trees, in woods : and that these superstitions still lingered in remote parts of Norway and Wermelandia as late as the year 1555." "It seems impossible," he adds, "to doubt, that both Trees and Serpents were worshipped by the

---

[1] *Tree and Serpent-worship*, p. 21.

peasantry in Esthonia and Finland within the limits of the
present century, and even then with all the characteristics it
possessed when we first become acquainted with it."[1]

This is important testimony, especially from one who does
not admit the events of Paradise to have been by perversion
the *origin* of Tree and Serpent-worship. According to Mr.
Fergusson, the worship of "Fire, Serpents, and Trees, in
woods," was carried from the Caspian Sea to the remotest
parts of Norway by one of the oldest routes of communication
between the East and West.

But it has been shown above, that the worship of Fire, Serpents, and Trees, was a part of that Babylonian system of the
worship of a false Messiah which was the source of the Pagan
mythology of the whole world : and also, that this Babylonian
system was indissolubly connected with reminiscences of the
Cherubim of Eden's gate, and of Eve in the first state of
innocence.

The inference is inevitable, that Tree and Serpent-worship
was derived from perverted traditions of the events narrated in
the first three chapters of Genesis.

Mr. Fergusson himself considers that the Scandinavian
" myth of the Yggdrasil ash is in the first place a *reminiscence
of the trees of fate and knowledge, in the garden of Eden.*"

And in like manner he regards the Persian and Indian
Homa tree as having had its origin in the same "*myth* as the
Trees of Life and Knowledge which grew in Paradise."[2]

But if the Trees of Paradise had their origin in nothing but
a "*myth,*" is it to be believed that such a false and idle story
would not only have been carried to the farthest regions of the
world, but have formed the basis of the religious creed of every
nation under heaven ?

" In Gaul, or France, and Great Britain, Tree-worship existed among the Celts, as among the Germans, till their con-

---

[1] Ibid., p. 22.   [2] Ibid., p. 24, 43.

version to Christianity:"[1]—which is the same thing as to say that it prevailed from the Alps and the Danube to the farthest extremities of the British Isles.

With regard to Tree-worship in *Africa*, what has been already stated from the testimony of Bruce is quoted by Mr. Fergusson—that the Shangalla, an Abyssinian tribe, "worship various *trees*, serpents, the moon, planets, and stars in certain positions". "It is, however," he adds, "on the West coast that the worship flourishes in all its pristine vigour."

As regards *America* also, Mr. Fergusson quotes authorities which go to prove that both Serpent-worship and Tree-worship prevailed over the whole continent.

Nor is this all—but, in accordance with what has been advanced above on this subject, he states that Tree and Serpent-worship was combined with *Sun*-worship. "The principal deity of the Astec Pantheon seems Tezcatlipoca, or Tona-catlecoatl, literally *the Sun-Serpent.*"

"Müller," he adds, "finds traces of Tree-worship all over the continent of America, and generally in juxtaposition, if not in actual connexion, with that of the Serpent."[2]

Tracing the course of human migration eastwards, we find the same ideas and practices every where prevailing throughout the vast continent of *Asia*.

Mr. Fergusson's testimony here also is important :—"Windischmann, who had probably rendered himself more familiar with the spirit of the Zend-Avesta than any other scholar, thus expresses himself on the subject. 'Homa is the first of the trees planted by Ahura-Mazda (the great god of the Persians) in the fountain of life. He who drinks of its juice *never dies*. According to the Bundehesh, the Gogard or Gaskerena

---

[1] Ibid., p. 28.   [2] Ibid., p. 37-39.

tree bears the Homa, which *gives life* and power, and *imparts life at the resurrection '."*

"In another place he says, 'From this it appears that the White Homa or the Tree Gokard is *the Tree of Life which grew in Paradise."*—" The Soma (or Homa) was unquestionably the greatest and holiest offering of ancient Indian worship'."[1]

Other authorities are here cited to show that Tree-worship prevailed from the banks of the Indus to China : that Serpent-worship was cultivated on the grandest scale in Cashmere, and extended southwards to Ceylon : and that in that island Tree-worship is still a custom of national importance. A "Bo Tree" sent from Buddh-gyâ, and planted there, has been re-verenced as the chief and most important "numen," or deity, of Ceylon for more than 2000 years, and is honoured to this day by the resort of thousands "to the sacred precincts within which it stands, to offer up those prayers for health and pros-perity which are more likely to be answered if uttered in its presence. There is probably no older idol in the world, cer-tainly none more venerated."[2]

Among the many reminiscences remaining in India of the primeval events of Paradise, is the following legend from the Hindû Shasters, which seems certainly to be a distorted tradi-tion of the Trees of Life and Knowledge, and of the doctrine of the Trinity.—"In the centre of the enormous plain of the earth, which is 250,000 miles in diameter, the loftiest of all mountains, Sumeru, rises to the enormous height of more than 200,000 miles ; it is crowned with three golden summits, which are the favourite residences of Brahma, Vishnu, and Shiva. At the foot of this mountain there are three smaller hills, placed like sentinels, on the top of each of which grows the mango tree, above 2000 miles in height. These trees bear a fruit as delicious as nectar, which measures several hundred feet in diameter. When it falls to the ground, juice exudes

[1] Ibid., p. 43.   [2] Ibid., p. 56.

from it whose spicy fragrance perfumes the air, and those who eat thereof diffuse a most agreeable smell for many days around them. The rose-apple tree is likewise grown in these hills, the fruit of which is as large as an elephant, and full of juice that at the season of maturity it flows like a stream, and whatever it touches in its course is changed into the purest gold."[1]

But no event since Mr. Layard's discoveries of the Assyrian sculptures has thrown so much light on the subject is the publication, in Mr. Fergusson's work, of the lithographs and photographs of sculptures found on the Topes of Sanchi and Amravati in central India. These Topes Mr. Fergusson considers to have been either the burying-places of chiefs, or shrines for relics. They were artificial mounds, covered with chunam plaster, with ornamental gateways, and surrounded with rails of stone-work. The gateways and rails were richly sculptured with representations appropriate to national worship: and it is from these sculptures, now brought to light, that so much additional information is obtained. Out of more than a hundred of these illustrations a few are here selected for description, as containing representations of the most important features of the worship of Trees, serpents, the Sun or Fire, and other symbols, showing an essential identity between the idolatry of ancient India and that of Assyria.

And as Hindúism and Buddhism are, in Mr. Fergusson's opinion, substantially identical,[2] his authority confirms the view that the idolatrous system of worship which prevailed in the Old World from the Japan Isles to Norway and Iceland, is one and the same origin.

Missions in Bengal illustrated, by the Rev. J. J. Weitbrecht.
65.
Tree and Serpent Worship, p. 71.

from it whose spicy fragrance perfumes the air, and those who eat thereof diffuse a most agreeable smell for many miles around them. The rose-apple tree is likewise growing on these hills, the fruit of which is as large as an elephant, and so full of juice that at the season of maturity it flows along in a stream, and whatever it touches in its course is changed into the purest gold." [1]

But no event since Mr. Layard's discoveries of the Assyrian sculptures has thrown so much light on the subject as the publication, in Mr. Fergusson's work, of the lithographs and photographs of sculptures found on the Topes of Sanchi and Amravati in central India. These Topes Mr. Fergusson considers to have been either the burying-places of chiefs, or shrines for relics. They were artificial mounds, covered over with *chunam* plaster, with ornamental gateways, and surrounded with rails of stone-work. The gateways and rails were richly sculptured with representations appropriate to the national worship : and it is from these sculptures, now happily brought to light, that so much additional information is obtained.

Out of more than a hundred of these illustrations a very few are here selected for description, as containing representations of the most important features of the worship of Trees, Serpents, the Sun or Fire, and other symbols, showing an essential identity between the idolatry of ancient India and that of Assyria.

And as Hindûism and Buddhism are, in Mr. Fergusson's opinion, substantially identical,[2] his authority confirms the belief that the idolatrous system of worship which prevailed in the Old World from the Japan Isles to Norway and Iceland, had one and the same origin.

[1] *Protestant Missions in Bengal illustrated*, by the Rev. J. J. Weitbrecht, p. 65.

[2] *Tree and Serpent-Worship*, p. 71.

PLATE V.

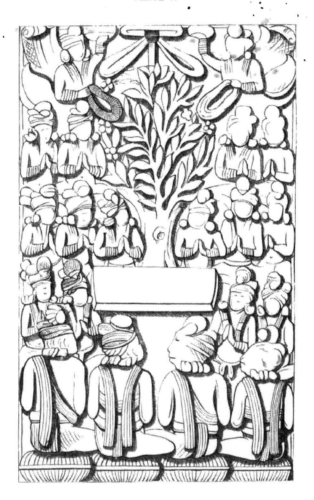

INDIAN TREE-WORSHIP, AND CHERUBIC FIGURES.

That origin could have been no other than corrupted traditions of the Trees, and Serpent, and Cherubim, of Eden.

In Plate XXIV. of Mr. Fergusson's work, are two lithographs
of sculptures on the gateways of the great Sanchi Tope, copied
from drawings by Col. Maisey; which Mr. Fergusson says
"may be taken as the typical form in which the Naga (or
Serpent-deity) is generally represented both at Sanchi and
Amravati."

One of these, reproduced in the accompanying Plate IV.,
represents a number of persons "worshipping the five-headed
Naga, who appears in a small hexagonal temple, raising his
head over what appears to be an altar. In front of him stands
a pot of fire: but what is still more remarkable is, that fire is
certainly issuing from the openings in the roof of the temple."
The Naga has the five-headed serpent-form usual in the
sculptures of these Topes.

Here, then, we have an evident combination of Sun (or Fire)
and Serpent-worship, as usual elsewhere.

In Plate V., from another of Mr. Fergusson's lithographs, we
have "the Sacred Tree, behind its altar, with its Chatta and
garlands, occupying the same position the Serpent did in the
other". Two flying female figures present garlands, approaching it on either side. The whole representation is undoubtedly
of similar import with the Sacred Tree of the Nineveh sculptures, with its attendant worshipping figures, and Cherubic
forms presenting offerings.

In others of Mr. Fergusson's illustrations there appears, in
attendance on the Sacred Tree, the *Garuda*, a bird-like figure,
concerning which he remarks that "it scarcely admits of a
doubt that the Eagle-headed deity of the Assyrians (the
Nisroch) became the Garuda of the Hindû mythology." [1]

Now as the Assyrian Nisroch was evidently the Eagle-
headed human figure copied from one of the Cherubim, we

[1] *Tree and Serpent-Worship*, p. 10.

M

have, in this sculpture of the Sanchi Tope, the same remarkable combination as in the Nineveh sculptures, of the Sacred Tree attended and honoured by Cherubic figures—memorials, beyond a doubt, of the Tree of Life guarded by the Cherubim in Eden.

In another lithograph of Mr. Fergusson's work, in Plate XXVI., is a figure "very common in these sculptures—a Winged Lion figure on which a man rides, bearing an offering." The resemblance of these figures to the Assyrian Winged Lions is too obvious to be mistaken, and is noticed by Mr. Fergusson in this place.

In his Plate XXXIX., there is another representation, here reproduced in Pl. VI., of Winged Lions, approaching much nearer in form to those of the Assyrian sculptures.

From the Amravati Tope there is a photograph, in Plate LVII. of his work, representing the same device, and still more closely resembling the Winged Lions from Nineveh. Mr. Fergusson considers them to be "lineal descendants of those discovered by Botta and Layard at Nineveh."[1] Rather, they are beyond all reasonable doubt direct reminiscences of the same Cherubic forms, and quite independent of the Assyrians, with whom it does not appear that the aboriginal Indian population had any other connexion than as being collateral offsets from the one family of the Ark. Moreover, while there is sufficient resemblance between the Indian and Assyrian sculptures to prove that they are meant to represent the same objects, there is also sufficient diversity to make it extremely improbable that they were copied the one from the other.

Another very remarkable coincidence is noted by Mr. Fergusson—that "at the great Pagoda at Rangoon *Winged Lions with human heads* guard all the *portals* leading to the enclosure in which it stands."[2] We could hardly expect, or even reason-

---

[1] Ibid., p. 118.   [2] Ibid., p. 170, note.

PLATE VI.

INDIAN WINGED LIONS.

ably desire, a more striking circumstantial proof how long and how far the *Cherubim guarding Eden's gate* had been remembered among the scattered families of mankind.

Again, in Plate LVI. of Mr. Fergusson's work is a figure thus described by him—" By far the most curious, however, of the episodes introduced into this frieze is that" which "represents Garuda, the bird of Vishnu, the dreaded enemy of the Nagas in all ages, holding in its beak, evidently for the purpose of destroying it, a five-headed Naga. It is difficult to guess what this can mean in a temple where the Naga is honoured almost as the chief god."[1]

The difficulty is easily solved. Vishnu is the second person in the Brahminical Trinity of Brahma, Vishnu, and Shiva: and his incarnation of *Chrishna* is beyond all doubt a traditional travestie of the Incarnation of the Son of God. Now one of the commonest representations of Chrishna depicts him in the act of *destroying a serpent*, whose *head he tramples under foot*— a signal memorial of the primeval promise that the Seed of the woman should bruise the Serpent's head. If, then, the Garuda is the bird of Vishnu, what more likely than that it should be represented as doing its master's work by destroying serpents?—" Garuda, Vishnu's Vâhana, the enemy of the Nagas," says Mr. Fergusson,[2] "is almost certainly the hawk-headed deity of Assyria." We have, then, only to suppose that as the hawk-headed Assyrian deity, the Nisroch, was a reminiscence of one of the Cherubic forms of Eden, the fancy of after times had assigned to it a function suggested by its bird-like head and beak—that of destroying the serpents which were understood to be the hereditary foes of its master Vishnu.

One more coincidence with the Assyrian and Egyptian symbols occurs in the Sanchi sculptures—the sacred emblem of the *Chakra*, or Wheel.

---

[1] Ibid., p. 169.   [2] Ibid., p. 70.

We have already seen that the *Circle and Wings*, sometimes with and sometimes without the *Serpent*, was a hieroglyphic of the Deity.

Now one of the most prominent and frequent devices of the Sanchi and Amravati Topes is a *Wheel*: and this Wheel is represented as *an object of worship.* In Plate XLIII. of Mr. Fergusson's work there is represented a Wheel mounted on a kind of pedestal, and hung with garlands, before which two female figures are kneeling in the attitude of worship. Two men are apparently turning the wheel—upon which Mr. Fergusson aptly remarks, " Is this the original of the Prayer-wheel of the Thibetans ? "[1]

In another engraving, Plate XLII., Garudas[2] or Devas are presenting offerings to the sacred Wheel.

Throughout the series of illustrations, the Wheel is one of the most abundant architectural ornaments ; in the Amravati Tope by far the most so of any. And it is repeatedly represented as being worshipped. " It was," says Mr. Fergusson, " evidently considered one of the principal emblems of the faith."[3] This is explained by the fact he elsewhere notes, that " the Chakra or Wheel, which occupies the principal place among Buddhist emblems both at Sanchi and Amravati, afterwards becomes one of the principal emblems of Vishnu."[4] And this fact altogether agrees with the known signification of the Circle and Wings in Assyria, Persia, Egypt, and elsewhere, as a symbol of the Divine Presence. It is also not a little significant, that the symbol of the Divine Presence should be regarded as the symbol of Vishnu, the *second* person in the Hindû Triad. For this fact evidently points to a primeval tradition not only of the Holy Trinity, but also of the Second Person in the Trinity being the WORD of God—the *Revealer*

---

[1] Ibid., p. 145.

[2] This word is applied to two different kinds of figures—1. Flying human figures. 2. The bird of Vishnu, the destroyer of serpents.

[3] Ibid., p. 223. [4] Ibid., p. 71.

of God to man, by whose personal Presence God Himself
would be present among men.

On the whole, Mr. Fergusson's artistic and elaborate work
cannot but be regarded as not only supplying a most important addition to the evidences of Tree and Serpent-worship
having been universal throughout the world, but also as proving
beyond all reasonable doubt that the principal features of the
Hindû and Buddhist forms of idolatry were just *reminiscences
of the events of Paradise*—although he does not himself draw
this inference from the conclusive evidences of it which his
own work supplies.   If anything, however, were wanting to
complete the proof that Tree and Serpent-worship had its
origin in the events of Paradise, it would be supplied by the
hopeless difficulty of every attempt to account for it on any
other grounds.
Of this difficulty Mr. Fergusson himself seems fully conscious.   "There are few things," he says, "which at first sight
appear to us at the present day so strange, or less easy to account for, than that worship which was once so generally
offered to the Serpent-god.   If not the oldest, it ranks at least
among the earliest forms through which the human intellect
sought to propitiate the unknown powers.   Traces of its existence are found not only in every country of the Old World,
but before the New was discovered by us, the same strange
idolatry had long prevailed there ; and even now the worship
of the Serpent is found lurking in out-of-the-way corners of
the globe, and startles us at times with the unhallowed rites
which seem generally to have been associated with its prevalence." [1]   It might, indeed, be thought that Mr. Fergusson's

---

[1] *Tree and Serpent-Worship*, p. 1.—Yet with strange inconsistency,
Mr. Fergusson says farther on—"And, if I am not mistaken, the
presence of such a form of faith may have influenced the early spread
of Christianity in these cities (of Asia Minor) to an extent not hither-

failure to meet the difficulty by any suggestion having even a
semblance of probability, might have induced him to pause
before proposing a theory as repugnant to reason as it is opposed to Scripture.

Nor is he more happy in trying to account for Tree-worship.
That must, indeed, be a hard case to prove, which requires us
to believe that Trees were worshipped because—in addition to
their beauty, their welcome shelter and shade, their flowers
and fruits—their *wood* was indispensable for various uses, and
"in ancient times it was from wood alone that man obtained
that fire which enabled him to cook his food, to warm his
dwelling, or to sacrifice to his gods."[1] We are painfully reminded of the Lord's scathing rebuke of the idolater of old—
"He burneth part thereof in the fire; with part thereof he
eateth flesh: he roasteth roast, and is satisfied; yea, he
warmeth himself, and saith, Aha, I am warm, I have seen the
fire: and the residue thereof he maketh a god"!—Isa. xliv.
16, 17.

To believe that the Scripture history of man's Creation,
Temptation, and Fall, is literally true—and that Tree and
Serpent-worship throughout the world had its origin in distorted traditions of those events, is easy, and consistent with
all history and existing facts. To believe that this worship
arose from any such ideas as those suggested by Mr. Fergusson, demands an amount of weak credulity of which no

to suspected"!—P. 20.—Does, then, that which is "*unhallowed*"
tend to the spread of that which is *hallowed*? The only recorded instance in which Serpent-worship came into contact with Christianity
was when the damsel at Philippi was through St. Paul's ministry *dis-
possessed* of a "spirit of divination"—literally, a spirit of "*Python*,"
the *Serpent-god;* for which offence against the Serpent-worshipping
Philippians he and Silas were stripped and scourged in the public
street, and then thrown into prison, and their feet were made fast in the
stocks.—Acts xvi. "What communion hath light with darkness?
and what concord hath Christ with Belial?"—2 Cor. vi. 14, 15.

[1] Ibid., p. 1.

man ever becomes capable till his mind has been warped from its rectitude of judgment by some over-mastering prejudice or other influence.

Moreover, Mr. Fergusson's theory not only rests on grounds altogether conjectural, but it is opposed to the facts of the case—even to facts adduced by himself. Nowhere is there any historical statement that Serpents were worshipped on account of their rapid and graceful motion without legs, as he supposes—nor that Trees were worshipped because they are beautiful or useful: nor does Mr. Fergusson produce a single historical authority for his theory.

But when the *reason*, as well as the fact, of the Serpent having been worshipped, is given in the historical authorities, it is always the supernatural *knowledge* attributed to it—and its supposed power of *imparting* supernatural knowledge, as in the Pythian oracles, for example: or it is its supposed power of conferring health, or some other blessing.—And in like manner, the fact that Trees were worshipped, is accounted for, not by their beauty, or usefulness for shade, food, or fuel—but by the supposed power inherent in certain trees of conferring *Life* and *Immortality*—as is specified respecting the Homa Tree in the authority adduced by Mr. Fergusson himself.

In short, all the facts of the case and all the testimonies of history point to the events of Paradise related in Genesis as the marvellous origin from which alone, by distorted tradition, so strange a worship could by any possibility have been derived.

CHAPTER XVII.

Self-worship—" Ye shall be as gods."—Pagan Hero-worship and Romish Saint-worship identical—Three Romish Saints manufactured out of one Pagan god.

BESIDES the material and traditional evidences already adduced, and others to be given hereafter, of the historical truth of Genesis, there are *moral* proofs of it, stamped upon the very soul and character of mankind, which may be read and known by all.

One of these may perhaps most fitly be noticed in this place —namely, the *nature of the temptation* which brought about the ruin of our first parents, compared with the actual character of man from that time to the present.

The first allurement presented by Satan to Eve—of course as being that which he judged most likely to succeed, because it approached her nature on its weakest side—was this—" *Ye shall be as gods.*"—Gen. iii. 5.

The temptation unhappily prevailed. The bait proved but too alluring—Eve listened—ate—and fell.

Not that this was the *only* object presented to her desires— but it was evidently the foremost and the most influential. She saw *also* that " the tree was good for food, and that it was pleasant to the eyes "—but these were clearly not the greatest attractions of that mysterious tree. They were not *peculiar* to that one tree—there were abundant other fruits in that garden of " Delight " equally " good for food, and pleasant to the eyes."

It was, above all, the belief that it was "*a tree to be desired to make one wise*" that prevailed with Eve to break through the awful prohibition and hazard the dreadful penalty. It was the idea that eating of that forbidden fruit would make them to "be *as gods*, knowing good and evil," that was the fatal charm which "brought death into the world and all our woe."

It appears then from the narrative that the Tempter hoped to excite in the minds of Eve and Adam the desire of being *wise so as to be like gods*—wise beyond the wisdom which God had given them—wise with a wisdom which God had reserved to Himself—and so, wise in such a manner as to be on a footing of *equality with God.* This was the nature of the temptation presented in the words "Ye shall be as gods."

Can we, then, find in history, and in the actual facts of human life and character at the present moment, any prominent and leading feature of man's nature such as that which caused Eve and Adam to desire to be "as gods"?

Is there any feature, in the past history or present character of mankind, more prominent than *Pride?*

The fatal triad of temptations contained in that forbidden Tree are well summed up in one verse of the New Testament— "All that is in the world, the lust of the flesh, and the lust of the eyes, and the *pride* of life."—1 John ii. 16.

And what else is Pride, in man, but the deification of man? What else is it but that *self-exaltation* which, in its utmost reach and ultimate tendency, aims at nothing less than to be "as gods"?

To suppose that any such tendency existed in our first parents before they fell, would be to suppose that their nature was not created upright—and would, indeed, make God to have been the author of sin. But there may be a *liability* to sin where no sin exists as yet : and however inscrutable to our minds may be the manner of sin's first entrance into an up-

right nature, we are at least left in no doubt as to the nature
of the sin into which Eve and Adam actually fell.

Those who wish to find Science opposed to Revelation would
do well to see whether, in the whole circle of moral science,
they can find a more profound truth than the identity of
pride—in its every form and every feature—in its highest
flights of ambitious desire, and its lowest depths of sullen
defiance—with the principle involved in Satan's successful
temptation, "Ye shall be as gods."

It is undeniable that here, as every where else, the Bible is
in the most perfect harmony with all history—that is, with the
history of all human action—all human attempts at self-ag-
grandizement and self-gratification—and even with all human
attempts at self-improvement *when unaided by the Bible itself.*
The history of mankind is a history of little else but the
actings of ambition, avarice, and lust—that is, of the development of the very principles which marked the first temptation
and the first offence. If the literal truth of Genesis be denied,
it certainly behoves those who deny it to show some more
probable reason of the remarkable *coincidence* of all subsequent
temptations with the temptation of Eve and Adam. Whatever
motives have led mankind to do evil at any time, are precisely
of the nature of those which led our first parents to do evil for
the first time. The things which tempted them are the same
which now tempt us—though not in exactly the same form.
The simple account in Genesis of the first offence, and con-
sequent fall, of human beings, is fully confirmed by the
universal history of mankind ever since—for all history demon-
strates that the motives which have produced all the crime and
all the misery which have deluged the world from that time to
the present, were the very identical motives which led to that
first offence and that fall. Without attempting the task of
following out this idea through the history of the world, we
may advantageously glance at a few of the most prominent
developments of that principle which was evidently the most

dangerous snare to Eve and Adam—the desire to be *as gods*.

Self-exaltation takes a double form. The pride which leads the individual first to magnify himself in his own eyes, leads him afterwards to magnify the species to which he belongs— as being, to a certain extent, identified with himself. *Family* pride, and *national* pride, are natural and obvious expansions of *personal* pride. And as the circle continually widens, it embraces at last the whole human race, and exalts universal human nature—as being that nature of which each individual feels himself to be a partaker.

And hence has arisen an almost infinite variety—as curious as it is melancholy—of *Self-worship*: that is, of the worship of *fallen humanity*—fallen human nature—whether by the actual deification of dead men and women, or by the inordinate exaltation of oneself, or the undue estimation of human nature in general. These different forms of *Self-worship* may perhaps be conveniently viewed under the three heads of *Hero-worship*, —*Ambition*—and *Humanity-worship*.

Not that this, or any other division, can be strictly correct. Pride is a thing of Protean diversity, and infinite subtlety. It so penetrates and pervades every feeling of each heart—whether viewed independently, or in relation either to God or man— that in any attempted classification of its effects, the divisions will be found to run into each other, in an endless complexity and confusion. The above classification, however, may serve to reduce into some kind of order the observations which follow.

Hero-worship has been a principal feature in the idolatry of every heathen nation, and in every corrupt professing Christian church.

It has been already shown how a world-wide system of idolatry began with the deification of Nimrod, as the pretended Seed of the Woman—and of his beautiful but profligate queen, Semiramis, as the mystic Woman, the Spouse of the Sun, and the Queen of Heaven.

This double deification became, in fact, the leading feature of all the corrupt religious systems of the whole world. Under a variety of names, and with a variety of attributes mixed up with those of other deified personages, Nimrod and Semiramis were worshipped among all nations.

In Assyria, Nimrod was worshipped as Bel or Baal, Tammuz, Moloch, and Molk-gheber, or "the Mighty King": in Egypt as Osiris: in India, as Chrishna and Iswara: in the farther East, as Buddha: in Scandinavia as Balder. In Greece, Italy, and Asia Minor he was the real original represented by all the names Apollo, Bacchus, Adonis, Æsculapius, Hercules, and Vulcan or Mulciber—which last is just *Molkgheber*.

In like manner Semiramis was deified in Assyria as Astarté or Ashtoreth, identical with the classical Venus or Aphrodité, the goddess of love and beauty—and also as Beltis (the feminine of Bel) signifying "My Lady", and exactly equivalent to *Madonna.* In India, she was worshipped as Isi or Paravati: in Egypt, as Isis: in Scandinavia, as Frigga. In the languages of Greece and Rome she was called Hera or Juno, "the Queen of Heaven"—Artemis or Diana—Aphrodité or Venus—Hestia or Vesta—Demeter or Ceres—Bona Dea, the "good goddess"—Alma Mater, the "sweet Mother". She was also doubtless in part the original of Cybele or Rhea, whom Dr. Smith states to have been the great goddess of the East:[1] but under this title she was confused with Eve—the attributes of the two original real persons having been partly assigned to one and the same deity, partly distributed among others: which is a frequent and natural characteristic of heathen mythology.

Noah also was deified after death. He was in fact no other than the original of *Dagon*, the Fish-god of Syria, Chaldæa, and Mesopotamia. He was otherwise called *Oannes*, "the Man of the Sea," or sacred Man-fish; and was represented either as

---

[1] Smith's *Classical Dictionary.*

half man, half fish, or as a man under a fish's body forming a
sort of cloak or covering—the fish's gaping jaws projecting
above the man's head like a mitre.   Such figures were discovered among the Assyrian ruins by Mr. Layard : and Mr.
Hislop has shown that this Dagon's *fish-head mitre* is the very
original of the mitre worn to this day by the Pope and Papal
bishops.   At Rome, the representative of Noah was *Janus*—
who was always depicted with two faces, one old, the other
young, looking opposite ways, to signify his having lived, as it
were, in two worlds, before the Flood and after it.   And as
the Pope borrowed his mitre from Dagon and his priests, so he
borrowed his *Cross-keys* from Janus and Cybele.   " Janus," says
Mr. Hislop, "bore a key, and Cybele bore a key : and these
are the two keys that the Pope emblazons on his arms as the
ensigns of his spiritual authority."[1]   In this, as in other
respects, Rome is the counterpart of Babylon.

It is not too much to say, that the idolatry of all heathen
nations has consisted very much in the deification and worship
of dead men and women.   Among the Romans the Lares, or
deified ancestors of the family, were worshipped in every
home ; and in great houses a separate apartment, called the
Lararium, was set apart for their images.[2]   Æneas, the
Trojan hero of Virgil's poem, is represented as carrying away
his household gods, as too important and sacred to be left behind, even though he had to fight his way through the burning city and through bands of victorious enemies.   To this
day the Chinese observe the same custom, and pay the most
religious veneration, and offer sacrifices, to their departed ancestors.

But we need not go so far for instances of this world-wide
superstition—this universal tendency of fallen and corrupted
human nature to deify itself.

[1] *Two Babylons*, pp. 302, 315.
[2] Smith's *Classical Dictionary*, Art. *Lares*.

The *Saint-worship* of the Church of Rome is of precisely the same nature as the Babylonian worship of Bel and the "Queen of Heaven," and of the old Pagan Roman worship of Jupiter and the whole Pantheon of heathen gods and goddesses. In fact, they are in part actually identical.

Under the name of the Virgin Mary, the Church of Rome worships *a heathen goddess*—the very same as the Babylonian Beltis, "the Queen of Heaven" mentioned by Jeremiah,— ch. 7. 18, and 44. 17, &c.;—the same as the Grecian Hera and Roman Juno, and Venus, and Astarté, or "Ashtoreth, the goddess of the Zidonians." The very names are identical in meaning. *Beltis* signifies "My Lady"—*Hera* signifies "Lady" —and *Madonna*, the Romish title given to the Virgin Mary, signifies "My Lady." *Juno* means "the Dove"—and the Dove is the well-known symbol of Venus or Ashtoreth. The "Queen of Heaven" was a title given to all these different goddesses—or rather to the one goddess represented by all these different names:—just as it is the Romish title given to the Virgin Mary at the present moment.

It is matter of history that the worship of the Virgin Mary was introduced into the Christian Church, in the fourth century, in imitation of the worship of the Pagan "Queen of Heaven"—and that the "unbloody sacrifice" of Rome, intro- duced at the same time, was identical with the "cakes" which had been from time immemorial offered by the Pagans to the "Queen of Heaven." These consisted of *round wafers*, sym- bolical of the *Sun*-divinity, or Babylonian false Messiah, be- lieved to have been the Sun-begotten Child of the Babylonian "Queen of Heaven". *Hence came the round wafer of the Romish Mass*, which has been adopted by the modern Babylon in- stead of the plain *bread* of the Lord's Supper.[1]

"Lady-Day", the 25th of March, was observed in *Pagan*

---

[1] For full proof of these facts see Hislop's *Two Babylons*, p. 232, &c.

Rome in honour of *Cybele*, another title of the Mother of the Babylonian false Messiah, long before the Christian era. The common appellation of Cybele at Rome was *Domina*, "the Lady"—exactly corresponding to *Beltis*, *Hera*, and *Madonna*.[1]

But indeed it was a common practice of the Church of Rome to conciliate and win over the heathens by transferring their Pagan worship to those Romish saints, male or female, who seemed most nearly to correspond in character with the Pagan gods and goddesses. In some cases the change was merely like putting a new name upon the old image, the deity represented by it being actually the same as before. "Thus the little temple of Vesta, near the Tiber, mentioned by Horace, is now possessed by *the "Madonna of the Sun."*[2] Now *Vesta*—the Grecian *Hestia* ("hearth" or "dwelling-place")—the same as the Egyptian *Athor* ("the habitation of God") was called by this name as being understood to be the *Dwelling-place*, or *Habitation, of Deity*—as being the Mother of the Divine Son. *Vesta* was thus only another title of the "Queen of Heaven". But she was also regarded as the tutelar goddess of the *Sacred Fire*, which was always kept burning in her temple : indicating that she was understood to be the mother of the *Sun*-begotten divine Child. Added to this, the care of her worship and of her Sacred Fire, was intrusted only to the *Vestal virgins*. Under all this symbolism, then, we have the clear intimation that the Pagan goddess *Vesta* was worshipped as the *Virgin-mother of the Sun-begotten divine Child*, or Babylonian false Messiah.—What, then, could be more significant than the fact that, when the priests of Rome desired to conciliate the Pagans, they changed the designation of the Temple of *Vesta* to that of the Church of the "*Madonna of the Sun*"? It was simply retaining the old divinity under a new name. The "Madonna of the Sun", or, "Our Lady of the Sun", was just another

[1] Ibid. p. 147.
[2] Dr. Conyers Middleton's *Letter from Rome*, p. 47.

name for the Pagan goddess Vesta. The debased Christians of that day might offer their devotions in that church to the Virgin Mary, raised, or rather degraded, to the rank of a goddess: while the Pagans would still continue, as of old, to burn incense there to the "Queen of Heaven". The worship of the Virgin Mary is expressly stated by Gibbon to have been borrowed from Paganism.—" The Christians of the seventh century had insensibly relapsed into a semblance of Paganism; their public and private vows were addressed to the relics and images that disgraced the temples of the East; the Throne of the Almighty was darkened by a cloud of martyrs, and saints, and angels, the objects of popular veneration; and the Collyridian heretics, who flourished in the fruitful soil of Arabia ('Arabia hæreseōn ferax,' Arabia fruitful in heresies) invested the Virgin Mary with the name and honours of a goddess."[1]

To which may be added the following explanation from Mosheim—"While they" (these women) "were mere Pagans, they were accustomed to bake and present to the goddess Venus, or Astarté, (the Moon) certain cakes which were called *collyrides*. And when they became Christians, they thought this honour might now best be shown to the Virgin Mary."[2] That is to say, they transferred to the Virgin Mary the worship and offerings they had been accustomed to pay to the "Queen of Heaven"—the supposed Mother of the Babylonian false Messiah, worshipped throughout the ancient heathen world under the various names of Venus, Astarté or Ashtoreth, Juno, Diana, Vesta, Ceres, Cybele, Rhea, &c.[3]

---

[1] Gibbon, *Decline and Fall*, ch. 50. vol. 5. p. 469.—"The Collyridian heresy was carried from Thrace to Arabia by some women, and the name was borrowed from the κολλυρίς, or cake, which they offered to the goddess."—Hottinger, *Hist. Orient*, pp. 225–228..

[2] Mosheim, *Eccl. Hist.*, vol. i. p. 410, quoting Schlegel.

[3] "The great goddess Diana, whom all Asia and the world worshippeth."—Acts xix. 27.

In like manner, "the Latin Church has not disdained to borrow *from the Koran* the Immaculate Conception of the Virgin mother." [1]

Nay more—one of the "*saints*" canonized and enrolled in the Calendar of the Romish Church is actually identical even in name with one of the gods of ancient Pagan Greece and Rome.—In that Calendar, the 7th October is set down for the festival of "*St. Bacchus the Martyr.*" Bacchus was the well-known god of wine and drunkenness : and he was believed to have died a violent death, which was afterwards fabled to have been suffered in behalf of religion and for the good of mankind. But Maimonides expressly states that the "religion" on behalf of which this Bacchus, or Tammuz, or Adonis, (for they are the same person) was put to death, was the worship of *the seven stars and the twelve signs of the Zodiac*—in other words, *Sun-worship* [2]—a statement which fully concurs with the other historical evidence that this Bacchus was identical with Nimrod, the Zero-ashta, (or Zoroaster) who was the reputed author as well as object of Fire-worship or Sun-worship. In the person, then, of "*St. Bacchus the Martyr*", the Church of Rome has actually canonized and still venerates the great arch-apostate Nimrod, the Babylonian false Messiah, and the ringleader of idolatry and heathen abominations throughout the world ! And what proves beyond a doubt the identity of the modern Romish "St. Bacchus the Martyr" with the heathen god of drunkenness and debauchery is, that the time of the Romish "*saint's*" festival, the 7th of October, is exactly the same with the season at which the Pagan Greeks and Romans celebrated the "Rustic festival," as it was called, of their drunken god Bacchus.

But the Church of Rome has a zeal for saint-worship which

---

[1] Gibbon, *Decline and Fall*, ch. 50. vol. v. p. 472.

[2] Hislop, *Two Babylons*, p. 89, quoting Maimonides, *More Nevochim*, p. 426.

N

is wonderfully prolific of saints. Not content with canonizing
the Pagan god of drunkenness under his Latin name of Bacchus,
it has canonized him a second time, and so made another saint
of him, under his Greek name of *Dionysus*—or, as it was
written in later times, *Dionysius.* "The Pagans," says Mr.
Hislop,[1] "were in the habit of worshipping the same god under
different names; and accordingly, not content with the festival
to Bacchus under the name by which he was most commonly
known at Rome, the Romans, no doubt to please the Greeks,
celebrated a rustic festival to him two days afterwards, under
the name of Dionysus Eleutherius, the name by which he
was worshipped in Greece. That 'rustic' festival was briefly
called by the name of Dionysia; or, expressing its object more
fully, the name became 'Festum Dionysi Eleutherii rusticum';
i.e., 'the *rustic* festival of Dionysus Eleutherius'. Now the
Papacy, in its excess of zeal for saints and saint-worship, has
actually split Dionysus Eleutherius into two—has made two
several saints out of the *double name* of one Pagan divinity;
and more than that, has made the innocent epithet *rusticum*,
which even among the heathen had no pretensions to divinity
at all, a *third;* and so it comes to pass that under date of
October 9 we read this entry in the Calendar: 'The festival of
St. Dionysius, and of his companions St. Eleuther and St.
Rustic'."[2]

In confirmation of these statements, it may be mentioned
that Dr. Conyers Middleton saw at Rome an altar erected to
St. Baccho.[3]

The patron saint of France, St. Denys, is none other but
this same St. Dionysius—the name *Dionysius* having been in
the course of time corrupted into *Denys.*

In short, the whole system of Mariolatry, saint-worship, and

---

[1] *Two Babylons,* p. 177.
[2] See Calendar in *Missale Romanum,* Oct. 9th and Oct. 7th.
[3] *Letter from Rome,* p. 53.

image-worship in the corrupt churches of Rome and of the East is but a continuation of the hero-worship of ancient Pagan Rome and Greece—the very same thing in reality, though the one be called Pagan hero-worship, and the other be dignified with the abused name and profession of *Christian* worship. Both alike consist in the deification and worship of dead men and women—and, in the instances just mentioned, the Church of Rome has not been ashamed to retain the adoration of the very same names, as names of Christian "*saints*", which had already, for ages before, been worshipped by the Pagans as those of deified heroes.

CHAPTER XVIII.

Same Subject continued.—Deification of Roman Emperors and Romish Popes and priests—Self-deification the real tendency of Romanism, Rationalism, and Atheism in every form.

NOT only were men and women worshipped as gods after death; in many instances they have been regarded as gods during life.

A familiar instance is the divine honour assigned to the Roman Emperors. Augustus Cæsar is continually flattered by the poet Horace as a god upon earth: and to show that this was no mere courtier's flattery, there needs only the express testimony of Pliny; who, when governor of Bithynia, wrote to consult the Emperor Trajan how he was to deal with the Christians in his province, and stated in his letter that one test by which he tried whether they were really Christians, or not, was to require them to *worship the Emperor's image.*[1]

Herein, again, Rome *Papal* is the counterpart of Rome *Pagan.* If the Emperor of ancient Rome was worshipped as a god upon earth, so is the Pope of modern Rome. Not only do the canonists of the Church of Rome assert that the Pope has power to overrule the laws of God Himself, but he has even been frequently styled by his adherents "our Lord God the Pope."[2] Nay, more than this, every Romish priest claims

---

[1] Pliny's *Epistles*, 10, 97, 98.
[2] Willet's *Synopsis Papismi*, vol. ii., p. 282.

that in the exercise of the priestly power he stands in the place of God.

There is no prerogative of God more absolutely exclusive—more inalienably belonging to God alone—than to be *the supreme Judge of what is right and what is wrong*—to pronounce finally and without appeal, *what is truth.*

It is obvious that any church—any system of "philosophy" —any individual—that claims to do this, claims thereby to exercise the prerogative of God—claims, that is, to *be Divine.*

The claim, again, to *direct the consciences of men*, is a claim to be "as God", and, in fact, to be God. For he alone is qualified to direct the consciences of men who is himself the supreme Judge of right and wrong.

Now these prerogatives have always been claimed by the Church of Rome. Every minister of that Church, from the Pope to the lowest priest, is supposed to direct the consciences of men in *the Confessional*, by virtue of an authority delegated by the Church.

Such an authority, however, can be grounded only upon the possession of *Infallibility.* Accordingly, Infallibility has always been assumed to reside in the Church of Rome by those who have advocated her claims.

It has been reserved for the present Pope to carry out these claims to the utmost extent of presumption and blasphemy, by proclaiming, in full conclave at Rome, that the Pope, and he himself as Pope, is *personally Infallible.*

This of course is the same thing as to pronounce himself to be God : and is so recognized by all parties, whether in the Church of Rome or out of it. It was even boasted by one foreign Roman Catholic journal that by the dogma of the Pope's Infallibility *a fourth person was about to be added to the Holy Trinity.*

Thus has the world witnessed the complete development of that principle of desire to "be as gods" which was stirred in the hearts of our first parents by the Tempter's suggestion.

Thus has the top-stone been put to that edifice of human pride which has been growing up for six thousand years. The deification of man, and defiance of God, seem to have reached their climax in the literal fulfilment of the apostle's prediction concerning the "Man of sin," or "Lawless one," who "opposeth and exalteth himself above all that is called God or that is worshipped; so that he as God sitteth in the temple of God, showing himself that he is God."—2 Thess. ii. 4.

It is, indeed, of the very essence of every false religious system to usurp the prerogatives of Deity. The Llama of the Buddhists is as much a god in their eyes as is the Pope in the eyes of Romanists : and the Hindû Brahmin claims and receives from his abject dupes a degree of honour almost divine.

But it is still more remarkable, and not a little instructive, that the very same tendency exists in the so-called *"philosophy"* which rejects all religious systems whatever—the "philosophy" which proclaims the freedom of human intellect, and claims an absolute immunity from all laws but those which each individual imposes upon himself.

This *self-deification of human nature* is co-extensive with the human race; and in the variety of its manifestations absolutely boundless. All history, all human character, are full of it. It is seen alike in the haughtiness of the despot, and in the voluntary humility of the devotee—in the God-defying insolence of a Nebuchadnezzar, and in the self-sufficient pride of a Diogenes.

Alexander the Great, the conqueror of Asia, who is said to have wept because there was not a second world for him to conquer, stood once by the side of the Cynic, whose tub was at once his home and his kingdom. The monarch, in the pride of royalty, asked Diogenes if there was any thing he could do for him. "Yes," said the philosopher, "you can stand out of my sunshine."—"Were I not Alexander," said the king, "I would wish to be Diogenes."—The difference between the two was a difference of circumstances more than of moral character.

The pride that towered above a conquered world was akin to the pride that scorned it. The man whose ambition grasped at every thing, and the man whose self-sufficiency wanted nothing, were mentally on a par—each in his own esteem superior to human weakness—less human than divine. In error, as in many other things, extremes often meet: and between the two extremes there is error of every conceivable and inconceivable diversity.

There is a similar coincidence between the claims of priest-craft and the pretensions of "philosophy", falsely so called. The Pope claims to be a God upon earth—the Rationalist "philosopher" demands to have no God but himself. The two start from opposite points, but arrive at the same centre—and that centre is the *deification of human nature* by each man in himself, and the deification of himself in that of human nature.

Let no one think that these pretensions, however extravagant, are mere jests put forward by those who find pleasure in paradoxes. They are held as practical principles by the whole school of "*advanced*" Rationalists in this latter half of the nineteenth century. They are put forward as the ultimate issues towards which all human progress is advancing, and in which all human society is to find its final and complete perfection.

This statement may seem, perhaps, exaggerated, to those who have not studied the subject. But it is nothing more than is borne out by the continual utterances of Rationalist teachers both in England and on the Continent, as reported in the public journals and elsewhere. The following sentence, from the pen of M. Scherer, in an article in the *Revue des deux Mondes* about seven years ago, may serve as a specimen. "When criticism shall have overturned miracles as useless, and dogmas as irrational; when there shall be no standard authority *other than every man's private conscience*; when, in short, man, having rent every veil and penetrated every mystery, shall contemplate the God he has been seeking face to face, *it will be found that the same God is no other than man himself*—man's conscience and reason personified ; and religion, on pretence of growing more religious, will have ceased to exist."

From the other side of the Atlantic we have a similar exposition of belief in the deity of human nature. "Calvin Blanchard described himself as a *Positivist*, and asserted that he was only 'falsely and libellously called a sceptic and an infidel.' He believed 'in Nature Omnipotent, self-acting, self-dependent, self-progressive to all-sufficiency.'" But this deification of nature is presently explained to be the deification of *human* nature—in other words, the deification of *man*, and consequently of Calvin Blanchard. "Nature's highest form is *mankind*," he goes on to say—"mankind, *the great continuous Being who will never die*"—and "Nature's highest function is being (and has been ever since the advent of mankind) manifested in Science and Art."

The *Daily News* recently gave the following description of this "New Religion." "Unlike the religions named after their founders, Positivism professes to have nothing personal to its author."—"Its teacher maintains that all other religions have been ancillary to the reception of this one by the human race, that the founders of other faiths have laboured to prepare the way for Auguste Comte. . . . . The aim of the system as a whole is 'the government' and 're-organization of Humanity.' Indeed, '*Humanity' is to the Positivists what a Deity is to others.* They make no profession about 'saving souls,' or holding out other than earthly advantages"—which apparently they consider alone to be *positive* advantages.

And these opinions are not confined to a solitary dreamer here and there, who might be supposed to be suffering from insanity. The professors of them have numerous followers both at home and abroad. They are found in the greatest centres of modern research and civilization—in London, Paris,

and New York. In France and England there are periodical
lectures, and so-called "Services", held for the dissemination
and celebration of the principles of the Worship of Humanity.
The *Pall Mall Gazette* lately published an account of an
annual meeting of the disciples of Auguste Comte at Paris,
held in the apartment formerly inhabited by their master, and
"sanctified", as they consider, by his occupation of it. The
object of this meeting was "to celebrate in common the
annual ceremony of the *worship of Abstract Humanity."* The
"Director of Positivism" exhorted his audience to "join in
spiritual communion with all their brethren in the faith,
especially in London and at Bradford, who were celebrating
with them at the same hour the Worship of Humanity."

Of this system one of the profoundest thinkers as well as
one of the soundest theologians of modern times, the late
lamented Dr. Jeune, Bishop of Peterborough, thus spoke :—
" Hear the motto prefixed to recent Positivist publications put
forth in the country by men of note ; a motto taken from M.
Comte, the author of the system. ' In the name of the past
and the future, the theoretical servants and the practical servants of Humanity are worthily assuming the direction of the
business of the world, and excluding for ever the political
supremacy of the slaves of God—Catholics, Protestants, Deists
—as men behind their age, and perturbators.' Do not think
this vaunt a mere hallucination. Facts justify it in some
degree. The Positivist school includes men who lead opinion,
and who play a part in politics. But man deposes God only
to take His place, and even Positivists can count Divine
honours. ' *Humanity*', they tell us, ' *is definitively substituting
itself for God*, without, however, forgetting the provisional
services.   *What is Humanity?* It is *the Great Being;* the
Great Being is the aggregate of beings past, present, and
future; not of all beings, but only of human beings; not of all
human beings, but only of those who freely concur in bringing
to perfection the universal Being. They are called convergent

beings.' But, I ask, who will want the past convergent, or the
future convergent beings? The living hierophants of the
school must be our Gods. Like the Romans, we shall be
governed by deified rulers.

"In the last and at the beginning of the present century it
was a material and mechanical Atheism which attracted the
vigour of scientific men. It was the Atheism which denies all
existence but the existence of matter—of matter eternal, and
containing a divinity called *Force* in every atom; the Atheism
which regards thought as the mere secretion of the brain, and
vice and virtue simply as products like sugar or vitriol: the
Atheism which sees order, but not design, in the universe—
laws, not Providence, in the course of things. To this blank
and revolting Materialism succeeded Pantheism, as revived in
Germany; the system which confounds the infinite and the
finite, and which makes God the sum of all things. God, it
teaches, is brutal in brute matter, mighty in the force of nature,
feeling in the animal, thinking and conscious only in man.
This system is, in its first aspect, more noble than material
Atheism, but in truth it is not less fatal to all that is noble
and good. It, indeed, *makes man*, nay, the beast that perishes
—nay, the very dung on the earth, *Divine*—but it also makes
God human, animal, material. It degrades what is high by
exalting what is low. Better to deny God, after all, than to
debase Him. Pantheism is, if possible, a worse Atheism.

"Of both these systems, Positivism—the system which at this
moment claims exclusive possession of truth: Positivism—for
such is its barbarous name, to which all thought (we are told
by a leading review) in Germany and in England, as well as in
France its birthplace, is now converging—speaks with no less
contempt, though with less hatred, than it speaks of Christianity.
Day-dreams, it says, all the assertions, all the negations alike, of
philosophers: impotent attempts to compass the impossibility.
Of God, if there be a God— of the soul, if there be a soul—of
Revelation, if Revelation there be—man can know, man need

know, nothing. Away then, it cries, with mere hypothesis. To the positive, to the material, to the teaching of the senses to observation of facts, philosophy must limit itself. This system is mean, though supercilious. Perhaps, however, Positivism rises in comparison with Atheism, which itself is less base than Pantheism, for it is better to ignore than to deny, as it is better to deny than to degrade God.

"Human reason, then, if left to itself, leaves us as to God a threefold choice—we may deny God, we may degrade God, we may ignore God. A noble result! a godless philosophy ends in suicide. So it will ever be. To quote from the noble close of the Dunciad :—

> 'Philosophy, which leaned on Heav'n before,
> Sinks to her second cause—and is no more.'

"At the present moment it is Pantheism, discarded though it be in Germany, which chiefly influences the Rationalists of France and England. Ministers of religion who yield to Pantheistic views do so in various degrees and inconsistently—perhaps not always consciously. It has its mitigated forms. Our Rationalists appear still to cling to a personal God, who is external to and above the world ; and thus they do not, like Pantheists pure and simple, make man and all other things Divine, and each man his own God. They do not deny Christianity—they claim to be Christians in a higher sense. But the supernatural in religion they assume to be impossible: and the supernatural is the substance of religion. They deny it in prophecy—in inspiration—in miracles: and *they make man, and each man, the sole origin and the supreme judge of religious truth.* They hold that there is no inspiration but that which belongs to all men, though in all men it varies in degree, according to the moral and intellectual culture of the individual. Unlike Socinianism, mitigated Pantheism acknowledges that the belief of the orthodox is found in Holy Scripture, but, unhappily, *it acknowledges in Scripture no authority superior to the internal criterion of man.* Exceedingly deceitful is the system, and to none more deceitful than to those who profess it. They can claim, and believe they feel, profound piety. They can speak with the fervour of mystics. They can dwell with reverence, as we do—nay, with enthusiasm—on the union of God and man in the person of the Lord, on the inspiration of God's written Word, on the Atonement of the Cross, on the Resurrection and Ascension of Christ. But alas! in the view of the many *that union is no more than the union of God and man in each of us,* and the Lord was more divine than we are only because He was more holy and more wise; and the Spirit which moved holy men of old was equally in Luther, or Bacon, or Shakspeare, or Raphael; and the Atonement reconciles not God to man, but only man to God—that is, to himself: and the Resurrection and Ascension of Jesus need not be historical facts (so a synod of French pastors has lately voted) but may be images merely of the ultimate triumph and enthronement of goodness and truth. They regard the devout sentiments and the high aspirations of the heart as the essence of religion, and Fetichism, Vedas, Korans, Scriptures, Creeds, as manifestations, more or less enlightened, of those sentiments, more or less true according to the advance of the times, but all relatively true. These several manifestations have been, they say, necessary stages in the education of our race. Pantheists can subscribe to all creeds, and minister in all churches consistently with their principles. By them all doctrines may be held or denied, or held and denied at once. They may be held in that they manifest religious intuition, and denied in that they fall below the culture of the inward light. The only heterodoxy is, according to them, exclusiveness. Dogma, they hold, must be banished from the Church. But the Bible is dogmatic and exclusive. Christ speaks with authority and not as the Scribes. He is the One Master. He is a jealous God. The Bible, then, while admitted to be

Divine, must, if Rationalism is to prevail, be convicted of being human too—that is, full of error and imperfection. It must come to be regarded as the mere voice of the congregation, as the expression of devout reason, and as subject therefore to the 'verifying faculty.' For the purpose of Pantheists, every objection devised against it by science falsely so called, or by the new criticism of Germany, must be sought out and complacently paraded. Its cosmogony must be proved to be unscientific and mere poetry, its facts unhistorical, its miracles legends or allegories, or natural phenomena, its prophets only fierce patriots who denounced kingly or sacerdotal usurpations, its prophecies fortunate guesses or prophecies after the event. It must be treated like any other book, and from every other book we should scout the supernatural. Criticism must reconstruct the history of the people of God, as Niebuhr, Michelet, or Bunsen have reconstructed each of them his own Roman history out of the compilations and legends of Livy. The Lord, too, must be shown to be human and like unto us, sin even not excepted. The true Christ had, we are told, been lost—criticism has recovered his lineaments."—"The human element—that is, error and imperfection—having once been annulled" (by the "verifying faculty") "in the Bible and Christ, the Bible and Christ shall be extolled, studied, venerated as Divine, held out as the noblest models and rules of life. Whole existences shall be devoted to the language, to the antiquities, to the history of the Bible. The story of Abimelech shall, if you will, be studied with more care than Christians have hitherto for the most part given to the words spoken by the Lord Himself. Every fragment shall be gathered that nothing be lost. Christ, too, shall be loved with more than a Christian's love. Christ shall make tongues eloquent. Christ shall be the whole of Christianity. *Let Him but bow down to the inward light,* to Him shall be given all the kingdoms of the world, and He shall be set on the pinnacle of the temple."

This witness is true.

And it is manifest that the tendency of every Rationalistic as well as every Atheistical system is to depose God in order that man may usurp His Throne—in other words, *every infidel system leads to the deification of man.* "Ye shall be as gods, knowing good and evil," may be adopted as the motto of Atheists, Rationalists, and infidels of every degree. The claim to make *unaided Reason* the supreme Judge of right and wrong, good and evil, independently and in defiance of Revelation, is of itself a claim to realize that godlike supremacy promised to Eve by the Tempter.

And therefore it is that the Bible is the great object of attack from every section of the infidel camp. Romanism and Rationalism alike aim at the overthrow of the Bible—though by opposite means. The Church of Rome would destroy its authority by making it subject and subordinate to the pretended infallible interpretation of the Church: thus making the Word of God of none effect by *human tradition.* The Rationalist would compass the same end by making it subject to the "verifying faculty": thus making the word of God of none effect by the pretended *inward light of human Conscience, Science, or Criticism.* Either system alike denies the authority of God, and exalts into its place the authority of man. Romanists, Rationalists, Atheists, and infidels of every sort, all alike do in effect claim to "be as gods, knowing good and evil" for themselves, without needing a revelation from God, and without submitting to His authority.

In the language of Bishop Jeune again, "'The Bible,' writes an eminent living Professor of the Sorbonne, 'would be a sad and fatal gift without a Divine Interpreter. It would be a firebrand cast into society. It would be a dead letter at the best.' In their disparagement of the Word of God, the Pantheist and the Romanist are as one. Both will love the Bible, if only they may interpret it."

The "Divine Interpreter" is sought by the Romanist in the infallible Church, or the infallible Pope—by the Rationalist or Pantheist in the inward light and the "verifying faculty."

The only *true* Divine Interpreter, expressly promised by the Lord Himself—the Holy Spirit, the Comforter—is by both alike rejected and despised. In that rejection, and the substitution of *an assumed Divine power in man of interpreting the Scriptures,* there is clearly involved the claim to "be as gods, knowing good and evil."

The deification of human nature is thus demonstrated to be the real aim and drift of every infidel theory: but the latest refinements—the most subtle and insidious form of this Satanic delusion—is put forward in the perversion of Christianity itself by representing the Lord Jesus Christ as merely a model of perfect *human* virtue.[1] The true Incarnation of Deity in "the man Christ Jesus" is denied, either expressly or by implication: and all that is so lovely and adorable in the holy Saviour is attributed to something Divine supposed to be inherent in every human being—the *fall* of man being of course, in defiance of all facts and common sense, coolly ignored.

Again we may say, extremes meet. The Polytheism of Greece and Rome made men equal to gods—modern Rationalism makes God, incarnate in the Person of Jesus Christ, no more than equal to man. In the Pagan mythology men were deified by being exalted to the level of God—in the modern so-called "more genial form of Christianity" men are deified by representing God as being on a level with man.[2]

But we must advance a step farther.—The corrupt instinct

---

[1] As, for example, in *Ecce Homo.*

[2] For farther proofs of the views here advanced, and illustrations drawn from the writings of French and German Atheists, see my answer to *Ecce Homo,* entitled *Ithuriel's Spear,* ch. xiii.

of self-glorification—the desire to "be as gods"—is not confined to any definite system either of priestcraft or of "philosophy" falsely so called. It is inherent in every human breast. It breaks out in a variety of ways absolutely countless, and almost infinite. Two or three only of the most prominent, as influencing not merely individuals but whole classes, will here be noticed.

The infidelity of " *Science,* falsely so called," is an obvious example, and specially conspicuous in the present day. "Modern Science," we are told, "has shown the Bible not to be historically true." This assertion of course proceeds upon the assumption that modern research is a surer criterion of the facts of Creation and of the world's early history than the revealed Word of God. But modern research has never yet succeeded in disproving a single miracle, or a single fulfilled prophecy, or a single historical fact, of the Scriptures. Now these miracles, fulfilled prophecies, and historical facts are just the proofs that the Bible itself *is* the Word of God. On the other hand, the alleged facts of Science, which are supposed to disprove the Bible, are not facts at all, but *inferences deduced from facts*, upon the supposition that certain things *must* have happened in such and such a manner—that certain processes *must* have occupied such and such a period of time—that certain things could not have literally happened as recorded in the Bible, because they are unlike anything we see now, contrary to experience, and the like. Therefore it is sagely concluded, that Moses was ignorant in comparison of modern "men of science"—that the book of Genesis is "poetry, not history"—that miracles were allegories, and that prophecies were written after the event. In short, all the so-called "scientific" objections to the truth of the Bible resolve themselves into mere probabilities and improbabilities at the best— to pass over the fact that no argument has ever yet been brought against either miracle or prophecy which is not an arrant "begging of the question". So that, in truth, the objections drawn from "science falsely so called" amount to this—that men think themselves wiser than God, and know better how the world was created than the Creator Himself.

Another manifestation of the same tendency is seen in the notion of *the perfectibility of human nature*, and the excellence of human virtue. This is the favourite idea of all mere human "philosophers", ancient and modern alike. "Indeed," says Archbishop Magee, "the manner in which some Socinians of the new school" (and, we may add, some in our day who are not called Socinians) "speak of their virtues, their merits, and their title to the rewards of a happy immortality, is such as might lead us to suppose ourselves carried back to the days of the old heathen schools of the Stoics, and receiving lessons, not from the followers of the humble Jesus, but from the disciples of the arrogant and magniloquent Chrysippus, Seneca, or Epictetus. When Chrysippus tells us, that 'as it is proper for Jupiter to glory in himself and in his own life, and to think and speak magnificently of himself as living in a manner that deserves to be highly spoken of; so these things are becoming all good men, as being in nothing exceeded by Jupiter':[1]— when Seneca pronounces that 'a good man differs only in *time* from God':[2] that 'there is one thing in which the wise man *excels* God, that God is wise by the benefit of nature, not by his own choice':[3] and that 'it is shameful to importune the gods in prayer, since a man's happiness is entirely in his own power':[4]—when, I say, we hear such language from the ancient Stoic, what *do* we hear but the sentiments of the philosophizing Christian of the present day? and on casting an eye into the works of Priestley, Lindsay, Evanson, Wakefield, Belsham

---

[1] Plut. *De Stoic. Repugn. Oper.* tom. ii., p. 1038, ed. Xyl.
[2] *De Provid.* cap. 1.
[3] *Epist.* 53.
[4] *Epist.* 31.

O

and the other Unitarian writers, do we not instantly recognize that proud and independent, and, I had almost said, heaven-defying self-reliance which had once distinguished the haughty disciple of the Stoa ? " [1]

The same remark would equally apply to our Rationalist writers of the present day—the authors of *Essays and Reviews, Ecce Homo*, and the like—as well as to the whole crew of French and German Atheists.

The idea of the perfectibility and virtue of human nature lies at the root of all democratic pretensions to sovereignty : and the great historian of the French Revolution, Alison, does not hesitate to affirm that this notion is the mainspring of revolutionary violence. " More even than by Mirabeau and Danton," he says, "the French Revolution was brought about by Voltaire and Rousseau." And what were their principles ? "Voltaire," says Alison, "thought that *by following the dictates and impulses of nature* man would arrive at once at the greatest happiness and highest destiny of his being." And again :— " In the fundamental doctrine of Rousseau's philosophy is to be found both the antagonist principle, in every age, of the Christian faith, and the spring of revolutionary convulsions all over the world. This is the doctrine of *human innocence and social perfectibility*." [2]

A similar remark applies to the *Liberalism*, so called, of the present day. The principle of Liberalism is " *Vox populi vox Dei* "—"the voice of the people is the voice of God ": by which is meant that whatever the people declares to be right and wills to be done, is right, and ought to be done, *without regard either to the revealed will of God or to any other rule whatever*. And what else is this but to *deify man*, by making man's wisdom the supreme Judge of right and wrong, and

---

[1] Archbishop Magee on *Atonement and Sacrifice*, vol. i., p. 176.
[2] See *Ithuriel's Spear*, p. 170, &c., for fuller illustration, and references, on this subject.

man's will the supreme authority and rule of action? And this is indeed the practical and constant principle of Liberalism, both in reference to religious truth, moral duty, and political supremacy. The question "What is truth," in religion, is decided by an appeal to *the majority*, not to the Word of God.

The inevitable result is disbelief of all religion whatever. The rejection of the only true guide—the Word of God— leaves the human mind to wander in darkness and hopeless error. The opinions of "the majority" are of course different in different ages and countries; yet all, according to the Rationalist, are equally true. But as these opinions contradict each other, the belief very naturally prevails that all are equally false. Hence it comes to pass that revealed Truth, being brought down to the bar of human judgment, and treated merely as one among many other forms of human opinion, is rejected with the same cold incredulity and contempt with which men disregard whatever does not please their humour, when it comes to them with no higher claim than human authority—for every man thinks his own opinion as good as his neighbours.

The result of this way of thinking—this so-called "philosophy"—is well described by a leading Liberal journal as an "aptness for universal unbelief, and for what may be described as a species of bitter and contemptuous universal charitableness," which is said to characterize "the cast of thought, the feelings, and the temper, of the highest order of London political, critical, and literary life."[1]

The world is an involuntary witness against itself. It is said that benighted travellers, in their efforts to find their way in a strange country, usually work round to the point from which they started, and find themselves just where they were. Unbelievers in Revelation seem to experience a somewhat

[1] *Pall Mall Gazette*, in a notice of Mr. Douglas Cook, late Editor of the *Saturday Review*.

similar issue.   Setting out in the dark, because they reject
the light of Revelation, they travel through the whole round
of human speculation, reason, and "science falsely so called,"
and end just where they began, in ignorance and error.   A
leading fashionable journal, and a leading fashionable Review,
concur in representing the tone of the highest order of political,
critical, and literary life in England as characterized by
"cynicism," "an aptness for universal unbelief, and a species
of bitter and contemptuous universal charitableness"—or, in
other words, a contemptuous rejection of all truth, and an
equally contemptuous indulgence of all error.

From the whole field of human scepticism we gather fruits
of essentially the same kind.   From the most abstruse reason-
ings of those who arrogate to themselves the exclusive title of
"profound thinkers," to the "Liberalism" of the demagogue,
and even to the cynical "*non-chalance*" of the London pleasure-
seeker, there is the same warp running through the whole
fabric of unbelief, however it may be diversified by various
colours in the weft.   Every unbeliever in Revelation believes
in nothing but himself—and does, in effect, set up his own
judgment and his own will as the supreme and only law.
Rationalists, Pantheists, Positivists, Atheists, infidels and
sceptics of every degree, together with demagogues and so-
called, but falsely called, " Liberals ", and money-seekers and
pleasure-seekers, "whose god is their belly "—Phil. iii. 19—
are all alike in one respect—namely, in the desire to "be as
gods."   Self, in one form or another, is their god—self-seeking
is their object, self-opinion is their law, and self-worship is
their religion.

If Genesis is "poetry, not history", how, then, is it that the
very principle which is there narrated to have been the temptation that "brought death into the world and all our woe", has
been found in practice to have been, from that moment to the
present, the world-wide temptation of our race, coextensive
with the human family ?.

Truly pride, or self-worship, bears witness to its origin, in the cold, heartless, hopeless "cynicism"—the death-like weariness of spirit—the dreary disgust of life and despair of good which even the unbelieving world's own organs avow to be the fruits of the loftiest human intellect apart from God and His revealed truth.

CHAPTER XIX.

Man a fallen being—objections to the Scripture account of Creation answered.—Proofs of the Fall—from the need of Education and Civilization—from the need of clothing—from the "pain and peril" of woman—and from the curse of labour.

ALL Scripture represents mankind as a *fallen* race of beings—fallen from a higher, purer, happier, more perfect state, into a state of moral depravity, intellectual incapacity, and bodily suffering ending in death.

The narrative of Genesis gives the history of this great and terrible change, and attributes it to wilful disobedience against God in the first human pair.

Now if this narrative is not literally and historically true, but only "poetical" and figurative, we must conclude that no such event as the Fall ever took place, and consequently that man is still in the same state by nature as when he was created.

If, on the other hand, the Scripture narrative *is* literally and historically true, then we shall certainly find the effects and evidences of some such fall in the present actual condition of mankind.

And, conversely, if such effects and evidences are found actually existing, then we must in all reason conclude that some such fall from original uprightness, purity, and happiness, must needs have taken place as the Book of Genesis records.

Do, then, the present actual nature and condition of mankind bear marks of having undergone some great alteration for the worse from what once they were ? Do we find that the facts of human nature, character, and life at the present moment bear out the narrative of Genesis ?

This is the question to which it will be the object of the present chapter to furnish an answer.

But before doing so, it seems necessary to notice a back-door of escape by which some sceptical objectors may run out from the argument altogether.

It is this :—That the Mosaic narrative of Creation itself is fabulous : and that consequently the present state of mankind, whatever it may be, is to be accounted for in some other way than by supposing any such event as *the Fall of man* to have taken place. That is to say, these objectors deny the very first statement of the Bible, that "in the beginning God created the heavens and the earth" : and they maintain that the world and its inhabitants came into being by some self-creative process.

This opinion is of course mere Atheism : but as it has been revived at this day by men of note and mis-directed science, it must not be wholly overlooked in this place.

It has been recently maintained by one writer of this school that "*creation* is only another name for our ignorance of the mode of production"—that new species "(man of course included) *must* have originated either out of the inorganic elements *or* out of previously organized forms ; *either* development *or* spontaneous generation *must* be true"—and the process is attributed to the "*self-evolving powers of nature.*" [1]

If this is all that can be said in favour of their theories by

---

[1] See the late Professor Baden Powell's article in *Essays and Reviews*—"On the Study of the Evidences of Christianity"—p. 166, 12th Ed.

men calling themselves "men of science" and "profound thinkers," it must be owned that they cannot say much. To assert that their theories *must* be true is a long way off from proving that they *are* true. In truth, such talk amounts to a confession that not a particle of proof can be produced for these very confident but very silly assertions—which are so far from having in them any science, that there is not even a grain of common sense in them. We ask, Why "*must* either development or spontaneous generation be true"? and no answer can be given but this—that a certain Professor, or a certain self-styled "man of science," has said so.—We ask again, What is meant by "the self-evolving powers of nature"? What is "nature"? and all the light we can obtain upon the subject from these professors of science is, that they themselves are in "*ignorance* of the mode of production."

Yet these are the theories put forward, with the loftiest assumption, as the latest improvements in knowledge, and the most advanced steps of "progress" in that course of scientific discovery which is to prove the Bible to be untrue!

If reason and common sense are to be our guides, it may perhaps seem to us more rational to believe that "in the beginning God created the heavens and the earth", than that the heavens and the earth created themselves—more rational to believe that God, having created the heavens and the earth, then proceeded to people them with creatures admirably adapted to inhabit and enjoy them, and crowned His work by creating Man upon the earth in His own image, endowed with wisdom and invested with authority to be God's own vicegerent over the works of His hands.

Reason also would suggest to us, that so far as all our observation, experience, and consciousness can reach, we find that all the works of *man* which are so framed as to serve a certain purpose, were framed with the *design* that they should serve that purpose. A watch—a steam-engine—an organ, were not constructed without a *design:* and that design was *in the mind of the artificer* before he constructed them. The watchmaker *intended* to make an instrument which should measure time—the steam-engine and the organ were *designed* for motion and music. But the machinery of the very simplest of the works of God is incomparably more exquisite and more complicated than the finest work of man's device. Is it not rational to conclude that, as the works of *man* are the works of a designing mind, so the works of "*nature*", which are immeasurably more exquisitely adapted to their purpose, were likewise *designed* for that purpose by a mind of infinitely superior wisdom? Yet if we were to reason about the works of man as Rationalists speculate about the works of God, we must come to the conclusion that the watch "developed" itself out of a stone, and that steam-engines and organs may have grown in a cabbage-garden. Such a conclusion would not be more absurd than the "science" according to which a man may have grown out of a mushroom, or a whale out of a Polar bear.

The rudest savage has more sense than such "philosophers." A missionary in Greenland was one day expressing to an Esquimaux, who had become a Christian, his astonishment at the ignorance and the stupidity in which he found this man's fellow-countrymen enveloped, in their notions concerning God, the human soul, and the duty of man towards the Great Spirit. "It is perfectly true," replied the Esquimaux, "that we have lived like ignorant Pagans, knowing nothing either of God or of the Saviour. Who was there to tell us any thing until you came amongst us? Nevertheless, do not imagine that a Greenlander never reflected at all. You shall hear my account of the line of reasoning which I have often followed. A *kajak*, (the canoe of the country) I said to myself, could not possibly construct itself, but must have been made by some one who understood this kind of work. And yet, the smallest bird that skims the air is better made than the most beautiful *kajak*. But no man knows how to make a bird. Then again, man was created more wonderfully than the rest of the animals on earth. Now, who created man? From his parents, without doubt, he received life, and they in their turn from their parents—but from whom did the first man receive his life, and whence did he come? It is said, out of the earth. Then why do we not see more men coming out of the earth now? Besides, the earth itself, and the sea, the sun, the moon, and the stars—whence came all these? There must, therefore, be a Being without beginning as also without end; and He must be infinitely more powerful, more wise, and more skilful than any man. He must also be very good, since all that He has made is so good and so useful. Oh if I could only know Him, how I would love Him! how I would honour Him! But who is there that has seen Him? Who that has spoken to Him? None of us. However, there may be, thought I, some men who have a knowledge of Him; how I wish I could find them and talk with them! This is what I used to say to myself. So then, as soon as I heard you speak of the Great Supreme Being, I believed with joy; and all that you announced to me was precisely that for which I had sighed so long." [1]

Will not this poor Pagan rise up in the judgment and condemn the "men of science," as they call themselves, who, with the full light of Revelation to guide them, shut their eyes against it, and prefer a darkness and a blindness worse than heathenism itself?

Dismissing, then, the absurdities of "science falsely so called", we return to the question whether the present actual state of the world bears marks of any such terrible event having taken place as *the Fall of man* described in Genesis. Are there any indications that the natural creation—earth, air, sea and sky, and the animal and vegetable worlds—have undergone any such change as would be involved in *the curse*—and that man himself, the noblest of all earthly beings, is not what once he was, physically, intellectually, and morally?

[1] *Rock*, July 28, 1869.

The favourite theory of those who deny the historical truth of Genesis is, that mankind are in a state of continual *progress* towards the perfection of their being : and civilization, education, and science, are relied upon as the means whereby this perfection is to be brought about. The "regeneration of society," is a thing of acknowledged necessity: and this necessary object is expected to be attained by a continual advancement in the arts, the sciences, and the conveniences of social life, and the humanizing and elevating effect which this improvement is imagined to be capable of effecting.

Now it is obvious that this very theory is a virtual acknowledgment of the fact that man is a fallen being.

For if not, how comes it that civilization, education, or improvement are necessary for mankind at all ? There is not another species of animals in all creation that stands in need of any such process. Every other kind of animal on the face of the earth is perfect from the first, and needs no artificial aid for the fulfilment of its appointed part in the great economy of nature. The horse which we see depicted in the carvings of Greece and Assyria two and three thousand years ago is precisely the same noble animal which we have now among us— and the fact that this noble animal, so evidently designed for man's use, still needs subjugation to man's will and purposes, is so far from being an argument against our conclusion that it confirms it. Man was placed by God in *authority* over all the lower animals, and doubtless with *power* to govern and control them all.[1] It is in perfect accordance with this statement that the lower animals are not now brought under subjection to man but by stratagem or force—for the *loss* of his original dominion over them was evidently a consequence of the Fall. When man threw off his own allegiance to God, he lost the allegiance of the subject creation to himself.

But we assert—in contradiction to the absurd theories of

[1] Gen. i. 26–28.

Darwin and others—that not an instance can be produced of any kind of animal having been essentially altered in its nature and natural properties since the world began. Lions have not become lambs—nor have wolves grown into shepherds' dogs.

Yet in defiance of all analogy, all history, and all known facts, we are told that man has grown up to the present condition of European civilization, from the "*state of nature*" in which he was first created, by his own unaided efforts through successive generations: and it is argued and expected, that a corresponding improvement for the future will complete the process of bringing the human race to a state of ultimate perfection both physical, intellectual, and moral.

And by a "state of nature" is meant a state of savage barbarism; such a state as that of the South Sea Islanders when they were first discovered, or of the Aborigines of Australia at the present moment—a state but little raised above the level of the brutes, and in some respects sunk below them.

Facts, however, are fatal to these fancies. Though it is *asserted* that men were created barbarians, and grew up into civilized and well-ordered societies by the force of inherent excellence of nature, *no instance of any such transformation has ever yet been produced.* The conclusion is inevitable that none ever took place. And it is mere idle talking to assume that any such thing *will* take place in future ages; since none has ever come to pass in the course of six thousand years.

And all history testifies that the natural process is just the reverse. Nations and tribes cut off from intercourse with the rest of the world do not improve—they invariably degenerate. The state of barbarism is not a "state of nature" in the sense usually intended. God never created savages—but men have *become* savages by a process of degeneration from age to age, and from a state of superior knowledge and mental culture. Though many instances can be shown of nations and tribes having been reclaimed from barbarism by the blessed influences of *Christianity*, in times comparatively modern, the very *earliest* uninspired records of the human race describe men as living, not in a state of barbarism, but in highly civilized societies.   The earliest histories of Assyria and Egypt represent those countries as civilized, not barbarous : and the lately uncovered palaces of the one, and the vast Pyramids of the other, are before our eyes to attest the truth of the representation.   None of the shallow "philosophers" of our day can point out the time when either the Hindûs or the Chinese were less civilized than at present.   The very exist- ence of the Sanskrit, now as a dead language, but containing the very fountains of all Hindû literature and religious creeds, is of itself a proof that the farther we trace back the history of any people the nearer we approach to the sources of their civilization.

The only exception to this truth is in the case of Christianity having been introduced among a people already sunk into a state more or less barbarous.

And this exception just completes the proof of what we are now insisting upon—viz., the truth of the Bible.   For if the Bible be, as we maintain, a revelation from God for the benefit of mankind, improvement must needs be one of its invariable results : and if, as, we farther maintain, man is a fallen and corrupted being, the Bible will prove to be the only adequate and sufficient means of his complete restoration.

The very fact, therefore, that man *requires* civilization, educa- tion, and improvement, points him out as an *anomaly* in creation. He is a broken link in the chain of universal being—a note out of tune amid Creation's harmony.

This is a remark forced upon us by the most cursory view of the case : and it is confirmed at every step in the course of a more detailed survey.   The Bible alone—and the Book of Genesis more especially—furnishes the key to unlock the mysteries and contradictions of man's nature and history.

It supplies, for example, the explanation of what would be otherwise altogether as mysterious as it is humiliating—the fact that man alone, of all created beings, requires *clothing*. One of the very first steps towards the civilization of a savage tribe is to clothe them—and absolute destitution of clothing is found only in connexion with the very lowest state of degradation and brutishness in which mankind have ever been discovered to exist. We ask, then, whence proceeds this primary necessity—this very first demand—of awakening sensibility? How comes it that man—the noblest being of earth's inhabitants—no sooner learns the first lesson of his education than he shrinks from himself, and from the exposure of "a state of nature," as a torture and a disgrace? Whence comes this intolerable sense of *shame*—this shrinking dependence upon an artificial covering—this dread of exposure, often stronger than the fear of death itself? There is nothing like it in all the rest of creation. Though "high art" pronounces the human form to be the most beautiful object of its study, the very first demand of civilized life is that it should be decently covered out of sight. And more than this—the sense of shame, and delicacy of feeling, become stronger just in proportion as the higher qualities of character are cultivated and improved. Together with the growth of all that is good and lovely in moral character there grows up a proportional sense of the degradation of "a state of nature."—How comes this?

Here is certainly a problem worth the study of those who set up "Science" and civilization as the true guides to human perfection.

It is impossible to deny the fact, and useless to evade it, that God's noblest work on earth is under a ban of dishonour and disgrace. Man is the only animal in creation that needs artificial clothing. Man is the only creature that comes into the world without a natural provision for its wants. Man alone, of all created beings, is overwhelmed with a sense of nakedness and shame. All other creatures are in "a state of nature ", and are in need of nothing—to man alone "a state of nature " would be a state intolerable and impossible.

We say, intolerable and impossible—for it is both. In every part of the globe except the warmer regions it would be impossible for mankind in "a state of nature" to exist at all: and even where this state is physically possible, it becomes intolerable at the very dawn of that state of civilization which is so much vaunted as the perfection of man's nature.

Now we maintain that the truth—the literal and historical truth—of Genesis is thus branded upon the very forehead of the human family. Why is there such a feeling as shame at all—or such a thing as need of clothing, not merely for warmth, but also for appearance? We challenge the whole crowd of atheistical and rationalistic "philosophers" to explain the mystery.

The Word of God explains it simply and sadly.—"They were both naked, the man and his wife, and were not ashamed." —Gen. ii. 25. This was a "state of nature" indeed—and the *only* state of nature in which God ever created man: a state in which man was "then most adorned, when unadorned the most", because adorned with that perfect purity of heart and integrity of mind which enabled him to look up into his Heavenly Father's face with confidence and joy. But the first act of disobedience was fatal—"the eyes of them both were opened, and they knew that they were naked."—Gen. iii. 7. Shame and fear fell upon them—they were seized with that mysterious and otherwise unaccountable shrinking from the light of day which is wrought into our very nature, and which is the very type and foreboding of that fearful agony of exposure which will overwhelm the ungodly when they stand in all the nakedness of a guilty soul before the Judgment-seat of God.—"Because thou sayest, I am rich, and increased with goods, and have need of nothing: and knowest not that thou art wretched, and miserable, and poor, and blind, and *naked:* I counsel thee to buy of me gold tried in the fire, that thou

mayest be rich; and white raiment, that thou mayest be
clothed, and that the shame of thy nakedness" (that is, thy
unforgiven sin) "do not appear."—Rev. iii. 18. From Genesis
to Revelation the Word of God is consistent and connected, as
inspired by the one Holy Spirit of God. *The sense of nakedness
is the consequence and type of Sin.* It is the awful warning,
branded by God Himself upon our very souls and bodies, of
the agonizing exposure and helpless wretchedness which will
overwhelm impenitent sinners at last.

Nor could the guilty pair dare to meet the eye of God or
the light of day till "unto Adam and to his wife did the Lord
God make coats of skins, and clothed them;"—Gen. iii. 21;—
an undeniable type and intimation of the great Atonement to
be afterwards made for sin by the death of the promised
Redeemer—as will be more fully shown hereafter. The fig-
leaves of their own devising were a miserable failure—and a
true illustration of the inability of man to cover the shame and
put away the guilt of past offences by any repentance or reformation of his own.

Another fact, equally anomalous and equally unaccountable
upon any natural principles, is the fact of the "great pain and
peril of childbirth". If we desire to arrive at truth, we must
dare to look facts in the face, and not seek to evade them
either on pretence of their being unimportant, or with a sneer
of ridicule. And here is a fact not to be disposed of either by
sneers of ridicule or smiles of contempt. Self-propagation is a
primary law of all animal and vegetable life—a law without
which that life must very soon become extinct. But in the
case of mankind alone, of all created beings, the continuation
of the race is attended with suffering, and even danger to life.

Again we challenge the whole circle of sceptical "philosophers" to solve the mystery. A fact so extraordinary, so
singular, and so terrible, must have a cause. Let Science, if it
is able, point it out: but if all science utterly fails here, let

those who deny the historical truth of Genesis confess that their system is futile and false.

It is a favourite theory with some of these so-called philosophers, that mankind are sprung, not from a single pair, but from several distinct families, created at different times and in different parts of the earth.   But, upon this theory, how comes it that the two last mentioned facts are *coextensive with the human race?*

The Bible explains this otherwise unfathomable mystery. "Unto the woman he said, I will greatly multiply thy sorrow and thy conception : in sorrow thou shalt bring forth children." —Gen. iii. 16.   Let but the words be allowed to mean what they must mean if they have any meaning at all, and all is plain.   The terrible infliction is seen to be a *penalty* imposed upon the race, on account of the sin of the one mother of us all.   "The woman being deceived was in the transgression ;" —1 Tim. 2. 14 ;—and, to this hour, throughout the whole habitable world, woman suffers the penalty which a mother alone can suffer.

The curse of *toil*, again, is another mystery of man's being which the book of Genesis alone explains.   Man alone, of all created beings, is condemned to toil.   There is not another species of animal on the face of the earth which is doomed to painful labour in order to procure the means of subsistence. The ant—the bee—the beaver, are no exceptions to this rule. There is nothing in their busy activity at all comparable to the exhausting toil of man.   "In the sweat of thy face shalt thou eat bread, till thou return unto the ground," is a curse not realized in the condition of any other creature but of mankind alone.   And of mankind it is true to the present hour. The daily bread is earned by daily toil—and the daily toil is never done till the weary limbs rest in the grave.

P

CHAPTER XX.

The literal truth of Genesis alone accounts for the existence of Death and Disease in man, created originally in the image of God—or for the miseries of mankind—or for the Curse evidently blighting and blasting the earth—or for the worst of all evils, Moral Corruption— or for the conflict between good and evil in the human Conscience.

THE *grave!* Yes—and here is another mystery—the solemn, ghastly mystery of *death*.

How is it that death has entered into the world—or *disease*, which is but the beginning of death ?

Here, indeed, mankind may seem not to be alone. The lower animals die, as well as man. Two things, however, are to be considered : first, that the death of a dumb animal is an event not of the same nature as the death of a man—and secondly, that the death of the lower animals is apparently in consequence of their sharing in the curse pronounced upon man. The death of a dumb animal is the *extinction* of the animal—the death of a man is but the temporary separation of the body from the soul which can never die. And the death of a man is as much more terrible than the death of a beast as an eternity of punishment is more terrible than mere annihilation.

We must say, then, bearing in mind the peculiar nature of the death to which man is liable, that he is in this respect also an anomaly in creation. Born immortal, yet doomed to die— conscious of his short and uncertain tenure of all here on earth, and forced to look forward to an eternity of existence in some unknown world—man, with a guilty conscience and a trembling heart, both sighs at his present lot, and fears and hates his future destiny. The enjoyment of life is chilled by the fear of approaching death—or if this be for a time overcome, it is only by an insane and reckless levity of mind—a complete oblivion of all but the present moment—such as that which prompted the heathen's motto, "Let us eat and drink, for to-morrow we die." Such a sentiment is an abjuration of humanity itself—a rejection of the very Reason which raises man above the brute.

And all these facts acquire a thousandfold intensity of force and meaning when it is considered farther, that man was *created in the image of God.* This is not denied, but, in a sense, admitted and maintained even by infidels themselves. "The image of God which is in every man" is a mode of expression familiar even to those who deny the very first principles of revealed religion. Taking the admission even as they mean it, we must say, that if the image of God, in *any* sense, is in man, it is strange indeed that man should be the wretched being that he is.

But there is nothing in infidelity more strange than its inconsistency—nothing in infidels more marvellous than their blindness in not seeing, or else their dishonesty in not duly accrediting, the plainest, saddest, and most terrible facts—as well as those which are most blessed and encouraging.

Now let a fair and intelligent survey be taken of mankind—not as poets dream, or "philosophers" theorize—but as the hard, coarse, vulgar facts and phases of every-day human life force themselves upon our notice. The man who shuts himself up in his study, and frames imaginary commonwealths based upon imaginary facts, is not a philosopher but a foolish dreamer. He may amuse himself, but he will never benefit mankind. If we must have philosophy, let us have a philosophy that deals with men and things, not as they might have been, but as they are.

And what a spectacle is presented to a thoughtful observer by the actual condition of mankind, even at the best! There is no country upon earth more highly civilized than our own—no country, that is, which has advanced nearer to that state of perfection which the admirers of human nature expect as the result of human development. And we survey this advanced civilization at the end of six thousand years of human "progress"—a time certainly long enough to bring out the real tendencies of human nature. And what do we see? such a state of virtue and happiness as we are taught to expect by the advocates of human perfectibility?

Let us glance first at the *physical* condition of man, and of earth his habitation.

Let any one take a walk through the streets of London, or any of our large towns, and note with observant eye and reflecting mind the objects presented to his view. Let him make his observations, not among the exceptional scenes of luxury and splendour which meet the eye in the parks and palaces of "the upper ten thousand," but among the masses—the millions—the throng—the multitude—who form the bulk and body of the population. These toiling, anxious, care-worn beings, hurrying to and fro with looks of excited hope, or lingering in desponding sadness—are these the creatures made in the image of God, and born for immortality? This incessant struggle—this continual battle for life—is this the state which God intended his noblest creature, man, to experience as what the Heavenly Father selected for the happiness of His children? We hear much from the Rationalists of our day about "the Fatherhood of God"—by which is meant that He is, in an equal degree and in the same sense, the Father of all mankind alike. Is this, then, we ask, the best that God has been able and willing to do for His children? What else is the condition of mankind in general but a condition of *penal servitude?* What is life, to the most, but a scene of condemnation to hard labour for life? Work—work—work—is the sum and substance of man's occupation here on earth—work, not as an occupation which can be assumed or laid aside at pleasure, but as the very condition of existence. Mankind must either work or starve. The primeval curse is still in force—and man must win his bread by the sweat of his brow. There is no intermission of his toil, except by that very institution wherein God has tempered judgment with mercy—the blessed Sabbath :—that very institution which unbelievers would sweep away if they could, so that the curse should be unmitigated as well as un-repealed.

According to human laws, penal servitude for life is the severest punishment next to death. But here is the fact before our eyes that all mankind are actually condemned to hard labour for life by the very necessity of toiling for bread. It may be said that this is only by the laws of nature. We reply, that it is an *exception* to the laws of nature. There is not another instance to be found throughout creation in which any one of God's creatures is forced to provide for its own existence by severe and unremitting labour.

And we say, that such a condition of life bears upon it the very stamp and character of being *penal*. The condition in which multitudes of mankind pass their lives is such, that if it had been imposed upon them by human laws it would have been felt to be a severe punishment. What is life to a man whose days are spent at the bottom of a coal-pit, or in a mine, or an iron-furnace, or a glass-house, or a pottery? What is life to one who has no leisure to enjoy it? The desk—the counting-house—the shop—the factory, are not scenes of enjoyment, but of compulsory toil, from which men gladly escape as soon as each day's toil is over. It makes no difference that the toil is not imposed by human law: the fact remains that it *is* imposed, and not undertaken of a man's free choice. There remains also the fact, that the necessity of toil is caused by such conditions as it belongs to the Creator alone to order and control. And these facts, taken together, do certainly constitute a real proof that man's condition in this present life has in it much of the nature of a penalty, a condemnation, and a curse. We rise up early, and late take rest, and eat the bread of carefulness. We spend our youth in a course of long and often severe training, in preparation for an after-life of labour, either of mind or body, still more arduous and exhausting. And this labour continues in general till death. Many, perhaps the most of men, die like a jaded horse in harness—some are able to realize the hope of their lives, and end their days in retirement and leisure. And what then? The very leisure they have coveted is to the most a burden and a misery. Where they hoped to grasp a treasure they find that they have but clutched at a shadow; disappointment sours their temper and embitters even their success; and they are forced to feel, if not openly to confess, that the end of all their efforts and hopes is "vanity and vexation of spirit."

Yet these are the most favourable cases. How much worse are others! See the crowds of wretched, haggard, starved, and squalid beings that move about—like spectres more than men and women—in the courts and alleys of our great towns. Follow the City Missionary and Scripture-reader to the murky dens and creaking garrets which none but such men dare or endure to visit—breathe, if breathe you can, the fetid atmosphere, and see the sickening sight, of fermenting filth and festering disease—discover the abodes where whole families cower and shiver in cold, nakedness, and hunger—where mothers pine and die in starvation, and babes hang in vain upon the withered breast—where men have shrunken limbs and trembling hands, and children have pale cheeks and hollow eyes—where hair grows grey almost in childhood, and almost infant fingers are worn with toil, and pinched with penury. These are facts ignored by the carpet knights of philanthropy—the advocates of human perfectibility—but they are facts only too familiar to the practical philanthropists who

busy themselves, not with weaving fine-spun theories of
humanity in their easy chairs, but in "*visiting* the fatherless
and widow in their affliction", in "dealing their bread to the
hungry and clothing the naked with a garment," and in carrying to the sick and dying that which alone can "comfort all
that mourn"—the glad tidings of a Saviour's love.

And these, and many more, are the facts we must confront
and account for. The few who are looked upon in the world
as fortune's favourites—the rich and noble, the princely and
the proud—may seem to be raised above the common level of
human suffering: though in truth it is not so—for none are
exempt from pain, disease and sorrow·; and the miseries of
disappointed ambition and wounded pride are often not less
bitter than more substantial griefs. But in any case, these are
the few—the very few—one in ten thousand—among the great
mass and multitude. Mankind in general do at the present
moment fulfil the painful part allotted to Adam and his posterity—"In the sweat of thy face shalt thou eat bread."
Every article of food and clothing is obtained by labour—and
the rich man who is "clothed in purple and fine linen, and
fares sumptuously every day", is dependent upon the toil of
the poor no less than the poor themselves.

And it is a notable fact that the vaunted civilization of the
day does nothing to mitigate the curse of labour; but on the
contrary greatly increases it by multiplying artificial wants,
and by stimulating to an enormous degree the desire of wealth
and luxury. The original sentence which condemned man to
labour, though severe, is merciful in its severity. In the corrupt moral state into which man has fallen by sin, the curse of
labour is more tolerable than would have been the curse of
idleness. The necessity of toiling for bread keeps men out of
evils infinitely worse than labour. It is certain that if the
earth should yield a spontaneous supply of all things necessary
for human wants, the world would speedily become one mass
of corruption not a whit better than Sodom and Gomorrha.

Moreover, there is mercy in the physical effect of labour upon the body, a well as in its moral effect upon the character. The ploughman's work is not only tolerable, but healthful. The simple labours of the husbandman brace the limbs, and invigorate the frame, of the labourer. And if mankind were content with the simple wants and employments of the agricultural and pastoral modes of life—such as we find described in the history of the Old Testament patriarchs—the miseries of human life would be reduced to a mere fraction of their present amount.

The enormous majority of human suffering is not what has been inflicted by God—it is what has been, and is, self-inflicted by man. It is not the labour required to procure the necessaries of life that causes the most part of human suffering, but it is the indulgence of human passions and vices. It is the love of money, the lust of riches, the thirst for gold—or it is ambition, the lust of power and dominion—or it is the love of pleasure, the lusts of sensuality, the low, debasing appetites of the body—it is some one, or all, of these that have deluged the world with misery. But this remark is rather in the way of anticipation.

In observing the facts and causes of human suffering, we must not pass over the evident disorders of the natural world.

The earth, man's appointed habitation, is in truth barely habitable for man. The Polar regions, with their eternal barricades of ice, forbid approach. The Torrid Zone, though not absolutely uninhabitable, is almost insupportable even to the natives, and deadly to all the rest of mankind. The burning sands of Africa and Arabia, the sultry plains of Persia and India, and the inhospitable and dreary steppes of Tartary, occupy large portions of the earth's surface. The vast interior of Australia is believed to be uninhabitable for want of water: and the immense continent of Africa remains to this day for the most part an unexplored and unknown country, save to its own barbarian tribes.

And while large portions of the earth are thus either inaccessible or ill suited to man, its very best and loveliest scenes are still visibly under the primeval sentence, "Cursed is the ground for thy sake: in sorrow shalt thou eat of it all the days of thy life: thorns also and thistles shall it bring forth to thee." There is no other weed on earth provided with such a profusion of winged seed, or which propagates itself with such disastrous rapidity, as the useless and noxious thistle. There is no other tree which so universally and so readily occupies waste ground as the prickly, torturing thorn. To this hour the primeval curse is carried into effect. The ground does not bring forth spontaneous crops of wheat and barley for man's use, but it does bring forth thorns and thistles for his punishment. The fact is unaccountable without the record of the Fall. Amidst all the wonderful and beneficent provision for man's wants which every where abounds—in earth, sea, and sky—there is provision also for man's punishment—the very provision declared in Genesis, and realized to the present hour.

In every department of nature there is evident *disorder*. The Greeks called the world by the beautiful name κόσμος— *order*—and order, the most accurate and exquisite, is its general characteristic. But this only makes the disorder the more strange and unaccountable. The yearly supply of rain, in India or Africa, fails, and hundreds of thousands of human beings perish of hunger. Earthquakes make the solid ground heave and undulate like water over thousands of miles in extent—the sea recoils, and returns in a wave which whirls the largest ships about like nutshells, and swallows up both ships and towns together—the ground itself opens, and engulphs a whole city in a yawning chasm. Volcanoes reveal the existence of vast oceans of fire beneath our feet, and threaten to make the overthrow of Pompeii no solitary example of their terrors. Fevers, pestilences, cholera, influenza, brood in the atmosphere and ride upon the breeze. Some secret influence poisons the air, and breeds potatoe-disease at one time, vine-

disease at another, dealing out famine and death through a
whole population. Even in the ordinary course of things it
may truly be said that the world swallows up its inhabitants.
If the land is beset with perils, much more so is the sea.   Three
thousand seamen are computed to perish annually around our
own shores : the bottom of the ocean is strewn with the bones
and treasures of shipwrecked men. Not a year passes but
storm and tempest, thunder and lightning, flood and fire, strike
down multitudes of the human family.   Health, and life itself,
are only maintained by a continual struggle against adverse
influences and besetting dangers.

And what shall be said of the awful fact that no man is sure
of life even for an hour ! How shall we account for the existence of an evil so terrific—a doom so dreadful—as *Death?* Is
it a part of man's original nature that he must *die?* Of all
created objects known to us, the human form and feature is
the noblest and the loveliest—of all loathsome things which can
meet the eye or sicken the heart, the most loathsome—the
most revolting—is a *corpse.* The one seems to be a concentra-
tion of beauty—a triumph (if so one may speak) of the art of
God Himself, delighting in His own works: the other a combination of all that is most repulsive—most ghastly—most
appalling.

Of all the foolish speculations of science falsely so called,
none is more foolish than the attempt to make out death to be
a natural event. How can that be natural from which every
feeling of our nature recoils with unutterable dread and horror?
How can that be natural which is the very destruction of
nature itself? The infliction of death is the severest penalty
of human law—the most terrible punishment for the most
atrocious crimes : how can it be consistent with this fact that it
should be an event only in the ordinary course of nature? It
is certainly more reasonable to believe that what is the heaviest
punishment man can inflict is itself inflicted as a punishment
upon man by his Maker. By the laws of man, the most guilty

of men are condemned to death—but by the decree of God, *all* men are condemned to death. Does God, then, impose upon a whole race of *innocent* beings the terrors and the dreadful doom which man himself inflicts only on the most depraved. and desperate of criminals?

But farther:—*Disease* is but the beginning of death: and disease is incidental to the whole family of mankind, and must come under the same general argument.

Is it consonant with our ideas of a benevolent Creator to suppose that He has made the very noblest of His creatures, without their own fault, subject to all the pain, misery, and mutilation caused by disease? Has God at once created in the frame of man the elements of perfect health and consummate beauty, and also marred His own work by implanting in it the seeds of every loathsome and torturing disease that can corrupt and destroy it? The disorders incidental to man are a multitude the very description of which fills volumes. They fasten like vultures upon our frames. They poison our blood —they corrupt our flesh—they corrode our very bones. They run riot in every tissue of our bodies—they torture us with excruciating agonies—they defy our skill, and seem to mock at our misery. And yet we are to believe that disease, as well as death, is a part of our original nature! No—it cannot be. Disease and death are the effects of a *curse*. They are *punishments*. Let them be regarded as such, and all inconsistency vanishes at once. Let the narrative of Genesis be admitted as historically true, and the mystery is unravelled—the facts of human life, and the facts recorded in Scripture, are found to be in perfect harmony.

But the darkest shadows which cast a gloom over man's condition are not those of mere bodily suffering, disease, or even death itself—dreadful as these are. There is a worse evil than any of these, or all of them put together—an evil which imparts even to death itself its bitterest bitterness—its sharpest sting.

This worst of all evils is MORAL CORRUPTION—the corruption of man's very heart and moral nature.

What a scene is presented to a thoughtful observer of the very commonest facts of human life! Our dangers, difficulties, and miseries are not such only as even the anger of a righteous God has inflicted upon us. Our worst evils are those which we inflict upon ourselves and upon each other. The world we live in is a world of violence and wrong—a very haunt of assassins and a den of thieves. Why is it that we are never safe for a single night but within bars and bolts, and have need to live like men in a besieged fortress, or an enemy's country? Every man's house must be his castle of defence, and every city and town must be guarded by patrols and policemen day and night, or else no man's property or life would be safe for a single hour. And as it is between man and man, so it is between nation and nation. Ten millions of soldiers at the present moment are armed and drilled, and kept ready by the mutual fears or ambitious designs of the sovereigns of Europe, to shed the blood of their fellow-creatures: and to no one object are the skill, and science, and energy of the nations so eagerly directed as to the perfecting of the most deadly weapons of destruction. And this too, not among savage tribes to whom the only known law is the law of the strongest, but among the most civilized and refined nations of the world. Why, we ask, are these things so? Even Rationalists admit that man was originally made in the image of God: how comes it, then, that men in the most improved social condition are like beasts of prey, always on the watch to kill, devour, and destroy?

Nor is the case better as regards the commercial transactions of life. Fraud as well as force besets us on every side. The ingenuity of lawyers is taxed to devise words exact enough to prevent men from overreaching one another—the tricks of trade are matters of universal complaint — "commercial morality" is become a bye-word of reproach. Neither rank, reputation, nor high professions afford any guarantee for even common honesty: and things are come to such a pass that enterprise is checked, and the business of the world is crippled, because no man knows whom to trust. The boasted science of the day is made instrumental for evil as well as good: and among the arts which are studied the most eagerly and practised the most successfully is the art of cheating.

The very necessaries of life are turned to our injury by the adulteration of almost every article of food: and the cleverness of the age is exhibited in the skill with which the fraud is concealed. The warmest advocates of the virtuousness of human nature are careful enough never to *act* upon their own principles. What would become of the honest simpleton who should manage his worldly affairs with unsuspecting confidence in the universal integrity of mankind—or who should believe that those with whom he has to deal are always as anxious for their neighbour's interest as for their own? If human nature were virtuous, the simpleton would be safe. Every man might then trust his neighbour with uncounted treasure, and a child might walk through all the streets of London, with a purse of gold in his hand, untouched.

But if the mere mention of such a state of happy innocence sounds like bitter scoffing—if almost every newspaper reveals some new atrocity of crime or some improved refinement of duplicity, we ask again, *Why* is it so? whence comes this amazing prevalence of evil—this teeming abundance of every thing base, sordid, and abominable—this rampant activity of every vile passion, every selfish instinct, every heartless motive? The wilderness of the natural world is not more overgrown with the thorns and thistles of the curse than is the field of the moral and social world rife with the vicious luxuriance of every immoral principle.

Here, again, is a fact which, but for the narrative of Genesis, must have remained for ever a mystery inscrutable to man : but which, viewed in the light of Scripture, is at least accounted for—however in its depths it must still remain, to finite minds, unfathomable.

The mystery of man's nature, however, is not merely the mystery of the *existence* of moral evil—which perhaps must always remain a depth impenetrable to our faculties. It is the *co-existence of good and evil in one nature* that baffles all human wisdom to explain. We can conceive of a nature absolutely good, and of a nature absolutely evil :—neither of these is wholly unintelligible. But a nature partly good, and partly evil—a being knowing good from evil—and not only so, but acknowledging the goodness of the good, and the mischief of the evil, and acknowledging too the duty of doing the good and shunning the evil, yet doing the evil and refusing the good,—this is a mystery utterly inexplicable by any principle known to moral philosophy.

To describe the enormous wickedness of the world would be a task beyond the reach of the most voluminous treatise— indeed, beyond the reach of all human language or thought : and even were it practicable, it would not be altogether to our present purpose. It is not merely that all human history is a history of covetousness, blood, treachery, pride, lust, false-hood, cruelty, intense and heartless selfishness—varied in an almost infinite diversity of manifestation : but it is that all this immensity of iniquity is practised by beings possessed of knowledge and feelings which condemn their own acts. The heathen poet's confession,

> ———Video meliora proboque,
> Deteriora sequor[1]—

was the sentiment of one who yet lived and died a profligate.

[1] Ovid, Met., 7. 21.

Three is a conscience in man which bids him do right—there are passions in man which impel him to do wrong. It is this contradiction and conflict of opposite principles in the same being—felt and acknowledged by every child of man—that is the mystery and enigma of human nature. The fact has been observed and commented upon by the sages of all antiquity: but in vain have they laboured to explain its cause.

The simple narrative of Genesis at once supplies the clue which enables us to thread the mazes of this labyrinth. A single act of wilful disobedience by man against his Maker unhinged the moral balance of his nature. The knowledge of good, the sense of duty, remained indelibly graven on his conscience: but the spirit which had cast off allegiance to God lost the allegiance of its lower instincts to itself. Man had become a rebel against God: and man's own passions became rebels against himself. Appetites adapted and intended to obey, began to get the mastery, and to rule. The being who had refused to be the willing servant of God became the slave of his own unruly lusts. And thus did man become a *fallen* being—fallen from the high office of God's vicegerent on earth, from the favour of his heavenly Father, and from the uprightness and self-government of his own moral constitution.

The narrative of this fearful depravation of man's nature is not merely credible, but thoroughly in accordance with the principles of true science. For it assigns an adequate cause to known effects: it solves the otherwise inexplicable enigma of man's self-contradictory nature: and it fully accounts for all the melancholy excesses of man's ungovernable passions throughout a blood-stained history of six thousand years. It explains how man was indeed first created in the image of God, and yet has sunk below the level of the beasts that perish. The glassy mirror of an unruffled lake reflects the sweet light of heaven and the face of nature: but the troubled water stirred by angry winds does but cast up mire and dirt. The same nature which, in its first perfection, reflected the image of God, is now but a troubled sea of conflicting passions. The image of God is lost, and can never be restored but by the same Almighty Creator who said at the first, "Let us make man in our image, after our likeness."

Thus is all Scripture in perfect harmony with itself, as inspired by the one mind and Spirit of God. Man's sin required an Atonement, without which it was impossible it could be forgiven consistently with God's own righteous law—and man's fall required a second creation of that image of God—that character of perfect uprightness, goodness, and truth—in which his soul was formed at first.

To meet the former necessity, the Son of God, as He himself declared, came into the world "to give his life a ransom for many"—Matt. xx. 28:—and with regard to the latter necessity, He said to Nicodemus, "Verily, verily I say unto thee, Except a man be born of water and of the Spirit, he cannot enter into the kingdom of God."—John iii. 5.

CHAPTER XXI.

The promise of a Redeemer—the universal practice of animal Sacrifice—
Cain both the first Ritualist and the first Rationalist—his offering
uncommanded and insincere—Animal Sacrifice divinely appointed as
the expression of Repentance and Faith in the promised Atonement.

THE sentence of punishment was not merely accompanied, but, with considerate tenderness, was even preceded, by a promise of mercy. "Unto the serpent he said, I will put enmity between thee and the woman, and between thy seed and her seed: IT SHALL BRUISE THY HEAD, AND THOU SHALT BRUISE HIS HEEL."—Gen. iii. 15.

In the promise that the Seed of the woman should bruise the Serpent's head, there was the first intimation that the case of the guilty pair was not altogether hopeless—for that of the woman's posterity there should arise a Deliverer who should destroy the Tempter and his power: and in the announcement that the Serpent should bruise the heel of the promised Deliverer, there was given an intimation that the work of deliverance would be effected at the cost of *suffering* to the Deliverer Himself.

Thus was the first outline sketched of the great work of REDEMPTION BY JESUS CHRIST—and presented before the downcast eyes of the trembling transgressors.

A farther intimation of the nature of the Redeemer's work

Q

was given when "unto Adam and to his wife did the Lord God make coats of skins, and clothed them."—Gen. iii. 21. As the permission to use animal food was not given till after the Flood, the animals whose skins were thus employed could not have been killed for food. It is evident that they were put to death for the *purpose* of using their skins as clothing. Whether they were offered in sacrifice to God we are not informed, nor is it material whether they were so or not. The significant fact remains, that the guilty pair were clothed each by means of the death of an innocent animal. A more expressive symbol cannot be conceived. As the shame of nakedness was relieved by the covering taken from animals slain for the purpose, so it was intimated that the shame of guilt could be removed only by the *death* of the promised Redeemer.

And thus was introduced the ordinance of SACRIFICE, as the appointed manner of approaching God in worship. Thus it was revealed that the only hope of forgiveness was wrapped up in the promise of a Deliverer who was to be the sinner's *Saviour* by being the sinner's *Substitute*. And the institution of Sacrifice was adapted, with admirable wisdom and fitness, to afford the sinner a means of expressing penitence for his sin, and faith in the promise of pardon through the promised Redeemer. Abel's offering of the firstlings of his flock was accepted because it was prompted by feelings of repentance and faith; Cain's offering of the fruit of the ground was rejected because it was made without regard to the appointed ordinance of Sacrifice—that is, without the acknowledgment of sin, and without faith in the promised Deliverer. And from that time forward, through all the patriarchal ages, and through all the elaborate institutions of the Mosaic Law, no worshipper could be accepted without Sacrifice—as the appointed mode of expressing "repentance toward God, and faith in our Lord Jesus Christ," the promised Redeemer—"the Lamb of God," which should "take away the sin of the world." When the one great and awful Sacrifice for sin was offered by Christ

Himself upon the Cross at Calvary, the *typical* meaning of all the sacrifices of lambs and of bullocks, from Abel's downwards, was openly declared.   The eye of faith was thenceforth directed to the "one sacrifice for sins for ever", which the Son of God had offered upon the Cross—and the typical sacrifices were no longer required to be offered.   The occasion for them had passed away ; since they had been replaced by the offering of Christ Himself.   The type had been superseded by the Antitype—the shadow by the substance.

Now one of the most remarkable facts in the history of mankind is *the universal prevalence of* SACRIFICE *as a mode of worship* among all nations.

And this fact amounts to a demonstration—as clear as any circumstantial evidence can possibly supply—of the literal and historical truth of Genesis.

If, indeed, there were any natural connexion between worshipping God and killing an animal, then the custom of animal sacrifice would be no proof that it was ordained by God and derived from the first human pair.   There is in all mankind, for example, a moral conscience, and a general sentiment of religion : but the common origin of all mankind from a single pair, though real, is not proved by the possession of a conscience and a feeling of religion ; because these are properties of human nature, without which a creature in human shape would not be a man, but a monster.   But it is otherwise with the custom of Sacrifice.   The general sentiment of religion is *natural* to man—but what natural connexion can be imagined between the sentiment of religion and the killing of an animal ? Viewed merely in the light of nature, there is absolutely no relation between them.   The two ideas have nothing whatever in common.   Be it so, that a feeling of gratitude to God, or a desire to enjoy His favour, should suggest the idea of making Him an offering ; yet what feeling could possibly suggest the idea that He would be pleased with cruelty inflicted upon an innocent and gentle lamb ?   The notion of a God who takes delight in the mere blood and dying throes of a harmless animal is absolutely revolting. The better feelings of our nature rise up in horror against such an idea : and the more we attribute to human nature of that goodness which Rationalists are so anxious to claim for it, the more must we repudiate, as impossible and incredible, the notion that any natural sentiment of religion could suggest the practice of animal sacrifices. Yet the practice has been universal, in all countries, and in all ages of the world before the Christian era.

Upon this point, all authors are agreed. No one, whether orthodox or infidel, ventures to deny the absolute *universality* of the practice.

Yet no one ever has given, or can give, any rational account of the *reason and origin* of it, except those who receive the testimony of Scripture that it was appointed by revelation from God.

Even the more reflecting among the heathens themselves, while conforming to the universal custom of sacrificing animals, wondered at their own act, in their ignorance of its origin. Spencer remarks—" The material of sacrifices (the flesh of cattle, and their shed blood, &c.) is so vile, and so far removed from the supreme majesty of God, that no one of any discernment but would easily judge that sacrifices are wholly superfluous and altogether unworthy of God. And indeed, so far were the politer heathens from thinking sacrifices agreeable to the nature of their gods, that it not seldom occurred to them to wonder *from what source* a rite so cruel, and so foreign to the nature of the gods, came into the hearts of man, spread itself so widely, and adhered so tenaciously to their customs."[1]

This ignorance of the origin of their own sacrificial system among the heathens is the more remarkable, inasmuch as they nevertheless regarded their sacrifices as *expiatory*, and offered them as such. "It is notorious", says Archbishop Magee,

---

[1] Spenser *De Leg. Heb.* lib. iii. diss. ii. c. 4, sect. 2, p. 772.

"that all nations, Jews and heathens, before the time of Christ, entertained the notion that the displeasure of the offended Deity was to be averted by the sacrifice of an animal; and that to the shedding of its blood they imputed their pardon and reconciliation. In the explication of so strange a notion, and of the universality of its extent, unassisted reason must confess itself totally confounded. And accordingly we find Pythagoras, Plato, Porphyry, and other reflecting heathens, express their wonder *how* an institution so dismal, and big with absurdity, could have spread through the world." [1]

Much greater is the marvel that the savage rite of *human* sacrifice has been almost, if not quite,[2] as extensively practised as that of inferior animals. For in this case, there was evidently a dread of the wrath of the gods, and a desire to avert it, as much more urgent than in the case of mere animal sacrifices, as the life of a man was esteemed of more worth than the life of a dumb animal. Accordingly, we find that among the Romans, as well as the Greeks, recourse was had to human sacrifices in cases of the greatest danger and emergency: and "among the Phœnicians it was customary, in great and public calamities, for princes and magistrates to offer up, in sacrifice to the avenging demons, the dearest of their offspring *as a ransom*".[3]

Now it cannot reasonably be doubted that a practice so unnatural and so revolting as that of sacrificing harmless animals, and still more, innocent persons—even unoffending children, the very sons and daughters of the sacrificers—must have had its origin in circumstances which had made a very deep and lasting impression on the minds of mankind. And the fact that this practice was universal throughout the ancient world,

---

[1] *Atonement and Sacrifice*, vol. ii., p. 51.

[2] Ibid, vol. i., p. 97.

[3] Ibid.—That the human and animal sacrifices offered by the ancient heathens were universally regarded by them as *expiatory*, is fully proved by this learned writer.

proves that these circumstances must have taken place before mankind had been scattered from the spot which had been the cradle of the human race. It could not therefore have arisen at any later time than when the whole of mankind were comprised within the one family of Noah.

But it did not originate with Noah. It had been in use from the time of Adam through all the ages down to the Flood.

We are thus thrown back, for the origin of Sacrifice, to the very time specified in Genesis—the time of Adam's fall, and of Abel's offering. We are shut up, by the irresistible logic of facts, to the conclusion that the practice of animal sacrifice could not, and did not, originate in any natural feelings of religion, but from the express appointment of God Himself. And the horrid customs of the heathen, in sacrificing human victims to their gods, are shown to have been merely corruptions of the primeval and divinely appointed ordinance, in which fallen man had been instructed to draw near to God with the blood of slain animals, in token of his repentance toward God, and his faith in the promised Redeemer whose blood was to take away the sin of the world.

The contrast between Cain's offering and Abel's is striking and instructive. Cain "brought *of the fruit of the ground* an offering unto the Lord." It was the offering of so-called "*natural religion*":—a religion in which there is neither acknowledgment of sin, nor faith in the Atonement of the Cross. —Abel's offering "of the firstlings of his flock and of the fat thereof" was the offering, not of natural religion, but of faith in God. It expressed both confession of sin, and faith in the promised Atonement.

Cain's offering was the offering of "voluntary humility", presumptuous self-will, and self-righteousness—both uncommanded, and insincere. That it was uncommanded, is evident from the history: that it was insincere, is evident from the fact that it was offered in disregard of the ordinance of Sacrifice as

THE Divinely appointed mode of approaching God in worship. As without sincerity there can be no real worship, so without obedience there can be no real sincerity.

And most curious and instructive it is to mark how, in this first recorded act of "voluntary humility" and "will-worship" there were contained the germs of every system of error which has afflicted the Church of God from that time to the present.

The course of error, as manifested first in the Church of the old world, and secondly in the Christian Church, has always divided itself into two main channels. The one may be described as *Formalism* or *Ritualism*, the other as *Rationalism*. The Formalist is distinguished by his rigid and exaggerated attachment to forms and ceremonies—the Rationalist by his contempt of them, and by his assertion of the supreme right of man to judge for himself, by his own natural reason, concerning truth and error in religion, and concerning the proper way and manner of worshipping God. The Formalist, or Ritualist, distorts and encumbers Revelation by ceremonial inventions, which, under the pretext of doing homage to God, do in reality dishonour and displease Him : the Rationalist, while equally professing a love for truth and zeal for God, contemptuously rejects Revelation, acknowledges no inspiration but the inspiration of each man's own mind and intuition, and denies the supernatural altogether.

In our Lord's time, the two "schools of thought," as it is fashionable now to call them, were very strongly marked. The Ritualists of that day were the *Pharisees*—the Rationalists were the *Sadducees*.

The Ritualists and Rationalists of our own time need no description. Under the former term is included the great apostasy of the Church of Rome, and the whole Ritualist and extreme High Church party nominally contained within the Church of England. Under the latter is comprised that whole "school of thought," unhappily too prominent in these times, whose opinions are represented in "Essays and Reviews", "Ecce Homo", the writings of Bunsen and the German Neologists, and more or less in too many of the popular periodicals and journals of the day. Socinians, Arians, Latitudinarians and Freethinkers of every grade, must take their place under the same general denomination of Rationalists.

Both alike—Ritualist and Rationalist—"make the word of God of none effect", but in different ways. The Ritualist overlays it with "traditions" and inventions of men, which in reality supersede it: the Rationalist undermines it by the claim to judge of its truth according to his own ideas of what is probable or improbable—rejecting whatever does not pass the scrutiny of his own "verifying faculty." The one destroys the effect of God's word by "*adding* to" it—the other by "*taking away*" from it.

But how are these two opposite systems of error both recognizable in the offering of Cain? The answer is easy. Cain was the first Ritualist, in that he observed a *form* of worship similar in pretence and in appearance to the appointed sacrifice, though essentially and radically different: he was the first Rationalist in that the form he chose to observe was one *devised by himself* according to his own notions of what was right and proper, and in open contempt of the revealed will of God.

Ritualism and Rationalism are not so widely different as they may at first sight appear. The North and South Poles are on opposite sides of the earth—but they agree in being both alike frozen regions of desolation and death. Ritualism and Rationalism are the two opposite Poles of error. In the first recorded example of them, both were united in one and the same individual: and from that time to the present, however antagonistic may sometimes have been their attitude, there has always been a strong sympathy between them. The Pharisees and Sadducees were agreed in condemning and crucifying the Lord of glory: and Ritualists and Rationalists, at the present moment, are working together, though in different ways, to undermine and overthrow the whole fabric of belief in Christian truth. Unbelievers of every sect can sympathize and combine in opposing the revealed and inspired Word of God.

The sum of what has been here advanced on the subject of Sacrifice is briefly this :—

It is a fact admitted on all hands that animal sacrifice has been a mode of worship universal among all heathen nations in all ages of the world, as well as among the Jews until the time of Christ.

This practice could not have originated in any natural sense of religion, but on the contrary is wholly abhorrent to nature: so that the very heathens themselves wondered what could have been the origin of their own practices in this matter.

Moreover, these sacrifices were always offered under the notion of making *atonement* for the offences supposed to have been committed against the gods, and of propitiating their favour.

The universality of the practice, together with its unnatural character, points to the fact that it must have originated when the whole human race was comprised within a single family or small community: and as the rite was not new in the time of Noah, it must of necessity be traced back to the very time of Adam himself.

So much we gather from the mere undisputed facts of history : but the *origin* of Sacrifice— the *reason* of its being practised both at first and ever afterwards—remains an inscrutable mystery until we have recourse to the literal sense and historical truth of Genesis. Admit this, and the mystery is solved. The fall of man by Adam's sin—the promise of a Redeemer in the Seed of the woman, who should be the sinner's Saviour by suffering death in the sinner's stead—the coats of skins—the appointment of Sacrifice as the mode ordained for the sinner to draw near before God with the expression of his penitence and faith in the promised Saviour—all these circumstances of the Scripture narrative at once supply the clue to the whole labyrinth of heathen ceremonies, and the key to unlock the treasury of revealed truth.

If no such actual facts had taken place as Genesis records, then the universal consent of all nations in offering expiatory animal sacrifices would have been simply impossible—sacrifices so unnatural, that natural reason or religion would never have prompted them, and so very cumbrous and costly that the introduction of them would certainly have been resisted with all the combined and overwhelming force of contempt, parsimony, and every mercenary motive.

To the unanswerable cogency of this argument may be added the internal evidence of truth supplied by the fact that, in the account of Cain's offering, there is wrapped up the double germ of all the religious, or rather irreligious, error which has been developed into the gigantic systems of Ritualism and Rationalism—in the widest sense of those terms —from that time to the present. If it be argued, that the very fact of this development makes it probable that the story of Cain's offering is just an allegory intended to point out the necessary tendencies of error in religious matters; we reply, that to have possessed such an insight, as is here supposed, into the tendencies of the human mind, would have required, in itself, nothing less than inspiration from God. If Moses wrote the story of Cain's offering as an allegory, to indicate that there existed in the human mind such undeveloped tendencies as have since produced the Pharisaism and Sadduceeism of the Jews, and the Romanism, Ritualism, Rationalism, and Neology of modern Europe, then indeed he must have possessed a knowledge more than human. He must have possessed that very inspiration which Rationalists are anxious above all things to discredit and deny. And so this argument would destroy the conclusion it was intended to support.

Cain's offering was a simple matter of fact : and it proceeded from those corrupt principles of combined unbelief, hypocrisy, and the pride of human reason, which are the very fruits of the Fall, and which have characterized every erroneous system of worship from that time to the present.

CHAPTER XXII.

The Cherubim of Eden's gate—identical with the "Seraphim" and "Living Creatures"—unquestionably the originals commemorated in the Assyrian Sculptures—in connexion with the Sacred Tree derived from the Trees of Knowledge and of Life—and the Circle and Wings symbolical of the Divine Presence.

"AND now, lest he put forth his hand, and take also of the tree of life, and eat, and live for ever: therefore the LORD God sent him forth from the garden of Eden to till the ground from whence he was taken. So he drove out the man; and he placed at the east of the garden of Eden Cherubims, and a flaming sword which turned every way, to keep the way of the tree of life."—Gen. iii. 22-24.

So says the sacred record—is it confirmed by facts? Is it attested by history?

Thirty years ago, these questions could have been answered, without hesitation indeed, but with incomparably less advantage than now. The researches of Mr. Layard among the Assyrian ruins have brought to light sculptures and engravings, which may well put to shame the cavillings of foolish men. Buried out of sight for twenty-five or thirty centuries, they have now marvellously risen up to bear witness to the truth, at a time when that truth is more keenly than ever controverted. It is as if they had been entombed for three thousand years on purpose that they might be kept in safety, till they were wanted, in these last days, to bear a last testimony to the Word of God.

The two subjects of the Tree of Life, and the Cherubim, are so interwoven that it will be convenient to treat of them together; though at the risk of some repetition of remarks already offered concerning the former.

What were the CHERUBIM—those mysterious figures placed around the flaming sword which guarded the gate of Eden and the Tree of Life? A clear understanding of this point is necessary in the first place.

They are mentioned first in the passage of Genesis just quoted.

They are mentioned next where Moses was instructed to make "two cherubims of gold, in the two ends of the mercy seat," in the Tabernacle in the wilderness.—Exod. xxv. 18. Figures of Cherubim were also interwoven in the vail of the Tabernacle, of blue, and purple, and scarlet, and fine twined linen.—The promise was added, "And there I will meet with thee, and I will commune with thee from above the mercy seat, from between the two cherubims which are upon the ark of the testimony, of all things which I will give thee in commandment unto the children of Israel."—Exod. xxv. 22. St. Paul alludes to them as "the cherubim of glory overshadowing the mercy seat."—Heb. ix. 5.—So also, God is spoken of as "the LORD of hosts, which dwelleth between the cherubims."—1 Sam. iv. 4, and 2 Sam. vi. 2.

In the Temple of Solomon, besides the two Cherubim overshadowing the Mercy seat, there were two colossal Cherubim, of "olive tree", overlaid with gold, in the Holy of Holies, facing the Mercy seat; and all the walls were "carved round about with carved figures of cherubims and palm trees and open flowers, within and without."—1 Kings vi. 23-29.

They are referred to in Psalm xviii. 10:—"And he rode upon a cherub, and did fly: yea, he did fly upon the wings of the wind:"—and again Ps. lxxx. 1:—"Thou that dwellest between the cherubims, shine forth:"—and Ps. xcix. 1:—"The LORD reigneth; let the people tremble: he sitteth between the cherubims; let the earth be moved."

Again, the prophet Isaiah received his commission from the Lord Himself seated upon a throne which was surmounted by these mysterious attendants. They are here called the Seraphims: but this is only another name for the same beings. —Isa. vi. 1-7.

Ezekiel also, in two separate visions, was permitted to see these, and has given a full description of their appearance,— Ezek. i.,—where they are called "living creatures": and chap. x., where they are again designated Cherubim. The two are expressly identified in verse 15:—"And the cherubims were lifted up. This is the living creature that I saw by the river of Chebar".

The last place in which they are mentioned in holy Scripture is in Rev. iv.: where they are, by a most unfortunate mistranslation, called in the authorized version "beasts." The word ζῶον, however, exactly answers to the "*living creature*" of Ezekiel, and should have been so rendered.

It is evident from a comparison of these various descriptions of the Cherubim, Seraphim, and "living creatures", first—that they are all identical with the Cherubim placed at Eden's gate. The composite figures described by Ezekiel, being compounded of the same parts and features as the others, are clearly of the same symbolical import, though combining in one figure the four faces which in the others are distributed among four separate figures. Secondly—it is manifest, that these Cherubim were ministers and attendants of the Lord Himself, and that their place was about the Divine Presence. Thirdly—they were manifestly appointed to be special witnesses and recorders of the great work of Redemption. This is evident from their distinctive position, overshadowing the Mercy seat in the Holy of Holies—bending over it and the Ark of the Covenant, the symbols of God's redeeming mercies—" which things the angels desire to look into."—1 Pet. i. 12. In this position also they were continually associated with the *Shechinah*—that dazzling light of glory which intimated the immediate Presence of God.

The same thing is evident also from their action described in Rev. vi., where they are employed to call St. John's attention to the opening of the Seals—each Seal introducing a vision of symbols marking the progress of events towards the fulness of time, when the mystery of Redemption should be unravelled, and the Redeemer's Kingdom set up.

All these circumstances must be borne in mind in order to a clear understanding of the appearance and meaning of the Cherubim of Paradise. The LORD God "placed"—or, *made to tabernacle*—" at the east of the garden of Eden, cherubims, and a flaming sword which turned every way, to keep the way of the tree of life."—Gen. iii. 24. Comparing the "flaming sword which turned every way", with Ezekiel's description of the "fire infolding itself, and a brightness about it"—"as the appearance of the bow that is in the cloud in the day of rain" : and again with the "fire between the Cherubims,"—Ezek. i. 4, 28, and x. 6,—we can come to no other conclusion but that the Cherubim "tabernacling" at Eden's gate, with the "flaming sword turning every way," were of a similar import with the fuller symbol of the Mercy seat and Shechinah of the Wilderness Tabernacle and of Solomon's Temple afterwards : and the addition in Ezekiel's vision of the appearance of the *rainbow* completes the symbolism of *mercy combined with justice* in the Covenant of salvation through the promised Redeemer.

It appears, too, from Gen. iii. 4, 5, that there must have been some visible tokens given of the acceptance and rejection of Abel's and Cain's offerings respectively—probably by fire lighting down from the "flaming sword," or Shechinah fire, upon Abel's sacrifice, (as Elijah's afterwards was consumed by fire from heaven), while Cain's offering was left untouched and unnoticed.

What, then, was the spectacle presented to the view of the worshippers at Eden's gate?

There was the "flaming sword, which turned every way "— the fiery Shechinah, waving like a brandished sword—symbolizing the Presence of God who, out of Christ, is "a consuming fire" to sinners, and barring against them the way to the Tree of Life.

There were the Cherubim—those mysterious beings who were the special attendants upon 'the Mercy seat, the peculiar harbingers of Redemption.

The whole group presented a striking symbolical representation of God's eternal Justice on the one hand, and of God's redeeming Mercy on the other. The *sword* is the symbol of *death*—the *Cherubim* were the symbols of *life*. And taken in connexion with the promise already given to fallen man, that *the Seed of the woman should bruise the Serpent's head*, they constituted a complete symbolism of *death incurred by sin*, and *life promised through Christ*. They were a combined type of the Law and the Gospel—that Law which was afterwards more fully given by Moses, and that Gospel which was typified in the Tabernacle and its sacrifices—that Law under which the Son of God, the Seed of the woman, died upon the cross, and that Gospel of life and salvation which through His death is preached in all the world to every creature.

But what were the forms and appearance of those mysterious Cherubim?

We turn to the fourth chapter of the Revelation. Around the Throne of God, from which proceeded *lightnings* and thunders—like the fiery sword, and lightning-stroke from Eden's gate—but which was encircled by the Rainbow of the Covenant, the token of redeeming mercy, "were four living creatures, full of eyes before and behind. And the first living creature was like a lion, and the second living creature like a calf, and the third living creature had a face as a man, and the fourth living creature was like a flying eagle. And the four

PLATE VII.

ASSYRIAN HUMAN-HEADED LION.

ASSYRIAN HUMAN-HEADED BULL.

PLATE VIII.

ASSYRIAN EAGLE-HEADED FIGURE, OR NISROCH.

ASSYRIAN WINGED HUMAN FIGURE.

living creatures had each of them six wings about him."—Rev.
iv. 1-8.

Now let any one who doubts the literal and historical truth
of Genesis examine the Assyrian sculptures in the British
Museum, and he will find reason to believe that the very
Cherubim of Paradise are there portrayed before his eyes.

The most conspicuous forms among these sculptures are just
four in number—and they might be correctly described in the
very words of St. John in the Revelation—the first like a lion,
the second like a calf (or bull), the third having a face as a
man, the fourth like a flying eagle. They are represented in
Plates VII. and VIII.

There is, indeed, this difference—that whereas the living
creatures of the Revelation had each six wings, the Assyrian
figures have but two.

But so also had the Cherubim of Solomon's Temple—as we
are expressly informed in 1 Kings viii. 7 :—" For the cherubims
spread forth their *two wings* over the place of the ark."

Now these were doubtless the identical Cherubims made for
the Tabernacle in the wilderness. For they are spoken of in
this place as "THE Cherubims": which would naturally mean
the same already so well known. Moreover, there is no mention of Solomon's having caused any new Cherubim to be made
for the Temple, except the two colossal Cherubs of olive tree,
—1 Kings vi. 23,—which were *additional* to the Cherubim of
the Mercy seat. It is therefore natural, and almost unavoidable, to conclude that in the *earliest* forms of the Cherubims
they appeared with but two wings.

Even putting aside, therefore, the fact that a certain latitude
and variety are observable in the combinations of the cherubic
forms, as they are described in the passages already referred
to, we have every reason to believe that in the Assyrian
sculptures there is actually before our eyes a portraiture
correct in all essential points of the forms of the Cherubim of
Paradise, handed down by tradition from the very time when

R

they overshadowed Eden's gate, or from the latest days when
they still remained there.   And as there is reason to think
that they were not removed till the time of the Flood, there
would, in this case, be many persons living after the building
of Nineveh to whose fathers the Cherubim of Eden had been
a familiar spectacle.   Shem lived five hundred years after the
Flood, and more than three hundred after the confusion of
tongues at Babel and the foundation of Nineveh by Nimrod.

In any case, it is certain that the Cherubim and flaming
sword at Eden's gate were a spectacle not likely to be forgotten
by posterity.   No sight has ever since been publicly seen on
earth at all comparable to that : and it would be strange indeed
that a sight of such surpassing and awful grandeur should have
been so long before the eyes of men, and not be commemorated
in some kind of sculptures and engravings by men well acquainted with the use of tools.

Moreover, there is a circumstance discovered by Mr. Layard
which cannot but be regarded as an additional proof that these
Nineveh sculptures were indeed traditional portraits of the
Eden Cherubim—they were placed at the *entrances* of the
temples.   "The winged human-headed lions and bulls", says
Mr. Layard, were the "magnificent forms which *guarded the
portals* of the Assyrian temples".[1]   What could be more
natural?   The Assyrians were familiar with the story of the
Cherubim guarding the portals of Eden : the figures of these
supernatural beings had been handed down in sculptures or
paintings from generation to generation : and the pride and
superstition of the Assyrian monarchs could find no more
ostentatious display, at once of royal grandeur and professed
religious zeal, than the adoption of the cherubic forms to be
as the guardian deities of their temples and palaces.

The four principal forms were those of a Winged Lion, a
Winged Bull, a Winged Man, and a man's figure with the head

---

[1] *Nineveh and its Remains*, vol. ii., 460.

and wings of an Eagle. The lion is represented in some of the sculptures with a human head.

The striking coincidence between these figures and the Cherubim seen by Ezekiel, has not escaped Mr. Layard; but he has fallen into a mistake as regards the relation between them. The resemblance is far too remarkable to be accidental: but in seeking to account for it, Mr. Layard assumes the Assyrian sculptures to have been the *originals* from which Ezekiel *borrowed* the description of the Cherubim in his vision. He says—"The resemblance between the symbolical figures I have described, and those seen by Ezekiel in his vision, can scarcely fail to strike the reader. As the prophet had beheld the Assyrian palaces, with their mysterious images and gorgeous decorations, it is highly probable that, when seeking to typify certain divine attributes, and to describe the divine glory, he chose forms that were not only familiar to him, but to the people whom he addressed—captives like himself in the land of Assyria. Those who were uncorrupted by even the outward forms of idolatry sought for images to convey the idea of the supreme God. Ezekiel saw in his vision the likeness of four living creatures, which had four faces, four wings, and the hands of a man under their wings on their four sides. Their faces were those of a man, a lion, an ox, and an eagle. By them was a wheel, the appearance of which 'was as it were a wheel in the middle of a wheel.'—Ezek. i. 16. It will be observed that the four forms chosen by Ezekiel to illustrate his description—the man, the lion, the bull, and the eagle—are precisely those which are constantly found on Assyrian monuments as religious types. The 'wheel within wheel' mentioned in connexion with the emblematical figures, may refer to the winged circle, or wheel, representing at Nimroud the supreme deity. These coincidences are too marked not to deserve notice; and do certainly lead to the inference, that the symbols chosen by the prophet were derived from the Assyrian sculptures. The symbolical figures of the Assyrians, as we might expect from the evident identity of the two nations, were placed, at a very early period, in the sacred edifices of the Babylonians ".[1]

Mr. Layard thus records his conviction that the coincidence between the forms of the Cherubim in Ezekiel's vision, and those of the Assyrian sculptures, is so complete, that *the one must have been borrowed from the other*. His testimony is all the more weighty because it is wholly independent and un-biassed. So far from seeking to uphold a theory, he was led by the singular coincidence to suggest a theory in order to account for it. And he has been led to propound a theory exactly the reverse of what is evidently the truth. He considers the description of the Cherubim in Ezekiel's vision to have been suggested to him by the Assyrian sculptures—not seeing that this idea is wholly inconsistent with the prophet's own express statement that the visions he saw were " *visions of God.*"—Ezek. i. 1. How could those visions be visions of God, if they were nothing more than imaginations suggested to Ezekiel by the Assyrian sculptures? He says expressly— " Now it came to pass in the thirtieth year, in the fourth month, in the fifth day of the month, as I was among the captives by the river of Chebar, that *the heavens were opened, and I saw visions of God :*"—how, then, could the stupendous appearances presented to his view be " symbols *chosen* by the prophet," and " *derived* from the Assyrian sculptures"? And whence were derived the similar appearances described by Isaiah, and by St. John in the Revelation—neither of whom had ever seen those sculptures? Can any thing be more strikingly—more startlingly—manifest, than the fact that the forms of the Assyrian sculptures were derived from the Cherubim—the same mysterious and awful beings who were first seen at Eden's portals, and afterwards shown in visions to Isaiah, Ezekiel, and St. John—whose golden images overshadowed the Mercy seat

[1] Ibid. ii, 464.

of Solomon's Temple—and whose forms had been so deeply impressed upon the memory of the beholders of Eden's gate, that they were reproduced in Assyria's temples and palaces, in those marvellous sculptures which Mr. Layard himself has brought to light after they had suffered an interment of three thousand years ?

Moreover, there is a passage in Ezekiel's prophecies which makes it a matter of certainty that the Cherubim of Eden were known among the *Phœnicians*—and if among the Phœnicians, they must have been no less known among the Assyrians. The passage is thus commented upon by the able author of *Armageddon :*—"This (28th) Chapter of Ezekiel contains a portraiture of that sacrilegious monarch Ethbaal, or Ithobaal, king of Tyre, who in his blaspheming pride assumed to himself divine honours ; and declaring that he was the very model of wisdom and beauty compared himself to one of the Cherubim of Eden, to one of the anointed ones of the Mercy seat.— The following is the sarcastically beautiful portrait given of him by the prophet—' Son of man, say unto the Prince of Tyrus, Thus saith the Lord God ; because thine heart is lifted up, and thou hast said, (impiously flattered himself by saying,) I am a God, I sit in the seat of God, (as in Thess. ii. 4,) in the midst of the seas ; yet thou art a man, (a mere worm,) and not God, though thou set thine heart as the heart of God : behold, thou art wiser (in thine own thought) than Daniel ; there is no secret that they can hide from thee. Son of man, take up a lamentation upon the king of Tyrus, and say unto him ; Thou sealest up the sum, full of wisdom and perfect in beauty, (in his own estimation the very exemplar of all perfection in his person, riches, power, and government.) *Thou hast been* (as thou boastest) *in Eden the garden of God ; thou art the anointed cherub that covereth,* (the mercy seat,) and I have set thee so : (I, thou sayest, have placed thee there :) thou wast upon the holy mountain of God ; thou hast walked up and down in the midst of the stones of fire. Thou wast perfect in thy ways from the day that thou wast created, till iniquity was found in thee. Therefore I will cast thee out, as profane, out of the mountain of God : and I will destroy thee, O (false) covering cherub, from the midst of the stones of fire'.—Ezek. xxviii. 2, 3, 12-16. The above prediction relative to the king of Tyrus is a manifest proof that notions of the Cherubim prevailed among the Phœnicians, which must either have been derived from the revelation of Moses, or from primeval traditions of the garden of Eden, or from both sources." [1]

This passage of Scripture is not only a manifest proof that the Phœnicians entertained notions of the Cherubim of Eden, but also that if they derived those notions from the writings of Moses, they understood the Mosaic narrative of the creation and fall of man, the garden of Eden, the Trees of Life and of Knowledge of good and evil, the Cherubim, and all the attendant circumstances, in a literal, and not an allegorical or poetical, sense.—If, on the other hand, they derived those notions from primeval traditions, it is no less manifest that they received those traditions as true accounts of real transactions, and not as poetical myths and allegories.

But farther—the evidence that the Assyrian sculptures were indeed memorials of the Eden Cherubim derives double force from the association of the winged figures with a certain *Sacred* TREE.—"The flowers on the earlier monuments," says Mr. Layard, "are either circular with five or more petals, or resemble the Greek honeysuckle. From the constant introduction of the tree ornamented with them, into groups representing the performance of religious ceremonies, there cannot be a doubt that they were symbolical and were invested with a sacred character. *The sacred tree, or tree of life, so universally recognized in Eastern systems of theology*, is called to mind, and

---

[1] *Armageddon*, vol. iii. 270.

we are naturally led to refer the traditions connected with it to a common origin. We have the *tree of life of Genesis*, and the sacred tree of the Hindhus, with its accompanying figures —a group almost identical with the illustrations of the Fall in our old Bibles. The Zoroastrian Homa, or sacred tree, was preserved by the Persians, almost as represented on the Assyrian monuments, till the Arab invasion." [1]

Now in the Assyrian sculptures, there are groups representing this Sacred Tree *with the cherubic figures.*

One of these groups consists of the Tree with a Nisroch, or Eagle-headed Winged human figure, on each side of it.

Another group has on each side of the Tree a Winged human figure in a kneeling posture.

On the embroidered dress of the king of Nineveh are groups of the Tree with winged griffins, one on each side.

But the most remarkable of all these groups is that in which the Tree has on each side a human figure in the act of worship, denoting probably the king and an attendant, and beyond each of these a Winged human figure: while *over the Tree* hovers the Circle and Wings, symbolical of the Divine Presence. [2]

Can any other rational account be given of these remarkable sculptures, especially the last, but that they commemorated the Shechinah token of the Presence of God, with the attendant Cherubim, and the Tree of Life, at the portals and in the Paradise of Eden ?

On a cylinder of green felspar, which Mr. Layard believes to be the signet of Sennacherib himself, is a group of the king and his attendant on either side of the Tree, which is surmounted by the winged Circle with *three* human heads, instead of the one figure which usually appears within the circle on the Assyrian monuments, sometimes armed with a bow and arrow, as the symbol of the divine Presence. The king, Mr. Layard

---

[1] *Nineveh and its Remains*, ii., 471.   [2] See Plate III., chap. xv.

says, "holds in one hand the sacrificial mace, and raises the other in the act of adoration before the winged figure in a circle, here represented as a triad with three heads. This mode of portraying this emblem is very rare in Assyrian relics, and is highly interesting, as confirming the conjecture that the mythic human figure, with the wings and tail of a bird, enclosed in a circle, was the symbol of the triune god, the supreme deity of the Assyrians, and of the Persians, their successors in the empire of the East." [1]

It was to be expected that so striking and impressive a sight as the Cherubim over Eden's gate would be commemorated far and wide in the monuments of posterity: but evidently, the traditions of them would be most vivid and correct among those nations who lived nearest, in respect both of place and time, to the locality and the date of their appearance; and would naturally become less distinct and less accurate in proportion as mankind were scattered farther from that locality, and were more urgently intent upon providing for the supply of their daily wants. A long time must needs pass before the wanderers into remote countries could be so far settled, and so far relieved from the daily struggle for life, as to have leisure to execute ornamental edifices and monuments. Necessaries must come before ornaments: and during the long infancy of a nation the arts alone or chiefly cultivated are unavoidably the useful, not the fine, arts. Meanwhile, the traditions of antiquity would run risk of falling more or less into oblivion.

Now this is exactly what has happened with regard to the Cherubim of Eden.

Assyria—in close proximity to the site of Eden—was the seat of the earliest colonization, and the speediest settlement of men into regular communities and social habits. Here, accordingly, the arts would soonest flourish, and be brought to perfection: so that the traditions which were embodied in

[1] *Babylon and Nineveh*, p. 160.

PLATE IX.

PERSIAN HUMAN-HEADED BULL.

those marvellous sculptures now before our eyes might be per-
petuated in carved monuments and engravings while still
comparatively recent and freshly remembered. The representations of the objects commemorated would be proportionally
correct.

On the other hand, the traditional representations of the
events of Eden among other nations are less correct, and less
prominent—and that too, almost in proportion to their remote-
ness, in place or time, from the events themselves. But it is
an indisputable and most striking fact that such representations *exist*, among the monuments of various nations: as well
as the traditions of them which, as has been already shown,
are found scattered throughout every nation under heaven.

In *Persia*, lying contiguous to Mesopotamia and the rivers
of Paradise, "the Zoroastrian Homa, or Sacred Tree, was preserved almost as represented in the Assyrian monuments, till
the Arab invasion"—as already mentioned in the words of
Mr. Layard.

At Persepolis, Sir Robert Kerr Porter discovered sculptures
not less remarkable than any found by Mr. Layard in Assyria
—Winged human-headed Bulls, of colossal size, and similar in
every essential particular to those of Nimroud. These gigantic
figures are described as beautifully carved, and measuring no
less than nineteen feet in height : and, like those at Nimroud,
they stand on either side of the *portals* of an ancient palace,
now in ruins.[1] See Plate IX.

And at Mourg-Aub, in the same country, on a marble pillar
attached to an ancient temple, he found a Winged human
figure, closely resembling those of the Assyrian sculptures,
only that it had four wings instead of two.[2]

[1] Sir R. K. Porter's *Travels*, vol. i., p. 591.
[2] Ibid., vol. i., p. 492. This intelligent traveller remarks that this
Winged human figure resembles nothing so much as the Seraphim of
Scripture.

We have thus two out of the four cherubic forms preserved with remarkable distinctness in Persia as well as in Assyria.

The Circle and Wings also, with a human figure in the centre, is a frequent ornament of the Persian sculptures.

In *India*, according to Mr. Layard, "the Sacred Tree of the Hindhus, with its accompanying figures, formed a group almost identical with the illustrations of the Fall in our old Bibles."

"The andro-sphinxes, and winged gryphons, with eagle heads, and lions with heads of men, of the *Egyptian* sculptures, which are seen in our Museums, and similar relics from the mounds of Nineveh, as well as of winged human-headed bulls and lions, and winged figures with baskets in their hands, some with the heads of eagles, some of men, and apparently partaking of the sacred symbolical Tree, or Tree of Life, have all one common origin, and are evidently corrupted and idolatrous similitudes of the Cherubim."[1]

The following testimonies are cited by the same author :—

"Clemens of Alexandria (says Smith) believed that the Egyptians imitated the Cherubim of the Hebrews in their Sphinxes and hieroglyphical animals.—*Patr. Age*, p. 169."

"Cory, Bonomi, Smith, all add their testimony of belief to this one common origin. 'It is a matter of curious enquiry (says Cory in his *Mythological Enquiry*) how mankind degenerated into the worship of animals, and the abominations of idolatry. Among the heathen, the Eagle was the token of the *ethereal power ;* the Lion of the *light ;* and the Bull of *fire, heat,* or *the Solar orb ;* though these distinctions are not always very accurately maintained. *These animals are, in fact, no other than the animals which composed the Cherubim* which, in the antediluvian, patriarchal, and Jewish dispensations, were placed at the entrance of Paradise, and afterwards upon the Mercy seat of the Ark. They were deemed oracular: and above them rested the Shekinah, the cloud of glory, the visible

---

[1] *Armageddon*, vol. iii., 271.

symbol of the presence of the Lord, who is represented as sitting between them. In the heathen Cherubim, among other remarkable variations, the head of the *serpent* is often substituted for the human head. The Seraphim are considered to have been similar: and the Teraphim were of the same form, but smaller figures, which were set up by individuals in their own houses, and to which they resorted for answers. (Zech. x. 2.) The Cherubim ·constituted the place of worship for all believers: they were termed the *pheni Elohim,* the faces, or presence, of God; and from them issued oracles. (Exod. xxv. 22.) It would have been a singular omission if the heathen, as they went off from the patriarchal worship, had not carried with them an institution so remarkable; accordingly, we find the figures worked into all their religious institutions, and the memory of them retained even to the present day. *The Cherubim may be found in every part of the heathen world;* and to the abuse of them, I believe, may be traced the worship of animals'.—Cory's *Myth. Enq.* pp. 99-104."

"These symbolical combinations, (says Mr. Bonomi) must be regarded as being derived from the traditional descriptions of the Cherubim which were handed down after the Deluge by the descendants of Noah; to which must be attributed their situation as guardians, as it were, of the portals of the palaces of the Assyrian kings,—*Nin. and its Palaces,* p. 133."

"So also Smith, in his *Sacred Annals, considers 'the identity of the animal worship of Egypt with that of the cherubic figures* to be proved by the fact, that the living Apis was required to have the marks of this *cherubic combination.* The selected animal must not only have a white crescent on his side, and a particular lump under his tongue, but also the resemblance of an eagle on his shoulders. And this, explained by antique bronze figures of Apis, gives, not the addition of an eagle to the ox, but the form of eagle wings on his shoulders, similar to those of the Nimroud sculptures. These marks, as Wilkinson observes, were undoubtedly supplied by the priests: but this rather corroborates the opinion that the cherubic form was the model to which the living animal was, as far as possible, to be conformed. We also find *a Sacred Tree* associated with all the sacred rites of this people, and *placed in such juxta-position with these cherubic sculptures*, as to lead to the conclusion that it was incorporated into this system as a memorial of the Tree of Life in Eden.'"

In short, the more extensively and profoundly we enquire into the idolatrous systems of antiquity, the more inevitably are we brought to these conclusions :—

First—That all the Pagan creeds and forms of worship throughout the world were substantially one and the same, and must therefore have had one and the same origin.

Secondly—That they all had their origin in corrupted and distorted traditions of the events related in the early chapters of Genesis : from which it follows inevitably that those events actually happened, and consequently that Genesis is literally true.

Of the former of these two conclusions we have very abundant evidence.

The classical Polytheism of Greece and Rome was but another version of the old creeds of Assyria, Persia, India, and Egypt—derived directly from them, and indeed the same in every thing but the names of their divinities.

The same original traditions have been shown to have been embodied in the worship of the Scandinavians, the Germans, Gauls, and ancient Britons.

They have been traced likewise in every part of America, where any religious observances can be traced at all.

Even the New Zealand and South Pacific Islanders, amidst all their savage barbarism, had retained relics of the memorials of Eden and the Deluge not to be mistaken.

And in various parts of Africa, besides Egypt, the same notions and similar religious rites are distinctly recognized.

Not only so, but we have express testimonies that the multitude of gods and goddesses worshipped by the ancient Pagans were but one and the same divinity under a variety of names and titles : as already shown in a previous chapter.

We have seen also that Sun-worship was an essential ingredient of all ancient systems of idolatry.

Now it has been abundantly shown, that the one personage really worshipped under the various titles of Adonis, Bacchus, Baal or Jupiter, Apollo or the Sun, and many other names, was none other but *Nimrod*, together with his wife Semiramis, as the Serpent-Sun-god, the Sun-begotten Seed of the Woman: and that the worship of this false Messiah and his supposed Mother, as the " Mother and the Child ", was THE ONE form of idolatry which had pervaded the world.

The inference is irresistible.   From Eden and its lost Paradise—from the thrilling story of man's creation, fall, and promised Redeemer—from the appointed sacrifices, ordained to shadow forth the Lamb of God who should take away the sin of the world—from these, and no other sources, was derived the traditionary worship which had filled the world.

There were indeed accessories and additions to this worship —there was Oannes, the sacred Man-fish, the Dagon of the Philistines, and the Janus of the Romans, of which the original was Noah: there was the mundane Egg, so prominent in heathen mythology, commemorating the Ark, from which, as from an egg, sprang the new population of the world: there were deified heroes and heroines, Nymphs and Naiads,

emperors or benefactors, imposed upon the credulity of the
multitude by fear, fancy, or flattery—but the system, in its
essence and main features, was every where one and the
same throughout the world, and traceable to one and the
same source—corrupted traditions of Eden and its memorable
history.

CHAPTER XXIII.

The Giants of old—and their houses yet standing—the Cities of Bashan and their Giant builders—identity of manners in patriarchal and modern times.

" THERE were giants in the earth in those days : and also after that," (viz. after the Flood) "when the sons of God came in unto the daughters of men, and they bare children to them, the same became mighty men which were of old, men of renown."—Gen. vi. 4.

So, again, it is written : and if any part of the sacred record might seem open to the suspicion that it was "poetry, not history"—allegorical or fabulous—certainly no part could be more so than this passage, together with others of a like import which occur later in the Scripture narrative. We are accustomed from childhood to the stories of giants in the Greek and Roman classic writers—and these stories are fables. —Are we, then, equally to conclude that the Scripture accounts of giants are poetical myths, which ought to be purged out of the Bible—upon the principle of the late Dr. Arnold, that the early Scripture history stands in need of being treated as Niebuhr treated the early history of Rome, by being cleared from the mists of fabulous antiquity ?

The Scripture narrative cannot be so easily disposed of as the story of Romulus and Remus being reared by a she-wolf. The facts of Scripture are spoken of plainly and positively.

They are related in language as far removed from "poetry" as it is possible for words to be. The narrative is circumstantial and detailed—the dates, and names of persons and places are mentioned, dimensions and descriptions given, and particulars specified which must either confirm the truth of the narrative, or expose it, if not true, to certain detection.

Such for instance is the account given of some of the giants. —"Only Og king of Bashan remained of the remnant of giants; behold, his bedstead was a bedstead of iron; is it not in Rabbath of the children of Ammon? nine cubits was the length thereof, and four cubits the breadth of it, after the cubit of a man."—Deut. iii. 11. The writer of this statement appeals to the eyes of living witnesses—a sufficient proof that what he states is neither fable nor "poetry," but fact. "Is it not in Rabbath of the children of Ammon?" If the bedstead was not still to be seen at Rabbath, or if the size of it was exaggerated, the writer would expose himself to certain conviction of falsehood.

This bedstead was above 16 feet long, and 7 wide; so that its occupant may reasonably be supposed to have been twelve feet in height.

A similar account is given of Goliath of Gath—1 Sam. xvii. 4. His "height was six cubits and a span"—or six cubits and a half—nearly twelve feet: his coat of mail weighed about 156 pounds, and the rest of his armour, in proportion, must have brought up the total of what he carried upon him to more than two hundredweight, besides spear and shield.—Other giants among the Philistines are spoken of in the time of David, whose strength and stature approached, though they did not equal, those of Goliath.

These are marvellous accounts: so marvellous, that nothing in the whole Bible can be pointed out having more of an air of romance, or "poetry," than these descriptions of the giants of antiquity.

But there are facts now existing which, even apart from the

Scriptural or any other history, are suggestive of the probability of such giants having once lived upon earth.

These facts form a testimony to the truth—the literal, historical truth—of the Scripture narrative, which can by no means be overthrown. And they seem, like the discovery of the Assyrian sculptures, to have been providentially brought to light in these latter days as if on purpose to convince the gainsayers.

The Bible tells us of "giants that were in the earth" in old times—a modern traveller is able to tell us that he has *seen their dwellings*.

The Rev. Mr. Porter has published a volume of such marvellous interest that, were he not a living witness to the truth of what he narrates, he might have fallen under the same imputation of having written "poetry, not history," which has been so unscrupulously cast upon the sacred writers.

"The cities," says Mr. Porter, "built and occupied some forty centuries ago by these old giants exist even yet. I have traversed their streets; I have opened the doors of their houses; I have slept peacefully in their long-deserted halls."[1]

Og, the last of the race of giants who inhabited northern Syria, was king of Bashan—and there, in Bashan, may be seen at the present moment such dwellings as giants alone would build. Describing Bashan, Mr. Porter says—"It is literally crowded with towns and large villages; and though the vast majority of them are deserted, *they are not ruined*.. I have more than once entered a *deserted* city in the evening, taken possession of a comfortable house, and spent the night in peace. Many of the houses in the ancient cities of Bashan are perfect, as if only finished yesterday. The walls are sound, the roofs unbroken, the doors and even the window-shutters in their places. Let not my readers think that I am transcribing

---

[1] *The Giant Cities of Bashan, and Syria's Holy Places*—by the Rev. J. L. Porter, p. 12.

a passage from the 'Arabian Nights.' I am relating sober
facts: I am simply telling what I have seen. 'But how,' you
ask me, 'can we account for the preservation of ordinary
dwellings in a land of ruins? If one of our modern English
cities were deserted for a millennium, there would scarcely be
a fragment of a wall standing.' The reply is easy enough.
The houses of Bashan are not ordinary houses. Their walls
are from five to eight feet thick, built of large squared blocks
of basalt; the roofs are formed of slabs of the same material,
hewn like planks, and reaching from wall to wall; the very
doors and window-shutters are of stone, hung upon pivots projecting above and below. Some of these ancient cities have
from two to five hundred houses still perfect, but not a man to
dwell in them."—P. 20.

Again :—"Moses makes special mention of the strong cities
of Bashan, and speaks of their high walls and gates. He tells
us, too, in the same connexion, that Bashan was called the
land of the giants (or Rephaim, Deut. iii. 15); leaving us to
conclude that the cities were built by giants. Now the houses
of Kerioth and other towns in Bashan appear to be just such
dwellings as a race of giants would build. The walls, the
roofs, but especially the ponderous gates, doors, and bars, are
in every way characteristic of a period when architecture was
in its infancy, when giants were masons, and when strength
and security were the grand requisites. I measured a door in
Kerioth : it was nine feet high, four and a half wide, and ten
inches thick—one solid slab of stone. I saw the folding gates
of another town in the mountains still larger and heavier.
Time produces little effect on such buildings as these. The
heavy stone slabs of the roofs resting on the massive walls
make the structure as firm as if built of solid masonry; and
the black basalt used is almost as hard as iron. There can
scarcely be a doubt, therefore, that these are the very cities
erected and inhabited by the Rephaim, the aboriginal inhabitants of Bashan : and the language of Ritter appears to be

true: 'These buildings remain as eternal witnesses of the conquest of Bashan by Jehovah.'"

"We have thus at Kerioth and its sister cities some of the most ancient houses of which the world can boast; and in looking at them and wandering among them, and passing night after night in them, my mind was led away back to the time, now nearly four thousand years ago, when the kings of the East warred with the Rephaim in Ashteroth-Karnaim, and with the Emim in the plain of Kiriathaim (Gen. xiv. 5). Some of the houses in which I slept were most probably standing at the period of that invasion. How strange to occupy houses of which giants were the architects, and a race of giants the original owners!—In size they cannot vie with the temples of Karnac; in splendour they do not approach the palaces of Khorsabad; yet they are the memorials of a race of giant warriors that has been extinct for more than three thousand years, and of which Og king of Bashan was one of the last representatives; and they are, I believe, the only specimens in the world of the ordinary private dwellings of remote antiquity. The monuments designed by the genius and reared by the wealth of imperial Rome are fast mouldering to ruin in this land; temples, palaces, tombs, fortresses, are all shattered or prostrate in the dust; but the simple, massive houses of the Rephaim are in many cases perfect as if completed yesterday."—Pp. 83, 84.

"Mr. Graham," adds Mr. Porter, "the only other traveller since Burckhardt who traversed eastern Bashan, entirely agrees with me in my conclusions. 'When we find', he writes, 'one after another, great stone cities, walled and unwalled, with stone gates, and so crowded together that it becomes almost a wonder how all the people could have lived in so small a place; when we see houses built of such huge and massive stones that no force which can be brought against them in that country could ever batter them down; when we find rooms in these houses so large and lofty that many of them would be considered fine rooms in a palace in Europe; and lastly, when we find some of these towns bearing the very names which cities in that very country bore before the Israelites came out of Egypt, I think we cannot help feeling the strongest conviction that we have before us the cities of the Rephaim of which we read in the book of Deuteronomy'."— P. 85.

To the same effect is the testimony of Ammianus Marcellinus, quoted by the same writer. "The towns of Bashan", he says, "were considered ancient even in the days of the Roman historian Ammianus Marcellinus, who says regarding this country —'Fortresses and strong castles have been erected by the *ancient inhabitants* among the retired mountains and forests. Here, in the midst of *numerous towns*, are some great cities, such as Bostra and Gerasa, encompassed by massive walls.'"

Another proof of the historical truth of the Mosaic narrative comes out here with regard to the *number* of these most remarkable and ancient cities. "The freshness and picturesque beauty of the scenery, the extent and grandeur of the ruins, the hearty and repeated welcomes of the people, the truly patriarchal hospitality with which I was everywhere entertained, but, above all, the convincing, overwhelming testimony afforded at every step to the *minute accuracy of Scripture history*, and the literal fulfilment of prophecy, filled my mind with such feelings of joy and thankfulness as I had never before experienced. I had often read of Bashan—how the Lord had delivered into the hands of the tribe of Manasseh, Og, its giant king, and all its people. I had observed the statement that a single province of his kingdom, Argob, contained threescore great cities, fenced with high walls, gates, and bars, *besides unwalled towns a great many.* I had examined my map, and had found that *the whole of Bashan* is not larger than an ordinary English county. I confess I was astonished: and though my faith in the Divine record was not shaken, yet I felt that some strange statistical mystery hung over the passage, which required to be cleared up.—That *sixty* walled cities, besides *unwalled towns a great many*, should exist in a small province, at such a remote age, far from the sea, with no rivers and little commerce, appeared to be inexplicable. Inexplicable—mysterious though it appeared, it was true. On the spot, with my own eyes, I had now verified it. A list of more than *one hundred* ruined cities and villages, situated in these mountains alone, I had in my hands; and on the spot I had tested it, and found it accurate, though not complete. More than thirty of these I had myself visited or passed closed by. Many others I had seen in the distance. The extent of some of them I measured, and have already stated. Of their high antiquity I could not, after inspecting them, entertain a doubt ; and I have explained why. Here, then, we have a venerable record, more than three thousand years old, containing incidental descriptions, statements, and statistics, which few even would be inclined to receive on trust, which not a few are now attempting to throw aside as 'glaring absurdities,' and 'gross exaggerations,' and yet which *close and thorough examination proves to be accurate in the most minute details*."—Pp. 85, 89, 90.

This testimony is invaluable and unanswerable. I have given it at some length on account of its extreme importance.

Even particulars so minute as the bars of the doors in these cities of giants are still traceable. Mr. Porter thus describes, among the ruins of Kenath, "the remains of a castle or palace, built of stones of enormous size. The doors are all of stone, and some of them are ornamented with panels and fretted mouldings, and wreaths of fruit and flowers sculptured in high relief. In one door I observed a place for a massive lock or bar ; perhaps one of those 'brazen bars' to which allusion is made by the sacred writers, (1 Kings iv. 13)."—P. 44.

Many of the names of the cities and provinces of Bashan are recognizable in their modern appellations ; some are even identical with those mentioned by Moses. "*Gaulanitis* is manifestly the territory of *Golan*, the ancient Hebrew city of refuge;

Auranitis is only the Greek form of the *Hauran* of Ezekiel, xlviii. 16 ; *Batanea*, the name then given to the eastern mountain range, is but a corruption of Bashan ; and *Trachonitis*, embracing that singularly wild and rocky district on the north, is just a Greek translation of the old *Argob*, 'the stony'."— *Kureiyeh* is "manifestly an Arabic form of the Hebrew *Kerioth*. Kerioth was reckoned one of the strongholds of the plain of Moab.—Jer. xlviii. 41." The name of *Kenath*—Numb. xxxii. 42—"was changed into *Canatha* by the Greeks; and the Arabs have made it Kunawât."—*Um-el-Jemâl* is the modern representative of the *Beth-gamil* of Scripture. *Bosrah—Salcah —Edrei*, the city of Og king of Bashan—with their peculiar positions and characteristics, all are recognizable at the present day.

The truthfulness of the narrative of Genesis is strikingly attested by the exact similarity of the state of the country, and the manners and customs of the inhabitants, to those described in Scripture. . "Bashan is, in many respects, among the most interesting of the provinces of Palestine. It is comparatively unknown, besides."—"The state of the country is so unsettled, and many of the people who inherit it are so hostile to Europeans, and in fact to strangers in general, that there seems to be but little prospect of an increase of tourists in that region. Both land and people remain thoroughly Oriental. Nowhere else is patriarchal life so fully or so strikingly exemplified. *The social state of the country and the habits of the people are just what they were in the days of Abraham or Job.* The raids of the eastern tribes are as frequent and as devastating now as they were then. The flocks of a whole village are often swept away in a single incursion, and the fruits of a whole harvest carried off in a single night. The arms used are, with the exception of a few muskets, similar to those with which Chedorlaomer conquered the Rephaim. The implements of husbandry, too, are as rude and as simple as they were when Isaac cultivated the valley of Gerar. And the hospitality is everywhere as profuse and as genuine as that which Abraham exercised in his tents at Mamre. I could scarcely get over the feeling, as I rode across the plains of Bashan, and climbed the wooded hills through the oak forests, and saw the primitive ploughs, and yokes of oxen, and goats, and heard the old Bible salutations given by every passer-by, and received the urgent invitations to rest and eat at every village and hamlet, and witnessed the killing of the kid or lamb, and the almost incredible despatch with which it is cooked and served to the guests,—I could scarcely get over the feeling, I say, that I had been somehow spirited away back thousands of years, and set down in the land of Nod, or by the patriarch's tents at Beer-sheba. *Common life in Bashan I found to be a constant enacting of early Bible stories.*"—"Away in this old kingdom one meets with nothing in dress, language, or manners, save the stately and instructive simplicity of patriarchal times." [1]

Since the above chapter was written, a book has been published by a recent traveller, Mr. Freshfield, in which some doubt has been cast upon the remote antiquity, and consequently upon the Giant origin, of the cities of Bashan. The cursory observation, however, of so hasty a traveller as Mr. Freshfield appears to have been, can hardly be accepted as of much weight against the far more careful and extensive researches of Mr. Porter and others: and besides this, there is internal as well as external evidence that Mr. Freshfield's conclusions are erroneous.

He considers the majority of the cities of Bashan to have been Roman: yet he admits without dispute that houses exist there "which may be of the time of Og, or they may not:" though he adds, "there is nothing to show that they were built by giants."

[1] Ibid., p. 18, &c.

But if there are houses, now standing, of the time of Og, the probability is that the majority of the houses are of the same date—even apart from the historical evidence of the Scripture narrative. For to suppose that they are for the most part Roman would be to suppose that the Romans selected the rocky, barren, forbidding district of Trachonitis for the purpose of settling there a Roman population beyond all comparison more dense and numerous than they ever placed in a similar extent of the most fertile and delicious country of their vast colonial dependencies.

Mr. Freshfield's principal argument for the Roman origin of the Bashan cities seems to be expressed in the following remark :—" Surely no one without a preconceived theory to support, will maintain that where every public building—whether temple, theatre, triumphal arch, tomb, or church—is of Roman or later date, the private dwellings are, as a rule, 1800 years older."

This argument might have some force if there were any reason to think that it was the habit of the people of Og's time to erect public buildings at all. It is almost a certainty that they erected none. In those rude and unsettled times the question was not how to adorn their cities or amuse themselves, but how to live. To till the ground for food, and build houses for shelter and walls for defence, were the urgent and imperative necessities which occupied attention. Nothing therefore could be more natural and probable than the very result which Mr. Freshfield thinks incredible—namely, that although the public buildings might be Roman, the private houses might be 1800 years older. And this is all the more natural from the massive solidity of their structure and the extraordinary hardness of the stone of which they were built : circumstances which would make small buildings equally enduring as more imposing edifices. To argue that because there are Roman temples and theatres in Bashan the houses must be Roman too, is not more convincing than to maintain that because London is a modern city therefore the Tower was not built by the Romans—or that because there exists a Cathedral at Salisbury, therefore Stonehenge is not a Druidical monument.

Then, we have the express testimony of Ammianus Marcellinus, quoted above ;—a writer characterized by Gibbon as " an accurate and faithful guide."[1] His statement is that " Fortresses and strong castles have been erected by *the ancient inhabitants* among the retired mountains and forests. Here, *in the midst of numerous towns*, are *some great cities*, such as Bostra and Gerasa, encompassed by massive walls."

This testimony is of itself fatal to Mr. Freshfield's theory : while it fully confirms the sacred narrative. It reduces almost to historical certainty the intrinsic probability that as a rule the private houses of the Bashan cities are of the time of Og and the Giants : though the public buildings, and a certain proportion of dwelling houses, as might be expected, were the work of the Roman conquerors, and the mere adventitious consequences of their temporary occupation of the country.

Mr. Freshfield's strictures on Mr. Porter's descriptions are far too vague and desultory to prove anything. There is but one instance mentioned by Mr. Freshfield in which he tested Mr. Porter's account of the dimensions of any of the Bashan buildings by actual measurement—viz., that of " the gates, 10 feet high, mentioned by Porter," at Kufr. And in this solitary instance Mr. Porter is misrepresented. He does not say that the gates were 10 feet high, as if he had measured them, which Mr. Freshfield's words imply : but only that the " stone gates (at Kufr) *about* ten feet high, remain in their places." He had evidently only guessed their height by the eye. And as Mr. Freshfield himself says, " the *doors* turned out to be 7 feet high, and did not fully fill the gateway which was a foot loftier," making the gateway 8 feet high, Mr. Porter's rough guess is no evidence of general inaccuracy.

[1] *Decline and Fall*, ch. 26.

CHAPTER XXIV.

The Exodus of Israel—the line of march—the Wady-el-Tih, or Valley of the Wanderings—the Wady-Mousa, or Valley of Moses—the Djebel Ataka, or Mountain of Deliverance—the Bahr-el-Kolzoum, or Gulf of Destruction—Serbâl the true Mount Sinai.

No part of the Scripture history has been more vehemently attacked by objectors and sceptics than the narrative of the Exode of Israel out of Egypt, and their forty years' sojourn in the Wilderness. The miraculous passage through the Red Sea—the Manna—the quails—have all been assailed with allegations of not being "historical"—that is, not *real*. From this of course it would follow that the narrative is not *true:* for it is idle to pretend that the writer of the book of Exodus did not mean to speak of the passage through the sea, the Manna or the quails, as literal facts, and therefore miraculous. The description of the crossing the sea is the description of a *miracle*—or else words have no meaning. "The Lord caused the sea to go back by a strong east wind all that night, and made the sea dry land, and the waters were *divided*. And the children of Israel went *into the midst of the sea* upon the dry ground: and *the waters were a wall unto them on their right hand and on their left.*"—Exod. xiv. 21, 22.

Now, if the retiring of the waters had been caused, as sceptics have pretended, by an extraordinary ebb-tide, the waters would not have been "*divided,*" but would all have receded in a southern direction, so that the Israelites would have *all* the

water on their right hand, and *none* upon their left. But the
narrative says that the waters were *divided*, and the people
went *into the midst* of the sea upon dry ground. The ebb-tide
theory is not an explanation of the words of Scripture, but a
point-blank denial of them.

Again—"the waters were *a wall unto them*, on their right
hand and on their left." A *wall of water* is certainly a phenomenon beyond the effect of any tide, however extraordinary!
The attempt to account for such an event by natural causes is
not merely absurd in the extreme—it is an unworthy evasion
of the history. It would be far more honest to reject the
whole account as absolutely false and fabulous. If the Exode
ever took place at all, it was miraculous from beginning to end,
and could be nothing else. The whole transaction was one
grand and continuous miracle—from the very moment when
the oppressed captives of Israel escaped from the iron grasp of
their Egyptian tyrants, to their final settlement in their promised Canaan. What else but a miracle could have forced the
proud and cruel Pharaoh to release his slaves—whom, after
their escape, he was so madly determined to recover? What
but a continual miracle could have sustained a multitude of
two or three millions, for forty years, in deserts where even the
passing traveller cannot linger for fear of perishing by thirst
and hunger? No greater difficulty besets the commander of an
army than that of keeping his soldiers provided with food and
clothing, even for a few months, and in a country not destitute
of supplies: and one of the indispensable requisites of war is to
keep communications open in the rear by which supplies may
be regularly conveyed to the scene of action. But Moses was
the leader of *two or three millions* of people, through a "waste
and howling wilderness"—destitute of supplies in itself, and
cut off from all communication with the rest of the world.
Without a miracle, the very existence of such a multitude in
such a desert, even for three days, was an impossibility: their
preservation for forty years was a miracle of forty years' dura-

tion. The only rational account to be given of their very
existence under such circumstances is that which is given in
the sacred record—"Thou shalt remember all the way which
the Lord thy God led thee these forty years in the wilderness"
—"and he humbled thee, and suffered thee to hunger, and *fed
thee with manna*, which thou knewest not, neither did thy
fathers know; that he might make thee know that man doth
not live by bread only, but by every word that proceedeth out
of the mouth of the Lord doth man live. *Thy raiment waxed
not old upon thee*, neither did thy foot swell, these forty years."
—Deut. viii. 2-4. Admit the miraculous nature of the whole
Exodus, and every part of it becomes at once intelligible and
credible : deny the miracles, and the whole history of it becomes a tissue of impossibilities and absurdities.

An instance of this truth meets us at the very outset, in the
line of march by which Moses conducted the people.

In the first place—if he were not acting under the express
direction of God, why should he have gone many hundreds of
miles out of his way at all, for no other object but to bring the
people into a barren and frightful desert such as is the Sinaitic
peninsula ? It is unaccountable and incredible that he should,
of his own mind, have led them into a tract of country not
only in the direction exactly opposite to their promised inherit-
ance, but also where speedy destruction must have been their
inevitable doom. They set out to go to Canaan—but he
conducted them to Sinai. The thing is incredible, unless he
were guided by Divine command.

Then again—supposing Sinai to have been his object, he
chose a line of march absolutely unaccountable except he were
divinely guided. The ordinary route to Sinai is round the
northern extremity of the Red Sea, at Suez—not *southwards*
towards its western shore—as any one may see by a glance at
the map. By going round the northern extremity of the gulf
he would have taken the only route by which it was possible
to reach Sinai without crossing the Red Sea—the same route

by which travellers proceed at the present day : and moreover, he would have placed the sea between himself and his enemies. But he took a *southerly* course—towards the western shore of the sea ; by which he went out of the direct route—placed the sea in front of Israel, *between* them and their destination—and advanced into a position from which it was impossible to with-draw without actually returning upon his own footsteps. In marching southwards, he was not on the way either to Canaan or even to Sinai—while on the right was Egypt—on the left the sea. To have brought the people into such a position was simply to betray them into the hands of their enemies, in case they should pursue them ; and to make it inevitable that they must in any case retrace their steps, *unless they could walk through the sea*. And all this must have been perfectly well known to Moses—for he was well acquainted with the country on both sides of the gulf.

Is it credible or conceivable that any sane man could have acted in a manner so absolutely senseless and suicidal ?

But grant that Moses was acting, as the narrative expressly states, *under the immediate direction of God*, and all is at once intelligible and consistent. Nothing but Divine guidance could have induced him ever to advance into such a position as was the camp at Pi-hahiroth—nothing but a miracle could have extricated him from it.

And what is the rational and natural explanation? Why, that Moses did act under Divine guidance—that he was pro-ceeding according to a plan already formed in the counsels of God—and that *a part* of that plan was to deliver the Israelites by dividing the Red Sea. That Moses should have acted as he did under Divine direction is credible, and consistent with the actual occurrence of the miracle : that he should have acted as he did without the consciousness of Divine direction, and implicit reliance upon Divine power, is absolutely un-accountable.

Moreover, the stupendous events of that time have been

remembered, in the country where they took place, from that
time to the present. They are commemorated by monuments
as lasting as the Pyramids—the *names* of the localities where
they happened. "The route," says Osburn, "by which Israel
moved on in mystic pomp from Egypt to the Red Sea, has
never been forgotten. It is called to this day 'Wady-el-Tih,'
the Valley of the Wanderings, and 'Wady-Mousa,' *the Valley
of Moses*. It is hemmed in by a conspicuous mountain terminating in a promontory which projects far into the sea. The
modern name is 'Djebel Atáka,' *the Mountain of Deliverance*,
in commemoration of the Exodus; and Pi-hahiroth is the
'Djebel-Abon-Deradj' of modern geography. The former is
a bold and lofty promontory, stretching for many miles into
the Kolzoum, or 'Bahr-el-Kolzoum,' *the Gulf of Destruction*,
the Arab name of the Gulf of Suez. The latter is a steep
limestone cliff, very rugged, abounding with caverns, and
answering to its ancient name, 'mouths of the caves.' Between
these two mountains is a sandy plain seven miles broad, well
adapted for the encampment of the vast host of Israel. It
forms the termination of the Wady-el-Tih on the shore of the
gulf."[1]

"This noble semicircle of precipices," says Dr. Bonar, "is
Ras Atákah, 'the head of Atáka.' It maintains its full height
for some twelve miles, and then drops right into the sea, eight
or ten miles down from Suez, leaving not a foot of land for
passage. Into this *angle*, formed by the sea on the one hand,
and Ras Atákah on the other, Israel marched: and here they
were 'shut in' (Exod. xiv. 3); while Pharaoh, coming from
the west, marched upon their rear, and cut off all retreat. It
is worth remembering that Ras Atákah is not the name merely
for the abrupt headland which shoots into the sea; it is the
name for the whole twelve miles of precipice which form the
termination of the range."[2]

[1] *Armageddon*, vol. ii. 441, &c., quoting Osburn's *Mon. Egypt.*
[2] Bonar's *Desert of Sinai*, p. 80.

"Had the Israelites," says the same author, "been seeking a straight road to Sinai, they would have kept more to the east. They would have turned leftwards into the desert of Shûr, thus getting at once beyond Pharaoh's reach, and avoiding the necessity of crossing the sea *at any point.* There were no geographical, and certainly no strategical reasons for their approaching it at all. In making for it, they were compelling themselves to take a circuit which, without one compensating advantage, threw them back upon Egypt, delayed their escape, brought them within an easy distance of Pharaoh, and gave him the choice of attacking them on flank, or rear, or both, just as might suit himself. They not only, however, made for the sea, but they persisted in keeping to the westward of it, and in pursuing their march southward, along the inside, or Egyptian, margin. Their natural course was to turn eastwards, at least when they came to the northern tongue of the sea, if not before. But instead of doing this, and thereby throwing the sea between them and their enemies, they continued their march to the south, deliberately interposing the sea, not between them and their enemies, but between them and the great object of their exodus, Sinai and its desert."

"Thus they voluntarily imposed upon themselves the necessity for crossing a gulf which they might easily have avoided. It was this singular position into which they had brought themselves, or into which Moses had brought them, that rendered their extrication so apparently impossible. Had any general done so with his army, his conduct would have been imputed to madness, or ignorance of the country. But Moses knew the region well. He had more than once gone to Sinai from Egypt, and was acquainted with the way. He could not but know that he was misleading Israel, unless he was conscious of a direct Divine guidance—guidance which for the time superseded and overruled his own judgment. His object was to reach the Sinaitic desert : he knew the way : he had the safety of two millions to consult for ; yet he turns away from Sinai, and throws a broad sea between it and Israel."

"But he was acting under the command of God. Ten miracles had already stricken Egypt to the heart, but another was needed still. Her first-born had perished, but her peers and princes remained. This last miracle is aimed at them. It was needed to overthrow the last relics of a nation's pride, and to overawe them in time to come. It was needed to strike alarm into the nations around; and to give Israel one proof more of what God was ready to do in their behalf. Such were some of our thoughts as we skirted the spacious plain that stretches from Ras Atákah to the sea. We seemed to trace the march of the multitude up to the point where the promontory stayed them; and we could not help concluding that in the whole transaction there must either have been an enormous blunder or a most signal miracle. Admit the miracle, and the narrative is as consistent and intelligible as the event is marvellous and Divine." [1]

So Israel passed through the sea on dry land. The same miraculous power which opened the way for them, restrained their enemies from overtaking them—Exod. xiv. 23-25: and, as soon as they were safe on the opposite shore, unchained the mysterious bonds which held the waters back, and overwhelmed their enemies in the foaming floods.

The onward march of the Israelites is traceable to this day, in the Sinaitic peninsula.

The *names* of certain localities on this, as on the Egyptian side of the Red Sea, mark their course. Immediately on the spot where the Israelitish host must have made their first encampment after crossing the sea, we are met with the *Ayûn Mousa*—the "wells of Moses."—"They are dug in the sand," says Dr. Bonar, "but not regularly built. Of these Israel drank—or at least of wells in this neighbourhood, for no where

---

[1] Bonar's *Desert of Sinai*, p. 83, &c.

else could they get water for many miles round." [1]—Farther on, in "the great and terrible wilderness," is a fallen fragment of rock, called *Hajir-er-R'kab*—the "stone of the rider"—"to which tradition assigns some niche in the history of Moses. The Bedaween seem to reverence it, and make it a resting-place. It is an immense fragment of rock which has fallen from the heights above into the plain, but beyond this it has nothing very notable about it." [2]—The locality of the waters of *Marah* is still recognized, and there is a well of bitter water still called by the Arabs *Murrah*, "bitter." Then, a day's march farther on, is *Elim*. "For there seems little doubt that this is really *Elim*. It is a stage beyond Marah, and a day's journey from the Red Sea—just as Scripture represents. It lies in Israel's route. It is just a spot for them to encamp in. If this be not Elim, then there is no other spot, on which the name can be fixed, which so exactly suits the distances, or to which the peculiar features so well apply. If this be not Elim, then Elim must have vanished from the desert, and this new oasis risen since the days of Israel. Not a very likely thing; for the upspringing of an oasis in the desert is as rare as the appearance of a new star in the sky. The 'threescore and ten' palm trees have multiplied into hundreds; but the 'twelve wells' have diminished, and the shallow excavations which now get the name of wells are scanty and brackish springs ".[3]

Then again, at another day's journey farther on, the same traveller writes—"Here the sea bursts on us, less than a mile off. We reach our halting-place at half-past five—the mouth of *Wady-el-Markhâh*, the 'valley of rest'—hard by the sea, and within sound of its soft ripple. The road from Ayûn Mousa had receded from the coast, so that for nearly three days we had lost sight of the sea. Yesterday it suddenly brought us to the sea again, and our morning ride had been along its margin. All this strikingly showed the minute

---

[1] *The Desert of Sinai*, p. 111.   [2] Ibid.   [3] Ibid. p. 123.

T

accuracy of the Scripture narrative regarding Israel's march—
'they removed from Elim and encamped by the Red Sea'.—
Numb. xxxiii. 10. To one who does not know the exact
geography of this region this might seem unaccountable; but
one who has been upon the spot knows that this is, if not the
only practicable route, at least the best one." [1]

Moreover, the whole desert, except the mountainous part
immediately about Sinai itself, bears to this day the name of
El Tih, "*the Wanderings*."

Once more:—There is a scene described in the Scripture
history, which, it may well be thought, must needs have left its
marks upon the locality where it took place, in a manner
recognizable as long as the world endures. It is THE GIVING
OF THE LAW ON MOUNT SINAI.

That scene was such as never took place in all the world
besides. The PRESENCE OF GOD was then manifested to His
chosen people Israel so as it has never been manifested elsewhere—and the terrors of the Law, that is, the terrible consequences of transgressing it, were then intimated in a manner
unheard of before or since.— " Moses brought forth the people
out of the camp, to *meet with God ;* and they stood at the
nether part of the mount. And Mount Sinai was altogether
on a smoke, because the LORD descended upon it in fire; and
the smoke thereof ascended as the smoke of a furnace, and
THE WHOLE MOUNTAIN QUAKED GREATLY. And when the
voice of the trumpet sounded long, and waxed louder and
louder, Moses spake, and God answered him by a voice. And .
the LORD came down upon Mount Sinai, on the top of the
mount."—Exod. xix. 17-20.

The inference cannot be better stated than in the following
passage :—

[1] Ibid, p. 135, &c. This excellent and intelligent traveller gives
here very abundant proofs that the Manna could not by any possibility
be the gum of the Tarfa tree, according to the ridiculous theory of
some sceptics.

"Now, if the Scriptural account of these miraculous physical phenomena contains any marks available for our guidance, in the ascertainment of the true Mount Sinai, it is perfectly clear that traces of these marks ought to be discernible on the face of that holy mountain. Thus, if, as Moses tells us, 'the whole Mount did quake greatly'; if the shock as of an earthquake rocked it literally to its foundations; if 'the earth did quake, and the rocks rent,' as we all know and believe they did at the time of the Crucifixion; it is most clear that we must look for marks of this wreck of nature, in any mountain of the Peninsula claiming to be Mount Sinai. Now, the very marks described and required in order to the verification are to be found at *Mount Serbâl*, and are not, it appears, to be found on any other of the reputed Mount Sinais. For the Wady Aleyât, on its northern face, is one vast chaos of ruins—of rocks precipitated from the face of the perpendicular mountain above by some great convulsion of nature. The face of the perpendicular summit, 2000 feet in height, has been *torn open*, and the only practicable ascent (as Mr. Pierce Butler ascertained) is up the chasms made by the fallen rocks below. There are no signs of volcanic agency. The shock, therefore, which thus shook the mountain, resembled rather that of an earthquake. Now compare these physical facts and features with what took place at the giving of the Law. 'And the LORD' (we read) 'came down upon Mount Sinai, *on the top of the Mount.*' Can words describe more graphically the precipitous summit of the Serbâl? Can facts attest more literally the awful sequel, than do the rifted precipice here beneath the feet of Jehovah, and the rent rocks of the Wady Aleyât in chaotic confusion below it? If, therefore, Sinai is still recoverable by its Scriptural signs, *Mount Serbâl is the true Mount Sinai.*"

Moreover, according to Mr. Forster, the name Serbâl, as derived from the Arabic, actually signifies *The Mount of God.*[1]

---

[1] Forster's *Israelitish Authorship of the Sinaitic Inscriptions*, p. 75, &c.

CHAPTER XXV.

The Sinaitic Inscriptions.

IN close and unavoidable connexion with the Exodus, a fact occurs too remarkable to be passed over in silence.

It is now about thirteen and a half centuries since an Egyptian merchant named Cosmas, and surnamed, from his voyages to India, Indicopleustes, made a journey on foot to the Sinaitic peninsula, and there was an eye-witness of the extraordinary fact that the rocks of Sinai were covered with innumerable inscriptions in a language now unknown. He published this fact to the world, from the seclusion of a monastery to which he had afterwards retired, in a work called *Christian Topography*.

His statement is as follows—"In the des............ Mount Sinai one may see, at all the haltin............... stones thereabouts, which have b.............oken ....ountains, inscribed with sculpt..................................elf, having traversed those pl...gs certain Jews havi...re numerous, so t...ew letters, pre...the unbeliev..........

1 ....

Coll. Nov.

And there—preserved even to *this* present time—are the mysterious Inscriptions still, just as they were seen and described by the honest Egyptian merchant-monk.

They have been observed and described by various modern travellers : various theories have been propounded to account for their existence, and various attempts have been made to decipher and translate them.

Two questions, of course, present themselves for enquiry :— Who were the authors of these mysterious writings ? and what is their meaning ?

And these two questions must be studied independently of each other. The circumstances of the case are so peculiar— so absolutely unique—that the authorship of them can be debated without respect to their meaning : and on the other hand, their meaning must be investigated on principles wholly unconnected with their authorship.

If, indeed, both the circumstances of the case, and the deciphered meaning, shall be found to *concur* in proving them to have been executed by the wandering tribes of Israel, the proof of their authorship will be so complete that nothing can be added to it. But the evidence of their authorship need not wait to be completed by the discovery of their meaning : though, of course, if the Israelites were indeed the authors of ____, their meaning must of necessity turn out to be such as ____lites would have been likely to express.

____e question is one not of mere probability, but of possi-____. I____t so much who were *likely* to have executed ____ inscriptions as who could *possibly* have done ____ the matter results from the very nature of

____ute from Suez to Mount Sinai the Inscrip-
____e eye of the traveller in the Wady Mokatteb,
____lley "—so called from the great number of
____. They are thus described by Lord Lind-
____entered Wady Mokatteb, a spacious valley

bounded on the east by a most picturesque range of black
mountains, but chiefly famous for the inscriptions on the rocks
that line it, and from which it derives its name; there are
thousands of them—inscriptions too—and here is the mystery
—in a character which no one has yet deciphered."[1]

Again—" The Sinaite inscriptions," says Dr. Robinson, " are
found on all the routes which lead from the west towards Sinai,
as far south as Tûr. They extend to the very base of Sinai,
above the Convent el-Arba 'in: but are found neither on Gebel
Mousa, nor on the present Horeb, nor in St. Catherine, nor in
the valley of the Convent; while on Serbâl they are seen on
its very summit."[2]

Professor Beer says—" These inscriptions exist at Mount
Sinai, or, more accurately, in the valleys and hills which extend from its roots as far as to the eastern shore of the Gulf,
so that those who at the present day travel from the monastery of Mount Sinai to the town of Suez, whichever route they
choose—for there are several—may see these inscriptions on
the rocks of very many of the valleys through which they are
conducted, even as far as to those parts of the coast which they
reach after accomplishing more than half their journey. Besides these places, similar inscriptions are found, and those in
great numbers, on Mount Serbâl, which is situated near the
south-western route; and likewise, though less frequently, in
some of the valleys which are to the south-west of Mount
Sinai."[3]

" But the valley," he adds, " which beyond all the rest claims
special notice, is that which stretches from the neighbourhood
of the eastern shore of the Gulf of Suez for the space of three
hours' journey in a southern direction. Here, to the left of
the road, the traveller finds a chain of steep sandstone rocks,

[1] Lord Lindsay's *Letters on Egypt*—Letter i., p. 176.
[2] Dr. Robinson's *Biblical Researches*, vol. i., p. 188.
[3] Beer, *Studia Asiatica*, Introd., pp. 1-15.

perpendicular as walls . . . these, beyond all beside, contain a vast multitude of tolerably well preserved inscriptions."

Another traveller found a multitude far more vast in another direction.—"For the so-called. Sinaitic Inscriptions," says the Rev. R. St. John Tyrwhitt, "they are doubly numerous, and much more legible (if one *could* read them) all along Wady Maghara and near the mines. The Mokatteb ones cannot be compared to them. No Hebrew or Greek occurs, as on the regular road to Sinai."[1]

So of the Djebel Mokatteb, another writes—"These hills are called Gebel el Mohatab, that is, the Written Mountains ; for as soon as we had parted from the mountains of Faran we passed by several others for an hour together, engraved with ancient unknown characters, which were cut into the hard marble rock so high as to be in some places at 12 or 14 feet distance from the ground ; and though we had in our company persons who were acquainted with Arabic, Greek, Hebrew, Syriack, Coptic, Latin, Armenian, Turkish, English, Illyrican, German, and Bohemian languages, yet none of them had any knowledge of these characters, which have nevertheless been cut into the hard rock with the greatest industry, in a place where there is neither water, nor any thing to be gotten to eat."[2]

Dr. Lepsius says—"I went the same evening up the Wadi Aleyat" (under Mount Serbâl) "and passed innumerable rock inscriptions". . . . "Distinguished from all the other mountains, and united in one mass, rises the Serbâl, first in a gentle slope, and then in steep rugged precipices, to a height of 6000 feet above the sea."—"It appeared to me very doubtful, when I was in the Convent at Gebel Mousa, whether it was the holy mountain on which the commandments were given or not.

---

[1] Galton's *Vacation Tourists*, art. "Sinai."
[2] From *A Journal from Cairo to Mount Sinai, by the Prefetto of Egypt, translated by the Rt. Reverend Robt. Clayton, Bishop of Clogher.*

Since I have seen Serbâl, and Wadi Feiran at its foot, and a great part of the rest of the country, I feel quite convinced that we must recognize Sinai in Mount Serbâl. The present monkish tradition has no worth in an impartial research."[1]

Mr. Bartlett writes—"In a short time after leaving the mouth of Wady Maghara the valley expands into a small plain, and suddenly contracts; it is here, on the right hand rocks, that the largest collection of the Sinaitic writings is to be found: they occur, indeed, in considerable quantity, and must have been the work of a large body of men. Wady Mokatteb is the name given to the spot. It is somewhat singular that there should be so many of them at this particular place; and some could only have been executed by means of a ladder, or at the least by clambering up the face of the rocks. They occur hence continually, though at intervals, all the way to Wady Feiran, and up to the very top of the Serbâl."[2]

Again—"While my guides and servant lay asleep under the rock, I walked round the rock, and was surprised to find inscriptions similar in form to those which have been copied by travellers in the Wady Mokatteb. They are upon the surface of blocks which have fallen down from the cliff, and some of them appear to have been engraved while the pieces still formed a part of the main rock. There is a great number of them, but few can be distinctly made out."—"The rock, though of sandstone, is of considerable hardness."[3] The inscriptions here described were in the Wady Naszeb.

Miss Martineau, describing the approach to the Wady Mokatteb from Suez, says:—"For six miles or so, now, we passed

[1] Dr. Richard Lepsius's *Letters from Egypt, Ethiopia, and the desert of Sinai*, p. 350.

[2] Bartlett's *Forty Days in the Desert*, p. 47.

[3] Burckhardt's *Travels in Syria and the Holy Land*, p. 477. Ed. London, 1822.

through rocks inscribed all over with characters which nobody can read. They are irregularly carved—some larger, some smaller, from, I think, nearly a foot high to half an inch. Those of us who had a good sight perceived that there were inscriptions much higher up than we had been given to understand by travellers. On many a smooth natural tablet, high on the face of the mountain, could I see mysterious lines like those below ; . . . but the unbroken mass of inscriptions were between the base and a height of twenty feet. Almost every large stone which lay in the valley also bore similar records. Some were rather lightly traced, little more than scratched, on the stone ; but many were deep cut." [1]

"Various travellers," says the author of *Stones crying out*, "agree in the report that, commencing near Suez, the Wadys Wardan, Maghara, Mokatteb, Feiran, and Aleyat, are all full of them ; and the last, Wady Aleyat, leads up to the five-peaked Serbâl, whose two easternmost summits, according to Burckhardt and Dr. Stewart, are covered with inscriptions. Ruppell finds them on the second peak from the west; Stanley saw them on the top of the third or central peak ; and Mr. Pierce Butler especially tells us that innumerable inscriptions clothe the northern side of the mountain."

The nature of the ground traversed in order to reach the localities of these Inscriptions is thus described—" Stewart descended from Serbâl as daylight was fading, and depicts the agony of walking when footsore over the loose angular stones of Wady Aleyat. He reached his tent utterly exhausted, and bruised with severe falls sustained by stumbling over rocks in the darkness ; and he elsewhere speaks of the 'avalanches' of rock and stone which during the course of ages have been brought down from the mountain by the winter torrents, and have so covered the Wady Aleyat as to suggest

---

[1] Martineau's *Eastern Life*, vol. ii., p. 238.

the idea that the clouds must have some time rained down boulders instead of hailstones."[1]

Once more—" In ascending the Wady Aleyât, on his way to the summit of Mount Serbâl, Mr. Butler observed traces of a path to the left, out of the usual track of the ascent, which led through a chaos of enormous rocks, evidently precipitated from the broken face of the perpendicular mountain above by some great convulsion of nature. Into this untrodden path he struck, and as he clambered through these wrecks of nature, he discovered, to his great astonishment, that hundreds upon hundreds of the fallen stones were covered with Sinaitic Inscriptions. So numerous were the instances that he added, he could state with safety 'that every second stone was inscribed.'"

"But there occurred a still more remarkable phenomenon. The granite rocks were largely interspersed with blocks of trapstone: a species of stone black on the surface, but lemon-coloured inside. Now this peculiar material had been studiously selected by the Sinaitic engravers, as the receptacle for their Inscriptions; and the consequence was that the Inscriptions carved on this material came out with the effect of a rubricated book or illuminated manuscript; the black surface throwing out in relief the lemon-coloured inscriptions. The proofs of thought and care, of taste and judgment, contained in this eclectic choice of material are such as to require no other comment than the statement of the fact."[2]

As to the extent of the Inscriptions, Mr. Forster adds— " Here, at least, all parties are agreed. There is no diversity of opinion as to the extent of the Sinaitic Inscriptions. Mr. Stanley here coincides with all preceding travellers. They stretch, on the western side of the peninsula, in broken or con-

---

[1] *Stones Crying out*, p. 222.

[2] Rev. C. Forster's *Israelitish Authorship of the Sinaitic Inscriptions*, p. 29, &c.

tinuous succession, from the vicinity of Suez, through the
Wadys Wardan, Sidri, Mahara, Mokatteb, Firan, and Aleyât,
(exclusive of those in the Wadys Nasb, Humr, and sundry
more), up the side and to the summit of the giant Serbâl,
whose lower part, the Wady Aleyât, is literally clothed with
them. They stretch, on its eastern side, in great numbers, in
the Ledja, along the table plain between the Wady Sayal and
the Wady el Ain, in the direction of Akaba. And they reappear in the vicinity of Petra and Mount Hor, only here
scattered and rare. In other words, they reach, on a rough
calculation, along lines of two degrees in both directions, exclusive of the few vestiges of them at Petra, and in the neighbourhood of Mount Hor. But their central site is around
Mount Serbâl, the leading avenues to which they throng in
innumerable multitudes."

The reflexions forced upon a thoughtful mind by these
marvellous facts are thus expressed in Mr. Lowth's interesting
work, *The Wanderer in Syria.*

"Thus we came to the Wady Mokatteb, the Valley of
Writings. On both sides of it—it was about sixty or seventy
yards broad, with perpendicular rocks on either side, starting
straight up from the level floor—high up on the face of the
cliffs, and low down on the large spreading slabs of sandstone,
were in immense numbers the Inscriptions, with occasional
figures of animals. You wonder how the places could have
been reached, at such perpendicular heights were some of the
writings. Although you cannot read a word of all this wide
amount of inscription, yet so great and general is the question
concerning the writers—Were they Israelites or were they not?
—that you gaze and stop, and gaze again, and you try to de-
decipher a letter in vain. You people the whole place with
living beings at this laborious and enterprising work, and you
are lost in wonder at such a remarkable and tremendous
amount of apparently useless labour and skill in these unten-
antable wilds.

"As you ride on thus, you quietly argue the matter. Here are miles and miles of writings, if they were drawn out into lines, and this requires that the writers must have been numerous. Their number and position oblige a long residence on the spot, for the work must have occupied a long time, the letters being large and deeply cut. The workmen must have used ropes or ladders, or have built up wooden machinery, to enable them to reach up from above or from below the places inscribed, all of which protracted labour involves considerable time and an acquaintance with habits of building on a large scale. The rude style of the greater part of the writings, and the finished sculpture of other portions, betray a people of various ranks in point of knowledge of art—a large and mixed people, and also accustomed to the presence of works of art on a magnificent scale; for how could an assemblage of common men have imagined and executed the gigantic and imposing work—'The Title'—the work measuring, as it is guessed by the eye, about one hundred feet of perpendicular height? Who could come here—what cultivated artists—what ingenious mechanicians of various trades—what crowds of untaught labourers would come and dwell in these savage deserts for the purposes of engraving sentences on bare rocks? Would the Nabathæans come here from distant places across the deserts to do this objectless work, far from all places of habitation? Would pilgrims in thousands stop on the way of their pilgrimage, and build scaffolds, and make ladders, and work skilled works in a place where death threatened them hourly? . . . You come to the conclusion that there is something in the matter of these inscribed rocks that is not in the usual and common course of human actions. You ride on with your thoughts pointing, whether you will or no, in the direction of the story of the wanderers fed and maintained by God upon these deserts for years and years, accustomed to see the works of art of Egypt, some of them skilled workmen of Pharaoh's buildings, habituated to scaffolding and ladders

. . . not now needing to work for their bread—idle, unemployed, ready for covering the rocks of the Wady Mokatteb, or any others, with their rude inscriptions."

Of all the Sinaitic records, the most extraordinary are the one last mentioned and another close to it, both described by the Comte d'Antraigues, a French nobleman who travelled in the peninsula with his suite in the year 1779. His account of them "was published originally in 1811, in the Posthumous Letters of J. G. Von Müller, the historian of Switzerland, a name so eminent in literature, before, at the call of Napoléon, he exchanged the path of 'quiet and delightful studies' for the cares of state." [1]

The following is a translation of the Comte's own words :—
"At five o'clock in the morning, on the 14th May, 1779, I put my whole caravan in motion, and we repaired to the Dshebel el Moukatab. It consists of two very lofty rocks, cut perpendicular, separated one from the other by 50 paces. It appears that their base has been hollowed by the action of the waters. . . . These rocks, covered with characters carved in relief, have none from their base up to the height of 14 feet 2 inches. The total length of the valley is 547 Paris *toises*.[2] The rocks are covered with characters up to their summits: the lines are straight, but their extremities bend up to the junction of the line above, and form a writing in furrows. On the right hand rock, in coming from Tor, there are in all 67 lines ; 41 on the rock to the left. The characters stand out one inch, and are one foot long. On the left side, on the highest part of the rock, are the characters which are called *The Title*. The reason of their having been called by this name is that the letters which compose it are 6 feet high, and stand out 3 inches. I caused them to be drawn with the greatest exactness. It would require six months of stubborn toil to draw the whole

---

[1] Forster's *Voice of Israel from the Rocks of Sinai*, p. 82.
[2] 1094 yards.

of these characters : it is a book *unique*, perhaps, under heaven, and the history of a people perhaps unknown." [1]

Of the forty-one line Inscription here described, the first line has been copied and brought to England—and of this a copy was furnished to Mr. Forster, who has succeeded in deciphering it by his Primeval Alphabet.

Such is a general description of these remarkable records graven upon the rocks of the Sinaitic deserts.

Who were the mysterious scribes? What people—what artisans—what industrious and persevering workers were they, who have left these singular memorials of their profitless labour and skill?

The question is one of transcendent interest. What if these Inscriptions are indeed nothing else but the sculptured records of Israel's forty years' sojourning in the Wilderness? What an unanswerable confirmation of that which, however, needs no confirmation—the truth of the Scripture narrative! And what stores of curious and instructive information concerning the details of those forty years' wanderings may yet be opened up by the copying and decipherment of these rock-sculptured records!

Now the idea which first occurs, that these Inscriptions were the work of Israel in their wilderness sojourning, is not only the most natural, but it is the only idea that is consistent with the facts of the case. The countless *numbers* of these Inscriptions—the *heights* at which many of them are found—the vast

---

[1] "Extract of a letter from M. le Comte d'Antraigues, ap. J. G. Müller, tom. vi. p. 330.—Von Müller saw no improbability in the assignment of an Israelitish origin to these monuments. . . . The writer whom *Napoléon* summoned to the offices, successively, of Secretary of State for Westphalia, and Minister of Public Instruction, will hardly, in our day, be taxed with credulity. At least, if he be, the charge will assuredly recoil upon the taxers."—Forster's *Voice of Israel*, p. 82, &c.

labour bestowed upon them—the difficult and almost inaccessible *situations* of multitudes of them—all combine to form a demonstration of the absolute impossibility of executing them without resources and opportunities as ample as the work is great. The workers must have been a multitude—they must have had ladders or scaffoldings of a great height—they must have had plenty of tools, and very abundant *leisure*, allowing them to choose their time, and take advantage of the opportunities of shade from the scorching sun of the desert, and not less from the fierce winds which frequently rage there, blowing up the sand in blinding clouds, and making it difficult and dangerous to use a ladder at all. All these considerations point out the absolute impossibility that these Inscriptions could have been executed by any mere straggling pilgrims or passing travellers. The work done is out of all proportion greater than any such desultory workers could possibly accomplish, even if they had the inclination to make the attempt.

These reflections would hold good even if the country were a land of ordinary fertility, and productive of ordinary supplies of food and water. But the weight of proof is altogether overwhelming when the greatest peculiarity of the whole case is taken into account—viz., that the country over which these marvellous records are scattered, to distances of about 150 miles apart, is a *stony desert*—interspersed indeed with narrow belts of pasturage in the bottoms of the valleys, but absolutely barren and destitute of all sustenance for human life. Food there is none—water is scarce and scanty, only found at distant spots known to the Arab guides, but undiscoverable by travellers without their aid. Even the Bedouin shepherd must carry his provision with him—and the "passing traveller" must not only pass, but pass on quickly too, for fear of dying by thirst or hunger in those savage wastes. Not even a moderately numerous caravan could remain for more than a day or two in any one spot, (except the Wady Feiran or some similar

oasis here and there), without an organized commissariat
bringing supplies from a distance.

This is the climax of the demonstration. The argument is
narrowed up to a dilemma from which there is no escape.
*Those Inscriptions were the work of men who had miraculous
supplies of food and water*—for it was impossible they could
either work or live there without such supplies. That such a
miraculous supply was given to Israel is matter of history: if
we refuse to believe the miracle we must believe the impossibility. Thus does the creed of the infidel recoil upon himself.
To believe the miracle requires only the common sense and
rational faith of a Christian—to believe the absence of the
miracle demands the capacious credulity of the infidel, who
strains out a gnat but can swallow a camel—who can remove
(*from his own sight*, at least) mountains of facts harder than
adamant, which demonstrate the truth of Scripture, and can
build up castles of vain theories out of fancies as visionary as
the *mirage* of the desert.

It is important to observe that, with the exception of a few
Greek and Latin sentences of quite a different aspect and
evidently more recent date, all the Inscriptions are so alike as
to be clearly the work of one single people. This fact is fully
admitted, and candidly stated, by Professor Beer himself, the
principal objector against their Israelitish origin. Beer says—
"The internal evidence of the writing is so uniform, that I
doubt whether the most ancient of the inscriptions was separated from the most recent by an interval of much more than
one age[1] (or generation)." If by an *age* Beer means a natural
generation, no expression could more accurately coincide with
the forty years of the Israelites' sojourning in the wilderness.
If, again, he means a century, still the exact uniformity of the
writing proves all the Inscriptions to have been the work of one
and the same people; and Beer's admission, taken even at its

---

[1] "Sæculum."—Beer, *Studia Asiat., Introduction.*

widest limit, restricts the whole mass of them to one hundred years, at the most, as the period within which they were begun and finished.

It is obvious that this admission of Beer's is fatal to the theory of the Inscriptions being the work of pilgrims or passing travellers. If this were so, each pilgrim or traveller would have carved his sentence in his own language, and this through-out the course of the hundreds and thousands of years since the desert was travelled at all. There would have been seen upon the rocks of Sinai specimens, not of one language only, and that one unknown, but of the languages and letters of all the nations within reach of the Arabian peninsula: and there would have been the marks of greater and less antiquity dis-cernible among them: whereas Beer, while attributing them to pilgrims, admits the absolute identity of them all in language and character, and limits them all to the space of one genera-tion, or, at most, one century.

Another important point is the *date* of these mysterious writings.

In the time of Cosmas they were believed to be the work of the Israelites of the Exodus, and consequently to be, even in his day, 2000 years old. This belief was confirmed to the eye of the Egyptian traveller and his companions by their appear-ance; and he especially notes a circumstance which subse-quent observation has proved to be a most important proof of their great antiquity even in his time. He says, that the In-scriptions were found "on all the rocks which had been broken off from the mountains." Now these inscriptions have since been ascertained to be in many instances *turned upside down* by the fall of the fragments: from which it follows that the inscriptions were made while these fragments were still part of the solid cliff. Those sculptured rocks had borne the brunt of ages before the time of Cosmas himself; till at length the wear and tear of tempest and torrent, scorching sun and searching blast, had loosened and rent the fragment from its bed, and hurled it into the depths below.

The testimony of Cosmas is unimpeachable. Beer himself quotes with approbation the words of the learned Montfaucon, —the editor of Cosmas's work—"What Cosmas reports of the inscriptions of this kind seen by himself, I think cannot be called in question by any one: for he is a truthful writer, and worthy of confidence, if any one is so."[1]

We have, then, express and indisputable historical testimony to the remote antiquity of the Sinaitic Inscriptions: and to the fact that in the time of Cosmas they were believed to be the work of the Israelites of the Exodus. That belief appears to have been universal: since Cosmas does not so much as hint at any other opinion being then entertained.

And if, five hundred years only after the Christian era, those Inscriptions were generally believed to be the work of Israel in the Wilderness, this alone ought to silence the modern sceptics who pretend to be better acquainted with ancient times than the people who lived in those times.

Moreover, this express historical testimony is borne out by the facts of the case: which present a chain of circumstantial evidence hardly less cogent than mathematical demonstration.

The combined force of the evidence both of history, and of visible facts existing at the present moment, must carry conviction to any honest mind.

But still, as other theories have been started, and have found adherents, it may be well to take some notice of them.

The principal objector, as already stated, is Professor Beer. His theory is, that the Inscriptions were the work of Nabathæan pilgrims to Mount Sinai, and were executed mostly in the fourth century. Yet Beer himself, who writes with an amusing simplicity, and a candour worthy of a better cause, immediately adds, that certainly he had never heard that there

---

[1] Beer, *Studia Asiat.*, Introduction.

ever were any such pilgrims, nor did he think it likely that
pilgrims from Palestine or Syria had at that time visited
Mount Sinai ; though it is true that Helena, the mother of
Constantine, had made a pilgrimage thither, and built a sanctuary on the spot.   But as a custom had grown up about that
time of making pilgrimages to sacred places, especially Jerusalem, " it might easily happen," he says, " that the desire of
visiting holy places might stimulate some tribes of Arabia
Petræa to go in considerable numbers, from religious motives,
to the sacred spots of their own country, Mount Sinai and the
valleys of the great miracles of Moses." [1]

The German Professor has much ado to conjure up his
Nabathæan pilgrims, and make them cover the rocks with in-
scriptions scattered along one hundred and fifty miles of desert.
True, he had never heard of any pilgrims whatever going to
Mount Sinai, with the solitary exception of the Empress

---

[1] The whole passage is such a curious piece of reasoning that I
give Beer's own words.—" Ipse primus (Cosmas) inscriptionum harum
nuntium viris eruditis suæ ætatis tradidisse videtur. Unde conjicimus,
ætatem harum inscriptionum tempore haud ita brevi superiorem esse
ævo Cosmæ. Crucis Christianæ figura Y, quæ in nostris inscriptionibus frequentior est quam ✝, num diu post Constantini ætatem . . . in
usu manere potuerit præter alteram, dubito.

" Itaque sæculo quarto maximam partem harum inscriptionum factam
esse existimo. Eo tempore apud Christianos maximè increbuerat mos
sacra loca, præcipuè Hierosolyma, cum exspectatione miraculorum
adeundi et religionis causâ peregrinandi, ita quidem ut sub finem ejus
sæculi Gregorio, episcopo Nysseno, necesse videretur ut peculiari
libello contrà hunc morem dissereret. Montem Sinai tum temporis
visitatum esse a Palæstinensibus Syrisve *verosimile vix est, certè desunt
testes :* quamquam haud negaverimus, Helenam, matrem Constantini,
ad eum montem religionis causâ profectam esse, ibique sanctuarium
erexisse. . . . Sed *facile fieri potuit,* ut illa sacrorum locorum visitan-
dorum cupido aliquot Arabiæ Petrææ tribus excitaret, ut suæ terræ
loca sacra, montem Sinai vallesque magnorum Mosis miraculorum per
aliquod tempus frequentes et religiosi adirent."—Beer, *Studia Asiatica,*
Introduction.

Helena: true, he thought it not likely that any should go there from either Palestine or Syria, (though from thence, if from any quarter, it was likely they would go); yet, as it was the custom for Christians to go on pilgrimage to Jerusalem and other holy places, it was just possible that pilgrims *might* go from Arabia Petræa (Nabathæans) in such multitudes as to cover the desert with the countless thousands of the Sinaitic Inscriptions[1]!—The Professor has omitted to inform us how, when they arrived at their destination, they managed to live without food or water, or where they obtained ladders and scaffolding: or how it is that the great majority of the Inscriptions are found, not on the route from Arabia Petræa to Mount Sinai, but far to the opposite side of it, where his pilgrims would have no occasion to go at all.

Beer's chief argument for a Christian authorship of the Inscriptions is the occasional occurrence of the character ✝, which he assumes to be meant for the Cross. But as even this character is too rarely found to sustain his theory, he farther enlists into his service the character Y, which occurs more frequently, and which he supposes to be another form of the Cross. True, he adds, with admirable simplicity, this form of the Christian Cross is unheard of—which may certainly be thought a difficulty in his theory:—true, he has never heard of any such form of the Cross among Christians: but this he thinks a circumstance of no great moment—it *may* have existed among Christians in *some* countries, in which *perhaps* male-

---

[1] Beer thinks the Inscriptions were executed in the fourth century, because it was at that time that the custom of pilgrimages had grown up. But Niebuhr says that "even in the *third* century these inscriptions had been mentioned by a Greek author"—(Niebuhr's *Travels*, vol. i., p. 200:) so that they existed before those pilgrimages were made which are supposed by Beer to have produced them. Beer attributes them to pilgrims from Arabia Petræa because "he does not see any other country which can be mentioned as so likely"!

factors may have been executed upon crosses of the furcated figure Υ !¹

The learned German Professor's theory, then, is this :—That the Sinaitic Inscriptions, in their countless thousands, were the work of Nabathæan pilgrims who, (so far as he, or any one else, knows) never existed : that they are proved to be the work of Christians by the occurrence now and then, though very rarely, of the sign ✝, and more frequently of the sign Υ ; which signs he takes to be meant for the Christian Cross, though there is no proof that either of them was so intended, and though a Cross of the latter form never was seen or heard of by any one. The fact that not a single particle of *proof* can be adduced in favour of his theory is a circumstance which the Professor treats with sublime unconcern : to say nothing of the still more inconvenient circumstance that his theory is opposed by the fact that people cannot live without eating and drinking.

Moreover, so learned a Professor, before he undertook to decipher Sinaitic Inscriptions, ought to have known that the character ✝ is not necessarily the sign of the Cross at all, but is simply a letter of the alphabet. It is just the letter *t*—the *tau* of the most ancient, as it is still the T of the most modern languages. It was variously written Τ, and ✝, and in other forms : and as the mystic Tau—the initial letter of Tammuz —it is found in the medals and monuments of Chaldæa, Egypt, Etruria, Rome, the Celtic nations, Mexico, Tartary and other

---

¹ Here again, I give Beer's own words, lest I should be thought to have in any way misrepresented his meaning, so as to produce so remarkable an argument.—"Ob hunc in inscriptionibus locum hoc signum crucis Christianæ figuram esse existimo, quæ in nonnullis regionibus usitata fuerit, in quibus fortasse malefici plerumque in cruces quæ hunc furcæ (Υ) figuram habebant, agebantur.   Cui sententiæ obstare videtur quod talis Christianæ crucis figura nova est, certè equidem *nullum ejus testem reperi :* sed hoc levioris momenti esse puto."—Beer, *Studia Asiat.,* Introduction, p. 13.

Buddhist countries, and, in short, in almost every Pagan tribe and people under heaven.[1]—So little does it make for Professor Beer.

Nothing daunted, however, by such considerations, other authors have followed in Beer's footsteps—the most noted of whom is Dean Stanley.

The Dean adopts the idea that the Inscriptions were the work of passing travellers.—"Their situation and appearance," he says, "are such as in hardly any case requires more than the casual work of passing travellers." Again—"*None* that I saw, unless it might be a doubtful one at Petra, required ladders or machinery of any kind. Most of them could have been written by any one, who, having bare legs and feet, as all Arabs have, could take firm hold of the ledges, or by any active man even with shoes. I think there are *none* that could not have been written by one man climbing on another's shoulders."[2]—Again, he would diminish the difficulty by reducing the number.—"Their numbers," he says, "seem to me greatly exaggerated." . . . "The Inscriptions straggle not by thousands, but at most by hundreds or fifties."

Now let any one compare these remarks with the descriptions given by all other travellers, and even by Beer himself, and judge whether the Dean's theory is not wholly irreconcileable with the facts.

The unanimous testimony of other travellers, as given in the extracts above, is entirely opposed to the Dean's statement. They declare that the Inscriptions are in countless thousands —that they are in every possible position, and at every height up to about a hundred feet from the ground—that they cover not only the sides of perpendicular walls of rock, to the height of twenty, thirty, forty, eighty, or even one hundred feet, but that they are found on the very peaks of the almost inacces-

[1] See Hislop's *Two Babylons*, p. 289, &c.
[2] *Sinai and Palestine*, p. 60.

sible Mount Serbâl, and in places so remote and rugged that
"passing travellers" would be likely to pass some other way,
and that none but curious explorers would penetrate there at
all. Is it likely that passing travellers would spend their time
and strength in clambering up the rugged precipices of a
mountain more than 6000 feet high, carrying with them chisels
and mallets, for the useless object of carving inscriptions which
might never meet the eye of man—and that, too, in such numbers that in the ravine discovered by Mr. Butler every second
stone is covered with them ?

The Dean says that most of those which he saw could have
been done by one man climbing on another's shoulders. He
has omitted to explain how any man balancing himself upon
the shoulders of another, and maintaining his position, as he
must do, by holding on to the rock, could at the same time
use a punch or chisel, and a mallet—which would require the
free use of both hands. And we must needs suppose that
those Inscriptions which the Dean did see were as nothing in
proportion to those he did not see. A man "on another's
shoulders" could not even touch the rock higher than about a
dozen feet from the ground : whereas the Inscriptions are
found at all heights up to eighty or a hundred feet, carved on
perpendicular walls of cliff. Did the Dean see, for instance,
those described by Mr. Grey, and carefully verified by Capt.
Butler and his brother[1]—many of which are described as
"high up"—"inaccessible"—"*inaccessible without a ladder*,"
&c. ?—Or did he see those marvellous monuments of patient
toil, daring, and skill, described by the Comte d'Antraigues—
the inscription in 40 lines of characters a foot high, surmounted
by "THE TITLE," in letters carved three inches deep into the
rock and 6 feet high—forming a sculptured face of cliff about
100 feet in height :—or the other in 67 lines, apparently on a

[1] See, for the full description, the Rev. C. Forster's *Israelitish
Authorship of the Sinaitic Inscriptions*, p. 17, &c.

similar scale of grandeur, and which, in proportion to the number of lines, must be very much higher? The expressions in the Comte d'Antraigues' description, "deux rochers, très élevés, *taillés à pic*," and "caractères *taillés en relief*," seem to imply that the perpendicular faces of the two cliffs had been smoothed in order to receive the inscriptions, and that the letters were actually *embossed* upon the surface by chiselling out the interstices—so that the letters of "The Title" stood out three inches, the rest one inch, from the face of the rock. If this be the true sense (and it is the literal sense) of the words, and if the Count was correct in his observation, the labour of executing the work must have been enormous; and the skill required could be possessed only by educated and practised artisans. It is needless to observe that the work could no more have been executed without scaffolding than could the building of a church tower.

The following description may serve to illustrate the nature of some of those situations where Inscriptions are found, and the probability that they might be executed "by one man climbing upon another's shoulders."—"Except to a daring cragsman some of the highest elevations now in question are absolutely inaccessible, being on the face of sandstone cliffs perpendicular as house-walls. Examples of this character are so important in the evidences, that I must give a specimen, *instar omnium*, from the account of it given me by Mr. Pierce Butler. His Inscriptions numbered I., II., III., IV.,[1] he discovered in the Wady Mahara; the first two at the height of thirty feet from the ground, the others a very little lower, on the face of a perpendicular sandstone cliff. To all appearance, those Inscriptions were wholly inaccessible; but the sandstone lying in strata presented seams at intervals of five or six feet; and Mr. Butler, accustomed to scale the face of the Giant's

[1] See Forster's *Israelitish Authorship of the Sinaitic Inscriptions*, p. 24.

Causeway, and of the other gigantic cliffs of the County of Antrim, contrived to climb this wall by means of its slight fissures, and holding on with the left hand, to copy with the right the Inscriptions which, by this perilous process, he had succeeded in reaching. His Arabs and his dragoman beneath gave him up for lost; repeatedly ejaculating, after their fashion, that he must be killed. To their utter astonishment, however, he descended in safety, bringing down fac-similes of the life-imperilling records." [1]

To pursue farther the *reductio ad absurdum* may seem to be a waste of words; yet for the sake of those who have not attended to the subject, and are therefore in the greater danger of being misled, it may be as well to point out the extreme labour and difficulty of executing these desert rock-writings. The reader will then be able better to form a judgment as to the probability, or rather the possibility, of their having been done by passing travellers.

Dr. Robinson, for instance, says that they occur "at such points as would form convenient resting-places for travellers or pilgrims during the noon-day sun" [2]—during "the mid-day halt," as it has been otherwise expressed. But Dr. Bonar states that, in the Wady Mokatteb, inscriptions are found in very great numbers on rocks where "from nine in the morning till three or four in the afternoon the sun never left them. They lie fully exposed to his rays." [3]

The conclusion is obvious. Would passing travellers be inclined to aggravate their weariness by working instead of resting? Would they choose to hazard their lives by sun-stroke in the almost insupportable toil of standing for hours under the scorching sun of the desert, for the purpose of carving useless inscriptions?

---

[1] *Israelitish Authorship*, &c., p. 23.
[2] *Biblical Researches*, vol. i. p. 128.
[3] *Desert of Sinai*, p. 166.

It is easy to *talk* about travellers doing this or that—the actual doing of the thing is a very different matter. The practical difficulties of sculpturing inscriptions on the rocks of Sinai may be judged of in some degree from the following descriptions of the labour of even *copying* some of them.

"On the fourth of this month (May 1845) I set out for Sinai; and on reaching the Wady Mokatteb, I and my people kept a sharp look-out for the writings. At the first graven rock which I espied, I ordered a halt. I then reconnoitred the neighbourhood, and found that if we tarried three days, or even two, our water and provisions would not hold out till the Convent, whither we must go to take in a six-days' supply for our return. The expense, too, of detaining the camels and Arabs would be not inconsiderable. I therefore determined to select only the best and clearest inscriptions for copying, and worked, almost unremittingly, from noon to sunset under a burning sun; my servant, and the Arab Shieck and his boy, holding an umbrella over me in turns. The next morning, before sunrise, I went to work again; and when the sun began to wax hot, I called my servant to bear the umbrella as before. He, having something to do in the tent, called the Shieck; and he, from out of a rocky cave where he lay, called the boy; and forth came the poor boy from another shady retreat, to face the fierce glare of the sun, wondering what could possess the Frangee to stop in this frightful desert, to copy these useless and, (as he thought) unintelligible writings. I worked till noon; and then took a slight meal, and set forth on my journey."[1]

The next extract is from the journal of M. Lottin de Laval: "who describes the character of the country, the sites of num-

[1] "*Extract of a letter from Rev. T. Brookman.*—One of his inscriptions sent to me is thus endorsed: 'No. 17. Mem. Many after this too much effaced to be read, *and many inaccessible without a ladder*'."—From the Rev. C. Forster's *Voice of Israel from the Rocks of Sinai,* p. 174, 1852.

bers of the Inscriptions, the appliances indispensable for the task of *copying* them, and the difficulties and dangers to be encountered in their application, in terms to which nothing can be added.

"'To the west of the brown Wan-dick, to the east of the land of shade, there I found the track of a wolf (*d'yp*) : and certainly, if these beasts of prey are numerous in the peninsula of Sinai, they must dine but very seldom ; for there is nothing, absolutely nothing, but stone, granite, and sand. The country becomes more and more dreary in proportion as one rises : the desolation is oppressive. A deathlike silence reigns in these frightful gorges, so rarely visited ; and they terminate in a steep ascent almost insurmountable. At the outlet of these rugged passes, at some distance, the gigantic peak of Djebel-Cédré suddenly rose at the bottom of the route like a castle wall : I thought for a moment that we should have to return back again to find a passage ; but, to my great joy, a narrow wady opened in a cleft, and I had not gone a hundred paces before I perceived, on the wall of rocks, some Sinaitic Inscriptions, the characters of which shewed themselves clearly upon a dark ground.

"'Firing immediately a pistol shot (from the Wady Maghara) the Sheik Saleh brought me my ladders" (30 feet in length) "and the necessary materials. The operation was of extreme difficulty in the midst of this inextricable chaos, and I did not well know how to make myself a scaffold. I had tied two of my ladders, the base of which I propped with blocks of sandstone on the steep declivity of the mountain ; but the violent wind which had been blowing for several days across the gorges of the peninsula, made them oscillate like a willow branch, threatening every moment to carry me away together with them into the abyss.

"'Leaving Wady Faran, I returned southwards by the Wady Zreitt, which is the last spur of the Sinaitic group. There is not perhaps under the sun so dreary a corner. The

ground is covered with black sparkling pebbles; one sinks in
quicksands where the sand crumbles every moment under the
feet of the camels; and at the end of this, to crown the work,
one descends a frightful defile abutting on the desert of Gah,
which stretches from north-west to south-east.

"'This desolate plain is the celebrated desert of Sin of the
Hebrews. The tempest, which had been blowing for a fortnight over Arabia, was there of terrific violence. The north
wind parched me to the very marrow; and to complete my
misery, it was impossible to pitch my tent. I arrived at the
palm trees of Tor on the evening of the second day, half-dead,
and spitting blood by mouthfuls.'"[1]

Such are some of the difficulties of attempting even to *copy*
the Inscriptions: what must have been the difficulties of *executing* them?

Besides the toil and danger of the work itself, the impossibility of even existing in the desert, without miraculous
supplies of food, long enough to execute the Inscriptions, is
thus commented upon by another traveller:—"No reflection
forced itself upon me so often or so urgently, in passing over
the track of the Israelites, as the utter and universal inaptitude
of this country for the sustenance of animal life. It seems
really to possess no elements favourable to human existence
besides a pure atmosphere; and no appearances favour the
supposition that it was ever essentially better. I am filled
with wonder that so many travellers should task their ingenuity
to get rid of the miracles, which, according to the narrative of
Moses, were wrought to facilitate the journey of that vast,
unwieldy host; when it is demonstrable *that they could not have
subsisted three days in this desert* without supernatural resources.
The extensive region, through which we were twelve days in
passing on dromedaries, is, and ever must have been, incapable

[1] *Archives des Missions Scientifiques*, 1er Cahier, Jan. 1851, p.
10-14: quoted in Forster's *Voice of Israel*, p. 188, &c.

of affording food sufficient to support even a thousand, or a few hundred people, for a month in the year. There is no corn-land or pasturage ; no game nor roots ; hardly any birds or insects ; and the scanty supply of water is loathsome to the taste, provoking, rather than appeasing, thirst. What could the two millions of Israel have eaten, without the miracles of the manna and the quails? How could they have escaped destruction by drought, but for the healing of the waters of Marah? a miracle that was probably repeated in the Wady Gerundel, and at the other salt wells on their route to Sinai."[1]

This is the language of consistency and common sense—which cannot be said of the theories of Professor Beer and others.

There is one thing more, which is important to the enquiry —What could have been the *motive* of those who spent so much time and labour on these profitless Inscriptions? Men do not toil without *some* motive. The common ambition of travellers could have little force to induce them to leave their names inscribed in those savage solitudes where few indeed would ever see the writings—more especially at inaccessible heights where none could read them. And to suppose that men would endure the toil of executing " The Title " and its 40 lines ensuing—a work which the Comte d'Antraigues estimated must have cost six months of "stubborn labour"[2]—merely to immortalize their folly, would be to suppose that they acted from motives which are not credible.

But suppose men to be placed in such circumstances that time hangs heavy on their hands—that inaction becomes a burden—that *ennui* oppresses them till the smartest toil would be a positive relief from the sorer drudgery of doing nothing— in this case it is not only conceivable, but morally certain, that

---

[1] Dr. Olin's *Travels in Egypt, Arabia Petræa, and the Holy Land*, vol. i. p. 381—quoted in Forster's *Voice of Israel from the Rocks of Sinai*, p. 39, 1852.

[2] The Count's words *dessiner* la totalité &c., seem to mean that it would take 6 months even to *copy* the whole of these two inscriptions.

even such profitless labour as that of the Sinaitic Inscriptions would be a welcome resource.

And such exactly was the case of Israel in the Wilderness— and such has never been the case with any other people, either there or any where else.

The idea of rock-writing was familiar to the Israelites and other Eastern tribes : as is evident from the often quoted words of Job—" Oh that my words were now written! oh that they were printed in a book! that they were graven with an iron pen and lead in the rock for ever!"—Job. xix. 23, 24. There was no lack among them of skilled artisans, accustomed in Egypt to sculpturing and scaffolding on a large scale: and there were the rocks all around them, inviting their skill, and offering the means of "killing time," if nothing better. What more natural—what more probable—one might almost say, more certain, than that they would beguile the tedious, weary days of their wilderness life in such works as the Sinaitic rock-writings?

CHAPTER XXVI.

Same Subject continued.—The Monuments of Sarbut-el-Khadem.

EVIDENCE still more striking, if not more conclusive, assigns to the Israelites the remarkable monuments at Sarbut-el-Khadem.

In 1761, the celebrated Niebuhr was conducted to this spot by his Arab guides through a mistake. He had inquired for the Inscriptions, but his meaning being misunderstood he thus became undesignedly the discoverer of one of the most interesting monuments in the world—the Cemetery of Sarbut-el-Khadem.

The spot is thus described by Dr. Robinson :—"Among the sandstone mountains on our right, the site of Surâbit-el-Khadem had already been pointed out to us." . . . "Crossing on foot a ridge of deep sand towards the West into a rocky ravine, we began the difficult ascent of the mountain at its South-east end.

"The mountain may be some six or seven hundred feet high ; and is composed entirely of precipitous sandstone rock, mostly red, but alternating occasionally with strata of different shades. A track leads up the toilsome and somewhat dangerous ascent, along the face of the precipice at the head of the ravine, marked only by small heaps of stones. Climbing slowly and with difficulty to the top, we found ourselves at

the end of three quarters of an hour upon a level ridge, connected with a tract of high table-land of sandstone formation,
much resembling the Saxon Switzerland, and, like it, inter-
sected in every direction by deep precipitous ravines: while
higher peaks of irregular and fantastic form lay all around us.
A short distance westward on this ridge, with a deep chasm
on either side, are situated the singular and mysterious monuments of Surâbit-el-Khadem. These lie mostly within the
compass of a small enclosure, 160 feet long from east to west,
by 70 feet broad, marked by heaps of stones thrown or fallen
together, the remains perhaps of former walls or rows of low
buildings. Within this space are seen about 15 upright
stones, like tombstones, and several fallen ones covered with
Egyptian hieroglyphics; and also the remains of a small
temple, whose columns are decorated with the head of Isis for
a capital. At the eastern end is a subterranean chamber excavated in the solid rock, resembling an Egyptian sepulchre.
It is square, and the roof is supported in the middle by a
square column left from the rock. Both the column and the
sides of the chamber are covered with hieroglyphics: and in
each of the sides is a small niche. The whole surface of the
enclosure is covered with fallen columns, fragments of sculpture, and hewn stones, strewn in every direction; over which
the pilgrim can with difficulty find his way. Other similar
upright stones stand without the enclosure in various directions, and even at some distance." . . . "These upright stones,
both within and without the enclosure, vary from about 7 to
10 feet in height, while they are from 18 inches to 2 feet in
breadth, and from 14 to 16 inches in thickness. They are
rounded off on the top, forming an arc over the broadest
sides.—Not the least singularity about these monuments is
the wonderful preservation of the inscriptions upon this soft
sandstone, exposed as they have been to the air and weather
during the lapse of so many ages. On some of the stones
they are quite perfect.

"This spot was first discovered by Niebuhr in 1761."[1]

The objectors who have spent so much fruitless labour in disputing the Israelitish authorship of the Inscriptions will have still more trouble here. Are these singular monuments also the work of pilgrims or passing travellers—these elaborately carved tombstones, this rock-hewn sepulchre? Did pilgrims or passing travellers not only sculpture the most laborious and lofty Inscriptions, but also construct a *cemetery?*

Niebuhr, at least, thought not so.—"Ne seraient-ce pas ici," he says, "*les sepulcres de la convoitise,* dont il est fait mention Nombr. xi. 34?—Il n'était point défendu aux Israelites d'employer les figures hiéroglyphiques, ni d'avoir des images d'hommes et de bêtes; il ne leur était interdit que de les adorer, et même encore aujourd'hui les Juifs gravent toute sorte de figures, et même des portraits, sur des cachets."[2]

Niebuhr, then, believed the cemetery of Sarbut-el-Khadem to be the Kibroth-hattaavah of Scripture—the "graves of lust," or greediness, mentioned in Numbers xi. 34.

The objectors have shown, in this instance, more prudence than candour. Why have none of them ever taken the slightest notice of this remarkable admission of Niebuhr's—the man, above all others, to reject every thing mythical or fanciful in ancient traditions and histories? Why, but because the admission from such a man is fatal to their foolish theories?

That the tombstones of Sarbut-el-Khadem are indeed those of the "Graves of Lust," is confirmed by the discoveries of Dr. Stewart—all the more conclusively because his testimony is of the nature of an undesigned coincidence.

Respecting the circumstance of the top of the hill being chosen as a burying-ground, it may be observed, that to bury their dead on "high places" was quite in accordance with the customs of the Israelites, but not at all with those of the

---

[1] Robinson's *Biblical Researches*, Sect. III., vol. i., p. 77, &c.
[2] *Voyage en Arabie*, tom. i. p. 191.

Egyptians. Mr. Forster remarks,—" They whose ancestors
filled the mummy pits of Thebes, or Memphis, would never
carry their dead out to Sarbut-el-Khadem ; but Moses himself
was commanded to go up to the top of Mount Nebo and die.
Aaron was to go up to Mount Hor, and die there. The
Israelites as well as the votaries of Baal were always wont to
worship on 'high places,' and it is clear from ' the sepulchres
in the mount,' mentioned in 2 Kings xxiii. 16, that they were
also wont to bury on ' high places.'

"Mr. Forster however considers that while Sarbut-el-
Khadem and the Kibroth-hattaavah of Numb. xi. 34, are one
and the same, it is yet self-evident that the scene of the
plague could not have been limited to this locality, or its
countless victims interred on one spot. The mountain-top
could have been the burial-place only of the guilty priests and
princes of Israel, as the costliness of the monuments and the
difficulties of the ascent combine to certify. The common
people, the guilty multitude, must have had other and numerous burying-places ; and the identification of the spot would
be incomplete could not this be proved to be the case. But
here a service of no common moment has been rendered to
Scripture history and evidences by Dr. Stewart of Leghorn,
who has recovered, in the adjoining wadys, at different and
distant points, a series of ancient tombs and cemeteries distinguishing the whole region, and called universally by the
Arabs, to this day, ' Turbet es Yahoud,' *the Graves of the
Jews.*" [1]

"After leaving that part of Wadi Mokatteb where the inscriptions are most numerous," Dr. Stewart says, " we still
continued to traverse it for about an hour and a half; latterly,
over rough uneven ground, till it ends in a pass or defile
somewhat resembling Budrah, which leads into Wadi Natet."

[1] *Stones Crying out,* p. 241.

. . . "It is a large triangular plain, having its apex eastward, and its base to the west." . . . "We kept well to the left, and at the point where Wadi Naserane strikes off to the left, we came unexpectedly on a large number of ancient tumuli, generally composed of heaps of stones thrown together." . . . "To whom do these graves belong? The Arabs declared that they contained none of their dead, for they never were in the habit of burying there—that they were very ancient, but that they knew nothing more of their history than that their fathers had told them these tumuli were the *Turbet es Yahoud* —'the Graves of the Jews:' and that among them they had never had another name." . . . "Can these be the graves of the Israelites, or can they belong to the age of the Exodus? Considering how superstitious the Arabs are with regard to the resting-places of the dead, and having regard to the little change which has taken place in their manners since the Bible days downwards, there is nothing incredible in the supposition that these cairns may have remained undisturbed since Israel's days."[1]

Again, he says—"Turning to descend the hill, my attention was directed to a number of cairns of stone which, from their blackened appearance, had evidently remained untouched for ages. Others, however, had been opened, and the stones were scattered about; a small hole had been made in the centre of each, probably in search of treasure. In two of those which were undisturbed a huge stone had fallen in from the top, revealing two narrow chambers formed of granite blocks, each of which could only have contained a single body.—The next day, as we travelled up the Wady Berah, we came upon more tombs, with several chambers in each. The *whole of this part of the wady*, opposite Tamner, *seems to have been covered with graves*, the stones of which are scattered abroad in all direc-

---

[1] Dr. Stewart's *The Tent and the Khan*, p. 96.—Edinburgh, 1857.

tions. There is no vestige of a town or village. The place is too distant from Feiran for these graves to have any connection with the ancient city there, and the idea of pilgrims having died here in such numbers is not to be entertained, even if the graves themselves did not betoken an earlier existence.

"Dr. Stewart, therefore, believes they are the graves of the Israelites, and the same as the graves of greediness at Kibroth-hattaavah. But if Wady Berah be indeed the Taberah of Scripture, if the Israelites marched this way, and died here, it may fairly be expected that their route shall be traced by their roadmarks, the Sinaitic Inscriptions. Dr. Stewart says nothing about these, but Dr. Robinson unconsciously comes in to supply the missing link of evidence.

"In passing through Wady Berah, the sepulchres and burial-grounds escaped his notice, but he observed and notices the usual writings. 'I struck across the valley,' he says, 'and on a large rock found four inscriptions in the usual unknown character. Just by our tent was also a huge detached rock covered with similar writings, but much obliterated. Indeed we found these writings at almost every point where the overhanging or projecting rocks seemed to indicate a convenient resting-place.'

"The occurrence of the Sinaitic inscriptions *in connection with the graves in Wady Berah* is a new point in the evidence, since, if it be admitted that the tombs are those of the Israelites, it is in vain to question the Israelite authorship of the adjoining inscriptions." [1]

Let all the facts above detailed be fairly and impartially weighed—and, in addition, one circumstance which has not yet been mentioned, viz., that the Inscriptions, the Sarbut-el-Khadem cemetery, and the *Turbet es Yahoud*—"the Graves

[1] *Stones Crying out*, p. 238, &c.

of the Jews," so called from time immemorial by the Arabs to the present hour—are all *on the ascertained route of Israel in the Wilderness*, or in the near neighbourhood—and can a doubt remain that the Israelites, and the Israelites alone, were the authors and artisans of the mysterious rock-writings of the Sinai desert?

CHAPTER XXVII.

Same Subject continued.—Mr. Forster's system of decipherment and translation.

THE proofs adduced above of the Israelitish authorship of the Inscriptions, it will be observed, are of a nature wholly independent of their *meaning.* Let it be granted, for argument's sake, that no successful attempt has hitherto been made to decipher them—still, the fact remains that they *exist :* and no rational account can be given of that fact, except by allowing that they were the work of Israel in their forty years' sojourn in the wilderness—simply because it is impossible that they could have been executed by any other people.

But if we proceed from the fact of their existence to inquire farther whether there is reason to believe that their meaning has been at all made out, here also we find an amount of evidence too great to be lightly disregarded.

There is one, and only one, system of decipherment as yet published which is worthy of serious attention—viz., that of the Rev. Charles Forster. If the correctness of his decipherments be admitted, the Israelitish origin of the Inscriptions follows as a matter of course—for they contain actual records, by eye-witnesses, of the events of the Exodus as they occurred. If, on the other hand, any one disputes Mr. Forster's conclusions, it behoves the objector to show cause why they are to be rejected. *This has never yet been done.* Several writers have denied that the Israelites wrote the Inscriptions—which amounts to an assertion that Mr. Forster's decipherments are wrong. But none of these writers, nor any one else, has shown *why* they are wrong. Unless this can be done, Mr. Forster's position remains impregnable.

Those readers who desire the opportunity of judging for themselves must of necessity be referred to Mr. Forster's own works, *The One Primeval Language*, and *Sinai Photographed*—the latter as splendid a work as it is valuable. A brief description of his method of proceeding, and a few specimens of the decipherments obtained, must here suffice.

It is no more than justice to Mr. Forster to point out that he has gone to work in a way the most strictly and rigorously scientific. The recovery of a lost alphabet is as much a matter of scientific induction as the discovery of a law of nature. And by strict scientific induction Mr. Forster's alphabet of the One Primeval Language has been constructed.

There is an affinity between all languages which points to the conclusion that the confusion of tongues at Babel consisted, not in a complete oblivion of the primeval language, and the creation of other languages absolutely new, but in the division of the one language into different *dialects*—sufficiently different to make the speakers mutually unintelligible. The principle therefore upon which Mr. Forster has proceeded, to use his own words, "is simply this: that the change miraculously wrought at Babel was not radical, but dialectic. It is thus enunciated by Philo Judæus: '(Mankind) paid the fit penalty for their daring, for they presently became many-tongued: so that, from that time forth, they could no longer understand each other, by reason of the diversity in the *dialects* into which the one tongue, once common to all, was divided.'" [1]

It is obvious, therefore, that the only principle upon which

[1] Forster's *Primeval Language*, Pt. II, p. 1, quoting Philo Judæus *de Confus. Ling.* p. 321, ed. fol. Lut. Par. 1640.

an experimental primeval alphabet can be framed is to assume that those characters in the most ancient dialects which have *similar forms* must be taken to have *similar powers.* This is Mr. Forster's principle—rigorously carried out in the construction of his alphabet, and likewise in the decipherment of words.

But suppose the word to have been thus deciphered—how is its meaning to be ascertained?

"This one primeval language", Mr. Forster states, "has been identified at Sinai, as to its vocabulary at least, *with the old Arabic:*"—and, "the old Arabic stands identified, historically as well as philologically, with the ancient Egyptian ".[1]

But moreover, "the Hamyaritic itself is chiefly that portion of the Arabic, of which Arabic scholars, from Pococke downwards, have so often observed that while it occupies more than one half of all the Arabic lexicons, it rarely, if ever, is met with in any Arabic writers. This was the statement of the case made to the present writer at Paris, in 1844, by one of the first Arabic scholars in Europe, who had been studying Arabic for thirty years without being able to account for the anomaly; but observed, 'The problem is now solved—this is the lost Hamyaritic.'

"In the decipherment, therefore, of all primitive tongues, the Arabic lexicon, more than one half of which has been heretofore a dead letter, is the proper standard of appeal".[2]

It follows therefore of necessity that if the experimental alphabet thus formed—by induction from all the most ancient alphabets—deciphers a word in an unknown ancient writing, and farther, if the word thus deciphered is found in the Arabic Lexicon, the sense given in that Lexicon is the true sense of the word.

---

[1] See *Prim. Language,* Pt. II, p. 2; and the proofs there adduced of this fact.

[2] Ibid. pp. 75, 76.

It is precisely thus that Mr. Forster has worked out his decipherment of the Sinaitic Inscriptions.

But before giving specimens of these, it may be both interesting and satisfactory to the reader to quote a few instances,
out of many, in which Mr. Forster's alphabet, together with
the Arabic Lexicon, has elicited singularly striking and conclusive proofs of its correctness in translating various other
ancient inscriptions beside those in the Sinai desert.

When the device of a medal, or sculpture, for instance,
plainly depicts an object, and thus explains its own meaning—
and the legend or inscription accompanying it is found to
express in words the same action which is represented in the
device, not a shadow of doubt can remain that the legend has
been correctly read and correctly translated.

The following are instances of this correspondence between
the device, and the legend as deciphered and translated by
Mr. Forster.

In the British Museum there is a tablet (figured in Mr.
Forster's Primeval Language, Pt. ii., p. 104), representing, in two
compartments, Egyptian chariots and horses. In the upper
compartment, the driver is seen reining in a spirited horse; in
the lower compartment he sits at ease with his back to the
horses, which are seen jaded and weary, drinking out of a
bucket. Between the two compartments, as if to show its
connexion with both, is a legend in only two characters. Mr.
Forster thus describes the decipherment :—"A friend brought
me a newly published volume containing this tablet, for the
purpose of trying whether any light could be thrown on the
picture from its inscription. Immediately on looking at the
single central word, I told him the word was *tis :* but that full
light could hardly be expected from one monosyllable. I
opened the lexicon, however, at the root *tis ;* and, to his great
surprise and my own as great satisfaction, read the *primary*
definition : viz. 'Exercuit et obsequentem reddidit equum'—

'*exercising and taming the horse.*'"   That the one word should thus give the *double* action of the picture ; it being, perhaps, the only one out of 50,000 Arabic words capable of doing so ; and that it should be fixed on *impromptu* from among its 10,000 roots, is, on the doctrine of chances, an amount of proof which it is easier to indicate than to compute."

Again, in Michaelis's *Monimenti Antichi*, Pl. LIV., there is an engraving of a wounded warrior, with the blood dropping from his leg which is pierced with an arrow.   The legend, which is Etruscan, is deciphered by Mr. Forster's alphabet to be *tanatā*. This word is found in Golius's Arabic lexicon, and is rendered —" Paulatim fluxit sanguis e vulnere"—"*the blood trickles down from the wound.*"

Michaelis translates the legend as. giving the *name* of the warrior, viz. *Tideus.* But, in Lanzi Saggio's work *di Lingua Etrusca*, &c., Vol. iii. Tab. 4, are two other figures of wounded warriors, each with the same legend *tanatā:* and in a loose leaf sent to Mr. Forster from some other work are still two more—these also having the same inscription. According, therefore, to Michaelis's translation, these *five* wounded warriors had all one and the same name—Tideus !

Farther—in Lanzi Saggio's work, Tab. VIII., is a medallion of two men sitting in a stooping posture opposite to each other, with one knee of each bent, and pressed against the bent knee of the other. The legend, read by Mr. Forster's alphabet, is *iatsi niā.* These two words are given by Golius—*Jatsi, " to sit together with knees joined " :—niā, " to bend oneself."*

A still more curious illustration is furnished by two medallions on the same loose leaf representing two men in the act of washing their heads.—One of these is leaning forward to hold his head over a basin of water on a tripod, and in an easy and careless manner sluices his long and dripping hair with the water.—The other, on the contrary, bends himself backwards or sideways over the basin, with a painful contortion, and is washing or combing his hair with evident pains-taking. The

legend on the former reads *siā:* which word is rendered by
Golius, and also by Freytag, "*to wash the head slightly, not so
as to make it quite clean.*"—The inscription on the latter is *hiā
niā*—rendered by the same authors, "*a method of combing without actually wringing, bending oneself.*"

In another ancient Etruscan medallion is a beautifully
executed head of a pretty and coquettish-looking girl, who
draws aside her veil while she casts a sidelong glance over her
shoulder with a most winning expression. The legend is, *āur
dā*—rendered by Golius thus: "*āur,* puella"—a girl: "*dā,*
convocavit, invitavit"—"*the girl calls, or invites.*"

Once more, an Etruscan engraving in Mr. Forster's possession represents a warrior wounded by an arrow in the hand,
and the surgeon with an expression of the tenderest care and
gentleness drawing out the broken end of the arrow with a
string. The inscription reads—*bur, āsa, ākab.* These words
are rendered by Golius thus: *bur,* "exploravit, probavit"—
āsa, "obligavit vulnus"—*ākab,* "nervo obduxit sagittam."
The whole, in English, would run, "*Examining and binding
up the wound, drawing out the arrow with a string.*"

Not only ancient Egyptian and Etruscan legends are thus
deciphered with unmistakeable certainty, but the Celtiberian
also, another primitive dialect, yields to the same test. On an
ancient Celtiberian silver coin or medal, in Mr. Forster's possession, there is a horseman represented with two horses in
full gallop, leading one and riding the other: a palm branch,
the ensign of victory, being held in his right hand. On the
obverse is the head of a young Roman warrior. The legend
of the former device is *janab*—"ad latus, seu a latere, duxit
equum"—"*to lead a horse at the side*"—which is thus explained
—"Cum in cursu certaminis aliquis a latere equi sui alium
ducit, in quem transilire possit si vereatur ne equus, cui insistit,
ab adversarii equo praevertatur:"—"when any one in running
a race leads at the side of his own horse another on to which

he may leap if he fears that the horse he rides may be out-stripped by that of his adversary."

Now between the Celtiberian language and the one primeval language of mankind there is a most remarkable affinity.

The Celtiberians of Biscay are identified by Humboldt with the Iberians.—Dr. Prichard says there is no doubt that the Basques, or Biscayans, are the representatives of the ancient Iberians, who belong to the very earliest stock of European nations; and that their language must have been in existence at a period long anterior to the migration of the Celtic nations into Western Europe.

And it is a most remarkable fact that the Celtiberian alphabet is nearly identical with the Hamyaritic. But the Hamyaritic language, again, is the same as the old Arabic—which is believed by the greatest Oriental scholars, such as Sale, Sir William Jones, and Polier, to be the nearest approach to the one primeval language.[1]

It is no wonder that an alphabet which deciphers with such evident correctness ancient Egyptian, Etruscan, and Celtiberian writing, should be equally successful with the Sinaitic Inscriptions; the vocabulary of which, as already observed, is identified with the old Arabic and the ancient Egyptian.

Dean Stanley himself, the most noted English opponent of the Israelitish authorship of the Inscriptions, yet *virtually admits the probable correctness of Mr. Forster's system of decipherment.*

The proof of this fact is as follows :—In Mr. Forster's *Voice of Israel* (Pt. I. of *The One Primeval Language*) at p. 104, may be seen three of the Sinaitic Inscriptions, each of which, by his primeval alphabet, gave, with slight variations, the following sense :

> " The red geese ascend from the sea,
>   Lusting, the people eat on at them."

[1] See Forster's *Voice of Israel* (*One Primeval Language*, Pt. I.) p. 180, Ed. 1851 : and Smith's *Dict. of the Bible*, under *Arabia*.

From this circumstance Mr. Forster was led to the conviction that the birds intended by the Hebrew word *Salu*, rendered *quails*, were not quails, but a reddish bird of the goose
species, and of stork-like (or crane-like) height. The name in
the Inscription was *Nuham*—its definition, "nomen avis rubræ,
quæ formâ anserem refert"—"the name of a reddish bird
which in form resembles a goose."

This conclusion, drawn solely from the alphabet and the
Arabic Lexicon, was signally confirmed, to Mr. Forster's "in-
describable astonishment," by Dean Stanley himself. The
Dean, in his *Sinai and Palestine*, quotes, as a confirmation of
the identity of Hazeroth, where the people "abode" for seven
days at least, with the modern *Huderâh*, the mention of *the
sea*, as being probably not far off—"There went forth a wind
from the Lord, and brought quails from the sea".—Numb. xi.
31. And he then goes on to say—"In connexion with this
incident of 'the quails,' may be mentioned the fact, that, on
the evening and the morning of our encampment, immediately
before reaching the Wady Huderâh, *the sky was literally
darkened by the flight of innumerable birds*, which proved to be
the same large *red-legged cranes*, three feet high, with black
and white wings, measuring seven feet from tip to tip, which
we had seen in like numbers at the first Cataract of the Nile.
*It is remarkable that a similar flight was seen by Schubert near
the very same spot.*"[1]

The Dean continues—"If a recent explanation" (Mr.
Forster's) "of the difficult passage in Num. xi. 31, be correct,
and the expression 'two cubits high upon the face of the
earth', he applied, not to the accumulation of the mass, but to
the size of the individual birds, the flight of cranes, such as we
saw, may be not merely an illustration, but *an instance*, of the
incident recorded in the Pentateuch." And in his unpublished
journal, "written under the immediate first impressions of the

---

[1] *Sinai and Palestine*, pp. 81-83.

astounding phenomenon he had just witnessed, he speaks warmly of it as a fact 'which will delight Mr. Forster'—as 'a curious coincidence with his view'—and as a discovery which makes his (Mr. Forster's) explanation of the 'two cubits *extremely probable*'.   He adds, that Schubert saw similar flights nearly on the same spot, which according to the usual theory '*must be close to Kibroth-hattaavah.*'   He mentions, last, what is omitted in the published account, the all-important fact that he and his fellows had eaten one of these birds upon the Nile, 'and had found it *very good food.*'"[1]

It need hardly be observed that this admission, by the Dean, of the probable correctness of Mr. Forster's decipherment and translation of the words *nuham bahari*—"red geese (or cranes) from the sea"—in three of the Sinaitic Inscriptions, amounts to an admission that Mr. Forster's system of decipherment and translation of the Sinaitic Inscriptions in general is probably the true one.

And a more startling proof, not only of the correctness of Mr. Forster's decipherments, but also of the historical and literal truth of the Pentateuch, can hardly be imagined.

In one of the Inscriptions deciphered by Mr. Forster there is a remarkable confirmation of the decipherment, similar in kind to that of the Etruscan and other medals above mentioned—there is a rude pictorial representation of the fact recorded by the words.   In *The Voice of Israel*, p. 56, is given, from a copy made by Mr. Grey, an Inscription with two rude outlines inserted among the letters.   Mr. Grey had appended as a note, at the foot of his copy—"*A quadruped opposite the last line but one.*"

Mr. Forster, following the sole guidance of his alphabet and Arabic Lexicon, as elsewhere, had translated the inscription as follows :—

---

[1] Forster's *Israelitish Authorship of the Sinaitic Inscriptions*, pp. 85, 86 : quoting Stanley's *Sinai and Palestine*, pp. 81-83.

"The People with prone mouth drinketh [at] the water-
    springs:
The People [at] the two water-springs kicketh [like] an
    ass:
Smiting with the branch of a tree the well of bitterness
    he heals."

At the time of making this decipherment Mr. Forster expressed to some friends his regret that Mr. Grey had omitted
to copy the quadruped, and requested them to note what he
then said, viz.—that whenever a perfect copy of the inscription should be taken, the figure of "a quadruped" noticed by
Grey would be found to be the figure of *an ass.* "It was,"
adds Mr. Forster, "more to my satisfaction than surprise that,
within the next day or two, the prediction was verified. An
Oriental scholar courteously offered for my perusal Professor
Beer's 'Century of Sinaitic Inscriptions'—a collection which
not only I had not seen, but of the existence of which I was
unaware; and there, on opening the book, I found a duplicate
inscription, and in it Mr. Grey's 'quadruped'—the figure of the
ass."[1]

And on Mr. Forster's showing the Inscription, with its two
outlines, to a Fellow and Tutor of Cambridge, who had just
returned from the East, he at once said, "Of the first of these
wells I can say nothing, for I did not see it: but here (pointing
to the second) is the well of Marah, by which I sat. It is
exactly of this shape, about five feet in diameter, and a stream
running from it in the direction here delineated." He farther
added, that when he was about to taste the water, his Bedouins
exclaimed, *Murrah, murrah* (bitter, bitter) thus pronouncing
undesignedly its Scripture name. That this exclamation is
their usual warning here, appears from its being mentioned by
other travellers. "How interesting," adds Mr. Forster, "the
circumstance, that a name and locality of the Exode, deter-

[1] *Voice of Israel,* p. 51, &c.

mined independently by other considerations, should be thus fixed by the fidelity of a rude outline three thousand three hundred years ago!"

The fact of the form of the well having remained unchanged for so long a time is accounted for by a circumstance mentioned by Mr. Bartlett—that "the small oval pool occupies the centre of a mound of *travertine*"[1]—which is a hard and close-grained stone.

One more example may be given of a decipherment confirmed by pictorial representation. In *The Voice of Israel*, p. 132, there is a copy of a Sinaitic Inscription, also furnished by Mr. Grey, consisting of four lines of written characters which, deciphered by Mr. Forster's alphabet and translated by the Arabic Lexicon, give the following sense:

> "Destroy, springing on the People, the fiery serpents;
> Hissing, injecting venom, heralds of death, they kill;
> The people, prostrating on their back, curling in folds,
> They wind round, descending on, bearing destruction."

At the side of this Inscription, running down the whole depth of it, as if to explain to the eye what is described in the words, there is the figure of *a serpent*, springing, in undulating curls, downwards upon its victim.

Concerning the passage of the Red Sea, we have:

"Fleeth the swift long horse, raising both feet together, going at full speed, his rider dashed to the ground: Pharaoh running with long strides like a fleet-horse takes startled fright, casting off violently with both hands, to quicken his pace, his helmet."

"The sea enters by night the People: the sea and the waves roaring:

---

[1] *Forty Days in the Desert*, p. 31.

Divideth asunder the leader the sea: its waves roaring. Enter and pass through the midst of the waters the People."

"The People pass quickly over, through terror, like a horse, the soft mud at the bottom of the sea."

"Weep for their dead the enemies, the virgins wailing. The sea pouring down overwhelmed them; let loose, to reflow, the waters."

"Fleeth the People: enter into the deep the tribes. Enter the water the People."

"The People enter and penetrate through the midst.

"The People are filled with stupor and mental perturbation,

"Jehovah although their keeper and companion."

"The People journeyeth through the passage terror-stricken: urges onward with slackened rein benignantly Jehovah the People. The People essayeth the waters: Pharaoh retrograding reins back his war-horse."

Again, the miraculous supply of water is thus recorded:—

"The People the hard stone satiates with water, thirsting."

"The hard rock water—a great miracle."

"The People wending on their way drink, drinking with prone mouth; gives them to drink again and again Jehovah."

The "*drinking with prone mouth*" recalls the distinction taken between the followers of Gideon who "*lapped*" the water, "putting their hand to their mouth," and those who "bowed down upon their knees to drink."—Judg. vii. 5. The former were chosen to be the means of defeating the Midianites, as being the most ready both in body and mind—the rest were rejected, as indicating by their manner of drinking a more self-indulgent spirit.

Another inscription, with a rude figure of a man lifting up both hands, is deciphered thus:—

"Prayeth unto God the prophet upon a hard great stone: his hands sustaining, Aaron, Hur."

"In a *wady* close to Serbâl is found the following:—

Y

'The People make many journeys, pilgrimizing in the vast wilderness.' "

" In Wady Mokatteb we have :—

'The People devour enormously and voraciously.'

'The People devour greedily, they drink like horses, they clamour tumultuously,

Disobedient to all authority.   Sucking the marrow from the bones,

Devouring flesh ravenously, dancing, shouting, they play.' "

"How similar this to the Scriptural account of them in Exod. xxxii. 6—quoted by St. Paul, 1 Cor. x. 7—'as it is written—The people sat down to eat and to drink, and rose up to play'." [1]

Once more :—" The celebrated Eastern traveller of the last century, Dr. Thomas Shaw, gives the following extract from Fra Tomaso de Novara, respecting one of these Inscriptions which he found graven on the rocks in the desert of Sin.   The inscription itself, and its almost fac-simile in Hebrew characters, are given in Dr. Margoliouth's work (*Pilgrimage to the Land of my fathers*).   It was rendered by De Novara '*a rain of Manna,*' in strong confirmation of the Israelitish origin of the Inscriptions ; and some remarks are added by De Novara in Italian, of which the subjoined is a translation—' I found these letters engraved on a large stone in the desert of Sin, where God sent Manna to the children of Israel; upon which appeared also engraved the drawing of an Omer, the measure with which they were to gather the Manna, as described in Exod. xvi.—Dr. Margoliouth entertained the conviction of the Inscriptions being the handiwork of the Israelites, without knowing the meaning of the characters since deciphered by Mr. Forster.   He even considers that *these Inscriptions are actually mentioned in Scripture*—namely, in Numb. xi. 26—' But there remained two of the men in the camp ; the name of the one

---

[1] *Stones Crying out*, p. 236.

was Eldad, and the name of the other Medad : and the Spirit rested upon them : *and they were of them that were written,* but went not out unto the Tabernacle : and they prophesied in the the camp.' The original words translated, *and they were of them that were written,* (says Dr. M.) are *w' haymah baccthoobeem,* which signify literally, ' *and they were among the Cthoobeem,*' or Inscriptions."[1]

However this may be, the coincidence of the Inscriptions answering, in so many instances, both to the facts of the Scripture narrative, and to the key which Mr. Forster has discovered—corroborated by the previous interpretation of De Novara—can hardly be accidental.

Not less striking than any of the preceding examples are those supplied by the hieroglyphics on the tombstones of Sarbut-el-Khadem. Copies of three of these were made by Niebuhr, and are reproduced in Mr. Forster's *Israel in the Wilderness,* p. 82, &c., from the plates in the first volume of Niebuhr's work. Those who doubt of the fact that Mr. Forster has discovered the true key to the decipherment of these remarkable hieroglyphics, would do well to examine for themselves these plates and the interpretations of them. " The reader," says Mr. Forster, " has here before him the irrefragable fact that the very birds which by every kind of evidence stand identified with the *salus,* or long-legged and long-winged fowls of the miracle, are the very birds depicted on the tombstones of Sarbut-el-Khadem—both standing, flying, and apparently even trussed and cooked. The inevitable inference is, that if symbolic writing be meant to convey any meaning at all, and if its meaning can ever be educed from the collation of the symbols with a known event of Scripture history in a known locality, these tombstones record the miracle of the ' feathered fowls,' and stand over the graves of the gluttons who consumed them.

[1] *Armageddon,* vol. iii., 480, 482, quoting Dr. Margoliouth's *Pilgrimage to the Land of my fathers.*

"Intermingled with the geese, the reader will observe a succession of hieroglyphic archers, kneeling (as in the Egyptian monuments) in the act of discharging their bows. There occur no fewer than eighteen in the first tombstone, and they reappear in the others. These figures are the well known Egyptian hieroglyphic for archers. But, as though to prevent mistake, or to silence scepticism, while all the rest are without their bows, at the end of the penultimate line of the first tombstone we have the figure of an archer kneeling in the act of shooting, fully equipped, with full quiver, bended bow, and presented arrow. In these unmistakeable symbols, therefore, we see represented unequivocally the means employed to bring down the 'feathered fowls.' For the Israelites were a nation of archers.[1] When, therefore, the *nuhams*, or long-legged geese, flew over the camp in clouds which darkened the air, they would fall by tens of thousands, as the arrows of six hundred thousand armed Israelites flew among them."

But if the figures of the hieroglyphics *suggest* the subjects they commemorate, the decipherment fully and most strikingly confirms their meaning.

Now in order to do justice to this fact, let it be remembered that Mr. Forster's decipherments are obtained by a process wholly independent of the pictorial illustration, though of course, if correct, they must entirely coincide with it. The picture is one independent witness—the decipherment is another.

The following sentences are selected from the sixteen lines of Niebuhr's first plate, as deciphered by Mr. Forster.

"At the flocks of fowls the mixed multitude sitting on their heels twang the bow."

"Casts to the ground the rapid-blowing wind, propelling, the *nuhams*."

"The oblivious owl snores heavily like the dying. The sepulchres digging, they bury their dead."

[1] Ps. lxxviii. 9.

"The owl ill-omened. Sudden death, the marrow corrupted, from greedily devouring the cranes."

"By the fat cranes visits with punishment God, causing ulcerations plaguing to madness."

"The sepulchre entombs the fugitives. The cranes, sea-brought, black and white, prepare for flight spreading their wings."

"Seized with sickness, give to destruction the gluttons, the red dusky geese"—(i.e., the red dusky geese give to destruction the gluttons seized with sickness).

The reader will not fail to observe the coincidence of the "sea-brought" cranes, and the "rapid-blowing wind," with Numb. xi. 31—"And there went forth a *wind* from the Lord, and brought *salus* (nuhams) *from the sea.*"

Nor will it escape notice that the "black and white" cranes, and "red dusky geese" are exactly the "red-legged cranes with black and white wings," seen by Dean Stanley on the very spot of the miracle.

Even the very time during which the feathered fowls were to be given is commemorated in these tablets. The Lord had said—"Ye shall not eat one day, nor two days, nor five days, nor twenty days, but even a whole month."—Numb. xi. 19, 20.

And in the second of Niebuhr's three tablets we read—

"They make ready, cooking, the flying prey, nourished and sustained by it for a whole month, spreading it out."

In the following sentence, from the third tablet, the very hill of Sarbut-el-Khadem on which the monuments are placed, as described by Niebuhr and others, seems to be intended: and *the Hebrews* are actually mentioned by name:

"A sudden death: greedily lusting after flesh, die the gluttons. The mountain-top ascend the Hebrews."

In the first of these three tablets, the *ostrich* is both depicted, and thrice mentioned—as,

"The gluttons twang the bow: they run to and fro like the

ostrich, the wounded prey hiding itself to die searching after, running at full speed, the wind blowing rapidly along the fugitives."

And the ostrich is a Scripture emblem of folly and want of natural affection,[1] expressly applied as such to God's people Israel—"The daughter of my people is become cruel, like the ostriches in the wilderness."—Jer. Lam. iv. 3.

Is it not, then, something more than an accidental coincidence—is it not a strong circumstantial proof of a common origin—that in a cave in the Djebel Maghara there exists, in a triple tablet of inscriptions discovered by Mr. Pierce Butler, "a living figure of the ostrich, so deeply sculptured in the rock as to set scepticism at defiance—so beautifully executed as to charm artists as a work of art—and so full of life and motion and expression, that (to use Mr. Butler's words) it looks as if it would fly out of the rock? As a work of art this life-like hieroglyphic stands in the most violent contrast to the lifeless, dry, conventional forms of Egypt."[2]

A glyphograph of this interesting rock-sculpture is here presented to the reader.

But the most remarkable of all the pictorial representations discovered in the deserts of Sinai is thus described by Mr. Forster:—"These monuments have lately received new and most valuable illustration from a fresh quarter, namely, the casts taken by Major Macdonnell, R.A., both of the triple inscription in the cave on Djebel Maghara, and of additional tablets in the excavated rock-chamber at Sarbut-el-Khadem.

"These casts are now deposited in the British Museum. By the kind offices of Lord Lyndhurst permission was obtained from the Trustees to have a selection from them photographed for the present work (*Sinai Photographed*). While engaged in his selection, our artist's eye was suddenly arrested at the

---

[1] Job xxxix. 13, &c.
[2] Forster's *Israel in the Wilderness*, p. 103.

PLATE X.

SCULPTURE IN THE DESERT OF SINAI.

PLATE XI.

SCULPTURE IN THE DESERT OF SINAI.

bottom of one tablet of it by the *living form* of a little child, kneeling devoutly, with upraised head and uplifted hand, obviously in the act of prayer—the very counterpart of Sir Joshua Reynolds's touching and celebrated figure of 'The Infant Samuel'!—The reader is here presented with the figure of the Mosaic 'Infant Samuel.'—Of this figure it may safely be affirmed that in the original it stands out as clear and salient as a work of high art engraved on a signet. And if the work be Israelite, was not this to be anticipated? For if we believe the Scriptures, this was the special vocation of those inspired artists, Bezaleel and Aholiab, of whom we read that 'they wrought onyx stones inclosed in ouches of gold, graven as signets are graven, with the names of the children of Israel.—Exod. xxxix. 6.[1]"

The accompanying Plate is a fac-simile of the figure in Mr. Forster's volume. That such a work should have been executed by pilgrims, or passing travellers, is simply incredible.

The examples now given of Mr. Forster's decipherments are but, as it were, a few grains of corn from the sack—samples of the harvest.

Those who desire to investigate the subject fairly and impartially will find in his remarkable volumes a mass of evidence which cannot be rebutted by flippant objections or self-confident assertions. Sceptics delight to throw doubts and dust over every discovery that confirms the truth of Scripture. They pervert the plainest truths, and ignore the most prominent facts, which condemn their flimsy theories. They meet the most convincing proofs by an incredulous smile, if not by a contemptuous sneer. But something more than either smiles or sneers will be required to shake the solid structure of proof which Mr. Forster has constructed:—proof which has convinced such men as the late Lord Lyndhurst, accustomed to weigh evidence as the habit of his life—the late Sir Robert

[1] Forster's *Sinai Photographed*, p. 65.

Inglis, and others, whose names are identified with intellectual power and moral uprightness—and which is confirmed by the collateral and independent testimony of some of the greatest of Oriental scholars.

The following fact, among others, is significant. In the year 1845, soon after the publication of Mr. Forster's *Historical Geography of Arabia*, and decipherment of the Hamyaritic inscription at Hisn Ghorab, Professor Lee of Cambridge wrote to the Syro-Phœnician Society, requesting them to call a general meeting to hear from him a paper in refutation of Mr. Forster's principle of the Primeval Alphabet. The meeting was held. About one hundred or more members assembled, among whom were many eminent men—Oriental scholars, men of science, and travellers to every part of the world. The paper was read by the Secretary, in the unavoidable absence of the Professor himself. The result was a unanimous vote against the Professor, and in favour of Mr. Forster's method.

CHAPTER XXVIII.

The present condition of the Jews, and their history for the last eighteen centuries, a demonstration both of the historical truth and the prophetic character of the Old Testament.

BENEATH the triumphal arch of Titus at Rome is a sculpture which stands as an eloquent though silent witness to the truth of God's holy Word.

That sculpture represents a procession of captives, among whom are seen carried aloft a seven-branched candelabrum, a table, and two long trumpets. The bearers are shown by their proud step and laurel-crowned heads to be conquerors.

Those bearers are Romans—that candelabrum is the Golden Candlestick of the Temple of Jerusalem—carried, with the Table of Shew-bread and the Silver Trumpets, in triumphal procession by the soldiers of the Emperor Titus, on his return to Rome after sacking and plundering the city and Temple of the Jews.

This sculpture casts a light absolutely startling upon the whole history of the Jewish people, and very specially upon the fulfilment of prophecy. It is at once a monument of the historical accuracy of the Mosaic books, and a token of the prophetical inspiration of Moses, in the fulfilment now before our eyes of the predictions he delivered to the Jews themselves thirty-three centuries ago. Like a coin or a medal, it stamps the character of truth and reality upon the records of the past.

The description of the Candlestick is given in Exodus xxxvii. 17-24. It was formed of an upright shaft, with three branches proceeding from it on each side: both shaft and branches being ornamented with knobs, almond-shaped bowls, and flowers—the whole beaten out of one solid mass of pure gold.

From the description in Exodus we turn to the sculpture on the arch of Titus at Rome—and there is the very portraiture in stone of the Candlestick described in the Scripture. Even the details are so exactly worked that any one after reading the sacred narrative and looking upon a photograph of the sculpture can recognize at a glance every particular, even to the embossed work of the shaft and branches.

Here, again, is a *fact*—and a fact which as much proves the reality of the whole Jewish system of sacrificial and typical worship as the discovery of a fossil bone of a Mammoth proves that Mammoths once existed. It carries us irresistibly back to the days of Israel's sojourn beneath the Mount of Sinai—to the ascent of Moses into the Mount of God—to the giving of the Law amidst the thunders and earthquake, fire and smoke, which announced the presence of Jehovah—to the framing of the Tabernacle and its furniture, and this very Candlestick, " according to the pattern which was shown" to Moses "in the Mount."—Exod. xxv. 40. It testifies to the fact that the Temple service was actually carried on from the time of Moses till the Temple itself was plundered and destroyed by the Romans. History explains how the Candlestick was carried to Rome, where its portraiture is still to be seen—the Bible alone explains how that Candlestick itself ever came to exist.

But history has nothing to record at all comparable to the marvellous spectacle presented to the eyes of all mankind, for the last eighteen centuries, in the preservation of the Jews as a distinct though scattered people. With this fact before our eyes we need not ask for any other proof of the reality of miracles. *Every Jew is a miracle*—for it is a miracle that a whole nation, numbered by millions, and driven by force, oppression, and persecution into every country under heaven, should exist at all as a distinct people for eighteen hundred years. It is a miracle, because it is an effect produced, not by means of natural causes, but in contravention of them. In the ordinary course of things, one nation mixed up among another nation becomes amalgamated with it. In our own country we have a sufficient proof of this. An Englishman is neither a Celt, nor a Saxon, nor a Dane, nor a Norman, but he is a mixture of them all. And no instance can be produced of any importation of foreigners into any country remaining long distinct from the native inhabitants. Neighbourhood naturally induces intermarriage, and intermarriage inevitably and speedily merges all distinct nationality. The Jews are the sole and singular exception.

They are far more than an exception. They are an exception under circumstances in themselves exceptional—circumstances such as to make the exception a hundredfold more wonderful. If a colony of New Zealanders had been brought over and settled in Kent a century ago, even then we should think it somewhat singular if any of their posterity were recognizable in the present day; though a New Zealander can still say that New Zealand is the home of his fathers. But what if the whole native population of New Zealand were now to be expatriated and deported to foreign lands, and forcibly detained in distant countries all over the world—what traces of them would remain after the lapse of a hundred years?

The Jews have been scattered for eighteen hundred years into every country under heaven—without a home on the face of the earth—without a vestige remaining to them of their country save its beloved name and cherished memory—yet the Jews are to this day, like grains of gold in the furnace, indestructible and unmixed in the midst of the nations. If this be not the effect of a special intervention of God which may truly be called miraculous, then let any laws of nature be pointed out capable of bringing about so remarkable a result.

If it be said, that the religious customs and prejudices of the Jews are a sufficient barrier against their becoming inter-mingled with other nations, then let it be shown how those religious customs themselves were ever established—and more-over, how they became so ingrained into the very soul of the Jew that he will sooner part with his life than his religion. Let it be shown how else those religious customs originated if not in the way narrated in the Books of Exodus and Genesis. But if they originated as Exodus relates, then Exodus is liter-ally and historically true—the Law was miraculously given to Moses in the Mount, written with the finger of God—and Moses was an inspired messenger and Lawgiver of God to the Jewish people.   Consequently the whole Pentateuch is the Word of God Himself.

But this is only a small part of the significancy of the past history and present condition of the Jews.   It is *a fulfilment of prophecy*, so signal and so startling that the man must be blind indeed who cannot or will not see it.   And this, at least, is a case in which it cannot be said that the prophecy was written after the event—for the event is before our eyes, and the pro-phecy is three thousand three hundred years old.

To say that the Jews have been preserved as a distinct people, though scattered through every part of the world, for eighteen hundred years, is but a small part of the truth.   They have been so preserved amidst an extent and severity of oppression unparalleled in the history of any other nation. They have been so preserved as the burning-bush in Horeb, from which the Lord called to Moses, was preserved in the midst of the fire.   They have been so preserved, in a furnace of affliction and cruel persecution such as must have annihilated any other people long since.   The word that cannot be broken had gone forth, that "the seed of Israel should not cease from being a nation before God for ever"—Jer. xxxi. 36 :—therefore

Israel must be preserved, and has been preserved to the present time. The word has gone forth to all the nations, that " he that scattered Israel will gather him, and keep him as a shepherd doth his flock "—Jer. xxxi. 10:—and Israel is preserved that this also may be fulfilled in its season.

Thus had the sure word of prophecy declared :—" It shall come to pass, that if thou wilt not hearken unto the voice of the LORD thy God, to observe to do all his commandments and his statutes which I command thee this day, that all these curses shall come upon thee and overtake thee" : . . . . . "The LORD shall cause thee to be smitten before thine enemies : thou shalt go out one way against them, and flee seven ways before them : and *shalt be removed into all the kingdoms of the earth.*"—" The LORD shall smite thee with madness, and blindness, and astonishment of heart " :—" and thou shalt be only oppressed and spoiled evermore, and no man shall save thee. Thou shalt betroth a wife, and another man shall lie with her : thou shalt build an house, and thou shalt not dwell therein : thou shalt plant a vineyard, and shalt not gather the grapes thereof. Thine ox shall be slain before thine eyes, and thou shalt not eat thereof : thine ass shall be violently taken away from before thy face, and shall not be restored to thee : thy sheep shall be given unto thine enemies, and thou shalt have none to rescue them. Thy sons and thy daughters shall be given unto another people, and thine eyes shall look and fail with longing for them all the day long : and there shall be no might in thine hand. The fruit of thy land, and all thy labours, shall a nation which thou knowest not eat up : and thou shalt be only oppressed and crushed alway ; so that thou shalt be mad for the sight of thine eyes which thou shalt see ".—" Thou shalt become an astonishment, a proverb and a byeword, among all nations whither the Lord shall lead thee."—" Thou shalt beget sons and daughters, but thou shalt not enjoy them : for they shall go into captivity."

" The LORD shall bring a nation against thee from far, from

the end of the earth, as swift as the eagle flieth; a nation whose tongue thou shalt not understand; a nation of fierce countenance, which shall not regard the person of the old, nor show favour to the young":—"and he shall besiege thee in all thy gates, until thy high and fenced walls come down, wherein thou trustest, through all thy land"—"and thou shalt eat the fruit of thine own body, the flesh of thy sons and of thy daughters, which the LORD thy God hath given thee, in the siege and in the straitness wherewith thine enemies shall distress thee."— "If thou wilt not observe to do all the words of this law that are written in this book, that thou mayest fear this glorious and fearful name THE LORD THY GOD; then the LORD will make thy plagues wonderful, and the plagues of thy seed, even great plagues and of long continuance, and sore sicknesses, and of long continuance."—"And the LORD shall scatter thee among all people, from the one end of the earth even to the other;" —"and among these nations shalt thou find no ease, neither shall the sole of thy foot have rest: but the LORD shall give thee there a trembling heart, and failing of eyes, and sorrow of mind: and thy life shall hang in doubt before thee, and thou shalt have fear day and night, and shalt have none assurance of thy life. In the morning thou shalt say, Would God it were even! and at even thou shalt say, Would God it were morning! for the fear of thine heart wherewith thou shalt fear, and for the sight of thine eyes which thou shalt see."—Deut. xxviii. 15-67.

The prophecy declared that all these miseries should overtake them in the event of their disobeying "the commandments of the LORD their God," but not otherwise. And accordingly, as long as they continued obedient they were blessed with liberty and prosperity. It was when they departed from their obedience that the threatened judgments actually overtook them.

In this case it was predicted that they should be "smitten before their enemies, and removed into all the kingdoms of the earth."—To say nothing of the captivity of the Ten Tribes, and their removal by Shalmaneser into distant countries from which they have never yet returned—to say nothing likewise of the seventy years' captivity of the Two Tribes in Assyria—the fulfilment of this prophecy of Moses is before our eyes at the present moment in the dispersion of the Jews into every country and nation under heaven.

Again—"Thou shalt be only oppressed and spoiled evermore, and no man shall save thee."—The fulfilment is a prominent feature of the history of Europe and of the world for eighteen centuries past. Oppression, robbery, injustice, and cruelty have been the portion of the poor Jew, with few exceptions, always and every where. In most of the principal cities and towns of Europe they were confined to a particular quarter of the town, in which they were usually locked up after a certain hour of the evening. In Austria they were forbidden the use of the baths, and even of the inns, frequented by Christians : and Christians were forbidden to associate with them. At Thoulouse it was the custom to smite them on the face at Easter. They were excluded by law from every dignity, office, and employment which might elevate or improve their condition. They were debarred from holding landed property, from exercising any civil or military office, and even from the right of citizenship. They were compelled to wear yellow clothes, peaked hats, and the like, as a badge of degradation. In Bohemia, Jewish criminals condemned to death were ordered to be hanged in a different manner from others, that their bodies might receive a different treatment.

The word of prophecy had said by Moses—"And I will scatter you among the heathen, and will draw out a sword after you."—Lev. xxvi. 33. And the sword has been drawn out against the dispersed of Israel so as it never was drawn out against any other people in the history of the world.

In the times of the Crusades, it was customary with the fanatical soldiers of the Cross, as they were called, before they marched for Palestine, to whet their swords by a general massacre of the Jews. At Treves, Metz, Cologne, Worms, Spires, and other towns on the Moselle and the Rhine, the Maine and the Danube, the Crusaders rushed upon the Jews, massacred all they could find, and pillaged their houses. Jewish women threw themselves into the rivers to escape their ruffian hands—parents slew their own children to save them from abuse and cruelty. The sword followed them even into Palestine itself. They were hunted down wherever they could be found, and it was considered equally meritorious to kill a Saracen or a Jew.

In the fourteenth century the fanaticism of the *Flagellants* gave a fresh impulse to their murderers. The Flagellants professed that their self-inflicted stripes were to serve as an atonement for the sins of their country. But the superstitious multitude were easily induced to believe that a better atonement would be made by the slaughter of "the enemies of Christ." They again rose upon the Jews. Throughout Silesia, Poland, Lithuania, Brandenburg, Bohemia, and other parts of Germany, the same atrocities were perpetrated as in the times of the Crusades.

In Spain, during the dark ages, dark indeed was the day of Israel's misery. At Toledo alone, four times a persecution was raised against them : in one of which, commenced by the bishop and terminated by the Crusaders, Abarbanel declares that more Jews were driven from Spain than left Egypt under Moses.[1]

At length, in 1492, under Ferdinand and Isabella, they were all ordered to quit the country under pain of death, unless they submitted to baptism. A miserable multitude, variously estimated at from 300,000 to 800,000, were driven from Spain. They were stripped of all their gold and silver, and the market

[1] Brooks's *History of the Hebrew Nation*, p. 506—which see for this and other particulars.

was so glutted by the forced sale of their other property that a house was given for a mule and a vineyard for a piece of linen. In some of the vessels in which they sailed, they were first carried out to sea and plundered of all they still possessed, and then the vessels were scuttled, and sunk with all on board. In others, they were first in like manner robbed, and then sold into slavery on the opposite shores, or landed and left to perish on a desert coast. A large number of them applied to the King of Portugal for permission to pass through his dominions. It was but turning from one oppressor to another—as their prophet had forewarned them—"as if a man did flee from a lion, and a bear met him: or went into the house, and leaned his hand upon the wall, and a serpent bit him."—Amos v. 19. The King of Portugal betrayed them. Not content with the offer of a large portion of their remaining effects, he waited till the whole number were in his power, and then perfidiously seized and condemned them to slavery unless they submitted to baptism. The children under fourteen years of age were at once taken from their parents and baptized; upon which many of the parents, on condition of having them restored, submitted likewise to be baptized. Others, preferring death, first slew their children and then themselves.[1] Those who had been baptized had but deferred their fate; for they were all soon after set upon and butchered, because some of them had been seen to smile at a pretended miracle. Those who succeeded in getting away from the ports of Spain, after having endured unparalleled cruelties from the Moors of Africa, found shelter at length in Constantinople, where, though despised, they have ever since been permitted to reside.[2] Since the destruction of Jerusalem by Titus, and the

---

[1] So had the prophet declared—"Death shall be chosen rather than life by all the residue of them that remain of this evil family, which remain in all places of the earth whither I have driven them, saith the LORD of hosts."—Jer. viii. 3.

[2] Murphy's *Portugal*, p. 695, quoted by Brooks, ibid.

z

slaughters which followed, no calamity so terrible has befallen the unhappy Jews as their expulsion from Spain.

England is not clear of Jewish blood. A massacre of the Jews at the coronation of Richard I. was considered by his subjects to have cast a lustre, instead of an indelible stain, upon the beginning of his reign. The persecution spread through the kingdom, and similar massacres took place in the provinces. In York, the Jews took refuge in the Castle, where they were besieged by the populace led on by one of the Canons of the Cathedral. After defending themselves till provisions failed them, the unhappy Jews, driven to despair, set fire to the Castle, slew their wives and children, and then each other—the Rabbi destroying himself last of all with his own hand. A place in York, called *Jew-bury*, is still remembered as the spot where their remains were buried.

The "spoiling", or plundering, too, of the Jews is among the familiar events recorded in English history. King John first inveigled them into his dominions by caresses and privileges, then seized and imprisoned them, confiscated their property, and tortured them to make them discover where their treasures were concealed. By this treachery he is said to have acquired sixty thousand marks—a vast sum in those days. Henry III. afterwards extorted from them more than double that sum; and then sold them to his brother Richard, with full liberty to plunder them as he pleased. His reign was likewise stained by the massacre of 500 Jews in London.

Edward I. in like manner played the extortioner, and then, having impoverished them to the utmost, in the year 1290, expelled them altogether from his dominions. Fifteen thousand Jews were conducted to the seaports, there robbed of the pittance left to pay their charges, and then for the most part thrown overboard by the sailors and drowned.

In France, they were over and over again oppressed, plundered, massacred, expelled. Every outbreak of religious

fanaticism, every pestilence or public calamity, was the signal
for an assault upon the unhappy Jew.

In the East, under the dominion of the Saracen conquerors,
they found no more pity than in the West. There is a wearisome monotony of suffering in their history. In the records of
almost every country under heaven there is a page blotted
with the tears and blood of oppressed and persecuted Israel.
Driven out of one country, hardly could they find another
where a refuge was allowed them. Truly and fearfully was
the prophecy fulfilled—"Among all these nations shalt thou
find no ease, neither shall the sole of thy foot find rest: but
the LORD shall give thee there a trembling heart, and failing
of eyes, and sorrow of mind: and thy life shall hang in doubt
before thee, and thou shalt fear day and night, and shalt have
none assurance of thy life."—Deut. xxviii. 65. The time was
come when according to another prophecy, "All that found
them devoured them, and their adversaries said, We offend
not, because they have sinned against the LORD, the habitation of justice: even the LORD, the hope of their fathers."—
Jer. l. 7.

The "giving of their sons and their daughters to another
people"—Deut. xxviii. 32—has been systematically practised
by their Roman Catholic persecutors for the purpose of forcing
them to be baptized. The case of the boy Mortara is a well
known instance even at the present moment.

The prophecy had declared—"The Lord shall bring a nation
against thee from far, *as the eagle flieth;* a nation whose tongue
thou shalt not understand, a nation of fierce countenance",
&c. . . . "and he shall besiege thee in all thy gates." . . .
"And thou shalt eat the fruit of thine own body, the flesh of thy
sons and of thy daughters, which the LORD hath given thee,
in the siege and in the straitness wherewith thine enemies shall
distress thee," &c. And so it came to pass. History relates
that while the *eagle-standards* of the Roman legions hovered
around the walls of Jerusalem, "one circumstance excited uni-

versal horror. Mary, a noble lady of Perea, in the delirium
produced by hunger, slew and boiled her own infant, and having eaten part of it, set the remainder aside. A party of ma-
rauders, allured by the smell of food, burst in, and charged her
with the crime of having *eaten*. She uncovered the remains of
her child, and with frantic irony invited them to partake of
her repast."

In the siege of Jerusalem, and the subsequent wars, not
less than two millions of Jews are computed to have
perished.

But there is one circumstance in the prophecy above all
others peculiar, and impossible to have been foreseen by any
human sagacity. There is no other nation under heaven so
degraded that their very *name* is a reproach. But to Israel it
had been declared by Moses—"And thou shalt become an
astonishment, a proverb, and a *byword*, among all nations
whither the LORD shall lead thee."—Deut. xxviii. 37.—So also
Jeremiah—"And I will deliver them to be removed into all
the kingdoms of the earth for their hurt, to be a *reproach*, and
a proverb, a *taunt* and a *curse*, in all places whither I shall
drive them."—Jer. xxiv. 9.

And the very name of *Jew* has been for ages, and is at the
present moment, a taunt, a curse, and a reproach.—"A short
time since," says a Jew, writing to his brother, "as I stood
before the house of a gentleman waiting for a friend, the child
of the gentleman, which could hardly utter a few sentences,
spit several times in my face, and said with its stammering
lips, 'You accursed Jew!'"[1] In Portugal the name was so infamous that the Christian who was called "Jew" by another
was permitted to stab the offender with impunity. In Germany
the Jews were stigmatized as cattle, by being forced to pay
toll for passing through the turnpike-gates. Toll-tables, we
are told, are still to be found there on which may be seen in-

[1] Herschell's *Brief Sketch*, p. 29.

scribed, "For a horse 2 kreutzers, a pig 2 kreutzers, a Jew 1 kreutzer".[1]

But the history of Israel's degradation and sufferings for the last eighteen hundred years in every country under heaven would fill volumes. Never did such a doom befall any other people, nor could any other people have undergone such a doom and still survived. The history of the Jews is unparalleled in the world, and absolutely unaccountable by any natural causes.

Yet Moses foretold it all—and that three thousand three hundred years ago—and with a graphic minuteness and detail which no power but Omniscience could supply. Are we now to be told that the coincidence is accidental, and the prophecy a fortunate guess?

If so, then let any author sit down and write the history of England even for ten years to come. The task would be easier than for Moses, if not inspired by God, to foretell thousands of years beforehand, with circumstance and detail, the dispersion, oppression, sufferings and reproach of the Jews for the last eighteen hundred years—to write by anticipation a history of events not only impossible to have been foreseen or conjectured by any human sagacity, but impossible even to have happened without a continual miracle.

It is related of Lord Rochester, that, while still a hardened infidel, he confessed, "I reject all argument with one single exception—that founded on the history of the Jews. That alone baffles my infidelity."

[1] Hirschfeld's *Strictures on the Jews*, p. 88, quoted by Brooks, p. 503.

CHAPTER XXIX.

The Two Mysteries.

"THE TESTIMONY OF JESUS IS THE SPIRIT OF PROPHECY."—
Rev. xix. 10. In other words, the one grand object of the
whole written Word of God is to reveal JESUS CHRIST, the
Redeemer of a lost world, the Saviour of lost sinners.

Therefore it was that Jesus Himself said to His disciples,
" These are the words which I spake unto you while I was yet
with you, that all things must be fulfilled which were written
in *the law of Moses, and in the prophets, and in the psalms, concerning me.*"—Luke xxiv. 44. Therefore it was that "then
opened he their understanding that they might understand *the
Scriptures.*"—That which they did not then understand was
that *all the Scriptures,* from Genesis to Malachi, spoke of *Him*
—spoke beforehand both of His sufferings, and of the glory
that should follow.—V. 26.

Now, this being the declared object of all Scripture— declared so to be by the Lord Jesus Christ Himself—it follows
inevitably that if the very first events recorded in Genesis concerning mankind did not really happen, *the whole Bible is false
together*, from beginning to end.

For if man never sinned and fell, as Genesis records, no
Redeemer was needed—no redemption was possible. If man
never fell from his original uprightness of nature, no renova-

ting, new-creating work of the Holy Spirit in the heart was
either requisite for man's salvation, or possible in itself. If no
such events ever happened as those related in the third chapter of Genesis, the whole fabric of Christianity falls at once to
the ground like a building without a solid foundation.

It is not the object of this volume to bring forward the
proper proofs of the Deity of Christ. These proofs are scattered throughout the whole Bible—the very gems and jewels
of the Saviour's crown, the very stars in the firmament of
Scripture. They are found in the express declarations of the
Psalms and Prophets—but above all in the Gospel histories.
His miracles—His prophecies—His promise of the Holy
Ghost and the fulfilment of that promise—His Resurrection
from the dead and Ascension into Heaven—His appearance
to Paul and to John, and other facts recorded by the Evangelists, are so many direct proofs that Jesus was, and is, true
and very God.

But what does belong to the design of this work, and is in
fact the practical conclusion of the whole argument here maintained, is to point out that the literal and historical truth of
Genesis is bound up in Christianity itself—is involved of
necessity in the whole testimony of Scripture concerning
Christ. If Christianity is true, Genesis cannot be false; it
cannot be either fabulous or allegorical, but must be historically true. If Genesis is not historically true, then Christianity
is an imposture and an absurdity.

But this is not all.

If Christianity is true—and if the historical truth of Genesis
is bound up in the truth of Christianity, we may reasonably
expect to find that the great truth of the *Deity of Christ* is at
least *implied* in the Mosaic records. Revelation was at first
but indistinct, and gradually clearer afterwards—like the dawn
of morning increasing more and more to the perfect day. It
would not have been in accordance with this design to make
known at once all the counsel of God concerning the promised

Redeemer, nor *how* He was to bruise the Serpent's head.   But
still we might reasonably expect to find that the outline of the
plan of Redemption, however incomplete, would be *comprehensive*—and would leave room enough for the gradual filling in
of the details.

Upon this most interesting and all-important subject we
have a double line of testimony—in the gradual development,
on the one hand, of the MYSTERY OF GODLINESS; on the
other, of the *Mystery of iniquity.*

The great Mystery of godliness is that "*God was manifest
in the flesh:*"—1 Tim. iii. 16: born of a virgin, and so made
man, in order that He might become man's Redeemer by
suffering death as an Atonement for man's rebellion against
God: and might also, as the fruit and consummation of His
Mediatorial work, become the delegated Sovereign over all
Creation, till all should be brought once more under subjection
to His Heavenly Father.   He was to be moreover the glorified
Head of a new-created and glorified Humanity for ever.

The Mystery of iniquity is Satan's travestie of the Mystery
of godliness: and it is a proof of the truth of Christianity, inasmuch as the existence of a caricature proves the existence of
the original which it misrepresents.   The great Enemy of God
and man, having prevailed upon our first parents to disobey
God's commandment, then endeavoured to deprive their
posterity of the promised salvation from the sin and death
they had incurred, by a system of counterfeits and delusive
substitutes.

That salvation was first announced in the Lord's declaration,
addressed to the Serpent-tempter, that the Seed of the woman
should bruise the Serpent's head.   It is abundantly evident
that the words were understood from the first, and ever afterwards, as conveying the promise of a Heaven-born Man,
who should redeem mankind by suffering death himself—a
Deliverer who should be the woman-born Son of God—both
God and Man in one Divine Person.

It has been shown in the preceding pages how advantage was taken of this promise to introduce a vast and world-wide system of idolatrous worship.

The Serpent, man's tempter and destroyer, was represented as being man's benefactor, by having endued mankind with supernatural and divine knowledge,—as being the author of divine inspiration, oracular wisdom, poetical genius, and the knowledge of all arts and sciences. Accordingly, the Serpent was the symbol of Apollo, Mercury, and other heathen deities, as already shown.

The Heaven-born Redeemer had been promised as the Seed of the woman. This was parodied by taking advantage of a quibble of words. *Zero-ashta* signified both "Seed of the woman" and "Seed of light," or of the Sun. Hence the promise of the Seed of the woman was perverted into a belief in a Deliverer who was to be the *Sun*-begotten Child of the woman. Nimrod had met with a violent death—it was represented as a death incurred for the benefit of mankind. Semiramis, his ambitious queen and widow, gave out that her deceased husband had been mystically born a second time as her son. And this trumpery trick, recommended to popularity by the seductive and licentious influence of the beautiful queen, became the origin of the worship of the Babylonian false Messiah, and his mother as the Queen of Heaven, throughout the world. It is also the real origin of the worship of the Virgin Mary by the Church of Rome—as is incontrovertibly proved by the authorities quoted in former chapters.

And out of these materials, varied and combined in endless confusion, arose the whole mythology of the heathen world. The worship of Juno the "Queen of Heaven", Venus the goddess of love and beauty, Cybele the goddess of agriculture, Bacchus (or Adonis), Apollo, Mercury, and the whole Pantheon of the principal gods and goddesses of Greece and Rome, can all be shown to be derived from the Babylonian idolatry. The Hindû Vishnu and Chrishna, and the Buddha of the farthest

East, are just impersonations of the primitive ideas of the Heaven-born Redeemer and His virgin mother, corrupted and distorted. It can be demonstrated also that the very worst and vilest abominations of the ancient idolatry arose out of a sensual interpretation of the highest and holiest truths concerning the regenerating work of the Holy Spirit of God.

All this is not conjecture or fanciful theory, but sober fact, attested by the history, traditions, and monuments, of all ages and countries. Heathenism itself, with all its unspeakable abominations, is thus compelled to be an involuntary witness to the truth that JESUS, the Redeemer promised from the first, is indeed very and eternal God. Heathenism is just a caricature of the Gospel which was preached to Adam : but even a caricature must have had an original, and however grotesque may be the portraiture, the existence of the caricature proves the *existence* of the original. Just so does the Babylonian idolatry prove the reality of the Gospel revelation, and consequently the reality of those events which gave occasion to that revelation :—the events, that is, narrated in the early chapters of Genesis.

But between the Mystery of godliness and the Mystery of iniquity there is one most important difference—not only the obvious and all-important difference that the one is a mystery of truth, light, life, and love, the other a mystery of falsehood, darkness, cruelty, and death—but also a difference in the *manner* of the mystery.

The Mystery of godliness is *the gradual revelation of God's hidden purpose of love to man*—from its first announcement in Paradise, to the Redeemer's Ascension from the Mount of Olives, and to His yet future Coming, and Kingdom, and glory.

The Mystery of iniquity is *the gradual covering up and disguising of God's revelation of mercy*, by a system of frauds, and mystification, jugglery of words, and confusion of ideas, and accommodation to man's depraved passions and pride. By the artful use of double meanings of words, and the clever adaptation of actual facts, the false Mystery was made to bear a deceitful resemblance to the true Mystery, so as to mislead the minds of men : and by a material and carnal perversion of the deepest and holiest truths, the Mystery of iniquity appealed directly to the master-passions of human nature—"the lust of the flesh" which brooks no restraint, "the lust of the eye" which pretends to make a heaven upon earth, and "the pride of life" which demands nothing less than that man shall be as God—his own master, his own regenerator, his own model of perfection, and the manufacturer of his own happiness. The result was that this corrupt system overflowed the world. The master-passions of depraved human nature have always proved themselves too strong to be held in check by any power but that of the renewing grace of God: and a system of professed religion which not only did not condemn, but permitted and positively prescribed, the indulgence of every dominant lust, gained, as it was likely to do, a world-wide popularity. It was celebrated everywhere throughout the ancient world with frantic excitement and licentious revels: and the more deeply the nations were imbued with its depraved spirit, the more completely was the Mystery of godliness hidden from their eyes. The description of the modern Babylon, the Church of Rome, "with whom the kings of the earth have committed fornication, and the inhabitants of the earth have been made drunk with the wine of her fornication",— Rev. xvii. 2,—was equally appropriate to Babylon of old and her worship of the false Messiah.

And as the Mystery of godliness is the gradual disclosure of God's plan of infinite and eternal love, revealed in clearer and clearer light, from glory to glory, till it shall at last shine forth in Heaven's own radiance—so the Mystery of iniquity is a gradual darkening and hiding of God's way of salvation from the eyes of those who turn away from the truth, till they are lost in the blackness of darkness for ever.

But so artfully is the concealment managed by the Enemy, that he deprives men of the blessing by seeming to give it to them. He gives them *something*—and something, too, which has some resemblance to the reality—so much resemblance as should serve to delude men of corrupt minds, and induce them to turn away their eyes from the spiritual reality, and accept in its place the fraudulent but more attractive counterfeit. A truly diabolical ingenuity of malice is apparent at every step and stage of Satan's cruel work. He promised to our first parents, as the reward of disobedience, the knowledge of good and evil. They obtained it—but it was by losing the good and falling into the evil. They came to know by bitter, bitter experience how good was the good they had lost—and how intensely and intolerably evil was the evil they had incurred.— Next, the very Tempter himself was represented as the bene- factor, instead of the enemy of mankind—and the fatal gift of the knowledge of all that was base and bad was set forth as a favour which God had enviously denied, but Satan had liberally bestowed.—Then, when their eyes were opened to see their own guilt and misery, the same art which had betrayed them to their ruin was employed to rob them of the promised remedy. God, with a Father's pity for His lost but still loved children, announced a plan of recovery devised in wisdom and love unfathomable, by which their sin would be condemned and punished, while yet the dreadful sentence of death should eventually be reversed by the inestimable gift of a new and blessed life. A Redeemer was promised to Adam and all his ruined race—a Redeemer who should be at once the Son of God, and also the Seed of the woman—God Incarnate by a human birth—Immanuel, "God with us"—God with us, by humbling Himself to become man, and as man to suffer the death which sinful man deserved—among us and for us—in our nature and in our stead—in the fearful agonies of Calvary.

All this, too, was travestied and misrepresented by the artifices of the Enemy. Woman had been the weak and guilty instrument of man's ruin by Satan—but she was also to be the forgiven and honoured instrument of man's Redemption by Christ. The same Enemy who had compassed man's ruin by means of her fall, would now complete their destruction by means of her false exaltation. The honour and love due to the promised Divine Redeemer should be transferred to His human mother: thus God would be robbed of His glory, and mankind deprived of salvation. The very mother herself should be personated by a pretender, so that men's eyes should be turned away from the truth. Eve first, and Semiramis afterwards, were dressed up in false colours as the Woman of the promised Covenant, or promise of redemption—the profligate queen of Babylon was worshipped throughout the world as the " Queen of Heaven"—and a child of her infamy was actually honoured as the "*Lord of the Covenant*", the promised Saviour. Thus, in the very outset of the Mystery of iniquity which originated in Babylon, and is continued to this day in the modern Babylon of the Church of Rome, sin was glorified and salvation frustrated.

Let the reader who doubts. the reality of this transfer and travestie ponder the following passage :—

"This son (of Semiramis) thus worshipped in his mother's arms, was looked upon as invested with all the attributes, and called by almost all the names, of the promised Messiah. As Christ, in the Hebrew of the Old Testament, was called Adonai, *The Lord*, so Tammuz was called Adon or Adonis. Under the name of Mithras, he was worshipped as the 'Mediator'.[1] As Mediator and head of the covenant of grace he was styled *Baal-berith*, Lord of the Covenant—Judges viii. 33. In this character he is represented in Persian monuments as *seated on*

[1] Plutarch, *de Iside*, vol. ii. p. 369.

the rainbow, the well-known symbol of the Covenant.[1] In
India, under the name of Vishnu, the Preserver, or Saviour of
men, though a god he was worshipped as the great 'Victim-
Man,' who, before the worlds were, because there was nothing
else to offer, offered *himself* as a sacrifice.[2] The Hindû sacred
writings teach that this mysterious offering before all creation
is the foundation of all the sacrifices that have ever been
offered since.[3] Do any marvel at such a statement being found
in the sacred books of a *Pagan* mythology? Why should
they? Since sin entered into the world there has been one
only way of salvation, and that through the blood of the everlasting Covenant—a way that all mankind once knew, from
the days of righteous Abel downwards. When Abel 'by faith',
offered unto God his more excellent sacrifice than that of Cain,
it was his faith 'in the blood of the Lamb' slain, in the purpose
of God, 'from the foundation of the world,' and in due time to
be offered up on Calvary, that gave all the 'excellence' of his
offering. If Abel knew of 'the blood of the Lamb,' why
should Hindoos not have known of it? One little word shows
that even in Greece the virtue of 'the blood of God' had once
been known, though that virtue, as exhibited in its poets, was
utterly obscured and degraded. That word is *Ichor*. Every
reader of the bards of classic Greece knows that Ichor is the
term peculiarly appropriated to the blood of a divinity. Thus
Homer refers to it :—

---

[1] "Thevenot, *Voyages*, Partie ii. chap. vii. p. 514."—This author gives
an engraving of a sculpture on an ancient Persian rock-temple, representing a Cupid sitting on a rainbow. The Grecian and Roman
Cupid was the son of Venus, who was the same as the "Queen of
Heaven." He was, in fact, the classical form of the mock Messiah.

[2] "Col. Kennedy's *Hindoo mythology*, pp. 221 and 247, with note."

[3] "Ibid., pp. 200, 204, 205. In the exercise of his office as the
Remedial god, Vishnu is said to extract the *thorns* of the three worlds.
—Moor's *Pantheon*, p. 12, 'Thorns' were a symbol of the curse.—
Gen. iii. 18."

'From the clear vein the immortal Ichor flowed,
Such stream as issues from a wounded god,
Pure emanation, uncorrupted flood,
Unlike our gross, diseased, terrestrial blood.'[1]

Now what is the proper meaning of the term Ichor? In Greek it has no etymological meaning whatever; but in Chaldee Ichor signifies 'The precious thing'. Such a name, applied to the blood of a divinity, could have only one origin. It bears its evidence on the very face of it, as coming from that grand patriarchal tradition that led Abel to look forward to the 'precious blood' of Christ, the most precious gift that love divine could give to a guilty world, and which, while the blood of the only genuine 'Victim-Man', is at the same time in deed and in truth the 'blood of God.'—Acts xx. 28.

"Even in Greece itself, though the doctrine was utterly perverted, it was not entirely lost. It was mingled with falsehood and fable—it was hid from the multitude—but yet, in the secret mystic system, it necessarily occupied an important place. As Servius tells us that the grand purpose of the Bacchic orgies 'was the purification of souls,'[2] and as in these orgies there was regularly the tearing asunder and the shedding of the blood of an animal, in memory of the shedding of the life's blood of the great divinity commemorated in them, could this symbolical shedding of the blood of that divinity have no bearing on the 'purification' from sin those mystic rites were intended to effect? We have seen that the sufferings of the Babylonian Zoroaster and Belus were expressly represented as voluntary, and as submitted to for the benefit of the world; and that, in connexion with crushing the great serpent's head, which implied the removal of sin and the curse. If the

---

[1] "Pope's Homer, corrected by Parkhurst. See the original in *Iliad*, lib. v. 339, 340."

[2] Servius, in *Georg.* lib. i., vol. ii. p. 197, and in *Æneid*, lib. vi. vol. i., p. 400.

Grecian Bacchus was just another form of the Babylonian divinity, then his sufferings and blood-shedding must have been represented as having been undergone for the same purpose, viz., for 'the purification of souls.'

"Now from this point of view, let the well known name of Bacchus in Greece be looked at. That name was *Dionusos*. What is the meaning of that name? Hitherto it has defied all interpretation. But deal with it as belonging to the language of that land from which the god himself originally came, and the meaning is very plain. *D'ion-nuso-s* signifies 'THE SIN-BEARER', a name entirely appropriate to the character of him whose sufferings were represented as so mysterious, and who was looked up to as the great 'purifier of souls'.

"Now this Babylonian god, known in Greece as 'The Sin-bearer', and in India as 'The Victim-Man', among the Buddhists of the East, the original elements of whose system are clearly Babylonian, was commonly addressed as 'the saviour of the world.'[1] It has been all along well enough known that the Greeks occasionally worshipped the supreme god under the title of 'Zeus the Saviour'; but this title was thought to have reference only to deliverance in battle, or some such-like temporal deliverance. But when it is known that 'Zeus the Saviour' was only a title of Dionusos[2] the 'sin-bearing' Bacchus, his character as 'the Saviour' appears in quite a different light. In Egypt, the Chaldæan god was held up as the great object of love and admiration through whom 'goodness and truth were revealed to mankind.'"[3]—"'The discloser of truth and goodness on earth was Osiris; and it is remarkable that, in this character of the manifestation of the Deity, he was said to be 'full of goodness (grace) and truth'.'"[4]

---

[1] Mahawanso, 31, apud Pococke's *India in Greece*, p. 185.
[2] Athenæus, lib. xv. p. 675.
[3] Hislop's *Two Babylons*, p. 100, &c.
[4] Wilkinson's *Ancient Egyptians*, vol. 4, p. 189.

Thus was the Holy One of God mocked in His sufferings, in the Mystery of iniquity, by the introduction of a suffering *false* Messiah : and thus was the faith of mankind diverted from the promised Redeemer, Jesus the Son of God, whose blood alone "cleanseth from all sin."

But the mockery went beyond this.

As Christ was fore-ordained first to suffer, and then to enter into His glory, so in the Mystery of iniquity He was mocked not only in His sufferings, but also in His glorious exaltation and Kingdom. "Osiris," says Wilkinson, "was called the 'Manifester of good,'" who "appeared on earth to benefit mankind.—He was also frequently styled 'Lord of the world,' 'Lord of Life,' 'the Eternal Ruler,' and 'King of the gods.'—We see in him the *goodness* of the Deity, which was supposed to have been manifested upon earth for the benefit of mankind, and in a future state the *Judge* of the world."[1]—"He was regarded," says Mr. Hislop, "as the pre-destined heir of all things ; and, on the day of his birth, it was believed that a voice was heard to proclaim, 'The Lord of all the earth is born.'[2] In this character he was styled 'King of kings, and Lord of lords,' it being as a professed representative of this hero-god that the celebrated Sesostris caused this very title to be added to his name on the monuments which he erected to perpetuate the fame of his victories.[3] Not only was he honoured as the great 'World-King,' he was regarded as Lord of the invisible world, and 'Judge of the dead': and it was taught that in the world of spirits all must appear before his dread tribunal, to have their destiny assigned them.[4] As the true Messiah was prophesied of under the title of the 'Man whose name was the Branch,' he was celebrated not

[1] Wilkinson's *Ancient Egyptians*, vol. 4, p. 320.
[2] Ibid., p. 310.
[3] "Russell's *Egypt*, p. 79."
[4] Wilkinson, vol. 4, p. 310-314.

2 A

only as the 'Branch of Cush,' but as the 'Branch of God,' graciously given to the earth for healing all the ills that flesh is heir to.[1] He was worshipped in Babylon under the name of El-Bar, cr 'God the Son.' Under this very name he is introduced by Berosus, the Chaldæan historian, as the second in the list of Babylonian sovereigns. Under this name he has been found in the sculptures of Nineveh by Layard, the name Bar, 'the Son,' having the sign denoting El, or 'God,' prefixed to it."[2]

"Thus daringly and directly was a mere mortal set up in Babylon in opposition to the 'Son of the Blessed.'"[3]

And, we may add, thus cunningly and cruelly were the eyes of men turned away from the Son of God, the promised Redeemer, the Saviour of sinners, through the surreptitious assumption of all His gracious attributes by a false Messiah.

One of the grossest corruptions of Christian doctrine perpetrated by the Church of Rome is that it attributes to the Virgin Mary a *participation* in the Saviour's work as the Mediator between God and man.

This, too, is a part of the original Mystery of iniquity—a continuation of the Babylonian apostasy.

[1] "This is the esoteric meaning of Virgil's 'Golden Branch,' and of the Misletoe Branch of the Druids. I may remark, in passing, on the wide extent of the worship of a sacred branch. Not only do the negroes in Africa, in the worship of the Fetiche, on certain occasions make use of a sacred branch,' (Hurd's *Rites and Ceremonies*, p. 375), but even in India there are traces of the same practice. My brother, S. Hislop, Free Church Missionary at Nagpore, informs me that the late Rajah of Nagpore used every year, on a certain day, to go in state to worship the branch of a particular species of tree, called Apta, which had been planted for the occasion, and which, after receiving divine honours, was plucked up, and its leaves distributed by the native prince among his nobles. In the streets of the city numerous boughs of the same kind of tree were sold, and the leaves presented to friends under the name of *sona*, or 'gold.'"

[2] *Nineveh and Babylon*, p. 629.   [3] *Two Babylons*, p. 104, &c.

In the Church of Rome the worship of the Virgin Mary, and the resort to her supposed intercession with God, far exceed the devotion paid to Christ.

So it was in Babylon and the heathen world. The worship of Semiramis as the "Queen of Heaven", under the various names of Ashtoreth or Astarté, Juno, Venus, Aphrodité, Diana, and other titles, came in time to eclipse the veneration paid to her son as the false Messiah. In China, to this day, the "Queen of Heaven" is honoured with a like devotion to that which the Virgin Mary receives in the Church of Rome.

The following account of the *heathen* worship of this goddess, and the assignment to her of the attributes and gracious offices of Christ, is equally applicable to the modern Babylon of Rome.

"In the uppermost story of the Tower of Babel, or Temple of Belus, there stood three images of the great divinities of Babylon : and one of these was of a woman *grasping a serpent's head.*" So also, "the Roman Church maintains that it was not so much the *Seed* of the woman, as the woman *herself*, that was to bruise the head of the serpent. In defiance of all grammar, she renders the Divine denunciation against the serpent thus : 'She shall bruise thy head, and thou shalt bruise *her* heel.'"[1]

"Whatever dignity the son was believed to possess, a like dignity was ascribed to her. Whatever name of honour he bore, a similar name was bestowed upon her. He was called Belus, 'the Lord'—she, Beltis, 'my Lady'. He, as the World-king, wore the *bull's horns*—*she* put on her own head a *bull's head* as the ensign of royalty. He, as the Sun-god, was called Beël-samen, 'Lord of Heaven'—she, as the Moon-goddess, Melkat-ashemin, 'Queen of Heaven'. He was worshipped in Egypt as the 'Revealer of goodness and truth'—she, in Babylon, under the symbol of the Dove, as the goddess of

[1] *Two Babylons,* p. 109.

gentleness and mercy, the 'Mother of gracious acceptance', 'merciful and benignant to men'. He, under the name of Mithra, was worshipped as Mesites, or 'the Mediator'—she, as Aphrodité, or 'the Wrath-subduer', was called Mulitta (or Mylitta) 'the Mediatrix'. He was represented as crushing the great serpent under his heel,—she, as bruising the serpent's head in her hand. He, under the name of Janus, bore a key, as the opener and shutter of the gates of the invisible world. She, under the name of Cybele, was invested with a like key, as an emblem of the same power. He, as the cleanser from sin, was called the 'Unpolluted god'—she, too, had the power to wash away sin, and, though the mother of the seed, was called the 'Virgin, pure and undefiled'.[1] He was represented as 'Judge of the dead'—she was represented as standing by his side, at the judgment-seat, in the unseen world. He, after being killed by the sword, was fabled to have risen again, and ascended up to heaven. She, too, though history makes her to have been killed with the sword by one of her own sons, was nevertheless, in the myth, said to have been carried by her son bodily to heaven, and to have been made Pambasileia, 'Queen of the Universe'."

"It is hardly necessary to say that it is this very goddess that is now worshipped in the Church of Rome under the name of Mary. Though that goddess is called by the name of the mother of our Lord, all the attributes given to her are derived simply from the Babylonian Madonna, and not from the Virgin Mother of Christ."[2]

If, in the Mystery of iniquity, the Divine Redeemer was

---

[1] The title of *Alma*, in the phrase Alma Mater, though as a *Latin* word it signifies "bland", or "fostering", has been shown by Mr. Hislop to be also a pure *Hebrew* word signifying a *Virgin*. It is the precise term used by Isaiah, ch. vii. 14, in predicting the birth of Christ.—*Two Babylons*, p. 109.

[2] *Two Babylons*, pp. 387–389.

thus mimicked and mocked in all His gracious offices, no less
so was the Holy Spirit of God.

It is abundantly evident that the ancient heathens were not
without some notions of the triune nature of the Godhead.
This is apparent in the Assyrian symbol of Deity mentioned
above, with three heads; in the Hindû triad of Brahma, Vishnu,
and Shiva: and in the *trefoil* grass used in worship from
remote antiquity by the Persians. In Egypt, it was expressed
in the three initial letters I.H.S. Those letters, now so commonly seen upon the coverings of our Communion tables, are
understood to mean *Iesus Hominum Salvator*, "Jesus the
Saviour of men": and they are adopted from the *wafer of the
Romish Mass*, upon which they are regularly stamped. But
from whence were those mystic letters originally derived?
They were in use for ages before the Christian era as a *heathen*
symbol: and, like many other things, were transferred by the
crafty policy of Rome from heathenism to the corrupted
Christianity of former days. In the idolatry of Egypt those
letters stood for *Isis, Horus, Seb*—that is, *the Egyptian trinity*
of Isis, the "Queen of Heaven", Horus her Child, and Seb the
father of the gods.[1]

It has been already shown how this Pagan trinity—so
generally recognized throughout the ancient heathen world—
was symbolized in the hierogram of the Circle, Serpent, and
Wings. The Circle signified deity in general, and in the
Assyrian and Persian forms of the symbol enclosed a human
figure to represent the father of the gods.—The Serpent, proceeding from the Circle, signified deity in operation, or the
creative and preserving energy of deity; and so, stood for
"the Second Mind", or second person, of the heathen trinity.—
The Wings—or, as in the fuller form of the Assyrian symbol,
the Wings and tail—of a *dove*, signified "*the motive and penetrative power* of God, which was called *Love*." The *third*

---

[1] *Two Babylons*, p. 239.

person of the heathen trinity, then, was symbolized by a
Dove.

The Dove is the very embodiment of gentleness; and
accordingly, as a natural symbol of love and peace, is adopted
in the Scriptures as an emblem of the Holy Spirit of God.

In the Mystery of godliness, the Holy Spirit is the gracious
Worker of that *new creation*, or new birth, by which the soul
of a man becomes "born of the Spirit"—John iii. 5; and so, is
made a child of God and an heir of glory.

Now all this, also, had its counterpart and counterfeit
in the Mystery of iniquity.

The holy and blessed work of a new birth by the Holy
Spirit is the life of the soul, and the only fountain of all holiness, joy, peace, and love.

The blasphemous perversion and carnal abuse of this truth
became, above every other corruption, a source of licentious-
ness which literally deluged the world with a flood of pollu-
tion.

Now, let the reader observe how this result was brought
about :—viz., by representing *Semiramis*, the beautiful but
,abandoned queen of Babylon, as *an incarnation of the Spirit of
God*.

"In Babylon, the title of the goddess-mother, as the Dwelling-place of God, was Sacca, or in the emphatic form, Sacta,
that is, 'The Tabernacle'. Now, in her, as the Tabernacle or
Temple of God, not only all power, but all grace and goodness
were believed to dwell. Every quality of gentleness and mercy
was regarded as centered in her; and when death had closed
her career, while she was fabled to have been deified and
changed into a *pigeon*, to express the celestial benignity of her
nature, she was called by the name of 'D'Iuné', or 'the Dove'
—or, without the article, 'Juno', the name of the Roman
"Queen of Heaven," which has the very same meaning; and
under the *form* of a dove, as well as her own, she was worshipped by the Babylonians. The dove, the chosen symbol of

this deified queen, is commonly represented with an olive branch in its mouth, as she herself in her human form also is seen bearing the olive branch in her hand : and from this form of representing her it is highly probable that she has derived the name by which she is commonly known—for 'Z'emir-amit' (Semiramis) means 'The branch-bearer'. When the goddess was thus represented with the olive branch, there can be no doubt that the symbol had partly reference to the story of the Flood ; but there was much more in the symbol than a mere memorial of that great event. A *branch*, as has been already proved, was the symbol of the deified *son ;* and when the deified *mother* was represented as a Dove, what could the meaning of the representation be but just to *identify her with the Spirit of all grace*, that brooded, dove-like, over the deep at the creation ; for, in the sculptures at Nineveh, as we have seen, the wings and tail of the dove represented the *third* member of the idolatrous Assyrian trinity. In confirmation of this view, it must be stated that the Assyrian 'Juno', or the 'Virgin Venus', as she was called, was identified with the *air*. Thus Julius Firmicus says :—'The Assyrians and part of the Africans wish the *air* to have the supremacy of the elements, for they have consecrated this same (element) under the name of Juno, or the Virgin Venus'.[1] Why was *air* thus identified with Juno, whose symbol was that of the third person of the Assyrian trinity ? Why, but because in Chaldee the same word which signifies the *air* signifies also the *Holy Ghost ?* The knowledge of this entirely accounts for the statement of Proclus that 'Juno imports the *generation of soul.*'[2] Whence could the soul—the spirit of man—be supposed to have its origin, but from the Spirit of God ? In accordance with this character of Juno as *the incarnation of the Divine Spirit*, the source of life, and also as the goddess of the *air*, thus is she invoked in the *Orphic Hymns :—*

[1] " Firmicus, *De Errore*, cap. 4, p. 9."
[2] " Proclus, lib. vi., cap. 22, vol. ii., p. 76."

O royal Juno, of majestic mien,
Aërial formed, divine, Jove's blessed queen,
Throned in the bosom of cœrulean *air*,
The race of mortals is thy constant care :
The cooling gales thy power alone inspires,
Which nourish *life*, which every *life* desires ;
Mother of showers and *winds*, from thee alone,
Producing all things, mortal *life* is known :
All natures show thy temperament divine,
And universal sway alone is thine ;
With sounding blasts of wind the swelling sea,
And rolling rivers roar when shook by thee.[1]

Thus, then, the deified queen, while in all respects regarded as a veritable woman, was at the same time adored as the incarnation of the Holy Ghost, the Spirit of peace and love. In the temple of Hierapolis in Syria there was a famous statue of the goddess Juno, to which crowds from all quarters flocked to worship. The image of the goddess was richly habited; on her head was a golden dove, and she was called by a name peculiar to the country, 'Seméion'. What is the meaning of Seméion? It is evidently 'The Habitation';[2] and the golden dove on her head shows plainly who it was that was supposed to *dwell* in her—even the Spirit of God. When such transcendent dignity was bestowed on her, when such winning characters were attributed to her, and when, over and above all, her images presented her to the eyes of men as Venus Urania, the 'heavenly Venus', the Queen of beauty, who

[1] "Taylor's *Orphic Hymns*, p. 50. Every classical reader must be aware of the identification of Juno with the *air*. The following, however, as still further illustrative of the subject, from Proclus, may not be out of place :—' The series of our sovereign mistress Juno, beginning from on high, pervades the last of things, and her allotment in the sublunary region is the air; for air is a symbol of soul, according to which also soul is called a *spirit*, πνεῦμα.'—Proclus, Ibid. p. 197."

[2] "From Ze, 'that', or 'the great', and 'Maaon', or 'Maïon', a 'habitation'; which, in the Ionic dialect, in which Lucian, the describer of the goddess, wrote, would naturally become Meïon."

assured her worshippers of salvation while giving loose reins to every unholy passion, and every depraved and sensual appetite—no wonder that everywhere she was enthusiastically adored."[1]

And no wonder, when the holiest truths of Divine Revelation were thus subverted, and their very symbols employed to sanction and encourage every sensual vice, that the ancient as well as the modern Babylon became the "mother of harlots and abominations of the earth."

Such are a few only of the facts floating on the mere surface of these "depths of Satan"—depths of impurity and wickedness, mysteries of darkness and death, too blasphemous and too revolting to be more than hinted at in these pages.

The Mystery of iniquity has also its "development." The word is a favourite one among the advocates of false religious systems. The theory of *development* is much insisted upon both by Romanists and Rationalists.

Now what is the difference between the *gradual revelation* of the Mystery of godliness, and the *development* of the Mystery of iniquity?

It is just the difference between the unfolding of a rose-bud and the growth of a rubbish-heap.

The whole rose is contained within the rose-bud before the bud begins to expand itself into the full-blown flower. So was the whole counsel of God, the whole Mystery of godliness, involved in the very first announcement to Adam of a coming Redeemer.

The rubbish-heap is but an accumulation of filth thrown together by the hands of men. Its growth is not an *expansion* of already existing parts by the power of an inward life, but the *addition* of new and dead matter heaped upon it from without.

There is nothing in the full-blown rose but what was con-

[1] *Two Babylons*, pp. 113-116.

tained in embryo in the closely folded bud; and so there is nothing, and never will be anything, in the fully revealed Mystery of godliness which was not contained and contemplated in it from the beginning.

But the Mystery of iniquity has been growing up for six thousand years, and is growing up still, by the continual addition of corrupt doctrines and practices one after another. The only kind of *life* existing in such a system is the working of corrupt human nature amidst the mass of accumulated errors —like the heat and fermentation of the dung-heap which at length reduces the whole mass into a state of uniform decay and rottenness.

There *is* such a life in the Mystery of iniquity. There is a corrupt principle which is working, and that with great activity —and which is working out a kind of development of itself. It is *the moral fermentation of fallen and corrupted human nature*—which is gathering heat and strength from the contact of man with man, the growth of population, the increase of means of communication, and the accumulation of the corruptions of one age upon those of former ages.

Romanism has quite recently accomplished a large addition to its rubbish-heap of false doctrines by casting upon it the monstrous dogma of the personal Infallibility of the Pope.[1]

So also Rationalism, by a most remarkable coincidence in time, and a most significant concurrence of corrupt principle, is at the present moment at the very same stage of its progress. The Rationalists of this day are insisting upon *their* particular claim to Infallibility—the infallibility of human Reason, and Science (falsely so called), and the "verifying faculty," and the supremacy of Conscience making man to be the only law to himself.

This process will culminate. There is every appearance of

---

[1] Promulgated by Pope Pius the Ninth at Rome on the 18th July 1870.

its going forward with increased and increasing activity and vehemence till it reaches a climax.

The climax will be the same in both "developments"—both of Romanism and Rationalism—viz., *the full development of Antichrist.*

The full revelation of the Mystery of godliness will be the full revelation of JESUS CHRIST as IMMANUEL—"God with us "—the *God-man.*

The full development of the Mystery of iniquity will be the open assertion of man's claim to be the *Man-God.*

This will be the full development of *Antichrist:* whether by Antichrist we are to understand a *system*, or, as some think, a *personal* Antichrist in whom the system will be completely matured and personified—the *focus* in which will be united all the converging lines of the lurid lights of Romish (or Ritualistic), Rationalistic, and infidel systems.

Whatever system, or representative of a system, shall be found holding this position at the appearing of Jesus Christ will certainly be that " *Man of Sin* ", or " *Lawless one*," " whom the Lord shall consume with the spirit of his mouth, and destroy with the brightness of his coming."—2 Thess. ii. 8.

CHAPTER XXX.

Same Subject continued.— Conclusion.

IT is worth observing how this subject throws light upon the difficulty, so ensnaring to fallen man, of believing in an *unseen and invisible God*. The difficulty is felt by every human being. The whole tendency of man's religious nature, (so far as it is religious at all) is to seek for a God whom he can *see*. Under the pressure of this feeling, the poor ignorant savage carves a block of wood or stone into an idol which his imagination invests with the attributes of Deity—and the politest nations of antiquity produced those statues which, as works of art, have been the admiration of all succeeding ages. The Greeks and Romans tried to realize the notion of God by distributing it into a multiplicity of deities which filled heaven, earth, sea, and the infernal regions—every grove and fountain, almost, had its presiding Naiad, Nymph, or Faun. The Hindûs enumerate ten incarnations of God, and reckon the whole number of deities at three hundred and thirty-three millions. The Romanist materializes God to his own apprehension by believing in a transubstantiated wafer—the Pantheist by considering all matter to be a part of God. The Atheist, foiled in his efforts to conceive of a God who cannot be seen, recoils with sullen disappointment into disbelief of the existence of any God at all. The Positivist refuses to believe in anything beyond the cognizance of his senses—the Humanitarian, in his search after the "unknown God", rests in the

sage conclusion that God is nothing else but *Human Nature*
—that is, himself.

Now in all these painful and doubtful conflicts of mind the
struggle evidently is to surmount a difficulty—the difficulty of
believing in an invisible God.

But how came this difficulty to exist at all?

Here, again, we must acknowledge that man's condition is
an anomaly in creation. The lower animals—all other animals
besides mankind—have a nature, capacities, and knowledge,
suited to their wants. They have no such contradiction in
their state of being as to feel the pressure of a want which it
baffles their power to relieve.

But man—in respect of that one question which his inmost
soul feels to be of paramount importance—is left, in his *natural*
condition, in the most distracting doubt and impenetrable
darkness. There is, indeed, evidence enough in the works of
Creation without, and in the moral Conscience within, both to
convince a reasonable man of the existence of a God, and to
convict him of guilt when he transgresses the laws of his very
nature and instinctive duty. But a natural *demonstration*, such
as we have in the case of all earthly things, we possess not in
relation to the being and attributes of God.

Yet this is a contradiction and an inconsistency in man's
natural condition. The fact is undeniable—the burden of it,
to a thoughtful mind, is intolerable—yet how is it to be explained or accounted for?

All human philosophy utterly fails to give any reply. The
sages of antiquity, and the "profound thinkers" in the present
day of boastful pretensions, are alike unable to solve the
enigma.

The difficulty vanishes, and the darkness melts into the
radiant light of truth and love, under the blessed beams of
Revelation.

We have every reason to believe that the absence of direct
and visible communication with God is simply a consequence

of the Fall of man. It does not appear that it existed at first
—in that happy Eden the newly created pair walked in familiar intercourse with their Creator, and in ignorance of nothing
but evil. Brief, indeed, are the notices we possess of that
brief time of joy : but all, as far as they go, indicate that God
made Himself intimately known by a personal appearance to
our first parents, being seen by them, and speaking to them
"as a man speaketh to his friend." And never was the approach of the Heavenly Presence the occasion of aught but
unutterable joy, until the fatal moment when guilt had brought
fear into their souls. Then, not for the first time, "they heard
the voice of the LORD God *walking in the garden* in the cool
of the day"—but then, for the first time, "Adam and his wife
hid themselves from the presence of the LORD God amongst
the trees of the garden."—Gen. iii. 8.

The sentence of death and the expulsion from Eden followed. Man became a wanderer upon earth, left to struggle
for himself : with only such tokens as were afforded by the
promise of a Redeemer, the clothing of skins, the institution of
Sacrifice, and the Cherubim and Shechinah at Eden's gate,
that the Presence of God was not withdrawn from him and his
posterity for ever.

Farther tokens were continually given afterwards *to those
who embraced the Covenant of promise*, and sought for mercy in
the appointed way, through faith in the promised Redeemer.

Abel's offering was accepted by some visible token, and
Cain's crime was rebuked by an audible voice of mingled condemnation and remonstrance.

And so, in all the ages afterwards, "God left not himself
without witness," even by personal appearances, and audible
addresses, to many of His own believing and obedient servants : as to Noah, to Abraham, to Jacob, and above all, to
Moses and the Israelites.

But the crowning act of manifestation was herein, that
"God, who at sundry times and in divers manners spake in

time past unto the fathers by the prophets, *hath in these last days spoken unto us by his Son*"—Heb. i. 1 :—the Son of God not only appearing to men, not only speaking to men, but Himself made man, both Son of God and Son of man. When men saw Jesus, they *saw God* in the midst of them. The consummation of the mystery of godliness, so far as it has proceeded as yet, is "God manifest in the flesh" in the Person of Jesus Christ.

Here, then, at last the weary search after truth, peace, and joy, has an end. Here, doubt is dispelled, difficulty vanishes, the great enigma is solved, the mental conflict is appeased. The heart that has longed—intensely longed—to *see God*, is satisfied :—*we see God in* JESUS. The perplexity which has distracted the unbelieving world for six thousand years is at once dissolved by a few words of Jesus, more sweet and precious than daylight to the eyes—"Have I been so long time with you, and yet hast thou not known me, Philip? *he that hath seen me hath seen the Father;* and how sayest thou then, Shew us the Father?"—John xiv. 9.

JESUS is Incarnate Deity : and this, not merely as bringing the *Presence* of God among us, but also as manifesting His *character*. Every act, word, and even look of Jesus was a manifestation of the character of God—and of His mind, intentions, feelings, and *heart* towards man. In the fullest possible sense, Jesus is "God manifest in the flesh."

A similar account is to be given of the question, so much agitated in these days, of "*the supernatural in religion.*" There are (so called) "philosophers" who object to revealed religion because it requires us to believe in the supernatural.

Must, then, our conclusion be this—that whatever is beyond and above the ordinary course of nature—or beyond and above the reach of our natural reason and faculties—is incredible and impossible?

This is a mystery inscrutable to reason and science, but clear even to a child in the light of Revelation.

It is only to *fallen* nature that religion is supernatural—and must be so.

To unfallen beings—as Adam and Eve in their innocence, and angels now—religion is not supernatural, but natural: to know God, to believe in Him, to love Him with all the heart, and with all the mind, and with all the soul, and with all the strength, is not supernatural, but natural:—so natural that it is the very essence of their moral nature, the very spring of their moral action, the very joy and sunshine of their existence. If to know and love God is, to us, above nature, yet to Adam and Eve it was so far from being above nature that it would have been far *below* their nature not to know, and not to love Him. Though the ability to know God, and the disposition to love Him, are not now formed in man otherwise than by a supernatural operation of the Spirit of God in the soul, yet to Adam and Eve this ability and this disposition were so natural that, without them, their nature would not have been what it was at all. Without the intuitive knowledge and love of God they would not have been made "in the image of God," but would have been far more like the beasts that perish.

Even this wonderful fact, however,—the fact that, in Jesus, God Himself is made manifest to us—would fail to satisfy an enlightened mind, if it did not include the means of *removing the terrors of conscience.* When "Adam and his wife hid themselves" among the trees of the garden, nothing was farther from their minds than the desire to see God. To *shun* His presence—to *escape* from His eye—to get beyond the reach of His voice and of His hand, at that awful moment was all their anxiety. They would doubtless almost have wished that the earth might open and swallow them up, or that the mountains and rocks might fall upon them, and hide them from the Presence of God for ever.

The Mystery of godliness, "God manifest in the flesh," is infinitely precious to *fallen* man, because it is the manifestation of God in Christ, "*reconciling* the world unto himself"—2 Cor. v. 19—namely, by Christ, "his own self, bearing our sins in his own body on the tree."—1 Pet. ii. 24.

To make *Atonement* for man's sin was the very first requisite for man's redemption; and therefore must needs be the very first object of the Incarnation of the Son of God for the purpose of being man's Redeemer.

God manifesting Himself in the flesh must needs manifest His attributes—His character.

Among these attributes, Truth, Holiness, and Love are prominent.

But what must be the effect of infinite holiness, righteousness, and truth, coming into collision with sin? Manifestly, sin must be condemned and punished.

What, again, must be the effect of infinite love looking upon the miserable condition of a sinner? Surely, to move the heart of God Himself with infinite pity and compassion.

Love would fain pardon the sinner—Justice and Truth demand the punishment of sin. The contrariety involves an apparent impossibility. In Christ alone the impossibility is removed.

God manifesting Himself in the flesh, in the Person of Jesus, manifested all His attributes in the most glorious manner. Justice was satisfied by the substituted sufferings and death of Jesus—Love was delightfully and rejoicingly satisfied in forgiving the sinner whose sins had been punished on the Saviour's Cross—and Wisdom, infinite and unfathomable Wisdom—was displayed in the plan which reconciled such apparent impossibilities. In the Cross of Christ God glorified in the highest degree all His own perfections—Holiness, Truth, Love, Wisdom, Power.

2 B

In the light of this truth, the Gospel according to the Evangelists is seen to be in exact accordance with the Gospel according to Genesis—the Gospel announced to Adam. The Atonement of Calvary corresponds with the sin of Eden—the promise that the Seed of the woman should bruise the Serpent's head was fulfilled when Jesus, hanging on the Cross, said, " It is finished," and gave up the ghost. But if Genesis is " poetry, not history," then Jesus needed not to have suffered death as an Atonement for man's sin. The fact that He did suffer death as an Atonement is a proof of the literal truth of the history of Adam's transgression. We cannot deny the one without virtually denying also the other.

Unbelievers cut the knot by denying both. To make their plan consistent, they deny the literal truth of Genesis, and assert that the Saviour's death was suffered only as an example of patience under injury.

It need only be remarked here, that this denial involves a denial of the plain words of the Gospel narratives as much as of Genesis. If a " *ransom* " and an " *example* " are one and the same thing, then words have no meaning. If Christ's " bearing our sins in his own body on the tree " means that He suffered a most cruel and unjust death only to teach us to bear patiently the wrongs which others may inflict upon ourselves, then it is perfectly consistent with truth to assert that black is white ; and it is impossible to affix any certain sense whatever to any history, book, or word, in any language.

But that which it is the particular object of the foregoing pages to point out is, that such a denial of the historical and literal truth both of Genesis and of the New Testament is in defiance not only of the plainest words of Scripture, but also of the history and traditions of all nations throughout the world ; and of facts only too familiar to us all, which can neither be denied, nor explained away as myths and allegories.

In taking the Word of God in its plain, literal, historical

sense, we are in accordance with the history of all nations, and the facts of human nature and experience all the world over.

But the foolish and dishonest pretence that Genesis is "poetry, not history," involves a defiant contradiction of the New Testament as well as the Old, an intolerable perversion of the meaning of language, and a total disregard of facts, experience, and history.

Moreover, the evidence of Truth is, and always must be, cumulative.

The great doctrines of Man's Fall by sin, Redemption by the blood of Christ, and Renewal by the Holy Spirit, are declared with increasing clearness throughout the Bible, from Genesis to Revelation.

They are in accordance with the universal experience of the *effects* of the Fall—both moral and physical—both in man, and . the whole natural creation.

They agree with the instinctive verdict of man's own consciousness, and especially with the inward testimony and felt requirements of Conscience.

They are confirmed by the existence of a world-wide system of idolatrous worship, in which every one of these three great central truths is actually travestied and, so to speak, caricatured, by a corrupt imitation.

And they point to a consummation in which the best and noblest aspirations of the best and noblest minds will be fully and for ever satisfied. They point to an immortality of pure and perfect happiness attainable through the obedience of faith in the Gospel, but not otherwise. Truth is exclusive, as well as comprehensive.

They anticipate, as a reality, that which the deepest instincts of our nature feel after, and cast about for, with an intensity of longing desire—the regeneration of the natural world as well as of human souls—an age of peace and plenty, purity, and beauty, love and loveliness, such as poets dream of, but the world refuses to supply; such as philosophy speculates upon,

but all human education and civilization utterly fail to produce.

The counsel of God will stand, though never so much
doubted or denied : and it will be accomplished in regard both
to the Mystery of godliness and the Mystery of iniquity.

The two Mysteries have been, for six thousand years past,
running their course side by side, like two parallel streams.
The gradual and majestic unfolding of the Gospel of the
blessed God has been, at every stage of its progress, overtaken
by a new and corresponding phase of Satan's counterfeit—up
to the present moment, when Ritualism (or Romanism) on the
one hand, and Rationalism (or intellectual Infidelity) on the
other, offer to simple and deluded souls the latest and the
most ensnaring imitations of "the truth as it is in Jesus."

But much more remains behind—a fuller development, more
open and more defiant opposition. The Mystery of iniquity
will be suffered to work till its real character shall be so
plainly manifested that it will cease to be a mystery. It will
at last show itself in its true and undisguised nature as "opposing and exalting itself above all that is called God or that is
worshipped." The full development of Antichrist will be nothing else but the full development of the claim of man to "be
as gods." Satan's first temptation to the first of mankind will
never cease to work till it results in a world-wide attempt to
overthrow the authority of God that man may exalt himself
into His place.

When this shall come to pass, then the Mystery of iniquity
and "the Man of Sin", or "Lawless one", will meet their
doom together. Then "the Lord Jesus will be revealed from
Heaven with his mighty angels, in flaming fire taking vengeance on them that know not God and that obey not the
Gospel of our Lord Jesus Christ: who shall be punished with
everlasting destruction from the presence of the Lord and
from the glory of his power, when he shall come to be glorified

in his saints, and to be admired in all them that believe."—
2 Thess. i. 7-10.

"The Mystery of God" will also be fulfilled in its appointed
season ; and will certainly issue in the establishment of the
Kingdom of our Lord and Saviour Jesus Christ—purchased
with His blood, created anew by His Spirit, and destined to
be the dwelling-place of IMMANUEL—"God manifest in the
flesh "—among His saints for ever and ever :—that Kingdom
in which shall be realized the anticipation of the angels' song,
" Glory to God in the highest heavens, and on earth peace, good
will toward men " :—that Kingdom of which it is written—" I
heard a great voice out of heaven saying, Behold, the tabernacle
of God is with men, and he will dwell with them, and they shall
be his people, and God himself shall be with them, and be
their God. And God himself shall wipe away all tears from
their eyes: and there shall be no more death, neither sorrow,
nor crying, neither shall there be any more pain ; for the
former things are passed away. And he that sat upon the
throne said, Behold, I make all things new."—Rev. xxi. 3-5.

THE END.

Sanson & Co., Printers, Edinburgh.

Second Edition, Price 7s. 6d.,

THE TREE OF LIFE;

OR,

REDEMPTION, AND ITS FRUITS IN GRACE AND GLORY.

CONTENTS.

LONDON: JAMES NISBET & CO., 21 BERNERS STREET.

SILVERDALE TRACTS.

No. I.—TAKEN BY SURPRISE: A Word for every one on Things which are coming on the Earth. 1d.; 7s. 6d. per 100.

No. II.—NOT TAKEN BY SURPRISE; or, the Servant ready when the Master knocks. 1d.; 7s. 6d. per 100.

No. III.—THOUGHTS ON WHAT *MAY* BE IN THE YEAR 1866 OR 1867. 1d.; 7s. 6d. per 100.

No. IV.—THE WINNING SIDE: On which Side are You? 1d.; 7s. 6d. per 100.

No. V.—OUR PRIEST: A word about Ritualism. 2d.; 15s. per 100.

No. VI.—"ONCE TO DIE, BUT *AFTER THIS*—" 1d.; 7s. 6d. per 100.

No. VII.—A GOOD TIME COMING. 1d.; 7s. 6d. per 100.

No. VIII.—FORETOLD AND FULFILLED: A Call to Awake. 1d.; 7s. 6d. per 100.

LONDON: S. W. PARTRIDGE & CO., 9 PATERNOSTER ROW.

Price 6s., Ornamental Boards,

ITHURIEL'S SPEAR;

OR,

IS THIS CHRISTIANITY?

BEING A VINDICATION OF CHRISTIAN DOCTRINE, AND AN
EXAMINATION OF THE BOOK CALLED *"ECCE HOMO,"*
BY THE TEST OF SCRIPTURE.

CONTENTS.

LONDON: JAMES NISBET & CO., 21 BERNERS STREET.

Lightning Source UK Ltd.
Milton Keynes UK
UKHW020742291222
414571UK00006B/376